Lady Frances

Lady Frances Balfour
By the kind permission of the National Portrait Gallery

LADY FRANCES

Frances Balfour,
Aristocrat Suffragist

Joan B. Huffman

Matador
9 Priory Business Park,
Wistow Road, Kibworth Beauchamp,
Leicestershire. LE8 0RX
Tel: 0116 279 2299
Email: books@troubador.co.uk
Web: www.troubador.co.uk/matador
Twitter: @matadorbooks

ISBN 978 1788035 057

British Library Cataloguing in Publication Data.
A catalogue record for this book is available from the British Library.

Printed and bound by CPI Group (UK) Ltd, Croydon, CR0 4YY
Typeset in 11pt Garamond by Troubador Publishing Ltd, Leicester, UK

Matador is an imprint of Troubador Publishing Ltd

MIX
Paper from
responsible sources
FSC® C013604
FSC
www.fsc.org

For Jim

TABLE OF CONTENTS

LIST OF ILLUSTRATIONS

PREFACE

I was initially moved to study the life of Lady Frances Balfour because her autobiography, *Ne Obliviscaris (Dinna Forget)*, was so incomplete, ending with her husband's death in 1911 and omitting the record of nearly 40 years of her work for women's causes. Moreover, the fact that she was a member of the aristocracy - a class whose women had been virtually ignored by historians of the late nineteenth century women's movement, but who had been active in the British women's campaign to secure the vote - drew my interest. But I suspected that I might find that Frances lent her name to the Cause more often than she actually worked for the movement.

I found, however, that the length and degree of Frances Balfour's service to the women's suffrage movement, combined with her great variety of efforts for other women's causes, merited a place for her in the forefront of those who helped break the social, political, and legal restrictions which constrained British women during the Late Victorian and Edwardian eras.

I have been fortunate in the large number of extant contemporary records, diaries, and letters to which I have had, in many cases, exclusive access. Frances herself saved most of her correspondence, and she left her papers to her sister-in-law, Lady Betty Balfour, who preserved many of the documents relevant to Frances's life and work, arranging the letters chronologically, typing and editing them to make them more readable. Even as edited, Frances's letters are quite interesting, and I have made an attempt in this study to incorporate her correspondence and diaries as much as is feasible in order to allow her to tell her own story.

One of the most difficult aspects of this biography concerned Frances's political interests. That politics had a major appeal for her sets her apart from most of the women of her day. In her case, politics was also family - her family life and her political life were one - and they are treated as such here. For all her interest in the subject, Frances does not appear to have ever addressed an audience specifically on a political issue (other than trying to convince MPs that they should give women votes). She did prepare some articles for publication in newspapers or journals, but articles written by women, especially political articles, were not always published, or if they were, were not given the attention that men's articles received. Further complicating a search for her opinions is the fact that she most regularly communicated her thoughts orally, not in writing, to the most prominent political leaders of her day: she either lived with them (Campbells and Balfours) or regularly visited them (the Cecils and the Asquiths). Since there are few large deposits of her letters in the archives of these families, I utilize short phrases which appear in her diary or the occasional sentence or paragraph touching on politics subjects, which she included in letters to family and friends.

I have sought the help of several ministers and academics for assistance with Lady Frances's interest in the Church of Scotland, but they are not to be blamed for any shortcomings in this work.

Since she and her family lived with Arthur, Alice, Betty, Gerald, and their children for six months of every year, these individuals figure more prominently in this biography than would ordinarily be the case, as does Eustace Balfour – not only because the man a woman marries says something about the woman (as do the lives of her children), but also because historians (Egremont, in particular) have in the past ignored or slighted Eustace, mistakenly dismissing him as a hopeless alcoholic who did not share the family brilliance. I have, nevertheless, maintained primary focus on Frances herself.

Joan B. Huffman, Macon, Georgia

ACKNOWLEDGEMENTS

I am indebted to a great many individuals and institutions for their assistance in facilitating this study, but to none more than to the late Gerald, 4th Earl of Balfour, who gifted the invaluable Frances Balfour Papers to the National Records of Scotland in the mid-1980s. Lord Balfour guided me around Whittingehame, and introduced me to his sister, Lady Evelyn; her author-husband, Michael Brander; and their son, Andrew Michael Brander. I am especially grateful to Andrew Michael for sharing with me his grandmother Jean's unpublished 'Notes and Observations upon the "Old Generation", the family of James Maitland and Blanche Balfour, of Whittingehame'.

I am equally indebted to a large number of additional relatives, all of whom proved to be delightful, helpful, and as Scottish as Frances herself. Frances's favourite granddaughter Elizabeth (Mrs Jocelyn) Gibb's warm smile, infectious laugh, and interesting habits gave me insight into the Campbell-Balfour mentality. I also wish to thank her twin daughters, Jean (Mrs Alexander) Lindsay and Alison (Mrs John) Watson, and their families for their assistance.

I am also grateful to Frances, the Dowager Lady Fergusson, eldest granddaughter of Frances Balfour, who graciously assisted me until her death in September 1988. Lady Fergusson's efforts were supplemented by those of her children: Adam and his wife Penelope (Poppet) provided me with much helpful family material, especially the Balfour *Book of Bosh;* answered many questions about the aristocracy and the family; and extended great friendship and warm hospitality to me on my numerous visits to their home in London. Adam, also an author, carefully read the manuscript; his brother Charles patiently answered my correspondence; and his sister Alice, Lady Renton of Mount Harry, explained British governesses to me.

Other family members who provided valuable assistance included Ian and Torquil, 12th and 13th Dukes of Argyll; Roderick, 5th Earl of Balfour; Elizabeth, the Duchess – Countess of Sutherland; Gerald, the 6th Duke of Westminster; Lord John Rayleigh; The Hon G R Strutt; Lady Kathleen Oldfield; Lord Henry Lytton Cobbold; Lady Rosalind Hayes, nee Finlay; Lady Richard Percy; Professor Jane Ridley; Alastair Anstruther; Penelope Jamison; Nora King, nee Balfour; John Balfour; and his wife, Dr Jean Balfour.

After family members, my greatest thanks must be extended to Miss Ierne Grant, without whose meticulous and patient copying – by hand – of most of the Frances Balfour materials in the National Records of Scotland this work might not have been possible.

From my editor, Karen Ferrell-White, I received splendid editing assistance and expertise which enabled me to bring Lady Frances's story to light.

Special thanks also go to my late friend and mentor, Dr J O Baylen, Regents' Professor of History for the University System of Georgia, for his encouragement in undertaking this project and for his assistance thereafter. I am also grateful for the hospitality provided by his wife Margaret on my numerous visits to their homes in Rottingdean and Eastbourne.

In addition, I have benefitted from the advice and assistance of several authorities on the British women's movement of the late nineteenth and early twentieth centuries. These included the late Dr Leah Leneman, Dr Elizabeth Crawford, Professor David Rubinstein, Dr Gail Savage, Professor Angela John, Professor Martin Pugh, Dr Janet Walker, Professor Olive Banks, Professor Joyce Bellamy, Professor Jill Liddington, Dr Elaine Harrison, Dr Lesley Orr Macdonald, Irene Cockroft, Amanda Mackenzie Stuart, David Mitchell, and Frank Sharp, JD.

Special thanks must also be given to Professor Ian F W Beckett, who patiently explained many aspects of British military history, kindly read the manuscript in its earliest - and longest - form and corrected military titles and other errors. I am also grateful to Professor Barbara Gilchrist, who searched the vault of Crown Court Church for the materials relevant to the rebuilding of the Church, and to Dr Kenneth Hughes, minister of the Church at that time. Alastair Sinclair and Dr John Holliday of the An Iodhlann, Tiree, patiently explained various historical events on the island. I am also indebted to Paul Harris for showing me around the impressively refurbished and renovated Whittingehame House.

I should also like to thank all of the library and archival personnel in Britain and the United States who have assisted me in obtaining almost all the material from sources outside my local area. I am especially grateful to Her Majesty, Queen Elizabeth II, and Pamela Clark, Deputy Registrar, and Julie Crocker, Archivist, The Royal Archives, Windsor Castle for letters pertinent to Princess Louise and the 9th Duke of Argyll; to Robin H Harcourt Williams, Librarian and Archivist for the Marquess of Salisbury, for opening and uncoding the materials at Hatfield House which were applicable to Frances Balfour; to Alastair Campbell Yg of Airds, Chief Executive of the 12th Duke of Argyll, for answering my numerous questions about the Campbells and Inveraray Castle; the congenial and helpful Nigel Hughes and the Grosvenor group; the Grosvenor Estate materials, City of Westminster Archive Centre; William W Ellis, Eileen Simpson, and

Carrie Jackson, the Eaton Estate Office; to the very knowledgeable David Doughan and his successors at The Women's Library of Great Britain: Elizabeth Chapman, Anna Towlinson, Angele David-Guillou, Graham Canfield, Sue Donnelly, and Heather Dawson, the London School of Economics Library, which now - fortunately - houses The Women's Library; to Dr Hazel Horn and the ever-efficient staff and leadership at the National Records of Scotland (NRS) for providing for computers to be used in the Reading Room of General Register House long before most other libraries allowed such; to Pat Borck, Anna Mancilla, Mary Morris and the rest of the library staff at Middle Georgia State University, Macon, Georgia; and to the staffs of the Bodleian, Nuffield College Library, and Western Manuscripts, Oxford University; Kate Parry and Girton College, Anne Thomson and Newnham College, and librarians at Trinity College and Churchill College, Cambridge University; Mary Sharp and Dr Alistair Cooke, the Carlton Club; Lord James Neidpath, Earl of Wemyss; Eton College; the Harrow School; the late Dr Daphne Glick and the National Council of Women of Great Britain; Clare Fleck, Knebworth House; The BBC Written Archives Center; the British Library; the National Archives (Kew); the National Portrait Gallery; the Huntington Library, San Marino, California; the National Library of Scotland; Dr Maureen Watry, Sydney Jones Library, the University of Liverpool; Eileen Hawkins and The Young Women's Christian Association of Great Britain; Dr Lesley Hall and Lalita Kaplish at the Wellcome Library; Jane Hogan and the Sudan Archive at the Library at Palace Green, Durham University; Professors David F Wright and Stewart J Brown of the University of Edinburgh; Kim Arnold and Bob Anger, Archives of the Presbyterian Church of Canada; Angela Macon and The British Architectural Library; Mrs Sylvia Barnett, OBE, and The Victoria League for Commonwealth Friendship; Victoria Moger and The Museum of London; The National Library of Australia; Michael Moss and the Library of the University of Glasgow; Christine Mackwell and the Lambeth Palace Archives; Cecily Greenhill and the Society for the Preservation of Ancient Buildings; Drs Waddell Barnes, Emory Johnson, Alex Weaver, L E Dickey, Waldo Floyd, Sr, and Waldo Floyd, Jr, Macon, Georgia; Steven Kerr, Royal College of Surgeons, Edinburgh; Laura Brouard, Lothian Health Services Archive; Professor Emeritus Neil McIntyre of the Royal Free Hospital School of Medicine; Estela Dukan, Royal College of Physicians of Edinburgh; Dr David J Kupfer, University of Pittsburgh Medical Center; Dr Caroline Acker and Susan Collins, Carnegie Mellon University; Clem Webb, Librarian, and Andrew Parsons, Curator, London Scottish Regimental Museum; Dr A R Morton, Royal Military College, Sandhurst; Judith Nefsky and Bob Kennell, Canadian Pacific Railroad Archives; Elizabeth Broekman and the Notting Hill and Ealing High School; H M Sherriff and St Columba's Church of Scotland, London; Debbie Youngs, North Mymms Park house; The Library of

Congress; The Victoria and Albert Museum; the Public Record Office; the Greater London Record Office; The London Metropolitan Archives; The Fitzwilliam Museum, Cambridge; the Central Library, Manchester; the William Perkins Library, Duke University; The Rare Book and Manuscript Library, Columbia University; the Staffordshire Record Office; The Modern Records Centre, University of Warwick Library; Cumbria Record Office; and the Reading University Library.

My thanks also go to the late Elizabeth, Lady Longford, Viscount Robin Bridgeman, Dr Donald Opitz, Dr Anne Bridger, Dr Jill Allibone, Dr David Nasaw, Dr Katharine Cockin, Dr Barbara Brandon Schnorrenberg, Dr Mary Vipond, Dr Paul Foos, M Andrew Saint, John Greenacomb, Jehanne Wake, Debbie Mays, Lance Thirkell, Mrs Ralph Oliphant, C H Cruft, Joyce Vann, Mrs J Bartlett, The Rev J E Stewart, The Rev Sigrid Marten, the Rev Creede Hinshaw, the Rev Wesley Smith, David Cockroft, Colin Shrimpton, Rosie MacIntyre, Penelope Adamson, Vivien Burgess, Claire Beckham, Dr Gwen Sell, Dr Dottie Brown, and Mrs Berniece Brewer.

Finally, as indicated in the dedication, I am especially indebted to all the members of my family - but especially to my husband Jim - without whose understanding and patience this study could not have been completed. Sadly, Jim died before the book was published. Still, it is, therefore, dedicated with love to Jim, Jean, Johnny, Jack, Ellie, Jill, Albert, and Rutledge.

Of course, none of the individuals nor institutions mentioned herein is responsible for the statements of fact or interpretations of material presented in the text. This responsibility is mine alone.

Joan B Huffman

Macon, Georgia

NOTES ON STYLE

Every effort has been made herein to shorten the references which are cited in the endnotes. Material taken from the Balfour Papers in the National Records of Scotland is cited by date and bundle only; i.e. FB to BB, 8 August 1898, 320. (The full citation is Frances Balfour to Betty Balfour, 8 August 1898, GD433/2/Bundle Number [320], National Records of Scotland.) The use of 'p' or 'pp' before page numbers in an endnote has been omitted in the footnotes.

The citation for minutes of the various committee meetings and reports of the numerous societies Frances belonged to only includes which society was meeting and the date of the meeting ('MEC, TAS, 8 April 1915') indicates Minutes of the Executive Committee, Travellers' Aid Society, and the date. Likewise, 'AR, LSWS, 1913' indicates the Annual Report of 1913 of the London Society of Women's Suffrage, etc.

In addition, I have preferred to use the following entry for articles in the *Oxford Dictionary of National Biography:* 'H C G Matthew, 'George Douglas Campbell, 8th Duke of Argyll, *ODNB*, article 4500'.

Efforts also have been made to make the text as easily readable as possible. All underlined words are those of the writers. In addition, an occasional misspelling or – more often – an abbreviated word, such as 'v.' for 'very' or 'recd.' for 'received' in the original, have been spelled out except when the material was written by a child. There are a few problems that have been dealt with by simply using the following spellings: Fisher's Hill (Fishers Hill), Nunkie (Nunk, Nunky), and Rosneath (Roseneath). I have also used exclamation points in a few places in this biography because Frances used them a lot!!

In addition, since **quoted materials from Frances' diaries are indicated in bold face**, the dates of the entries are provided in endnotes only if they are not obvious from the text. After 1877, Frances' diaries, which were appointment books, were usually three *inches* wide by five *inches* long, and each open spread covered an entire week.

In 1911, the Conservative party supposedly changed its name to the "Unionist Party," but this name appears never to have replaced 'Conservative Party.' Therefore, since Frances was a Unionist and not a Conservative per se, I have employed the term Unionist/Conservative throughout the book after 1886 rather than limit the reference to one or the other. In the interest of space, most of the noble titles to which many of the friends of Frances were entitled have been omitted, though I have tried to remind readers of her title by calling her 'Lady Frances Balfour' near the beginning of each chapter.

In quoting from newspapers, the page numbers have not been given because they are missing in many of the clippings inserted in the Balfour Papers, and the relative ease of finding such material in the digitized online versions available today, which stress key words, makes it unnecessary. All the quotations at the beginning of each chapter (both in the title and in the quotes before the narrative begins) are Frances's unless otherwise identified.

For ease of consulting, I have provided inclusive dates for the events covered in each chapter.

ABBREVIATIONS AND NICKNAMES

The following abbreviations have been employed in the footnotes and occasionally in the text:

FB – Lady Frances Balfour
EJAB – Mr Eustace Balfour
BB – Lady Betty Balfour
GWB – Mr Gerald Balfour
AJB – Mr Arthur Balfour, later Lord Balfour
ABB – Miss Alice Balfour
Alison – Miss Alison Balfour
Joan – Miss Joan Balfour
Oswald – Mr Oswald Balfour
Frank – Mr Frank Balfour
RAL – Lord Robert Arthur Lytton Balfour, 3rd Earl of Balfour
Salisbury – Lord Salisbury, 3rd Marquess
Ldy S – Lady Salisbury, wife of 3rd Marquess
Robert Cecil – Lord Robert Cecil
RBF – Sir, later Lord Robert B Finlay
MGF – Mrs Millicent Garrett Fawcett or Mrs Henry Fawcett
AM – Dr Sir Arthur Mitchell
MM – The Very Rev Dr Mitford Mitchell
DD – Edith, Mrs Alfred Lyttelton

The following abbreviations have been used to indicate the appropriate libraries:

NRS – National Records of Scotland, formerly the National Archives of Scotland, formerly the Scottish Record Office (SRO)
BL – British Library
LSE– The London School of Economics, which now houses The Women's Library of Great Britain, formerly the Fawcett Library

HH – Hatfield House

Organization abbreviations include:

BSF – British Salonika Force
CCCWSS – Consultative Committee of Constitutional Women's Suffrage Societies
CUWFA – Conservative and Unionist Women's Franchise Association
FLD – Freedom of Labour Defense
JPC – Joint Parliamentary Committee
LS or LSWS – London Society for Women's Suffrage
LSWH – London Scottish Women's Hospitals
NCW – National Council of Women
NSWS – National Society for Women's Suffrage (pre-1888)
NUWSS – National Union of Women's Suffrage Societies
NUWW – National Union of Women Workers
NVA - National Vigilance Association
ODC – Open Door Council
SPG – Six Point Group
SPAB – Society for the Protection of Ancient Buildings
SPS – Sudan Political Service
SWH – Scottish Women's Hospitals
TAS – Travellers' Aid Society
TWL – The Women's Library of Great Britain
WLF – Women's Liberal Federation
WLUA – Women's Liberal Unionist Association
WMP – Women's Municipal Party
WSPU – Women's Social and Political Union

Almost all the Balfours, Campbells, Cecils, and their closest friends had nicknames:
Aggie - Alice Balfour
Alice Jem or Alice Cran – Lady James Salisbury
Arker – Lord Arthur Strutt, later Admiral Strutt
Ba, Baffy – Blanche Campbell Balfour
Bear – Lady Frances Balfour's nickname for Gerald Balfour
Betty, Bet[t]s, Bettina, or Bina – Lady Elizabeth Balfour, nee Lytton
Bob or Bobs – Lord Robert Cecil
Cat, Old Cat – Gerald's nicknames for Lady Frances Balfour
Chief, Nunkie, Old Man – Arthur Balfour, later Lord Balfour

Conny – Lady Constance Emmott, nee Campbell
Con – Lady Constance Lytton
Constance – Lady Battersea
Despot – Lord George Campbell; to his grandchildren he was 'Pardie'
Evey – Lady Evelyn Campbell
Fa – Lady Frances Balfour, nee Campbell
Fish – Lord William Cecil
Fluffy – Florence, Lady William Cecil
Froggy – Lady Mary Glyn, nee Campbell
Granny, Mimi – Duchess Amelia
Gubbit, Annie – Alison Balfour
Georgy – Lady Salisbury
Gwenny, Tim – Lady Gwendolen Cecil
Jem – Lord James Cecil (4th Marquess)
Libby – Lady Elizabeth Clough-Taylor, nee Campbell
Linky – Lord Hugh Cecil
Melcho – Lady Mary Elcho
Nell, Nelly, Hell Nell – Eleanor Cole, nee Balfour
Nelly – Eleanor, Lady Robert Cecil
Nigs or Ned – Lord Edward Cecil
Nunkie – Arthur Balfour, 1st Earl of Balfour
Nunky G – Gerald Balfour, 2nd Earl Balfour
Peter, Pete, Ux (for Jupiter), Saul - Eustace Balfour
RAL – Lord Robert Arthur Lytton Balfour, 3rd Earl of Balfour
Robin – Lord Robert Strutt
Savage – Dr Arthur Milne
St O – Oswald Balfour
Teddy – Rev Edward Carr Glyn, later Bishop of Peterborough
Vi (pronounced VEE) – Lady Victoria Campbell
Wang – Mabel Palmer – married Earl Grey
"The White Man's Burden" – Frank Balfour

Other friends of the family were also given nicknames:

Biba - Lady Rosemary Finlay
The Castle - Lord Robert Finlay
Chimes - The Very Rev Dr Robert H. Story
Colinton - The Very Rev Dr Norman Maclean

Fairy – Mrs Anderson
Hamish - The Very Rev Dr James McGregor
Lord Hi – Dr Sir Arthur Mitchell
Mitty - The Very Rev Dr Mitford Mitchell
St Andrew - The Very Rev Dr A J Milne

Lady Frances's pseudonyms included: 'Ne Obliviscaris,' 'Grille,' 'Churchman,' 'Ethica', 'Joshua Hosh'

PROLOGUE

On a cold December evening in 1909, Lady Frances Balfour sat calmly on the platform in Aylesbury Town Hall, waiting to speak to a 'largely attended' suffrage meeting, when a 'working man' shouted angrily, 'It's a woman's place at home to cook a man's dinner or breakfast. We don't want women in Parliament. We want men who can speak, and do justice to the working man'.[1] Getting to her feet, Frances strode to the podium, looked serenely at the audience, and said in her beautiful, low voice, '[T]he man's question [is] easy to answer, for it [is] not suggested that women should sit in Parliament [and] not cook their husband's dinner'. But, she added, chivvying the man and his mates even more, 'if every woman in the country refused for three weeks to cook any dinner, they would get the vote immediately'. The place erupted with noise (including laughter). She waited, again calmly, as order was restored and then resumed her speech. Another interruption soon arose, and once more she waited, gazing around the audience, showing no fear and no inclination to leave the field. When this second disturbance subsided, Frances 'continued her address with perfect composure until the noise grew so loud that her words were not audible a couple of yards away'. This time, 'The chairman vainly appealed for order', and though Frances never lost her composure or that personal power that characterized her, she realized that this storm was not going to pass. She sat down; she was the only one that night who was heard at all, and this was the only time in her career when her speaking was stopped.

In the late 1860s, British women began a prolonged campaign to get the right to vote. The acknowledged leader of these non-militant suffragists – as they were called – was Millicent Garrett Fawcett. The movement was chiefly undertaken by middle class women, but there was one aristocrat in its leadership, the only noblewoman – and the only Scot – to have a British leadership role in the campaign. Called Mrs Fawcett's 'First Lieutenant', Lady Frances Balfour worked tirelessly for 30 years for votes for women. Unlike many of the others who toiled in this field, however, Lady Frances did not stop there but worked equally hard and long for rights for women in general. This is her story.

CHAPTER ONE

'Emancipation was a Passion'[2]
(1858-1877)

'It is well-known, that much, both
of what is good and bad in the
Scottish national characters, arises
out of the intimacy of their family
connections'.

Sir Walter Scott,
Heart of Midlothian

'. . . [I]t is all same go out
learn lessons and so on'.[3]

Lady Frances Balfour, nee Campbell, was every inch a politician: women's causes were her campaigns and the women of Great Britain her constituency. In her desire to influence others, Frances mirrored her father, the 8th Duke of Argyll, a prominent political figure of the 19th century, who was regarded as one of the best orators in the House of Lords.[4] Denied the forum of Parliament, Lady Frances resorted to writing and public speaking to inform her family, friends, and country. If the 8th Duke of Argyll had a political heir, it was Frances, not her MP brothers, on whom the mantle of an old, politically prominent family fell.

From the impressive Armory Hall and the numerous, somber pictures on the walls of Inveraray Castle, the 'fairytale highland home'[5] of the Dukes of Argyll, Frances would have been reminded continually that she was descended from a great number of Scottish generals, martyrs, and Protestant warrior-leaders who rendered service to crown and country. Her Campbell ancestors were Celtic settlers of Western

Scotland; the Dukes of Argyll are Scotland's second most senior peerage.[6] The Campbell chiefs fought on the side of Robert the Bruce during the wars of national independence against England, most conspicuously in 1306 and 1314 in the Battles of Methven Park and Bannockburn. The Campbell chiefs were also known for their work on behalf of the Protestant Reformation in Scotland, their championing of Presbyterianism over Episcopacy, and their support for the Protestant Succession during the English civil wars of the seventeenth and eighteenth centuries. The 4th Earl of Argyll 'was the first person of importance in Scotland who embraced the Protestant religion'.[7] The 8th Earl and 1st Marquess of Argyll was the Commander-in-Chief of the Covenanter army during the English Civil War of the 1640s. Depending on the political realities of the moment, he supported either Charles I or Oliver Cromwell – and paid for those switched positions after the Restoration of Charles II: the 1st Marquess was beheaded for treason in 1661.

Nineteenth-century Britons were probably most familiar with the 2nd Duke of Argyll (1680-1743), who earned a 'military reputation . . . second only to that of [the Duke of] Marlborough in the War of Spanish Succession.'[8] An ardent supporter of the Act of Union with England in 1707, the 2nd Duke also led the royal forces which suppressed the Jacobite rebellion in Scotland in 1715. The British throne thus secured for the Protestant Hanoverians, the 2nd Duke was subsequently honored with a large memorial in Westminster Abbey and immortalized by Sir Walter Scott as the hero of *The Heart of Midlothian*.

During most of the eighteenth century, the Dukes of Argyll wielded great political power in Scotland. As the most influential leaders of the Whig Party (the Tories were identified with Jacobitism), the 3rd Duke (1682-1761) – proclaimed 'the uncrowned King of Scotland'[9] – and his brother, the 4th Duke (1693-1770), virtually ruled Scotland as a personal fief mid-century.[10] Frances's father and brother, the 8th and 9th Dukes, also had leading roles in British governmental affairs in the 19th and early 20th centuries, but were the last Campbells to do so. The virtual demise of power of the House of Lords during the twentieth century, however, has resulted in a decline in influence of the British nobility in the affairs of state.

In 1844, Frances's father, George Douglas Campbell, married Lady Elizabeth Leveson-Gower, eldest daughter of the 2nd Duke and Duchess of Sutherland, heirs to the oldest earldom in Scotland.[11] Like the Argylls, the forebears of the Sutherlands were warriors and lieges of the Scottish kings. In 1847, Frances's father became the 8th Duke of Argyll, making him *MacCalein Mor*, Chief of the Clan Campbell. The striking and beautiful Inveraray Castle was the seat of an estate estimated in 1883 as having approximately 175,114 acres, and generating an annual income of £50,842.[12]

The current structure, based on a sketch by Vanbrugh and begun in 1743, replaced a 15th century castle. Its appearance today reflects changes made after a fire in 1877 and another in 1975. It rests below Dun Na Cuaiche, a high promontory. (The three-hour trek to the top was a favourite but challenging walk for Frances as she was growing up.)

Frances's maternal grandmother, Harriet Elizabeth Georgina Howard, daughter of the Earl of Carlisle and one of the most widely respected women of her day, was a powerful example in her granddaughter's life. As Whig Mistress of Robes for Queen Victoria and in constant attendance on the Queen, she held the highest social-political position among non-royal women in Britain. Supported by the wealth of an estate which (in 1883) comprised 1,358,545 acres and generated an annual income of £141,667,[13] she was one of the most influential political hostesses of her time.[14] She was also a woman of strong, independent convictions, not easily swayed by popular notions of right and wrong. It was her maternal grandmother's independence and courage that Frances lauded in her autobiography, *Ne Obliviscaris (Dinna Forget)*. She wrote of a woman unafraid of using the influence bestowed by rank and social prestige: 'Not all used it', she asserted, 'but Harriet, Duchess of Sutherland did her part, and round her gathered without distinction of creed or party, those who needed a champion'.[15] Her grandmother's example is clearly visible in Frances's choices and behavior during her long career of fighting for women's rights.

Frances's mother, too, was a notable woman. Oblivious to many practical concerns, the Duchess of Argyll was a woman of strong religious belief and, according to Frances, a woman of 'uncommon intellect.'[16] A pioneer in her own right, she was the first president of the Edinburgh Ladies' National Education Association, founded in 1870 to provide medical education to British women. A 'beautiful woman' with 'great stateliness and dignity', the Duchess kept one 'somewhat at a distance', though 'she was very kind and considerate'.[17] One of the governesses once said of her that 'the Duchess possessed all the big coins of character but none of the small change'. Above all, 'she hated gossip'.[18] These two women subtly influenced the woman Frances became.

Frances was one of 12 children, 11 of whom were born between 1845 and 1859; the last, Constance, was born five years later.[19] The Duke's estate generated a considerable annual income, and one of the Duke's preoccupations was improving his properties; he was, however, saddled with large inherited debts, which he worked during his entire life to repay.[20] He was not, unfortunately, a shrewd financial manager[21] and was plagued by financial woes throughout his life.

A Renaissance man, the Duke's interests were not confined to politics and his estate. During the early 1850s, he made his mark in science when he discovered in 1850 that volcanic eruptions of an earlier age on the Scottish island of Mull had occurred not under the water but above it.[22] Argyll's speech to the Geological Society in 1851 and his paper on the subject, published in the *Journal of the Geological Society of London* in May 1852, 'paved the way for all that has since been done in the investigation of the remarkable history of tertiary volcanic action in the British isles'.[23] The Duke subscribed to the cataclysmic school of geology; he was not a Darwinian evolutionist. His 'intellectual output – unusual for a duke – was one of the most thoroughgoing attempts of the second half of his century to defend a Christian (or at any rate a deistic) individualist position'.[24] He was elected a Fellow of the Royal Society in January 1851 and served as Chancellor of the University of St Andrews from 1851-1900; Lord Rector of Glasgow University from 1854-56; and President of the Royal Society of Edinburgh, 1860-64. In addition, he was a published poet and a 'competent' artist.[25]

Historically, the two major interests of the Campbell family were politics and the Church of Scotland. At age 19, Frances's father launched his public life with the publication of an article on the great crisis then confronting the Church of Scotland, a struggle which culminated in The Disruption of 1843. The main issue at hand was the appointment of parish clerics by lay patrons who were usually the great landowners – and the Argylls were 'perhaps the largest owners of church patronage in Scotland'.[26] Frances's father favored changing the law to allow congregations to veto the appointment of ministers unacceptable to them, a position favoured by the fundamentalists, but he was not prepared to accept the 1843 secession, when two-fifths of the Church of Scotland's ministers walked out of the General Assembly, the governing body of the Church, and formed the Free Church of Scotland. Frances's family remained true to the Church of Scotland.

The Duke's first opportunity to serve in government occurred after the fall of Lord Derby's government in autumn 1852. Argyll was essentially a Whig – that is, a conservative Liberal, not an unusual political position for many mid-nineteenth-century British landlords. Thus, the coalition government formed by the Earl of Aberdeen in December 1852 was the ideal entry into the government for Argyll. He was offered Lord Privy Seal on Christmas Day 1852. In his acceptance letter to Aberdeen, Argyll noted that his definition of good government included 'the uniting of steady progress and a liberal policy with a firm and jealous attachment to all the old institutions and the traditionary principles of the English people'[27] – all positions evident in the political philosophy Frances developed.

After studying an issue privately, Frances's father always determined what course of action he believed was correct for himself and for his party and then, taking his stand, championed – but according to Frances never argued[28] – his beliefs with all the forcible language at his command.[29] The Duke, his self-confidence sometimes bordering on arrogance, occasionally got carried away, but he was an effective defender of the Liberals in a predominantly Tory House of Lords.[30] And while he was at times a maverick, he was not a political dogmatist; his liberalism was marked by integrity and tolerance.[31] All these traits were echoed in Frances's behaviors and beliefs throughout her adult life.

With a growing family and the need now to remain in the capital for the entire Parliamentary session, the Duke in 1852 purchased a London residence on Campden Hill in Kensington, adjoining Holland Park; he renamed the property Argyll Lodge. 'If you were "in Society" it was necessary to be seen at Holland House (Lady Holland), Sion [Syon] House (Duchess of Northumberland), Argyll Lodge (Duchess of Argyll), and at Osterley Park (Countess of Jersey)', according to Lady Aberdeen.[32]

After receiving a copy of *Uncle Tom's Cabin* from its American author, Harriet Beecher Stowe, the Duke regularly denounced slavery and championed the work of the American abolitionists. Thus, the abolition of slavery and the outcome of the Civil War were two of the first political issues about which Frances heard as an adolescent.

> Emancipation was a passion of the purest and highest belief, in the heart of my home. I have always believed that this atmosphere . . . lay at the root of my intense conviction that the subjection of any race or nation, be they black or white, male or female, was a thing against the laws of God and man. I hold the belief that the American Civil War first set the civilized world seriously to think, whether the inequality of sex, could be as little defended, as was slave holding.[33]

When in 1855, as a result of the Crimean War debacle, Aberdeen's Ministry fell and gave way to Lord Palmerston's Administration, the new Whig leader reappointed the Duke to office. 'Pam' successfully defended his Government in 1857 and again in 1858, but it fell on 19 February 1858. Argyll was thus out of office only hours before the birth of Frances.

'Baby [Frances] is a beautiful creature, so jolly and firm', wrote the Duchess of Argyll to her sister-in-law, Lady Emma Campbell – 'Aunt Dot' – a few months after Frances's birth.[34] The tenth child of the Duke and Duchess of Argyll, Lady Frances Campbell was born Monday, 22 February 1858, at her parents' four-acre London residence.

She apparently began life as a healthy child, but at about age 2 ½, her mother recorded that 'Little Frances was threatened two months ago with hip joint mischief, and Syme [her doctor] prescribed bandaging with a splint and perfect rest. She was laid up for eight weeks, and is now toddling about the house, but is not to be allowed to go out walking this winter'.[35] Thus began an enforced bed rest regimen for what was probably congenital hip dislocation.[36] It was a treatment to which Frances would be subjected until her 19th year.

It was an excruciating routine for the energetic girl: the two-year old Frances lay motionless in her bed, bound tightly to a splint. Though she could hear her sisters and brothers in the rooms and halls around her, she must stay in "Counterpane Lane"[37]. On a string above her head, strung from post to post of her crib, Blondin, who wheeled a barrow filled with his family,[38] provided some distraction. Seldom visited by siblings or parents, she spent weeks, even months, in the forced stillness of the effort to correct her displaced hip. She longed to '[toddle] about the house', to run with her siblings, to ride horses – even to fence with brother Archie[39] – as she grew up; but these enjoyments were denied her. Except for the hour of tea, when Frances was carried into the Castle's beautiful drawing-room, where she could see the Beauvais Tapestry and the gilded ceiling and from which she could look out a window, she was alone most of the time. Despite these treatments she endured for 16 years, there was no improvement. One leg was forever shorter than the other, forcing her to wear a built-up shoe to ameliorate a limp.

As she grew, she learned to endure – to endure the enforced stillness, to endure the lack of companionship which she craved, to endure the pain from which she would never escape. Her self-reliance, her concentrated intellect, and indeed her 'temper', as she called it, which she exhibited (and with which she struggled) as an adult can be traced in large part to her early experience with these harsh efforts to remedy a condition which the treatment never corrected. Writing as an adult, she said, 'My character was undoubtedly too pugnacious, largely because of the physical fight that was associated with my early youth.'[40] Of course, children of this time were not 'spoiled' by parents or servants, and most children – including Frances – were taught not to weep except in 'real' emergencies, nor was one supposed to complain.

Fortunately, Frances was born into a household whose servants were unusually devoted to them. She fondly recalled that many 'sleepless hours [were] soothed by [the] vigil' of 'Nana', Elizabeth Campion, the Nanny,[41] who instilled in Frances the habit of deferring to her father. Elizabeth King, the head housekeeper, was also a significant force in her life, King's fervid fundamentalism being reflected in Frances's religious beliefs.[42]

Frances and her sisters were educated by a governess, Georgina Johnstone, an Englishwoman whose interesting nickname was 'Pock', short for Pock Pudding.

Frances remembered the self-taught Pock with great affection, but she did not praise the education she received at Pock's hands ('The teacher in the parish school could have instructed in a more effective way'[43]). Frances was quite impressed, however, with the 'cultured atmosphere which hung around this learned lady'[44] and with the example which Pock set in her lifelong pursuit of knowledge, which Frances came to emulate. Frances's actual education seems to have been somewhat lacking, however: she knew some history, literature, and grammar; her knowledge of foreign languages and geography was scant; and she was particularly deficient in arithmetic because she was not expected to keep books or do more mathematically than make change.[45] Frances probably began her schooling earlier than most girls because she could read by age four (she 'read widely' during the many hours she was confined to bed). In fact, she would prove to be the most intellectual member of the family.[46]

At mealtimes and tea, Frances and her siblings learned much from their parents, especially about politics and history. In an age when most children only got to 'visit' with their parents for a short spell each day – one hour in the evening being the norm – the Campbell children were regularly included in the family entertainments and festivities both at Inveraray and in London, and encouraged to participate in the conversations, which were 'spirited and heated'.[47] This practice was instrumental in creating the person Frances would become. The Argylls entertained many of the leading intellectuals of the time, including the Poet Laureate Alfred, Lord Tennyson; philosophers John Stuart Mill and Thomas Carlyle; the Christian Socialist Charles Kingsley; the Tractarians Edward Pusey and John Keble; the American poet Henry Wadsworth Longfellow; and most of the luminaries of the Church of Scotland and the Church of England. In a culture in which women were not welcome as speakers on platforms, Frances acquired some of the arts of public speaking by participating in the dinner table talk and discussions with guests. The family's extensive library also provided some of Frances's education. Except for the works of Sir Walter Scott, however, it apparently contained little fiction. Thus, it was Scott that Frances read in her youth, and it was always 'Scott, of course',[48] whom she read to her grandchildren. (When passing Scott's monument in Edinburgh, she even required any children with her to bow.)

Frances and her sisters, however, learned few of the skills most Victorian women cultivated – embroidering, crocheting, painting, playing the piano, and singing – though Frances did learn to knit, probably to occupy her thoughts and hands during the lengthy bouts of bed rest. By the age of nine, she could draw reasonably well, but Frances could neither play a musical instrument nor sing and, since she was – like her father – tone deaf, she had very little appreciation of music cxccpt for 'the Pipes'.[49]

Sadly, in 1863, the then-widowed Duchess of Sutherland, already troubled with cataracts and diabetes, was diagnosed with cancer. Her last attendance on Queen Victoria was the marriage at Windsor Castle of the Prince of Wales to Princess Alexandra in March 1863.[50]

Frances began her life-long habit of writing in a diary as a child, though she found it difficult at first,[51] primarily due to the tedium of her daily routine: '**it is all the same go out learn lessons and so on**'.[52] Many of her entries, which give a picture of her daily life at Inveraray, also speak to the monotony of a Victorian girl's life even that of an aristocrat [as given]:

> **Thursday 22 Au [1867] this morning we went a little way but it begane to rain in the afternoon Victoria and I went with Mama and [Aunt] Dot in the carriage and we named a little stream 'bubble' stream and a nother step stream. Mary walked with Miss Doeling.**[53]

> **Friday the 23 Au . . . Baby [Conny] and Mary[,] Baker [Conny's nurse] and I went to Baby's garden. I made another road. Miss Isa Cumming and here brother came here this evening she is not very pretty.**

> **Saturday the 24 this morning we went with Evey and Vic and Knowles by the riverside and worked a little in Baby's garden Mr Richmond came to day he is to paint our to heads [Frances and Mary].**

Often, she vowed that she would wait for '**something important to happen**' before writing anything more in her diary, and indeed, there are gaps of time between some entries.

Frances did not have many opportunities to make close friends with those outside her family circle. As she later put it, 'We used to be told that it was unnecessary for us to go to children's parties, as we were a party in ourselves'.[54] In truth, 'the children's party, the kindergarten, the idea that youngsters must be given companions of their own age . . . did not exist' in Victorian and Edwardian Britain.[55] Thus, except for the occasional visit of a family friend who might bring along a daughter or a son (most of whom were older than Frances), the Campbell girls had only each other, their parents, and their servants for company. Such exclusiveness was not altogether conducive to the development of good social skills (though all the adults around her devoted much time to correcting her manners, speech, and habits – very likely the source of her own lifelong tendency to 'correct' others). Frances never learned the tactfulness and sensitivity to the feelings of others that most people with a less segregated or insular upbringing acquire. On the other hand, the tolerance of differences, the more liberal political views espoused (Scotland had the '"most democratic aristocracy in the world"'[56]), and the kindness encouraged by the Argylls made Frances less elitist and more sympathetic to others.

Of all her sisters, Frances was closest to Victoria, her comrade in infirmity: Vi contracted infantile paralysis in 1859 and eventually was fitted in Paris with steel braces, on which she relied for the rest of her life. When Vi went to Brighton early in September 1867, Frances wrote: **'I miss Vict – awfully it is so dull without her and Knowles** [Victoria's companion and caretaker]'.[57]

Frances was particularly happy when, in autumn 1867, her oldest sister, Edith, became engaged to marry Earl Percy, heir of the Duke of Northumberland. **'Lord Percy asked Edith to marry him and she said yes O it is so nice Edith is very happy he is not handsome but very good natured and nice it is dilicious'.**[58]

The next fall brought grief; in October 1868, Frances and her sisters received the news at Inveraray **'that all was over [with Grandmother] it is very very sad she had great pain before but near the end she had none we ought to be very thankful . . . . Mama says she looks quite beautiful'.** The Duchess of Sutherland was buried in the family mausoleum at Trentham. The Prince of Wales, who laid a wreath on the coffin, served as a pallbearer.[59] Frances's mother was subsequently appointed The Queen's Mistress of the Robes.[60]

Lady Edith Campbell married Lord Percy in the parish church of St George's, Notting Hill, London, on 23 December 1868. Frances, age 10, was a bridesmaid. In 1869, Frances was again a bridesmaid when her brother Archie and Janey Callander, considered 'the most beautiful young woman of her day',[61] were married.

During the Parliamentary sessions, the Argylls lived in London, where the girls' walks were confined to Rotten Row, the area of Hyde Park where the British upper class went 'to see and to be seen'[62] by their social equals. Since 'all "ladies" lived under constant surveillance',[63] young girls appearing outside their home had to be accompanied by a chaperone. The Campbell girls, except for Frances, also took riding lessons while in London; Frances wished to ride, but Sir Prescott Hewitt advised on 18 February 1869 against riding just **'yet'**. Unfortunately, Frances was never able to ride, but – to compensate – she became a good 'whip' or driver of a pony cart.[64]

One illness especially distressed the family in 1869. After missing the family's carriage sent to pick her up at Lochgoilhead on a cold day in December, the Duchess traveled to Inveraray Castle in an open carriage, arriving late at night unusually cold and tired. During the night, she suffered a stroke; she remained in critical condition for several weeks. The Duchess's health had improved by February 1870, but her 'walking [was] a miserable attempt still'.[65] She made only a partial recovery.

The 1870s began with the engagement and marriage of Frances's eldest brother to Princess Louise, a daughter of Queen Victoria and Prince Albert. This marriage marked a major departure for British royalty. No child of a reigning English monarch had married a commoner since 1515, but the Queen, who now relied on her daughters to fill Prince Albert's place, sought for Louise a non-royal husband who would 'reside nearby'.[66] Lorne, well-known to the Queen, emerged as the major candidate.[67]

The Princess Louise and the Marquis of Lorne were married 21 March 1871 in St George's Chapel at Windsor. Only Libby was a bridesmaid, but the rest of the Campbell children were invited to Windsor Castle, where they saw Princess Louise in her wedding attire before the ceremony. '[The] first sight of Princess Louise in Windsor's long corridor, remain[ed] imprinted on my memory. A vision of beauty . . .', the 13-year old recalled. 'I fell in love with her at once. . .'.[68] The marriage, which Queen Victoria proclaimed 'the most popular act' of her reign, was hailed as 'striking a "democratic note" in the royal family'.[69]

Since 'spectacles were not becoming to a young lady',[70] Frances had been prevented from getting help for her shortsightedness. Now, Princess Louise bought Frances her first pair of glasses and thus 'transformed her existence'.[71] The reality of having a Royal in the family soon became clear to the Campbells, including the enraptured Frances. Louise was unable to attend many family events because the Queen demanded so much of her daughter's time. By 20 March 1872, Frances was less forgiving of Louise's absences. She recorded, '**Louise <u>as usual</u> unable to come**' to a large dinner party of 19 people. The Campbell children's lives went on, however, Royal connection or no.

That the early teen years were a trial at times for Frances is apparent from her diary entries. On one occasion, she '**had a delightful row with Pock on my supposed gaucherie**'.[72] She ruefully recorded on 14 February 1872 that she '**got one valentine Mary two**' and sadly stated on 28 February that her '**poor red-pole**' – birds were the only pets the Campbell children were permitted to have – had died. Her chaffinch, a present from her brother George on 29 February, died on 11 March. She replaced the dead birds with a '**nice green linnet**'. Repeatedly, she concluded that life was '**Such a bore**', a favourite expression for her frustration.

Birthdays, however, were always special days: on her fourteenth birthday 1872, Frances, Victoria, Evey, and Mary were taken to Madame Tussaud's: '**We were told not to go into the Chamber of Horrors but we saw everything else**', reported Frances. On 29 February, she, Evelyn, and Mary spent the evening with Princess Beatrice at Buckingham Palace. '**A nice evening on the whole but rather nervous[.] Prince Arthur came in**'.

Between 1858-1874, as Frances was growing up, her father was unusually busy with political work. Following the fall of the Derby government in 1859 over the issue of franchise reform, the Whig-Liberal Lord Palmerston replaced Derby as Prime Minister, and Argyll was back in the cabinet, again as Lord Privy Seal. On Palmerston's death in 1865, another Liberal leader, Lord Russell, replaced 'Pam' as Prime Minister. But the Government's preoccupation with its new electoral reform bill from 1866-1867 brought about the fall of the Russell Administration and Argyll's exit from government, which proved only temporary. When the Liberal Party returned to power in December 1868, William Gladstone, now Prime Minister, gave Argyll the India Office.

By the early 1870s, Frances, who shared the Campbell interest in politics, now regularly included political news in her diary. One event which evoked much comment by Frances was the illness of Edward, Prince of Wales. In November 1871, the heir to the throne fell victim to typhoid fever, the same illness that had killed his father ten years earlier. Perilously close to death by December, the Prince gradually rallied and survived the affliction. On 27 February, a Thanksgiving Service attended by the Queen and Prince of Wales was held at St Paul's Cathedral in London. Frances and her sisters attended: '**A thing never to be forgotten[.T]he music was beautiful. . . . Queen tremendously cheered. . .'.** Frances's enthusiasm for the reception accorded the Queen reflected the change in the popular feeling for the monarch, whose virtual seclusion following Prince Albert's death in 1861 had given rise to Republican sentiment.

Though young, Frances sensed that the Thanksgiving service did much to strengthen the monarchy. It is not clear whether Frances kept a diary from 1873-1876, but none can be found in the Balfour Papers; there is thus no intimate record of her daily life during her mid-teens.

The Gladstone government fell in 1874, when the Conservatives, led by Benjamin Disraeli, were victorious. By this time, Frances's brother Lorne was a Member, having first been elected – he was unopposed – in 1868. Since he had never spoken in the House of Common, however, his performance in Parliament had been disappointing. The election brought Irish Nationalists into Parliament, and Argyll, already displeased with the Radicals in the party, professed to be relieved to be rid of ministerial responsibilities.[73]

The year 1877, which began with Queen Victoria's being proclaimed Empress of India, found Frances, now age 18, at Inveraray, where she endured another bout of confinement because of her hip. This time she was not permitted to join the family for **'meals downstairs'** for 18 days.[74] By this point in her life, Frances found her confinements all but intolerable: though an adult, Frances apparently was not permitted to have any say in the treatment for her hip problem, even when it was obvious that her condition could not be corrected by enforced bed rest. At one point this January, she 'lost her temper badly',[75] and she had a row with her father. That he sympathized with her was apparent when, after Frances **'ran off and spent the afternoon upstairs,'** he 'sent me the jolliest letter',[76] and a day later permitted her to review his sums.

Frances's turmoil was also undoubtedly exacerbated by an inner conflict: she was at the age when she had to think about her future, and she wanted to be 'useful' to family, friends, and society (as *noblesse oblige* – and her upbringing – dictated). Frances desired to become a nurse, a strange choice for one who was lame, but she had an additional handicap: young women of the aristocracy (and many in the middle class) did not have 'careers'. Aristocratic women in Victorian Britain were expected to marry and preside over large households. Frances quickly learned that almost everyone opposed her desire for a career in nursing, and she soon informed her father that she had **'[given] up thinking of the [Nursing] Institute and resolved to be a help and comfort this winter not a beastly hindrance'.**[77]

It is quite likely that Frances's decision as an adult to work for women's equality with men was made because of all the prohibitions with which she was surrounded in her early life. She was told that she could not walk about without a chaperone, wear glasses, ride a horse, or be a nurse. Perhaps the strongest force that pushed her toward her work for women, however, was the fact that she would not be allowed to participate in the political process the way her brothers and her father could. The continual emphasis on what she could *not* do undoubtedly made her determined to be an instrument of change for women.

CHAPTER TWO

'Many plans for the Future' [78]
(1877-1879)

'Mr Balfour very nice'.[79]

'My life is in some senses more
lonely and empty of interest than
yours ought to be, because a
woman must keep more or less in
a "trivial round"'.[80]

By 1877, Lady Frances Campbell was preparing to take her first Communion, that pivotal point at which girls were 'out of the schoolroom' and ready for entry into Society.[81] Frances was nineteen years old and – her mother's reservations notwithstanding – desired to make her debut. She declared that she had **'Many plans for the future.'**[82]

At the same time that she prepared for her Communion, she was taking classes for her formal presentation at Court. This was no small undertaking. A Court dancing master taught required lessons in how to hold a long train, to walk erect in ostrich feathers and a tiara headdress, to bow before the Queen when presented, and to execute nine or ten deep curtseys to other royal family members before retiring from the Presence.[83] Frances made few remarks about her preparation and presentation at Court in her diary, and only once did she refer to her dancing tutor Talloni, who **'put me through my facings'** and was much **'encouraged'** by the lesson.[84] Given her physical difficulties, it must have been a challenging regimen. On 14 March 1877, she was presented by her Aunt Constance, Duchess of Westminster (her mother was too ill to attend).[85]

Frances's debut was followed by her first ball, on 15 March at Grosvenor House, the home of the Duke and Duchess of Westminster. Described as a 'very beautiful' young woman,[86] Frances did not lack for attention. Her golden red hair and whitest of skins made her quite noticeable at the dances and parties she attended during her Season. Though she did not like dancing,[87] she acknowledged that being 'out' was about the only way to make acquaintances – and meet prospective husbands. And she knew that marriage would bring a measure of physical and emotional independence: she would be freed of chaperones and compulsory bed rest.

Though Frances was apprehensive about her prospects, her fears proved unwarranted: she met Eustace Balfour during her first Season, at a ball at the home of Lord and Lady Goschen. '[M]y hostess brought into my vision, and introduced me to the most gigantic young man I had ever seen [Eustace was 6'5"]', she recalled.[88] 'The tall youth . . . was very thin, and had a face of great pallor, surmounted by a shock of dark hair, and a serious expression. Thus, I first met my future husband. . . '. At a breakfast at Chiswick on 4 July, she commented, '**Mr Balfour very nice**'. The final event of the Season was a 'drum' at Lord Salisbury's London residence in Arlington Street. Frances recorded in her diary that she '**saw [a] good deal [of] E. Balfour**'[89] that evening, and since her family was 'not then intimate with that illustrious family', Frances concluded that Eustace had probably persuaded his Aunt, Lady Salisbury, to invite her and Evey to the soiree.[90]

At their Highland home at Inveraray for their annual family holiday in 1877, the Campbells were awakened on the night of 11 October by a great fire which threatened the castle. Aroused by New, the Butler, Frances and Mary – in their 'stupefied funk' – got into their dressing gowns, seized their parrots from their cages, and fled into the hallway, where they met Lorne, who led them to the room where the rest of the family were gathered.[91] The large central hall – the chief family gathering site – and its roof were destroyed. Miraculously, no lives were lost, although 'some forty or more people' had been in the castle.[92]

Despite her enlarged social calendar, Frances was greatly interested in the Eastern Question, once more in focus with the Balkan tensions of 1870s. Britain had followed a pro-Turkish policy since the 1850s, largely because of Russian expansionist plans in the Balkans; that policy was now jeopardized by a reign of terror unleashed by Abdul Hamid II's Turkish irregulars against the Bulgars, in which thousands of Christian subjects had been massacred. Britain went to the brink of war to compel a revision of the harsh terms imposed by Russia on Turkey in the San Stefano Treaty. As the question was resolved at the Congress of Berlin (1878), Frances was no doubt intrigued by the work of Lord Salisbury, Foreign Secretary, who was assisted by Eustace's older brother Arthur Balfour, in his first foray into foreign affairs.

When Frances and her family returned to London for the opening of Parliament in 1878, she found Eustace Balfour waiting to resume his courtship. He invited her to lunch with him and his sister, Evelyn, Lady Rayleigh at his home in Addison Road. Following the meal, she and Eustace walked in his 'little garden, escorted by the chaperones behind'.[93] Frances regretted that she 'tactlessly chose' for her topic of conversation 'the subject that all politically minded people were thinking about at the time, namely the Eastern Question', as she quickly learned that Eustace desired 'not [to] waste time in discussing politics'.[94] Thus, both Frances and Eustace discovered early in their courtship that their interests differed.

Since there is no diary for 1878, we do not know all the times that she saw Eustace after this luncheon, but on Good Friday, 19 April, she attended a performance of Handel's 'Messiah' in Albert Hall with Eustace, Arthur, and Evelyn, following dinner at Carlton Gardens, Arthur's home in the capital. To Frances, the evening 'was one of life's great experiences',[95] an assessment no doubt associated with the other significant event of the day: Eustace's proposal. For the rest of her life, Frances attended a performance of the 'Messiah' every Good Friday as a commemoration of their engagement. Before she could accept, however, her parents sent her to Edinburgh to allow them time to consider the proposal. In truth, the Eastern Question so divided Britons that, for a time at least, the Argylls hesitated to let Frances marry 'a nephew of Lord Salisbury', a Conservative.[96] It was George, the brother to whom she was closest, who helped his parents overcome their Whig prejudices, and Eustace and Frances officially became engaged. While she was still away from London, though, a tragedy greater than the fire afflicted the family.

After her debilitating stroke in 1869, the Duchess of Argyll had continued to suffer additional strokes in the 1870s, becoming progressively worse following the fire at Inveraray Castle. On 24 May 1878, while attending a dinner party at the home of Lord and Lady Frederick Cavendish, the Duchess slumped unconscious over the table and was carried into the study. Four doctors and two nurses were immediately summoned to attend her, but the Duchess, who was only 54 years old, died at 3:30 am without regaining consciousness.[97] The cause of the Duchess's death was 'cerebral apoplexy', but most of the family agreed with Queen Victoria, who believed that "the poor Duchess of Argyll's illness is entirely the result of over exhaustion from having twelve children".[98] After Dean Stanley 'conducted a private service in St Faith's Chapel, Westminster Abbey for the family',[99] the Duchess was buried at Kilmun, the Campbell burial ground on the Holy Loch.

The Duke of Argyll did not resume his daily routine in the autumn – 'The memories [were] a trial to all'[100] – but instead took the family to Cannes for the winter. It was Frances's first trip abroad.

Born on 8 June 1854, Eustace James Anthony Balfour was the youngest of eight children of Lady Blanche Gascoigne Cecil and James Maitland Balfour. The Balfour family home, Whittingehame,[101] was an 86-room, unadorned, Neo-Classical residence on a 10,000 acre farming estate in East Lothian in southeastern Scotland. Sadly, Eustace had no memory of his father, who had died of tuberculosis in Madeira in 1856.

Like his brothers, Eustace attended The Grange, a private school at Hoddesdon in Hertfordshire. All the Balfour brothers went on to Eton or Harrow. For all but Cecil, learning came relatively easily, and the Balfour boys were competent students. Eustace was only eight when he was enrolled at The Grange (Arthur was 11);[102] when Eustace finally reached the age when most students entered, the Headmaster, Rev Charles Chittenden, reported that Eustace 'shows a good deal of intelligence in his answers and remarks',[103] adding that he had performed 'remarkably well' in the math classes to which he had recently been exposed. Just as Frank would shine in science and Arthur and Gerald in philosophy, Eustace would excel in mathematics. Arthur and Gerald attended Eton and majored in philosophy at Cambridge; Frank, Cecil, and Eustace studied at Harrow and preferred the sciences or mathematics at Cambridge. Remarkably for upper-class Victorian Britain, all the Balfour children except Arthur were accomplished pianists, playing Handel, Bach, and Beethoven with ease.[104] For their love of music, Frances nicknamed the Balfours 'The B. Flats'.[105]

Eustace entered Harrow on 20 January 1869, staying only until sometime during the first term of 1870. During that brief stay, however, Eustace's performance was 'invariably near the top of his class in the main areas of study, i e Classics, Mathematics and Modern Languages'.[106] Eustace was sent at some point after the first term of 1870 to be tutored for Cambridge by George Faithfull, a cousin of Eustace's mother's assistant, Emily Faithfull. At his small school at Llanwenarth Rectory, Abergavenny, Faithfull immersed Eustace in mathematics, reporting in November that Eustace had completed the six books of Euclid, and that '[S]uch good mathematical work is not often seen'.[107]

Before Eustace could leave for Trinity College, Cambridge, his mother died (May 1872), and Arthur (who had come of age in 1869) and Lord Salisbury became the guardians of Eustace and his brothers Frank and Gerald. Faithfull continued to work with Eustace until he entered Trinity in Michaelmas Term 1873. At Cambridge, Eustace's extra-curricular activities included membership in Magpie and Stump, a well-known debating society.[108] After missing the Honours examination in Mathematics due to illness, Eustace received the BA degree in 1877.[109] It could not have been easy being perceived as only an average student in a family of high achievers, yet Eustace's education was as demanding as his brothers'. Based on the evidence, he excelled in several areas, and all the Balfour brothers had a more challenging educational regimen than that which was given most boys of their class.

While still a student at Cambridge, Eustace became apprenticed to the architect Basil Champneys and worked with him for three years,[110]apparently completing his training shortly before his marriage to Frances in 1879. Champneys' work included Newnham College, Cambridge.

Interestingly, the initial engagement of Frances and Eustace, in spring 1878, was very brief. When they discussed religion, Eustace apparently disappointed Frances: 'They were engaged for a day . . . [before 12 May] but had a broil on religion' and Frances called their engagement off.[111] Mrs Charles Sartoris, Janey's sister, explained, 'I believe Eustace said he did not believe in the devil. . . '.[112] With the Campbells in Cannes that holiday, Eustace journeyed in December to the Mediterranean to win Frances back. Working out the details of the betrothal was not easy. Eustace gave Frances a Bible[113] and a copy of his mother's prayer, which Frances declared was 'quite beautiful'.[114] Frances and her family engaged Eustace, also reared in a home where religion was important,[115] in several discussions on the subject during his visit. They presumably received satisfactory responses from him: Mrs Sartoris recorded that: '. . . either he has swallowed Satan, horns, hoofs and tail or love will still be lord of all and Frances has left his conversion to be "continued in our next"'.[116] On Christmas Day, he informed Alice ('Aggie') 'Frances and I are engaged [again]', news which he asked Alice to share with other members of the family.[117] He ended his letter by declaring that he was 'in 7th heaven' and imploring Alice to write to Frances.

By 3 January 1879, Frances had received letters from Nora, Alice, and Arthur. The letter from Alice revealed her need for Frances's love: 'I feel you to be my sister already, tho' I do not know you personally. And I must love anyone who has made my Eustace so happy as you have done. . . . I hope you will love me in return. I want your love so much . . . '.[118] The romantic Frances enthusiastically responded in kind: 'I do not quite know how to answer your letter, for I cannot tell you how I feel all your love and welcome'.[119] She then admitted, 'I have been dreadfully frightened that you would not approve of me and that Eustace had made a great mistake, but after all the letters I got yesterday I can never feel that again'. The two women in the Balfour household (Nora and Evelyn were no longer at home) thus began a close, friendly relationship that endured for several years.

The Duke of Argyll had agreed in his marriage settlement with the Sutherlands that each of his children born after his heir would receive a portion of £25,000 for a dowry.[120] Divided among eleven children, however, the funds actually available amounted only to small dowries. That Frances did not bring substantial funds to the marriage, though, seems to have been no deterrent to Eustace. He apparently had an income of approximately £1,000 a year[121] (£2,000 or more was viewed as the 'ideal'[122] – the average middle class income at this time was £100-300[123]), and he already owned a house at 32 Addison Road in Kensington, London.

Frances, who insisted on a Church of Scotland service, wanted to be married in Westminster Abbey, but the Abbey was restricted to Church of England ceremonies, so she settled on St John's Presbyterian Church in Allen Street, Kensington.[124] Frances was precluded from attending dances and large dinner parties in her and Eustace's honour because she was still in mourning for her mother, a restriction that lasted for twelve months.[125] However, she purchased a trousseau, made numerous calls with Eustace on relatives, and received a large number of wedding gifts, including a gold bracelet set with diamonds from 'the ladies of Inveraray'.[126] To allay any fears that Eustace might have about her ability to have children or about her health in general, Frances arranged for Eustace to meet with Sir Prescott Hewett.[127]

Frances further used the weeks preceding the wedding to become better acquainted with the Balfour family. By this time, the two eldest Balfour sisters had married (Evelyn married John W M Strutt, later 3rd Baron Rayleigh, in 1871, and in 1876, Eleanor, called 'Nora', married Cambridge Professor Henry Sidgwick). Although she was grateful for all their kindness, getting accustomed to her new family required some adjustment. During an evening at Carlton Gardens listening to Evelyn and Eustace play duets on the piano, Frances reminisced, **'I sat in the gloamin fire & thought me ain thoughts'**.[128] On 21 March, she admitted to her diary that she had **'Fearful homesickness. I do so long to say goodbye to the old hills'.** Frances had not been back to Inveraray since the fire (the Castle was let after it was rebuilt), and she missed her home more than usual.

Frances was also learning to reconcile her interests with those of Eustace. In many ways, it was a case of opposites attracting. While Frances's major interests were politics and religion, Eustace's were music, art, and architecture, and all things military. Frances's preferences in music extended only to hymns and massed choirs.[129] As far as politics was concerned, Eustace disliked the subject, though his sympathies lay with the Tories. The two did, however, share an interest in art. She liked colours, especially brilliant sunsets and interesting skies; Eustace once teased Frances about 'never ending a letter without [a description] of a sunset'.[130]

Frances appreciated the Balfour family's discussions, which ranged across a wide spectrum of topics.[131] Arthur Balfour had already embarked on a Parliamentary career, having been elected in 1874 for Hertford; Frances thus had at least one

Balfour with whom to talk politics. In her autobiography, Frances described the Balfours: 'old for their years', the 'conspicuously talented' Balfours' 'logical faculties bordered on the dry as dust' and – unlike her family – 'their emotions were held in strict control.'[132] 'Intellectually proud and ambitious', they were 'the epitome of the Lowland Scot'. 'Into the midst of this exclusive family I came, an unadorned, unrestrained, and totally illogical Celt'. Frances well understood why her relationship with Eustace worked: the Balfours were unusually tolerant of the opinions and prejudices of others, and, moreover, they admired Frances's sharp intelligence.

The date set for her wedding – 12 May 1879 – was dictated by her father's projected journey to Canada to visit Lorne, who shortly after their mother's death had been appointed Governor-General of Canada. The Duke therefore 'hastened' Frances's marriage so that she might be 'settled in her new life' before he departed for Canada in late May.[133] (Her brother George's marriage was also hurried: he married Sybil Alexander on 8 May, the week before Frances's nuptials.)

The wedding of Frances and Eustace was performed by Dr Story, with the Very Rev Dean Stanley pronouncing the blessing.[134] Libby, Evey, Mary, and Connie were bridesmaids (Victoria was ill).[135] Gerald Balfour was Eustace's best man. It was primarily family members who were invited to the nuptials since the Campbells were in mourning.[136]

Frances and Eustace spent the first part of their honeymoon at Whittinghame – **'I like the place much, a great spirit of peace over it all',** recorded Frances.[137] Alice, who now presided over the Balfour homes for her brother Arthur, took great pains to make Frances feel welcome.

Frances's addition to the family brought one unusual gift to the Balfours. She and her siblings had been taught not only to be 'intimate friends' with the people on the estate but to learn from them.[138] The Balfours, on the other hand, had remained aloof from both their neighbours and their retainers.[139] Frances was especially troubled by their 'high degree of insensitivity to the feelings of others':[140] on one occasion, she recalled, they even ran to hide behind a large tree when confronted with company. 'In course of time I broke through the barriers . . . and made many a warm and understanding friendship'.[141] In addition, she occasionally assisted troubled estate people. When she learned that Margaret Wood, sister of the Whittingehame Keeper, was 'living in great poverty in Stenton', Frances gave her a weekly allowance, unbeknownst to Alice, for the rest of Margaret's life.[142]

Frances and Eustace remained at Whittingehame until 29 May. After a stop in Edinburgh, where they visited 'Hamish'- the Rev James Macgregor – they finally arrived at her beloved Rosneath, another Campbell Castle, on 31 May. Frances, who was still miserably homesick, was ecstatic: **'Got "Home" about 8 P M Such a**

glorious evening . . .' . Before returning to London, the newlyweds finally visited the rebuilt Inveraray Castle, with its new conical towers like those at Balmoral and Dunrobin Castles: **'The place looking lovely',** she declared.[143]

Following their honeymoon of five weeks, Frances and Eustace returned to London on 18 June. Frances was now mistress of her own home, a house in Kensington she was **'delighted with'** and which would become her 'much loved home'.[144] The most distinctive feature of Frances's new three-story home was its drawing room, with its rich grey oak paneling, installed by Eustace prior to the marriage. The room spanned the depth of the house. Eustace had also added water closets to the home, and his friend William Morris, whose company created some of the most fashionable interiors of the day, decorated the Balfour dining room,[145] which featured a dumb waiter.

Frances's home was quite small compared to the houses in which she had grown up and those she visited at regular intervals; Inveraray Castle, for example, had 88 rooms.[146] Her daughter Baffy later admitted, 'I was aware that our house was smaller than almost any other house I knew . . . ', but her mother was 'deeply attached to the little house'.[147] Because of their limited income, Frances and Eustace at first employed only two or three servants at a time when the average number of servants in North Kensington was eight per household.[148] Even after the birth of their first child, they only had four servants in the house: a cook, a parlourmaid, a nurse, and a nursemaid.[149] By contrast, there were 20 servants at Whittingehame,[150] 27 at Argyll Lodge,[151] and more than 80 at Inveraray. That Frances was constrained to be cost-conscious and frugal throughout her life is apparent in her frequent diary references to the cost of such expenditures as railway tickets, wages for servants, and prices of books. Frances saved on transportation costs by traveling third class on trains and by using the omnibus around London,[152] behavior most unusual for one of her class.

Once settled into her new home, Frances began the Victorian routine of paying and receiving visits, lunching out, and leaving cards. It was an arduous process with rigid etiquette, the violation of which marked one as an outsider.[153] Still, Frances found time hung heavy on her hands. She noted in her autobiography that for non-working women 'there was very little [to do] in England that was outside the scope of what used to be called Church work'. [154] To occupy herself and to fulfill her obligations to charity, she joined Lady Mary Fielding's Working Ladies Guild (July 1879), which laboured to alleviate poverty among middle class women;[155] she awarded prizes at a flower show for window gardening in Notting Hill; and she visited Victoria in Brighton. She spent most of her time, however, visiting family members who lived in London. These activities, however, could not keep someone as energetic as Frances busy. As she later admitted to Lord Lytton (1887), 'My life is in some senses more lonely and empty of interest than yours ought to be, because a woman must keep more or less in a "trivial round"'.[156]

And she was still homesick. Much as she loved Eustace and the Balfours, adjusting to married life was not easy. Victorian women – whose sphere was in the home – were supposed to provide their husbands with a refuge from the harsh realities of the commercial world and public life. Strong-willed and independent-minded, Frances Balfour was never the home-bound, self-effacing wife that Victorian women were expected to be, though she certainly tried to be the wife she believed Eustace deserved. She lamented her perceived shortcomings repeatedly in her 1879 diary: **'Was not good to [Eustace] failing always & not making him really happy'**,[157] and **'God help me to be a better wife'**.[158] On their first anniversary, however, Frances's diary entry noted, **'A year of untold happiness, may God spare us for many another to each other'**.[159] Her love for her husband was evident throughout her life.

Like most people of their class, Frances and Eustace made weekend visits to the homes of family and friends. They most often visited Hatfield House, home of Lord and Lady Salisbury; and Cambridge, where Nora, Frank, and Gerald were in residence in the late 1870s and early 1880s. In addition, Frances and her family lived approximately six months of every year with Arthur and Alice at Whittingehame, from the holiday period which began in August through the New Year's celebration in mid-January.

Frances's first non-family friends were Eustace's artist associates, especially Edward Burne-Jones and William de Morgan. Eustace's association with these Pre-Raphaelites and Arts and Crafts figures came largely through his active support of the Society for the Protection of Ancient Buildings (SPAB), nicknamed the 'Anti-Scrape Society' for its 'opposition to the practice of scraping the original plaster off medieval walls'.[160] Eustace was a charter member of the organization, formed in 1877 by William Morris to protect buildings of historic and architectural significance from those who wished to tear them down or those who 'threatened to restore' them in an arbitrary architectural manner.[161] Eustace played a significant role in the Anti-Scrape Society for many years. In addition to serving as a member of 'the Committee', the Society's administrative council, Eustace also made evaluations of buildings that the organsation sought to preserve.

It was probably through the SPAB that Eustace made the acquaintance of architect Hugh Thackeray Turner, the Society's Secretary after 1883. In 1885, Eustace and Thackeray created Balfour and Turner, whose office at 9, Buckingham

Street (later 20, Buckingham) off the Strand was the office of the SPAB; the Society provided the space in order to make the poorly-paid position more attractive to Turner.[162] From 1883 to 1911, the SPAB was virtually run from Balfour and Turner's office. The firm's total production exemplified 'charm, originality, and . . . ability', according to one knowledgeable evaluator.[163]

Perhaps as an adjunct to his interest in architecture, Eustace became fascinated with photography, purchasing his first 'photo apparatus' during the holiday season of 1879.[164] Balfour family photos feature few portraits of him because he was usually the one behind the camera.[165]

In the early years of her marriage, Frances was shy and self-consciousness around strangers. She credited Edward Burne-Jones for helping her overcome her reticence.[166] In 1880-81, while painting her portrait at Eustace's insistence, Burne-Jones was able to gradually 'draw her out' by talking and reading to her.[167] Unfortunately, she was not very successful in cultivating the kind of close friendship – the kind she preferred – with Burne-Jones's wife, Georgiana. Having spent long periods alone as a child and adolescent, Frances both longed to be the centre of her husband's attention and yearned for friends who would write to her *every day*, thus demonstrating that they thought of her continually. It was a desire few, including Georgina, were willing to fulfill.

By September 1879, Frances was expecting her first child. Though she never wrote details about her pregnancy in her diary or her letters, she did keep a careful record of her pregnancy (at the beginning of the 1880 diary, she noted '21 weeks'). Her first child, named Blanche Elizabeth Campbell, was born at 4:30 am on Sunday, 23 May 1880. It was not an easy birth and, in her autobiography, Frances disclosed that she was 'dangerously ill [possibly of Puerperal fever] for a short time' after her baby's birth.[168] Eustace therefore received most of the congratulatory messages, which included one from Edward Burne-Jones, who wrote, 'I am so glad, and nothing is so nice as a daughter. There should be nothing but daughters. . . '.[169]

Frances's autobiographical comment on the birth of her first child was typical of her strong pronouncements: 'The woman who does not feel that the greatest event in her life, next to her marriage, is the birth of her first child must indeed be a congenital idiot.'[170] Although Frances supposedly disliked nicknames, her daughter was never called 'Blanche'. She earned her nickname, 'Baffy', by correcting her doctor when he referred to her as 'Baby': she informed him that she was 'Miss Baffy', her early attempt at 'Balfour'.

Frances and Eustace asked Arthur Balfour to be Baffy's godparent since 'he is the possession that is of the greatest value to her'.[171] Clearly, from the beginning of their relationship, Frances looked up to Arthur and deferred to him as did other family members (particularly Alice). Indeed, Arthur would gradually take the place of Frances's father in her life.

A few weeks before Baffy's birth, Britain had held a general election – the Midlothian Election of 1880 – and members of both the Balfour and Campbell families were involved in the campaign. Gladstone, using the 'Bulgarian Atrocities' agitation, achieved an overwhelming victory, with the Liberals acquiring 414 seats to 238 for Beaconsfield's Conservative Party and 60 for Charles Parnell's Irish party. Frances followed the election closely. On 1 April, she gloated, '**The Liberals are having the best of it**'. She also noted that '**Arthur is safe**'. *The Times* speculated that the Duke of Argyll would be the next President of the Council,[172] but Frances noted on 26 April that '**Papa has accepted [the] Privy Seal**'.

Argyll's tenure in the new Gladstone administration was short-lived. In April 1881, unhappy with Gladstone over the Irish Land Bill, which provided Irish tenants with the 'three F's' of fixity of tenure, fair rent, and free sale, Argyll resigned, one of the first casualties of Gladstone's Irish policy. Argyll's objection to the Land Bill was based on his strong support of English landowners in Ireland. Within one week of the Duke's resignation, Lord Beaconsfield died, on 19 April 1881. Though her parents loathed 'Dizzy', Frances – already making astute political assessments – eulogized Disraeli as '**A great man gone and the face of party politics I think changed**'.[173]

Marriages continued to expand the family. On 17 July 1880, Elizabeth (Libby) married Major Edward Clough-Taylor in St Mary Abbot's Parish Church in Kensington. Thereafter, Frances would see little of Libby, whose husband was appointed to a post in India.[174] Meanwhile, the Duke of Argyll had begun to court Amelia Marie Anson, a 35-year old neighbor at Cannes who was the widow of Col Hon Augustus Henry Anson, former MP for Lichfield. Three years after the death of his wife, the Duke married Amelia on 13 August 1881 at Inveraray Castle. None of the Campbell children except Colin attended the ceremony; Frances was being treated for phlebitis and could not have attended the wedding.[175] On 14 August, Frances wrote, '**May I be such a daughter to her as my mother would wish**'. Duchess Mimi, as she was called, became a much-loved family member.

Frances and Eustace also lost some important figures in their lives during this time. The year 1880 closed with the death from Bright's disease of Frances's Aunt 'Conny', the Duchess of Westminster. '**How glad our mother must be**', Frances recorded.[176] Cecil, after forging Arthur's name to some cheques, settled in disgrace in New South Wales, Australia,[177] where he died on 3 April 1881 following a seizure from an 'aggravated cerebral disease' and a fall from his horse.[178] The death of Dean Stanley 18 July 1881 brought more sadness.

CHAPTER THREE

'[Y]ou are one of us now, you know!'[179]
(1882–1886)

'His Ex[cellency] says I am
becoming a regular "lobbyist"'.[180]

'Nothing but Ireland this
session[!]'[181]

The year 1882 began with Lady Frances Balfour and Eustace preparing to leave for Canada. Frances's brother Lorne was without an official hostess: Princess Louise, having been injured in a sleigh accident in 1880, was still recuperating in London. Lorne asked Frances to fulfill the Princess's duties for the various functions associated with his position as Governor-General, but especially those surrounding the opening of the Canadian Parliament in February. Frances reported the news of the impending Canadian trip to Gerald, now in Italy, noting that Arthur highly approved, his 'only objection [being] . . . that he thinks my presence there will probably cause a split between the mother country and the colony!'[182] Meanwhile, William de Morgan joshed Eustace: 'It will be a great satisfaction to see you return safely with all your toes on . . . .'[183]

After a bitterly cold, ten-day crossing of the Atlantic, which featured 'one incessant gale, varied by two hurricanes'[184] and a 52-mile journey by rail from Halifax, the Governor-General's party arrived in Ottawa on January 23 and were met by dignitaries. The cold was extreme, plunging to 24 degrees below zero during their first night in town and 34 below the following night. When they reached the residence of the Governor-General, Rideau Hall, the grey stone, Scottish-style edifice which Princess Louise had pronounced 'hideous',[185] Frances reported to Gerald that 'Lorne is in a state of radiant bliss being back in his beloved "land of ice and snow"'.[186] She noted that the Canadians loved her brother for his devotion to their country and were proud that he had been successful as Governor-General.[187] Only 33 when appointed, Lorne was the youngest person to serve in that position.

Frances's opinion of the Canadian people was by turns critical and complimentary. 'We are getting hardened to endless rounds of rough, vulgar [commonplace], uninteresting, loud, clever, shrewd, seldom exactly intellectual people, but always kind, open hearted, well meaning, well wishing souls', she declared to Gerald, in a sentence which she described as worthy of the American press.[188]

As hostess for the Governor-General, Frances was required to attend all the social functions during the Parliamentary season. The most important of these activities were dinners, skating and tobogganing parties, and theatre attendance. Frances admitted that skating parties, 'a large feature in Canadian entertaining', were 'rather my bane'.[189] Her shortened leg kept her from participating in the skating, but she was nevertheless expected to attend all the parties, where she stood in the cold 'hour after hour'.[190] But Canadian skating was not what the British practiced: 'Here no one thinks of being content with straight ahead skating', but preferred figure skating. She loved watching 'the good Canadian skaters. . . . [T]he absolute sense of their security, the perfect grace of every turn and movement is beautiful'.[191] The evening skating party hosted by Rideau Hall on 25 February was, according to her, 'a wonderfully pretty thing, all the rinks & slides are lighted up with lanterns, and there is a bon fire, & a band and fresh air & no necessity to recognize anybody'.[192]

She could participate in tobogganing, but it, too, was different from what she had experienced in Britain. The slide was some sixty to seventy feet high and sloped at a steep angle, which made the speed considerable. 'You feel as if you left your heart on the top, and at the bottom one lies gasping'.[193] Still, enjoying the sensation, she went down the slide three times on her second day out (26 January). Rideau Hall hosted its first big tobogganing party on 4 February for 400 guests, and Frances was pleased that it was a '**success in spite of wind and snow**'.[194] Frances and Eustace liked the activity so well that they brought toboggans home with them to Whittingehame, where tobogganing became a popular recreation with all the Balfours.[195]

The Governor-General and his guests attended almost all the performances presented at the theatre in Ottawa. In fact, Lorne has been credited with 'help[ing] make theatre-going an activity which Canadians could respect and emulate'.[196] Frances generally enjoyed the theatre, though she deemed some performances in Canada commonplace or inferior. She was, however, '**much amused**' by Gilbert and Sullivan's *Patience* (20 March), and she rated actress Genevieve Ward's performance in *Forget-me-Not* '**very good**' (23 March).

Since conversation was the entree of any meal as far as she was concerned, Frances preferred dinners for entertainment. At the official dinners, which were given by the Governor-General for Members of Parliament and various important visitors to Ottawa, Frances enjoyed conversing with ministers and politicians, but she admitted that 'it was sometimes difficult to get the ministers to talk . . . seriously with her since they did not have a high opinion of women's intellect.'[197] About Canadian women, she told Arthur Balfour that '. . . I have heard no woman mention politics or even seem to know what they mean, or mention a book – disgusting!'[198]

Frances and Eustace attended dinner parties almost every night while in Canada, especially when the Canadian Parliament was in session. She was especially impressed with Judge Johnson, a 'witty, brilliant French scholar', but he had one flaw: 'the infamous way he treated his very nice[,] rather stupid wife, and the way he allowed her to be treated by her stepdaughter who was pleased to describe her as "a d--d fool" to one of our party'.[199] Frances was not above correcting the manners of young Canadians. On this occasion, she 'sharply' informed the stepdaughter. . . 'that we were not in Billingsgate . . . '.[200]

In addition to all her other obligations, Frances returned an '**immense number of calls**'[201] on those who had welcomed her to Ottawa. In a letter to Gerald, she explained '[e]veryone calls, and you must return them all, asking for everybody to leave a card is a great insult. Our list already numbers over a hundred, and Parliament and the MPs, and their wives have not come yet'.[202] The Prime Minister's wife, Agnes Macdonald, was ill during this time and unable to have guests, to assist Frances, or be present at all the events she normally would have attended: thus even more responsibility fell on Frances. Driving the sleigh herself, Frances made calls on at least thirteen occasions.

Both the political and social Seasons began in Ottawa with the Opening of Parliament. In its coverage of the Opening, *The Daily Citizen* observed, 'The absence of the Princess is, of course, a matter which all will . . . deplore, and one for which even the presence of the amiable Lady Frances Balfour, sister of His Excellency, can hardly compensate, welcome as her presence will be this season to Canadian society'.[203] By 1882, many Canadians had become convinced that the Princess, by then able to travel around Britain and to the European continent, did not like Canada and therefore was using her convalescence from the sleigh accident as an excuse not to return.

The Opening of the Canadian Parliament on 9 February 1882 was like its British counterpart: a formal affair, which featured a speech 'from the Throne' by the Governor-General, written by the Government in power, which was the Liberal Conservative party. Frances attended the Opening and reported that it was '**an**

impressive sight', and that her brother's speech was '**long and prosperous**' (the government had a surplus of $4.1 million for 1881-1882).[204]

Following the Opening of Parliament, the first of five state dinners at Rideau Hall was held for some of the Members. Since all those in attendance were male, Frances did not appear at the dinners, but went to the receptions afterwards. Two days after the Opening, the Governor-General hosted a Drawing Room in the Senate Chamber of the Parliament Building. In the ballroom, where the presentations were made, Lady Frances passed first before His Excellency, after which she stood '**an hour and five minutes**' greeting those being presented. *The Ottawa Daily Free Press* reported that the Drawing Room was 'one of the largest held in recent years' and 'some six to seven hundred attended'.[205]

The last of the formal events of the Parliamentary season were the state balls, two of which were necessary because of limited space in Rideau Hall. When newspapers reported that Eustace danced with Mrs Russell Stephenson, Frances observed to Arthur, 'Eustace is adored by the womenkind, more than is good for him'.[206]

Thanks to her father, Frances had always had a keen interest in politics, but she had never attended the daily sessions of the British Parliament before her journey to Canada. As an official hostess for her brother, she now found herself often in Parliament and enjoying the experience. 'You hear in the Canadian Parliament the most wonderfully exciting speaking in the way of violence. The Finance Minister is a splendid speaker, and Sir C[harles] Tupper [Minister of Railways and Canals] is a master of violent invective',[207] she recorded.

Frances had an opportunity to practice her own political skills on the Minister of Agriculture, J H Pope. An emigration society that Frances supported sent two ladies, one of whom was a German, to Ottawa seeking '1,000$' to bring Germans, 'who were much wanted', to Canada.[208] 'I chaffed and bullied the rather important minister [of Agriculture] till he was obliged to come off his high horse, & made us very fairly hopeful of success, & then I led my petticoat regiment off to Sir John's [Sir John Macdonald, Prime Minister of Canada] rooms, & I think they will get what they want. His Excellency says I am becoming a regular "lobbyist"'.[209]

Though he had satisfactory employment up to this time, most of Eustace's architectural work had come from family members. His first commission had been to design the memorial to Frances's mother: a Coffee House near the pier in Inveraray.[210] He also made some alterations to the 'club and recreation rooms'[211] of the castle, and he designed an enlargement of the Balfour family's hunting lodge, Strathconan, for Arthur. Eustace would not be able, however, to fill all of his time with architectural projects for family members, so while he was in Canada, he explored some opportunities for other work in addition to architecture. He entertained an offer to work in London as a land agent for a Col Dennis and even considered settling British emigrants on Canadian land himself. Eustace also strongly considered investing in land from the Canadian Pacific railway and even wanted Arthur to invest as well. Since the trustees of Balfour's estate 'did not think that land in Canada was a good investment', nothing came of the plans.[212] Frances later remarked that '[t]wo more unsuitable settlers in virgin soil, could hardly be imagined, and I at least was well pleased with the decision . . . '.[213]

At the invitation of Judge Johnson, Frances and Eustace interrupted their stay in Ottawa to visit Montreal for a week in March. They were special guests at a performance of the Victoria Skating Club, where a 'Welcome' banner and 'Scotch tunes' greeted them.[214] Frances found the show captivating and breath-taking: 'Out and away the prettiest sight we had ever seen.'[215] A 'Gothic temple' with its 'mass of pinnacles, columns & gables', all of solid ice, dominated the rink. 'At eight, some 400 skaters, dressed as Zulus, Saracens, and Crusaders', among others, came on to the ice 'skating most beautifully, some round and round, some backwards, others making marvelous jumps in the air'. Coloured lights 'turned the ice bright red, livid white, purple, [and] green', 'altogether a most fascinating & fairy like sight'. After the show, they were treated to an oyster supper. Frances exclaimed, 'Oysters raw best of all!'

Frances loved Montreal, which was an older, more culturally advanced city than Ottawa: 'The number of churches and its situation reminds one rather of Edinbro', she reported.[216] And in spite of her antipathy for Roman Catholicism, Frances praised the convents she visited, especially Sacred Heart, where she was **'much struck with the quiet life'**.[217] She admired the work of the Sisters of Charity (affectionately known as the Grey Nuns or Grey Sisters). 'I had great fun with the Grey Sisters, put on their dress & pleased them all like a pack of babies. Told them if they would undertake to dispose of Eustace I would come & stay with them'.[218] Frances also visited St Andrews Church in Montreal, where her friend and confidant, Rev Dr Robert Story, was ordained into the ministry in 1859.[219] She **'thought much of Chime**s', her nickname for him, while she visited the church.[220] On their return to Ottawa, she recorded having **'enjoyed our visit much'**.

The Balfours prepared to return home at the end of March, though Frances **'felt parting with Ian [Lorne] much'**.[221] **'It has been a happy time'**.[222] Before leaving, they presented Lorne with a sketch by Eustace, a watercolor by Alice, and 'Eustace's head for the Royal Canadian Academy which opens in April'.[223] The founding of the Academy in March 1880 had been one of Princess Louise and Lorne's pet projects.

On the return trip, Frances and Eustace briefly toured several cities in eastern

Canada, including Niagara, Toronto, and Montreal. Unlike her father during his visit in 1879, Frances declined an opportunity to visit the US. She was anxious to get back to Baffy and Britain, and she disliked America, which she called 'a shoddy Republic'.[224]

The return voyage, begun 1 April, was preferable to that from Britain to Canada, and Frances coped a little better. She was able to go on deck by the fourth day, and on the seventh day attended a concert, which the passengers staged and at which Eustace played the piano. Despite the fact that this trip was an improvement over the first crossing, Frances never lost her dread of ocean travel, refusing for the rest of her life any trips that necessitated ocean voyages.

By 11 April 1882, Frances and Eustace were back in London and reunited with Baffy. Frances expressed surprise that 'people seem glad to see us again'.[225] On their first visit to Cambridge after returning from Canada, Frances and Eustace learned about the death of Charles Darwin, a close friend of all the Cambridge Balfours. Despite his differences with Darwin on evolution, Frances's father was a pallbearer for the famous scientist, who was buried in Westminster Abbey.[226] By now, Gerald had completed his studies at Cambridge, where he 'came fifth in the classical tripos'[227] and where he held a Fellowship in Philosophy in 1878. He had given up the Fellowship by 1881, and was in Florence studying philosophy.

A death in May 1882 brought national anguish. Lord Frederick Cavendish, newly-appointed Irish Secretary, and Thomas Henry Burke, Under-Secretary, were murdered in Phoenix Park by Fenian terrorists, only two days after the diplomats' arrival in Ireland. The very public knifing of two prominent British officials shocked both Britain and Ireland and, once more, hindered rapprochement in Anglo-Irish relations. 'I never saw such a general gloom thrown over all society,' Frances reported.[228]

A great personal loss for the Balfour family was the death in July of Francis (Frank) Balfour. A prominent scientist, Frank was the 'central figure'[229] of the talented Balfour family at this time. An Honours graduate of Trinity College Cambridge, Frank was elected a Fellow of the Royal Society and a Fellow of Trinity College in 1878.[230] In 1880-81, he published his two-volume *Treatise on Comparative Embryology*, 'which laid the foundations of modern embryology'.[231] The following year, his stature in the scientific community was such that he was invited, at age 31, to succeed eminent biologists at both Oxford and Edinburgh, but he elected to stay at Cambridge, where he was appointed the first Professor of Animal Morphology, a chair created for him. Weakened by typhus during winter 1882, he decided to recuperate by mountain-climbing in France and Italy, where he fell to his death while descending a secondary peak of Mont Blanc.[232] On learning of the tragedy, Eustace left immediately for Italy, where Gerald joined him.

Frank's body arrived at Whittingehame on 4 August; at noon the next day, the Rev Dr James Robertson conducted Frank's funeral. 'On [the coffin] was a small thick wreath of "Edelweiss", placed there by some Alpine friend. I thought', wrote Frances, 'how appropriate the name of the flower was to the noble and pure spirit that had been taken away'.[233] As a memorial to their brother, Alice and Nora bought land to build a laboratory, named after him, for the two women's colleges at Cambridge.[234]

Frank's death was the catalyst of a change in Frances's relationship with both Gerald and Alice. Though he had always accompanied Frank on his mountain-climbing trips, Gerald had remained in Florence this time and was overwhelmed by grief and guilt; Frances, who had a deep capacity for empathy, recorded in her diary (5 August) that it was he whom '**I feel for most in all this trouble**'[.] According to Betty, thereafter Alice 'noted a growing tie of understanding and intimacy between Frances and the brothers, and a diminution of interest in herself. Here began a bitter misunderstanding between the two women which increased as life went on . . . '.[235]

Alice had the responsibility of managing Arthur's three households. However, her preoccupation with 'organisation' and her desire for 'perfection'[236] irritated Frances, who was not a 'details' person and had no faculty of organization. Self-conscious and insecure because of her physical appearance (she was 'short and dumpy' and had a cleft palate)[237], Alice compared herself poorly to Frances: 'Everything I do will be wrong', her niece remembered her saying.[238]

Frances's growing sense of security and belonging in the Balfour family also contributed to the rift. At first, Frances had made concerted efforts to include Alice in visits to family and friends[239]; now she drew close to the brothers as well, bantering with them about their aloof, philosophical bent. In addition to being physically attractive and having a beautiful voice, Frances had considerable intellectual talent. When Alice visited him in Florence during 1882, Gerald reported to Frances that Alice had asked him to read poetry to her (as he had read to Frances). 'Reading poetry to Aggie is not quite the same as reading it to the old Cat [Frances]', Gerald remarked.[240]

Alice was unmarried and claimed that she would prefer to have her own establishment,[241] but though she owned a residence at Moatlands in Sussex, her obsessive love for Arthur, combined with her insecurity, kept her from even attempting to create her own life as an artist and lepidopterist at which she was quite talented – her collection is housed in the Royal Scottish Museum.[242] Adding to her insecurities was the fact that her 'open admiration' irritated Arthur and 'made his friends feel unwelcome at Whittingehame'.[243] Indeed, he showed more genuine affection for Frances,[244] which must have devastated Alice. With his mother gone and his sisters Nora and Evelyn no longer at home, Arthur appears to have appreciated the intellectual stimulation Frances brought to the household.[245] There was no sudden rupture, however, between Frances and Alice in 1882; in her 1883 diary, Frances mentions being with Alice on some 26 different occasions, and in 1884, 24 times, lunching, driving, attending plays: their relationship continued to appear normal for several years, though they were in reality drawing apart.

Frances's greatest wish had been that Eustace would choose a political career; it was where her deepest interest lay, and she had hoped that through her husband she could participate vicariously in the political debates raging through the land but in which she, as a woman, could have no actual role. However, after they returned from Canada, to her great disappointment, he decided not to enter politics. Gerald, still studying in Florence, tried to console Frances by pointing out Eustace's abilities, which were not of a political bent. Noting that he had 'a nature . . . exquisitely refined', Gerald believed that Eustace 'should have been lord of a great Estate, with nothing to do but to improve it and the people on it'.[246]

In 1882, unable to find enough work in architecture to keep him busy, Eustace joined the London Scottish Volunteer Rifle Regiment – the military was his other chief interest. This decision, of course, affected Frances's social life. Since 'Society dined out on Wednesdays and Fridays', the nights when the London Scottish drilled in Westminster Hall, and, since husbands and wives attended social affairs only as 'couples',[247] Frances now lost the opportunity to attend numerous dinners and parties where she might have been able to mingle with politicians and discuss affairs of state with the politically knowledgeable and influential. As Max Egremont so succinctly summarized, 'Lady Frances was one of those Victorian women who, restricted by the subservient position of their sex, were in an almost permanent state of intellectual frustration'.[248] Eustace's decision meant that Frances would not find in her husband the close intellectual companionship she desired, thus bringing closer the day when Frances would seek to participate in the life of the nation in her own right.

Between 1882 and 1884, Gerald and Frances came to know and understand each other much better, and Gerald fell in love with her.[249] On her part, Frances not only needed companionship and love from her close friends, but also needed to return affection. After Eustace, the first male on whom she doted was Gerald. The relationship did not always run smoothly, however. Frances's was a mercurial personality: she was calm, quiet, and reasonable at times, but at others could fly into a passion at the slightest provocation. Not surprisingly, her relationships with many family members sometimes became strained. At one point Gerald wrote, 'The truth is, that when you are in such a frame of mind my love for you is no longer the same'.[250] Frances frequently apologized for her temper, asserting on more than one occasion to Gerald that '. . .when I quarrel with you, it is not because I deliberately wish to quarrel but that most human thing temper arises, explodes and passes away, short if violent'[251] (a statement which suggests that Frances did not believe that she had control over her temper).

When Gerald was in Florence, 'one day a week was kept for the letters to and from Frances'.[252] In his correspondence, he assured her that there was little danger of a 'serious misunderstanding' between them, because 'you are one of us now, you know!'[253] Gerald's feelings for Frances undoubtedly developed from his unmarried state and his lack of direction. Still, Gerald acknowledged to Frances that '[B]etween us there is a bar for ever fixed, setting limits which love may not overpass'.[254] Some historians of the Balfours have asserted that Frances's idolization of Arthur meant that it was he whom she loved most,[255] but in truth, of the brothers, it was Gerald for whom Frances had the greatest life-long affection, though her true love – her romantic love -- was always reserved for Eustace.

In a decade of many disappointments and difficult choices, marriages and family celebrations provided a respite for Frances. In July 1882, her sister Mary married the Hon Rev Edward Carr Glyn, called 'Teddy', the Anglican Vicar of Kensington and Rector of St Mary Abbot's. In October 1883, Lady Maud Cecil married William Palmer, Viscount Wolmer, only son of the first Earl of Selborne. Shortly after her marriage, Maud wryly observed to Frances, 'It's rather a bore getting into a new family – worse than new stays on the whole'.[256] Maud, a feminist, would become one of Frances's staunchest allies within the women's movement. Maud's husband, Wolmer, was Lord Chancellor in Gladstone's Liberal Government. In 1886, however, he joined the Liberal Unionists over Home Rule for Ireland and 'in all but name [became] as devoted a Conservative as any Cecil'.[257]

Frances undertook her first speaking engagement in 1882 when, after returning from Canada, she was asked to talk to members of the British Women's Temperance Society in Scotland about her experiences in the colony. Frances may have developed her first bit of feminist anger over the response that she received after this from the Northumberlands while visiting Alnwick Castle. 'No sooner had I begun to feed than Edith asked me how "it had gone off?"'[258] Frances described what followed: 'Percy gravely and sadly from his end of the table put the case[,] "Had I spoken extemporare?" "Yes". "For how long?" "3/4 hour". "Did Eustace approve?" "How could you!" This from Edith. . . . My blood was up and . . . I replied my quarrel was the audience only consisted of women'. It would be a while before Frances spoke publicly again, but here the future feminist spokeswoman and orator had had her 'Baptism of fire'.

On a visit to Inveraray in 1883, Frances and Eustace acquired a collie named Cromarty, who became Eustace's most beloved dog.[259] 'Cro', whose sense of direction was poor, caused the Balfour family no small amount of trouble – he was often lost in London, forcing the family to place advertisements and make many fruitless journeys before they found him.

Family and friends continued to assist Eustace's architectural career. In 1880, he designed the Lodge at Melchet Court, home of the Lords Ashburton in Hampshire, and worked the next year on the Manse in Tiree.[260] In July 1883, he completed St Mary Magdalene church in Hatfield Hyde. Commissioned by his uncle, Lord Salisbury, this attractive chapel was the first church Eustace designed, and it was built before he became partners with Thackeray Turner. Of course, with his architectural commissions all out of town, Eustace was often away from home during this decade. When his work necessitated he be gone for more than a day, he wrote Frances every day, often including political news that he believed might interest her.

This difficult period in Frances's early married life, 1882 to 1884, ended on a happier note. After being placed on bed rest (she almost went into labour in October), Frances gave birth to her second child, a son, Francis Cecil Campbell Balfour (called Frank) on 8 December 1884.

Through all of these personal events, Frances remained absorbed in the chief political events of the day. Much of Gladstone's Second Ministry (1880-1885) was occupied with Irish affairs. Led by Charles Stewart Parnell, Irish MPs now demanded Home Rule. Gladstone tried placating the Irish, and he tried coercion, but nothing seemed to work. In frustration in 1882, Frances moaned: 'Nothing but Ireland this session[!]'[261]

After Ireland, the major political topic most interesting to Frances was Lord Randolph Churchill's challenge to Sir Stafford Northcote. Following the death of Disraeli, Lord Beaconsfield, in 1881, the Conservative Party leadership was shared by two men: Eustace's uncle, Lord Salisbury, who led his party in the House of Lords; and Sir Stafford Northcote in the House of Commons. Churchill in particular favoured Salisbury for leadership of the party, declaring 'An Opposition never wants a policy: but an Opposition, if it is to become a strong Government, must have a leader'.[262] Arthur, too, was concerned about Northcote's deficiencies: 'The condition of the party is even more unsatisfactory than it was when you

[Salisbury] were here. We are trampled on by the Govt. and we make no sign. We have no organization. We have no leader: – or rather our leader is . . . a source of weakness rather than strength'.[263]

Churchill countered Northcote's weakness by creating within the Conservative ranks a 'ginger' group'[264] called the Fourth Party which led the attacks on Northcote and with which Arthur Balfour was 'loosely' associated.[265] Northcote's weakness ultimately provided the impetus for Arthur to develop his own parliamentary gifts.

For Arthur, dealing with Churchill's challenge was awkward.[266] On the one hand, he undoubtedly agreed with Churchill on many issues, but he understood that these direct challenges to Northcote embarrassed many in the party. In an 1884 letter to Gerald, Frances declared: 'It is one of the things worth living for, to see how the Party will manage [Churchill], and what will be his end'.[267]

The major political battle of 1884 concerned the franchise. By the early 1880s, momentum was building for another extension of the vote, this time to agricultural workers who had been omitted in the Reform Bill of 1868. Meanwhile, British suffragists – most of whom were Liberals – had gained considerable support both inside and outside Parliament for giving the vote to women on the same terms men enjoyed. Gladstone, however, refused to add the women's clause to the bill, asserting that it was more than it could carry. When Woodall's Amendment, which would have given women votes on the same basis as men, was defeated by a vote of 271-135 on 12 June, with some 107 supposed 'supporters' voting against the bill,[268] the suffragists were both dejected and outraged.

Like her father (who opposed votes for women), Frances supported the franchise reform bill of 1884 as submitted by Gladstone. She later noted in her autobiography that the women learned valuable lessons – 'smooth stones for our slings'[269] – from the 1884 debates, but she did not mention that she herself played no supporting role in the women's fight in 1884.

Meanwhile, a crisis in the Sudan alarmed British citizens. When the public learned in February 1885 that Khartoum had fallen to a Muslim religious leader who proclaimed himself the 'Mahdi', or 'Messiah', and that General Gordon, sent to evacuate British and Egyptian citizens, had been killed, there was great grief and anger. Frances's daughter Baffy remembered that it was the first time she had seen 'grown-up people cry'.[270] Gladstone's government did not long survive the disaster in the Sudan. As Frances noted, 'The bugles that sounded the "Last Post" for Gordon, sounded also the fall of the Liberal government'.[271]

At the same time that Irish home rule, franchise extension, and problems in the Sudan commanded the attention of Frances and her family, developments on the

Isle of Tiree, one of the Hebridean islands owned by the Duke of Argyll, became troublesome. Though the island had lost a significant portion of its population to the 1846 potato blight,[272] by the 1880s, the remaining crofters, beset by a severe agricultural depression, were hurting. Gladstone secured the enactment of the Crofters' Holdings Act of 1886, which established an independent Crofters' Commission to fix rents, provided security to the crofters who paid their rents, protected their right to bequeath their crofts to family members, and awarded compensation for any improvements made by crofters who gave up their holdings. The act, however, provided little additional land or compensation for lost crofts, and resulted in continued agitation.

Little unrest had occurred on Tiree until 1886, when the islanders wanted Greenhill Farm, whose lease had expired, to be divided into additional crofts; instead, the Duke leased the farm to Lachlan MacNeill, brother of the president of the Land League in Tiree. In May, a hostile crowd prevented MacNeill from taking possession of the farm and 'turned out 55 cattle and 17 horses of their own on to the ground'.[273] Frances's father, 'nearly apoplectic with rage',[274] ordered notices of interdict to be served on 51 renters in Tiree, but officials attempting to serve the notices were unsuccessful. Thus, one of Arthur's first duties as Secretary for Scotland in Salisbury's 1886 Government involved sending troops (250 marines, 120 sailors and 40 policemen) to Tiree. There was no fighting, but eventually eight men were prosecuted and served time in prison for trespassing.

Absorbed by politics, religion, and science, the 8th Duke of Argyll appears to have been somewhat out of touch with the crofters' circumstances and unreceptive to their entreaties for change. But British farmers like the Duke were also troubled by the agricultural difficulties: they had been plagued by a series of bad harvests in the last quarter of the nineteenth century and by the flood into the country of cheaper grains from America. The Disraeli government in power in the late 1870s refused to impose tariffs on grains, thus contributing to a lingering depression from which the aristocracy never recovered. (Arthur's income from his farm-lands was also drastically reduced by the mid-1880s:[275] he leased Strathconan to the Guinesses, and when the lease expired, sold the property in 1891 to 'Mr. Coombe, a brewer', for £98,000.[276]

The disturbances on Tiree were a life-altering event for Lady Victoria Campbell. As the news of the unrest on Tiree reached the Campbell household in 1886, Victoria, who had pledged her service to God following her recovery from a lung abscess in 1868-1870, began spending more of her time on the troubled island, eventually moving there in 1891. Victoria's work on the island consisted mainly of promoting religious and social organizations like the Woman's Guilds and the

YWCA and providing technical training for many of the island's residents.[277] She organized classes in painting, lacemaking, and needlework for women and training in such crafts as woodcarving and joinery for the men. She established milk and soup kitchens for the needy and obtained Jubilee Nurses for the care of the inhabitants. She also worked to secure the construction of a pier for the island, and, writing under the pseudonym 'Hebridean', was one of the island's best-known publicists.[278] In fact, Victoria was much beloved by the residents, who recognized her dedication to them and appreciated her 'pluck' in working with them.

CHAPTER FOUR

'What an interesting Parliament it will Be'[279]
(1885-1889)

'Everywhere in the streets we were
the popular candidate. . . .'.[280]

**'I have gained Betty, [and]
Lord L[ytton]. . . '**.[281]

Lady Frances Balfour's first personal experience with the election process came when the Liberal Government in power under Gladstone's leadership since 1880 finally fell on 8 June 1885. The Queen summoned Eustace's uncle, the Marquis of Salisbury, to the Castle and asked him to form a new Government. Lord Salisbury, now Conservative leader, assumed office pending an election that would be fought by the new electorate produced by the Reform Bill of 1884.

In the December election, Gerald accepted the invitation to challenge the sitting Liberal Member for Central Leeds, Sir John Barran. At the suggestion of party organizers, Gerald asked Lady Frances Balfour to join him in Leeds as 'an "ornament"'[282] during the final five-day push to polling day. Her excitement was obvious as she drove around with Gerald on a 'beastly day'[283] – cold and wet – to the seven polling stations, where Gerald spoke to those assembled. 'We had the carriage open and beat Barran and his womenkind who were driving about shut up (Booo-oo-o!)', she exclaimed. Gerald's prospects appeared better with each stop: 'Everywhere in the streets we were the popular candidate.' When their work was finished, they journeyed to the Town Hall, where 'there was no sign for ages'. Finally the 'announcement came: 314! How splendid it was . . .'. Besides lending a female presence to his campaign, Frances brought her name, which was in itself an advantage: 'One of [Gerald's] supporters referred to Papa's visit to Leeds &

illustrated how times had changed by one of Papa's daughters being on the platform that night!! The audience rose and screamed for some minutes, and I grinned like a Cheshire cat. At the end G[erald] and I went out arm in arm . . . . The noise was stunning'.

The badly-divided Liberals managed to win the election, thanks to the expanded franchise, but 86 Irish MPs held the balance of power in the new Parliament. His previous constituency abolished by the new boundaries, Arthur now secured a seat for East Manchester. Frances observed, 'What an interesting Parliament it will be'.[284]

From 1880 to 1885, Frances's political perceptions changed significantly: having enthusiastically exclaimed in 1880 that the Liberals were having the best of it, she wrote in 1885 to her friend Walter Pollock, editor of the *Saturday Review*, that, 'No one in England is realizing the truth about the [elections in Scotland]. . . . Never have [Conservatives] polled so heavily in Scotland'.[285] She added, 'If real good candidates would stand for some of these constituencies a very different return would be made. . . . Nothing is so difficult as to put heart into a long beaten party [in Scotland] but every effort ought to be made to do so'.

By this time, Gladstone had become convinced that some measure of Home Rule for Ireland was inevitable, and the Grand Old Man was back in office in January 1886, though leading a still badly-divided party. When he presented his Home Rule Bill to the Commons on 8 April, there were numerous opponents of the bill, including the Protestant majority in Northern Ireland, who threatened revolt if they had to submit to a Catholic Government in Dublin. But the biggest hurdle was Chamberlain, who resigned his Cabinet seat during the debate on the bill, when he spoke strongly and eloquently against it and helped bring on its defeat.

Family members at Hatfield endured a suspenseful evening awaiting the vote on the bill. 'Lady Salisbury was in her best fight mood, the light of battle shone in her eyes, which were never far away from his Lordship',[286] Frances enthused. It was past two in the morning when the results were finally shouted by Linky (Hugh Cecil), who had waited at the telegraph office for the news. Gladstone resigned and new elections were called for July 1886.

Gerald's election experience in 1886 was not as positive as his '85 event because the Irish opposed him in this campaign. This time, Gerald enlisted in his fight his Uncle Salisbury, who spoke in Leeds on 18 June. Frances again accompanied Gerald on the final five days of the campaign, and in spite of the Irish vote, Gerald held his seat, but only by a majority of 13 votes. Frances, ebullient, declared it '**A great victory!**'[287]

Meantime, Gladstone's Liberal opponents hurriedly organized a new party, the Liberal Unionists, who, together with the Conservatives, trounced the Liberals, securing 395 seats to the Liberals' 275. Though Salisbury returned to office in August 1886 with a majority of 120 seats, the Unionists held the balance of power. Frances now supported the Unionist Party, a workable compromise for one now in a staunchly Conservative family and a sentiment which continued through her life; she insisted even a quarter of a century later, saying, 'How can Scotland want Home Rule, when England and Scotland have one flag and one country?'[288]

When Salisbury formed his second ministry, Arthur, again victorious in Manchester, was named Secretary of State for Scotland, and Randolph Churchill was made Chancellor of the Exchequer and leader of the House of Commons. During the crofter crisis of 1886, Salisbury raised Balfour to the cabinet, where he served as a 'counterpoise' to Churchill.[289]

As disturbing as was the split in the Liberal Party and the resulting three-party general election of 1886, a far more radical development on the political scene was the success of socialism in Britain in the 1880s. By the mid-80s, the Henry Hyndman-led Social Democratic Federation (SDF), William Morris' Socialist League, and the Fabian Society had all been launched as avowedly socialist societies and were gaining converts, especially among the working class. The downturn in the economy in the mid-1880s offered these societies opportunities to popularise their doctrine and to gain the attention of the public with demonstrations against the 'heartless' economic system of capitalism. In February 1885, the SDF sponsored a march of the unemployed from the Embankment to Downing Street and eventually to the Local Government Board, where G W E Russell, Parliamentary Secretary to the Board and friend of Frances, received a deputation of unemployed workers asking for assistance. When Russell's response failed to contain any promises of direct assistance, the unemployed passed a resolution which declared in language which the British public was unused to hearing that 'This meeting of the unemployed . . . considers the refusal to start public works to be a sentence of death on thousands of those out of work . . . . Further, it will hold Mr G. W. E. Russell and the members of the Government . . . guilty of the murder of those who may die in the next few weeks . . .' .[290] Among those who signed the resolution was 'John E Williams, labourer'.

In February 1886, with the economic distress among the working class even more severe, the SDF rallied the unemployed in Trafalgar Square. When violence seemed imminent, the SDF agreed – at the suggestion of the police – to move its meeting to Hyde Park. As the crowd made its way down the Mall, trouble developed when men in the fashionable clubs taunted the 'rabble', who answered with stones, some of which broke windows in the buildings along the Mall. The violence spilled over into Mayfair, where the crowd broke windows of private homes and shops, including that of Frances's sister, Edith, future Duchess of Northumberland, who lived in Grosvenor Square. Frances's daughter Baffy, much excited by the commotion, recalled that from the disturbances she 'first knew the meaning of envy', and that she had 'implored' her parents to move to Grosvenor Square, so as to be where the action was.[291]

In an effort to help ease the volatile situation, Frances asked another friend, Arnold White, First Secretary of the American Legation, 'for an "unemployed" to clean [her] windows'.[292] To her surprise and bemusement, White 'answered [her] appeal by sending "Williams the Socialist!"' Conceding that she was 'concealing [the hiring of Williams] from [Eustace]', Frances humorously noted, 'I suppose he is honest. I shall pursue him fr[om] room to room and converse with him. He will have an intimate knowledge of my house when he leads a mob down Add[ison] Road'.

Revolutionary Socialism in Britain lost much of its threat – and steam – when the Socialists chose to pursue the matter of free speech and respond to the closing of Trafalgar Square through the courts and the formation of a new organization, the Law and Liberty League.

During the same year that Frances helped Gerald win re-election, the equanimity of the entire Campbell family was shattered by Frances's brother Colin's divorce trial. For eighteen days in November and December 1886, Britain was titillated by 'the longest, most sensational divorce trial in British history'.[293]

Though he had been 'looked upon as a young man to watch',[294] the indolent Colin disappointed his family by becoming engaged in 1880 against their wishes to Gertrude Blood, a woman he had known only three days. Colin's medical problems caused the wedding to be postponed and, after two unsuccessful operations, the choice was between postponing his wedding once again or beginning his married life unable to consummate the union. Urged on by her parents, Gertrude chose marriage, agreeing to nurse her husband until he was well, and the wedding ceremony took place on 21 July 1881. Unfortunately, Colin spent most of his first two years as a married man in a separate bedroom, recuperating from his physical problems, other minor illnesses, and two more surgeries.[295] Meanwhile, Gertrude spent little time nursing her husband and much time entertaining mostly male visitors, alone.

Gertrude later testified that beginning in November 1881, she fought an 'illness' that was '"the result of sexual intercourse"'[296] with her husband, an illness she could not identify and about which she had heretofore kept silent. In July 1883, after learning from Colin that his doctor had pronounced him '"perfectly cured"',[297] Gertrude left him, declining ever to be '"touched by [Colin] again"',[298] though she was willing to continue to be his wife so long as he made no sexual demands of her. This offer rejected, Gertrude filed for judicial separation in August 1883 on the grounds of cruelty, claiming that Colin had forced her to share his bed while suffering from a communicable venereal disease.

Gertrude won her request for a legal separation, meaning that the jury found Colin guilty of 'legal cruelty',[299] that is, of infecting Gertrude. The news of the separation, together with the 'sordid details' of the failed marriage, was 'widely disseminated';[300] Princess Louise, among others, refused to receive Colin thereafter.[301]

Petitions for divorce were finally presented by solicitors for both parties in November 1884, with Gertrude now accusing her husband of adultery. At this time under British law, a wife had to prove adultery plus desertion or cruelty, while a husband only had to prove adultery in order to secure a divorce. Advised by two solicitors and 14 barristers, the spouses in *Campbell* v. *Campbell* found their divorce trial the chief item for all the major British newspapers from 27 November to its end on 20 December.

Robert Finlay wasted little time in debunking Gertrude's charge that Colin had committed adultery with a servant, Mary Watson; two doctors testified that she was a virgin. Most of the trial was taken up with testimony and cross-examination of various servants, cabmen, and other observers of the Campbells' domestic and social lives – what *The Times* called the 'malicious gossip of servants'.[302] James O'Neill, a butler to the Colin Campbells, testified that, looking through a keyhole, he had seen Lady Colin with her breast bared, lying on the carpet with Captain Shaw, Chief of the Metropolitan Fire Brigade, on top of her.[303] Gertrude's lawyers asserted that it would have been impossible to see through the keyhole because of brass coverings on both sides of the door that closed over the keyhole when there was no key in the door. However, members of the jury asked to see the door and keyhole, and their examination revealed that the brass escutcheons did not close when the key was removed.[304] Additional 'sensational' testimony included the assertion by one servant that Gertrude had had a miscarriage several months after she and Colin no longer '"lived as man and wife"'.[305] This was refuted by none other than Britain's foremost obstetrician, Dr Braxton Hicks.

Three of the men named as having a sexual liaison with Gertrude, including Shaw and Blandford, brother of Lord Randolph Churchill and later 8th Duke of Marlborough, denied it; a fourth, Col (later General) William Butler, a well-known military figure, declined to appear at the trial and thus made no denial.

On 20 December 1886, after a long evening of deliberations, mostly caused by Butler's lack of denial, the jury found that neither Colin nor Gertrude had committed adultery (it was later suggested that 'the jury believed that a woman might have an affair with one man, but not with four'[306]). It was a decision which greatly disappointed the Campbells. Since neither party had proved adultery, no divorce was granted.

The Victorian era was the 'Age of the Stork', and even dissemination of birth control information could bring prosecution for publishing 'obscene' literature. Thus, when the Campbell divorce trial was finally concluded, *The Times* let loose with a barrage of criticism of both parties, criticism which was echoed in many other papers. Noting that 'any decision is to be welcomed that rids us of an unsurpassably offensive business', *The Times* approved the fact that 'the two persons whose disputes have let loose this flood of filth upon the public' have their relative positions 'unchanged by the verdict'.[307]

Like the rest of her family, Frances was deeply embarrassed by the trial and the notoriety which it generated. On 27 November, she recorded in her diary that she was **'very low about Colin and all the horror of it'**. When the trial was over, she called the outcome **'A terrible shock. We hoped the jury would disagree'**. The year's end found Frances at a family party at Hatfield, where **'Aunt G[eorgy] disturbed the last night of the year by a very violent attack on C[olin]. I went to my room and watched it out quite alone, with many sad and burning thoughts'**. In fact, the trial brought on 'attacks of depression and nervous agitation' for Frances which lasted well into 1887.[308]

Frances was eventually able to overcome her bouts of depression through hard work, the usual solution to her emotional problems. By mid-February 1887, she was able to attend two large teas in Leeds, lunch parties, and meetings of the Primrose League: 'There is life in me yet!'[309] In November 1888, Colin, who had been called to the bar from Middle Temple[310] just before his trial, moved to Bombay, where he worked successfully[311] as a lawyer until his death.

Frances's main response to the trial was her withdrawal for a time from some of her public duties. When she offered to resign as President of the Travellers' Aid Society, however, the Executive Committee asked her to remain in the post. She agreed, but she did not resume regular attendance at the meetings of the Executive and General Committees until 1889-1890.

In 1887, Gerald found a wife, later described as the 'good angel' of the Balfour household.[312] Lady Elizabeth Lytton was the daughter of the Earl of Lytton, who was about to become Ambassador to France at this point in his distinguished diplomatic career. Frances first met Betty, age 20, in May 1887 at a ball at Hatfield House where Frances was serving as chaperone to her sister Conny. Betty's first impression of Frances provides valuable insight into Frances's demeanour, carriage, and personality:

I remember thinking her beautiful, and interesting. She [wore] a green and gold gown that evening which set off her wonderful gold red hair, and whitest of white skins. She wore pince-nez which she constantly knocked off impetuously when contradicting something said. Her movements were all quick, even her walk, in spite of her limp, and her talk eager and emphatic but never noisy. She had a beautiful low voice, and when uttering her fiercest most denunciatory words she did not raise it. She had a look of great breeding, and no affectation, or pomposity. She had gaity, but no frivolity. She enjoyed keenly, but things that amused most people did not amuse her, and when bored she always showed it.[313]

Though she declared to Betty that she and Gerald 'were made for each other', Frances admitted to herself that it was **'a bitter evening'** for her when she learned of their engagement (22 July). Frances was very sentimental about the past, and the breaking up of any aspect of her 'old life' affected her deeply.[314] But Frances candidly wrote Betty: 'I have never had any intimate woman friendship and I should like to have one and that that one should be yours would be very perfect . . . . I think you will have many disappointments for I don't think I am very nice on the surface, at least my candid friends always tell me so'.[315] After declaring to Betty that she had won 'the heart of one man in many thousands', Frances hastened to assure Betty that she loved seeing Gerald form 'those ties which his heart has longed for' and that Betty was taking 'nothing from [her], except his constant presence'. Most importantly, she pleaded with Betty to 'trust me, and care for me. At first because I love him, and in time for myself if you can'. Betty answered Frances's letter, which she found 'deeply touching' and 'generous', by declaring that 'it has already made me love you for your own sake'.[316]

On 25 July, Frances visited Betty at Knebworth, the ancestral estate of the Lyttons, where she found Betty **'very dear'** and noted that Betty made everything **'peaceful'**. One development greatly pleased Frances: by August, Gerald had leased 67 Addison Road, just one block from the home of Frances and Eustace;[317] and of course, when they were not in London, the two families would share Whittingehame with Arthur and Alice. More importantly, Betty agreed to correspond *daily* with Frances; thus Frances gained the 'intimate woman friendship' she had always desired. During the summer holidays in 1887, Betty visited Whittingehame; Frances left the estate for five days specifically to make Alice more comfortable in her first meeting with Betty.[318]

Several severe health problems delayed the marriage. First kidney trouble, then typhoid fever complicated by pleurisy struck Gerald during the autumn, and as

Gerald's life hung in the balance, Frances and Betty consoled each other and had numerous long talks about the future.

When Betty and Gerald finally married on 21 December in the spacious drawing room of Knebworth House, **'everything [was] beautifully done'**, according to Frances. Though she was **'not unhappy'** at the event, Frances observed on the last night of 1887 that it had been **'a year full of sad and many changes. [Dr] Story leaving Rosneath, Gerald's marriage, and Arthur's engrossment in political life'**. She reflected, however, that **'I have gained Betty, [and] Lord L[ytton]. . . '**.

It was Lytton who most clearly understood Frances's distress, and during the summer and autumn of 1887, he wrote several letters to her in which he consoled and even flattered her (Lytton was known to be 'a flirt'[319]). Lytton opined that he did not believe that 'Arthur [would] ever replace Gerald in [Frances's] life', and 'he never did', according to Betty.[320] Gerald, too, sought in his letters to allay Frances's fears about her future relationship to him. 'My darling, don't think I shall forget you. Catkins are not so easily forgotten! There is a very warm corner in my heart, which I promise to keep for you, <u>whatever happens</u>'.[321] Frances gradually developed a deep friendship with Lytton, who returned her affection. Betty's sisters Constance – called Con – and Emily both claimed to 'be fond of her',[322] though Emily commented that having both Frances and Betty around '. . . was like having three mothers'.[323]

During 1887, Frances's work for women included honoring the queen on her fiftieth year on the throne. This time-consuming duty entailed organizing the collection for the Women's Jubilee Fund in her ward, Holland Park and Kensington. The women's gift to their monarch provided for a statue of her beloved husband, the Prince Consort, at Windsor and funds to help the Queen's Jubilee Nursing Institute. On Jubilee Day, 21 June, Frances participated in many of the events and was present at a party at the Foreign Office which she claimed was attended by **'75 royalties'**. When the Queen laid the cornerstone for the statute of Prince Albert at Windsor, Frances and Baffy were present as guests of Princess Louise.

By now, Baffy was ready for more formal schooling than that which Frances had provided for her in the nursery. Despite Frances's low opinion of her own educational regimen, Baffy followed the same curriculum, probably because her mother knew no other. Baffy began working with her first teacher in London in January 1887.

Baffy recorded little about the subjects she studied except to note that she had no instruction in arithmetic.[324] Frances's children also received no significant musical education nor any instruction in the theatre – Baffy noted that her mother, 'who dramatized everything in real life, disliked the dramatic form of literature, and never read or encouraged the reading of any play, not even those of William Shakespeare'.[325] These omissions are surprising given the Balfour interest in music, sciences, and maths. Occasionally forced by family and friends to 'broaden' her horizons, Frances met Ellen Terry and Henry Irving and attended some of their performances, even taking Baffy to see them and, in one of her many contradictions, eventually becoming a good friend of Terry.

Perhaps the greatest tribute to Frances's educational choices was that Baffy's instruction was carried on unconsciously. She was never 'measured' on her educational attainments, and it 'never occurred to her to wonder whether [she] was 'backward', or 'forward', 'clever or stupid'.[326] As a result, she noted, she spent little time thinking about herself and much more time thinking about those with whom she lived and from whom she learned much.

As for reading matter, Baffy explained that her mother 'had a flair for choosing the right books for the right ages, and the child's library that she collected . . . survived the changing taste of three generations, and the competition of many new classics'.[327] Noting that 'the faintest flavour of slang condemned a book', Baffy related that her mother insisted that her children read only 'good English'.[328] Frances facilitated her daughter's wish to learn French and German in order to read books in these languages – though Baffy was warned against reading 'Uncle Arthur's "dreadful collection" of French novels'.[329]

The two subjects on which Frances specifically undertook to instruct her children were politics and religion, as Baffy recorded: 'The multiplication tables might remain a sealed book, but if you had asked me the difference between a Conservative and a Liberal Unionist, I could have told you by the time I was ten'.[330] She could just as easily have said age six or seven. At a time when many parents paid little attention to their children, Frances treated hers as if they were as interested in political campaigns, church affairs, or family events as she was. In 1886, she sent Baffy a telegram announcing Uncle Gerald's victory in Leeds. Baffy was only *six* years old.[331] In the same year, Frances took Baffy **'to see the Queen pass on her way to open Parliament'**[332] and later **'to see the Queen at Ken[sington] Pal[ace]'**,[333] where Louise and Lorne now lived. In 1891, Baffy had her first visit to the House of Commons, where the Speaker showed her around and allowed her to sit in his chair.[334] As for church schooling, Frances had her children learn by heart 'the metrical version of certain psalms and paraphrases of the Church of Scotland'.[335]

Frances was a dominating presence in the lives of her children and those of her extended family. She was also a powder keg which regularly blew. Her temper, as she called it, was frequent enough and furious, and whoever happened to be nearby felt her rage. These 'storms', as family members called them, were devastating, and the individuals on whom they most often fell were her children, and sometimes Betty's. No doubt they got used to the storms after a while, but the severity of her remarks were not easily forgotten – nor forgiven. One comment which has been passed down about her standards was a remark she made to Baffy when Baffy was 15. "'You do not seem to have the zest for life that I had at your age, but keep your elbows off the table and read Sir Walter Scott. . . and the rest may come'".[336]

No doubt, home life held more tension for the younger Balfours when Frances was around, but the tension, if inhibiting, was also creative. Baffy related that Frances was 'no tyrant. . . . Her children were neither plagued, nor protected, by rules, routine, or steady discipline, and with the perpetual tension which her presence produced there was also perpetual variety, interest, and plenty of laughter . . .'.[337] Frances wanted the best for her children, and she understood that they would be more likely to achieve their later goals if she set the bar high for them when they were small. Every child might not have fared equally well under such a regimen, but in the ultimate test, she did not fail her children – or Betty's. As adults, they were all generally considered to be individuals of intelligence, substance, and high character.

Frances not only lost Gerald to marriage in 1887, she also lost Arthur to a new post in Ireland, a move that was part of Salisbury's strategy for overcoming the political difficulties which befell his Government in late 1886-early 1887. When Salisbury refused to force W H Smith, Secretary for War, to make reductions in his defense budget, Churchill resigned. Political difficulties were not over for Salisbury, however (Frances observed, 'Everything was a crisis'[338]). On 12 January 1887, Northcote collapsed and died; and when Sir Michael Hicks-Beach, Chief Secretary of Ireland, resigned due to failing eyesight, the Government's fate was precarious.

Salisbury rallied, however, thanks in no small part to Arthur. In March 1887, Salisbury appointed him Chief Secretary for Ireland, a post full of political and governmental pitfalls. Frances decreed that 'the Hour and the man' had come.[339] The Prime Minister believed that if Ireland were governed with a firm hand for 'twenty years'[340] and given genuine land reform, it might be made ready for self-government in the future. As Secretary of State for Ireland, Arthur pursued the policies which Salisbury had been advocating for the rebellious country.

Continued agricultural depression in Ireland had brought fresh agitation in the winter of 1886-87. Using a new Crimes Act, Balfour moved quickly to quash rebellion. He banned the National League and 'was prosecuting no fewer than eleven MPs' at one point in December 1888.[341] His actions were not popular; after the discovery of a plot by American Fenians against his life, he began carrying a pistol, and throughout his service as Chief Secretary, Arthur was provided with police protection. During a golf outing at North Berwick in September 1887, Frances recalled, 'We amused ourselves trying to make out A[rthur]'s detective, . . . a guardian of the name of Pope . . .'.[342]

Understanding that distress in Ireland was genuine, Arthur also turned his attention to land reform and conciliation. Still, 'Bloody Balfour' pressed on and was so effective that by 1890, 'crime was lower than it had been at any point in the previous decade'.[343]

Meanwhile, another Irish drama was playing out in Parliament. When pressured by Gladstone to choose between himself and Parnell, who was a co-respondent in a divorce petition, Irish Nationalist MPs, though long familiar with Parnell's affair with Mrs Kitty O'Shea, nevertheless ousted Parnell as leader of the Irish party in Parliament. Frances, for whom loyalty was of paramount importance, was incensed by the disloyalty displayed by the Irish party in Parliament against their leader of many years. A student of Parliament, she recognized that Parnell was a brilliant political tactician. Always given to exaggeration when aroused (her 'white heat'), she declared that Parnell was 'essentially made to govern Ireland, and the Irish, and what we ought to do is to build a wall (like the Roman Wall) around Ulster, and leave the rest of Ireland to him'.[344] This outburst has caused some historians, incorrectly, to believe that Frances changed her mind about Home Rule.[345]

The years at the close of the 1880s were a time of considerable physical and emotional distress for Frances. Her brother Walter was in significant difficulty, both personally and financially. To avoid another divorce trial for the family, he was living apart from his wife Olive, who was 'cohabiting with a lover'.[346] On 3 May 1889, the family learned by telegram that Walter had died of dysentery in the Cape Colony, where he had gone to recoup his fortunes. The London Campbells had a private service for Walter, the first of the siblings to die. It was conducted by Dr Story on 6 May, the day Walter was buried in South Africa.

On 23 June 1889, Betty had her first child, her daughter Ruth. Later the same year, while at Whittingehame, Frances gave birth to her third child, Joan Eleanor Campbell. Ruth and Joan would be half of the Balfour group known as 'Us Four'.

Sorrow over Walter's death caused some emotional problems during Frances's confinement. 'She thought [Walter] was calling her . . . . [She] tried to get out of bed to go to him, and wept bitterly when [her nurse] held her down'.[347] According to Betty, this was the beginning of 'mental trouble, which hereafter was apt to recur'.[348] In point of fact, Frances had been prescribed bromide – illegal today – which can produce 'mental aberrations, lethargy . . . and other assorted symptoms'.[349] Significantly, Frances did not have a recurrence of 'mental trouble' once she no longer took the medicine.

One sure source of happiness for Frances was the company at Hatfield House, where she spent much time in the 1880s and '90s. 'Christianity, intelligence, conversation, honesty and a sense of humour were all-important'[350] to both Cecils and Campbells. For their part, the Salisburys enjoyed her company and made her welcome. In Lady Salisbury, Frances found a woman much like herself: long on intelligence and short on tact, Lady Salisbury was opinionated and unafraid to voice her views.[351]

In a biography of Lady Frances Balfour, some mention must be made of the emergence of 'The Souls', as the 'loosely-aligned group of British intellectuals and wits' came to be called in the late 1880s. The acknowledged leader of the fashionable set was Arthur Balfour; his sisters-in-law, Frances and Betty, easily qualified for membership in the aristocratic 'constellation'.[352] The originators of the group (the Tennant sisters) and some of its brightest members (Ettie Grenfell, Frances Horner, D D Lyttleton) were all friends of the Balfour women. Writing at a later date, Frances acknowledged that people at this time were expanding their thinking as well as their boundaries,[353] and that 'the coming generation', which challenged the old Society, had grown 'impatient of the many bonds and restrictions which admittedly bound them'.[354] Frances and Betty shared most of the interests with which the Souls are identified. They loved literature, art, and music, were avid readers, disliked cards and gambling, had inexpensive hobbies, often traveled third class, and enjoyed playing paper games.[355] Most of all, however, the Souls valued good talk, and their conversations were intellectual, animated, and anti-Philistine.[356]

Regardless of any brilliance or excitement it offered, this new coterie was irreverent and shocking to established Britain. And it was also often adulterous. The high moral standards and strong ethical imperatives by which Frances and Betty conducted their lives precluded full membership in The Souls, though both were certainly regarded as peripheral members.[357] Frances also differed with the Souls in her support for some reformist causes. She welcomed greater freedom for women in all aspects of life, and she laboured throughout her adult years to improve the lives of women; in addition, she was keenly interested in politics and the affairs of government, subjects many of the female Souls ignored. If it is true that the Souls – like the Spartans – left nothing behind but their fame,[358] the same cannot be said of Frances.

From 1882 to 1894, Eustace Balfour worked his way up through the ranks of the London Scottish Volunteer Regiment.[359] He had joined the Volunteers as a private; with the resignation of Lt Col W F Nicol in 1894, Eustace assumed command of the London Scottish and was promoted to Lieutenant-Colonel.[360] Interestingly, It has been claimed that Col Balfour was better known in Scotland than Arthur,[361] a Prime Minister of Great Britain. The London Scottish, identified as a 'class' corps,[362] boasted many socially prominent Scots and was considered a 'smart' group with which to be affiliated.

Eustace was a serious observer of all aspects of the military and author of a number of letters and articles on 'the problems of home defence and volunteer reform'.[363] To compensate for the lack of cavalry support, he was, 'before the advent of the automobile,'[364] a strong proponent of bicycles for use by the homeland security forces. In 1887-88, he sat on the War Office Committee on Volunteer Military Cycling and drafted the first official 'Drill of a Cyclist-Infantry Section'.[365] Experiments such as those suggested by Eustace for utilizing bicycles offer examples of the way Volunteers initiated and tested new theories, which has been declared one of 'their greatest contributions to the Army'.[366]

Balfour demonstrated great concern for increasing the efficiency of the troops so that they were not inferior to regular troops in their training. Eustace was one of the foremost advocates of utilizing some of the Volunteers as adjuncts to the regular army in times of war. Frances remembered that 'Volunteers and their place in the Army, or rather the fight that they . . . should be recognized as an integral part of the Army, became very much the uppermost thought with him'.[367] It was an uphill battle, however, because regular Army soldiers and officers tended to disparage the efforts of Volunteers.[368]

By 1890, Frances was beginning to rebound from her troubles. It began with her confiding to Betty that a phase of her life – from 1882 through 1889 – had finally passed and with it, she declared, her youth. She was now determined to be 'content and at peace'.[369] She began her transformation by making a valiant effort to heal the rift which had widened between her and Alice and 'be real friends again'.[370] Ironically, Alice almost prevented the reconciliation by informing Frances on the same day of Frances's resolution that Eustace had not returned two hampers which he had taken to camp at Wimbledon *two years* earlier and that she believed 'it would be "fair" to charge him "half-price"' for the missing items.[371] It was this kind of pettiness which Frances found so irritating and frustrating. Nevertheless, Frances remained true to her vow, and her parting with Alice on this occasion was accompanied with hugs and tears.

More importantly, in 1889, Frances finally found the 'Cause' which she had been seeking throughout the 1880s. She was always happiest when busy, and the British women's struggle to get the vote would prove to be a great fight which would occupy much of her time in the coming years.

CHAPTER FIVE

"Our [Parliamentary] champions are rather Pitiful" [372]
(1885-1895)

'I am doing my best'. [373]

'It is good for me to have to be
universal peace maker'. [374]

When W T Stead, director of the *Pall Mall Gazette*, published a series of articles in 1885 detailing his purchase of a 13-year old girl from her alcoholic mother for £5 for the purpose of prostitution, he created a fire storm. Stead's exposé of the white slavery trade stirred the consciences of the nation, and Frances began her work for women not in the votes for women campaign, for which she is best known, but by answering Stead's call to fight the evil. In her autobiography, Frances decreed that Stead's crusade was 'one of the finest things for women ever done by man'. [375]

Women's responses to Stead's revelations differed substantially from men's. The National Vigilance Association (NVR), also formed in 1885, was a male-dominated society which, by targeting the brothel keepers and procurers involved, primarily concentrated its efforts on the legal aspects of the suppression of trade in persons. [376] Women, however, wanted to prevent young girls from falling prey to the procurers, and to that end chose to create an organisation that would interact directly with the potential victims. [377]

By December 1885, a scheme for the 'protection of female travellers' had been devised under the auspices of the YWCA. [378] In the plan of work carried out by the new association, 'station-visitors' met trains coming into rail stations in London and offered assistance to any young women who arrived 'alone and friendless' [379] and 'without appointment'. [380] The station-visitors also 'warned' naïve young women 'loitering' in the station 'against the advances of strangers' and 'direct[ed] them to a safe home, Travellers' Friendly, or employment agency'.[381] The new association enlisted the support of various railway companies so that the station-visitors had official status and wore a badge.

A central office secretary managed the headquarters of the organisation and coordinated the activities of the general committee and the station-visitors. Organisations assisting the society financially, such as the Girls' Friendly Society, the Church of England Emigration Society, and the YWCA, were represented on the general committee, as the governing board was called. The first meeting of the General Committee of the Travellers' Aid Society (for Girls and Women)[382] (TAS, or Society), as it officially became known, was convened in February 1886, with Frances serving as president. No records exist of how she was recruited or when she was offered the presidency. She had attended none of the preparatory meetings, but Frances had earlier had discussions with Stead on his plans for an expose and was a supporter of his efforts.[383]

Though the organization always befriended women who arrived without an appointment, in 1886, the emphasis began to shift for the station-visitors, who now began by prearrangement to meet young women arriving from out of town. Girls seeking their assistance or those asking the society to meet their kinswomen and who could afford it were charged a small fee – one shilling – plus the 'small' travel expenses of the station-visitor.[384] However, no more than 25 percent of the TAS budget was ever met by charging fees.

The work of the TAS quickly spread to areas outside the London rail stations. In the first year of its existence, the TAS began cooperating with the Jewish Association for the Protection of Girls and Women – which employed an agent who could speak several languages – to meet young women arriving on ships at the London docks. In addition, ships of 45 steamship companies, which visited ports around the world, displayed TAS-provided placards and handbills, which advertised the names of women volunteers in foreign countries who would render aid to young female ocean travellers needing assistance.[385]

As awareness of the Society grew, women in numerous smaller towns across England offered to meet trains in their communities. By the end of its first year, the TAS reported that organisations were also being formed in Scotland and Ireland, and in the second year societies were created in Boston, New York, Montreal, Halifax, Brussels, Geneva, Copenhagen, and Adelaide. Soon other countries developed their own internal networks for meeting travellers, thus extending the British system to communities all over the world. All these foreign organizations were completely independent, but they often submitted reports of their year's work to the London-based founder, which published the accounts in its annual reports.

By the end of 1886, the TAS reported that the organization had met 136 girls at London railway stations, assisted 70 girls who sought the help of the station-visitors after arriving in London, served 60 young women sent to the central office by station officials, and aided nine young women who had been sent from the London docks. In addition, some 300 Englishwomen in the counties and 77 women in foreign ports were helping with the society's work – an impressive record of achievement for its inaugural year.[386]

The YWCA subsidized the society during that year, but by the end of the next, the TAS was able to raise enough funds itself to support its work. Throughout the remainder of its independent existence, the TAS was self-sustaining, though funding for the Society was a perennial concern.

The largest expense that the TAS incurred each year was for salaries of its employees, a station-visitor and a secretary of the central office being the initial salaried members of the staff. The first station-visitor was Ellen Rowe, who defined the role during her lengthy tenure with the society. The demands made on the station-visitor were considerable. She was expected to meet girls at all hours, seven days a week,[387] sometimes with insufficient information. One year, for example, a foreigner wrote asking the TAS to meet her sister. "'You will easily recognize her, because you met me fourteen months ago, and we are very much alike'" was the only information given.[388]

Rowe's demanding schedule took its toll. In 1893, she was stricken with rheumatic fever, which was 'caused by a chill taken while meeting a girl at the docks between 5 and 6 am on a wet morning'.[389] She was incapacitated for seventeen weeks but resumed her work later that year. However, her health remained delicate, and in April 1896, her tenth anniversary with the organization, the executive committee awarded her a pension, a benefit which the society now began to provide for all its salaried employees.[390] After Rowe's retirement in 1896, the TAS significantly increased its staff to handle its growing workload.

The TAS enjoyed impressive growth during the years following 1886. During each of its first 28 years of existence, the society assisted more girls and raised more money to support its work than in the previous year. The number of organisations assisting the TAS also grew. By 1910, twenty organizations were represented on the general committee of the society, which meant that the general committee went from 34 members in 1886 to 83 members in 1909. The executive committee, which began with 16 members in 1886, boasted 48 members by 1907.

The experiences of individual women and young girls served each year by the society illustrate better than statistics the need which existed for the society. In 1900, for example, the TAS befriended two young mill hands from the North of England who had been lured to London to train for a life on the stage. At 3 am on a Sunday morning, a man met the girls at a London station, took them to his room, locked them in, and then left the premises. Terrified, the girls 'screamed and kicked'[391] until the landlady heard them and opened their door. Since there was nowhere for them to go, the girls fled back to the rail station, where a station attendant fed them and then delivered them to the TAS office; the parents were notified of their whereabouts and arrangements made for their father to pick them up. Before leaving London, however, the young girls gave 'evidence before a magistrate in order that . . . [their pursuer] might be brought up on [charges] . . . '.[392] In 1901, a 'foreign Jewess' visiting London took the wrong omnibus and became lost.[393] Eventually the police took her to a police station, where she became quite frightened. 'What was only fright and distress was mistaken for lunacy', and the girl was taken to an Asylum.[394] Eventually, the dock agent, who could speak Polish, found her, secured her release, and sent her on to America. These stories and others which were related in the society's annual reports served to remind subscribers on whom their money was being spent.

When the Society moved its accommodations from the old YWCA premises to 3 Baker Street in 1896, the new headquarters provided lodging for 'two belated travellers and two resident officials of the Society' as well as office space and a servant's bedroom.[395] Eustace's firm, Balfour and Turner, 'volunteered' their services and directed the work of preparing the new premises.[396]

Over the years, the TAS attracted the support of several well-known British leaders. Queen Victoria became Patron of the Society in September 1891 and subscribed £5 annually to its work until her death in 1901, when her place was taken by Queen Alexandra. In 1911, Queen Mary became patron. Frances undoubtedly secured these supporters. As the husband and daughter of the founder of the YWCA, Lord Kinnaird and Lady Emily Kinnaird were important liaisons between the TAS and the YWCA, and both played prominent roles in the TAS for many years.

Few organizations have been served as loyally and steadfastly by one individual as was the Travellers' Aid Society by Lady Frances Balfour. Her attendance at the various TAS meetings was impressive, particularly when one considers the amount of time she spent away from London and her increasing obligations to other women's rights organisations. During her tenure of office, Frances attended 97 of the approximately 150 meetings of the general committee. The Society's chief governing body, the executive committee, convened the most meetings yearly; from 1890-1901 (when records of this committee cease), Frances attended 78 meetings out of 146, averaging almost six meetings a year (out of ten usually held). Moreover, Frances was present for 65 of 129 meetings of the house and staff committee, though she was only required to attend meetings which concerned staffing matters.

Frances also served the society as author and editor: most letters, reports, and releases were submitted to her for approval and editing prior to their publication. On more than one occasion, the Executive asked Frances to write a 'begging letter of her own'[397] to be used to solicit funds for the society. In 1901, when all attempts to locate a hostess for a Drawing Room meeting failed, Frances wrote a 'begging letter' to *The Times*, which brought in £34.[398]

One of the most noteworthy features of the TAS work was its close collaboration with the Jewish Association, a collaboration that was honored at the 'Coming of Age' celebration in 1906 and in the annual reports. Speaking at the celebration, F L Lucas noted that while '. . . so many associations are anxious to be doing everything themselves, neither the Jewish Association nor the Travellers' Aid Society cares for anything but that the work shall be effectually done, and that, . . . the co-operation of the two Societies ensures'.[399] Lucas; Lady Battersea; and her sister Mrs Eliot Yorke, who represented Southampton on the executive, were long-time executives of both the TAS and the Jewish Association and were an integral part of all the work done by both organisations. Such close collaboration, while not unknown in Britain, was not the norm in the anti-Semitic atmosphere of late nineteenth – early twentieth century Europe.

In addition to her own yearly subscription, Frances raised considerable funds for the Society. In May 1902, with the Society's emergency fund exhausted and the Boer War limiting donations, Frances and Betty were hostesses for a sale of work at a garden party at Frances's residence that raised over £105.[400] In 1904, Frances raised £12 from her friends in order to keep the Society from having to borrow money.[401] Another garden party at her home in 1905 featured a fencing match, pipers, and Highland dancers; and in 1909, one featured a performance of *As You Like It*. These parties raised £103 and £63 respectively. Of course, Frances also gave gifts, such as the 'chair-bed,'[402] to the Central Office.

Like many leaders, Frances acted as conciliator among disputants in the organization. The TAS operated under the auspices of the YWCA but was otherwise an independent body with its own constitution. An avowedly Christian organization, the YWCA expected members of the General Committee to subscribe to its statement of beliefs.[403] However, in 1894, some of the 'secular' members of the General Committee refused to sign the YWCA Basis. Working with Lord Kinnaird, Frances effected a compromise whereby the TAS continued its association with the YWCA. On this occasion, as on a few others, Frances expressed her awareness that 'It is good for me to have to be universal peace maker'.[404]

Lady Frances Balfour, who used dates loosely, stated in her autobiography that she began her work for women's enfranchisement 'about 1887'.[405] Records indicate, however, that she did not become a member of the Central Committee of the National Society for Women's Suffrage (CCNSWS) until June 1889. The leaders of the organization at this time were Millicent Garrett Fawcett and Lydia Becker.

Frances also claimed that she was never asked to join the campaign for votes for women until 1889;[406] this statement bears further analysis. It is certainly true that most women in her class were not supporters of votes for women, and considered those who were to be 'wicked, immodest and unwomanly'.[407] Moreover, her father was not in favour, and this likely explains why she waited as long as she did to become fully active. However in the Balfour-Cecil homes, she was surrounded by women sympathetic to women's suffrage. Nora Sidgwick, Alice Balfour, Gwendolen Cecil, Maud Wolmer, Clara Rayleigh, and Evelyn Rayleigh favoured votes for women before 1887 (though they did not belong to any suffrage societies). In any case, by the late 1880s, Frances's reservations had surely broken down, female relatives' arguments carrying weight with someone already intensely interested in politics and government.

When the use of paid canvassers – all men – was outlawed in 1883, the Conservatives were the first to mobilize their women for this work, in the 'Primrose Dames' (established in 1885).[408] Having canvassed for Gerald in 1885 and 1886, Frances was an early recruit. She was made a 'Dame Princess' of the Primrose League in Leeds in January 1887, where she had accompanied Gerald to a political meeting.[409] Frances not only worked for the Dames herself but also recruited members for the league, bragging to Bob Cecil in 1886 that she 'got George Darwin to join' it.[410] Once involved in elections, women like Frances were soon arguing that if they '[were] fitted to influence the votes of others by political argument, they [could not] be unfit to vote themselves'.[411] The women's very effective work for their respective parties 'broke down the belief that politics was exclusively a "man's job"',[412] and the closer association of women with the political parties now enabled them to secure a regular hearing at the hitherto male-dominated party conferences. As a result, the Conservative Party passed women's suffrage resolutions at its annual conferences in 1887, 1889, 1891, and 1894.

It was one thing to be sympathetic to Unionism/Conservatism; it was another to join an avowedly Conservative body. Thus, Frances instead joined the Women's Liberal Unionist Association (WLUA) at its creation in 1888,[413] and was a member of its executive committee from its inception, as was Mrs Fawcett.

In spring 1889, Frances was a guest of Clara Rayleigh at a Drawing Room for suffrage[414] and in April attended her first women's suffrage meeting: her sister-in-law Nora Sidgwick spoke in Westminster Town Hall.[415] Surely each of these events was an invitation to support the Cause. Though Frances did not remember being specifically invited to join the suffragists, the steps through which she came to be not just a member but a leader are clear.

The *immediate* impetus for Frances's joining the women's campaign, however, may have been the Anti-Suffragists' Appeal, published in the June 1889 issue of *Nineteenth Century Review*, the same month Frances joined the Central Committee. It was signed by 104 British women *against* the proposed extension of the suffrage. The suffragists answered the appeal with 'A Reply', signed by at least 2,000 women and published in the July issue of *Fortnightly Review*. Frances's name, by rank and precedence, appeared second in the list. Since a significant number of the women who signed the Anti-Suffragists' Appeal were members of the aristocracy,[416] Frances's name and title were persuasive in rebuttal.

Procedural changes had reduced the possibility of debate on private Members' bills, and, though there were 343 MPs amenable to women's suffrage after the 1886 election, there had been no debate on the women's bill from 1886 to 1890. Frances's earliest correspondence with Mrs Fawcett concerned this problem. Frances appealed to the Liberal Unionist MP Robert Finlay for information about the bill's chances in 1990; he reported that 'Women's Suffrage has been rather unlucky in the ballot. We stand first in the list for Wed[nesday] the 13th May, wh[ich] is rather late . . . '.[417] Saying 'I am doing my best', she reported to Fawcett that Gerald would vote for the bill but was 'not enthusiastic' and that Finlay would only abstain from voting since his Liberal Unionist leaders opposed the bill. She also informed Fawcett that the Government would take all the time before Christmas. Finally, she opined, 'I wish we could fall into the hands of some really good and well known MP, our [Parliamentary] champions are rather pitiful . . .'.[418]

With her numerous contacts within the House of Commons, Frances very quickly became the main liaison between the suffragists and Members of Parliament. Indeed, as the proposed date of the debate neared, she alerted Fawcett to a possible problem: 'I think I had better tell you something that passed at Arlington Street [Salisbury's London home] today. [Salisbury] said 'You must look after [W H] Smith. I have done my best, & have now turned Arthur on to him'. She added, 'I knew of course to what he was alluding, so I said 'but he has <u>promised</u> the day'. He ans[were]d. 'You don't know Smith as I do, he will get out of it if he can. . .'.[419] True to Salisbury's prediction, the women were foiled by the 'political chicanery'[420] of Sir Henry James and their old nemesis Gladstone: after Gladstone questioned the 'fairness' of excluding one Wednesday, James moved that all Wednesdays be taken for Government business, and the House concurred 218-159.[421]

The suffragists faced an additional thorny problem. While most of the women's supporters were Liberals, most of the Liberal leadership in the Victorian-Edwardian eras – especially Gladstone and Asquith – strongly opposed votes for women. And while most Conservatives supporters did not favour women's suffrage, the Tory leadership, especially Disraeli, Salisbury, and Balfour, were sympathetic to the women's claims. Hence, neither party was ever willing to make women's enfranchisement a party issue, causing the suffragists to regard votes for women as a non-party issue.[422]

Even after the Reform Act of 1884, which enfranchised some labourers – the last major male group to be enfranchised – only about 60% of British males (around 8 million men) had the vote: there were still property and residence qualifications for voting. Women suffragists demanded the vote on the same terms as men, but women would not be able to qualify with the same property as their husbands. It was therefore estimated that only about 1 million women would be enfranchised if women age 21 got the vote at this point. Women thus enfranchised were believed by the Liberals to likely be Conservatives; hence, the Liberal Party leadership did not support votes for women even though they could surely have crafted a bill that could have assisted their party.

Almost from the beginning of her association with the suffragists, Frances was enlisted as a speaker for the women's Cause, and she understood her value in this role: when aristocratic ladies embraced an activity, it broke down the barriers for all women.[423] In addition to her class, her Balfour name was a drawing card, and many more citizens would turn out to hear The Lady Frances Balfour than might listen to, say, Lydia Becker or Helen Blackburn, despite these women's obvious value to the Cause and popularity with supporters.

After the death of Lydia Becker in 1890, the suffragists' undisputed leader was Millicent Garrett Fawcett, who was intelligent and focused but not 'passionate' or 'stirring'.[424] In a movement generally lacking charismatic and inspirational leaders, Frances became the most exciting advocate for women's enfranchisement. Besides her rank and her name, critical to her effectiveness was her voice, which was always described as low and rich, possessing a lyrical, almost musical quality. She was reputed never to raise her voice, never to be strident or jarring – no small boon to the suffragists, for whom the 'womanly' image was most important.

Dora D'Espaigne Chapman's interview of Frances, published in *The World's Work* in 1907 and one of the few Frances ever gave, offers a compelling analysis of her effectiveness as a speaker: '[W]hen [Lady Frances Balfour] warms to her subject she does not betray it in any of the restless feminine ways of the town-bred speaker.'[425] Her voice, Chapman said, 'does not alter, she uses no gesture –

curbed by a platform, her absolute repose of manner is a thing to wonder at, and to remember long after the dramatic oratory of others is forgotten'. Frances herself often commented on the suffragists' insistence on being 'lady-like'; she understood that Members of Parliament would never support a measure such as votes for women if they believed it would jeopardize marriage or 'existing society'.[426]

Thanks to a 'shift amongst the Conservatives',[427] the suffragists were successful in bringing in a women's parliamentary franchise measure in the Commons in 1892. As a result – and possibly in anticipation of an election to be held later in the year – Conservative MP Albert Rollit, who secured the earliest ballot, piloted a bill now taken 'unusually seriously by both sides'[428] to a vote in the Commons in April.

Arthur Balfour spoke impressively for the women's measure, no doubt at Frances's urging. To those who argued that most women did not want the vote and that women had not identified specific grievances which needed redress, Arthur pointed out that there had been no 'widespread desire on the part of labourers to obtain the franchise in 1884', and that the grievances of labourers 'were never discovered before the vote was conferred'.[429] Responding to the assertion that women could not fight for their country, Arthur observed that 'the enemy is fought by a disciplined force raised in the country and the chief duty of ordinary citizenship consists not in shouldering the rifle and going to the frontier, but in paying the bill', and 'that is a duty which the people whom we wish to enfranchise under this bill can perform'.[430] For all his lack of vehemence on the issue, Arthur was basically sound in his arguments for the women's Cause (he simply believed there was no valid argument against the vote for women who qualified the same as men). No one had to put words into Arthur's mouth, of course, but one wonders how much Frances's discussions with him about the issues surrounding women's voting prepared him for such a speech: she was called 'A[rthur] Balfour's Egeria'.[431] The CCNSWS was so impressed with Arthur's speech that they reprinted it for sale to interested citizens.[432]

When the vote on the Second Reading of the bill was taken, the women's measure was defeated by only 23 votes. Most importantly, 78 Conservative MPs voted in favour of the legislation (compared to 64 against),[433] and Conservatives would be in power for all but three of the next thirteen years. Unfortunately, just when they might have helped women, the Conservatives found themselves in alliance with the Liberal Unionists, the faction of the Liberal Party most opposed to women's suffrage (only nine Liberal Unionist members voted for the women's bill in 1892[434]), and hope for governmental assistance for the women's bill seemed slim.

In the lead up to the vote in the House of Commons, Frances and Fawcett spoke in St James's Hall at a joint meeting of suffrage societies in support of Albert

Rollitt's bill. Frances also canvassed for the suffrage in the lobby of the House on the evening of 25 April, helped sponsor a Conversazione for the Cause on the evening of 26 April, and attended the Commons debates on the women's bill on 27 April. Afterwards, she recorded in her diary that there had been a '**splendid division for us**'and that within two days the women were making plans for their next '**moves**'. Though she had always been interested in parliamentary debates, Frances had not attended sessions on a regular basis before this date, but during the next two years, she gradually became a fixture in the Ladies' Gallery.

This same year Frances was elected to the Executive Committee of the CCNSWS, her first leadership position in the suffrage fight. At a time when most women's organisations were headed by a member of the aristocracy, the entire suffrage effort was by contrast comparatively devoid of noble supporters. There were only three titled women on the Executive: Frances; Clara, Lady Rayleigh; and Louise, Lady Goldsmid; and of these, only Frances would play a leadership role in the votes for women agitation.

Their near success in 1892 galvanized the suffragists and 'sent a thrill of fresh life through the Committees'[435] in anticipation of the 1893 parliamentary session. By the 1890s, many suffragists believed that petitions – their usual appeal to Parliament – had become stale and lacked the impact the women wished to make. '[T]o utilize the reviving energy',[436] the suffragists decided in 1893 to remind all Members of Parliament of the support that the suffrage Cause had in their constituencies.[437] To this end, they proposed a Special Appeal with signatures of women throughout the United Kingdom, to be collected by members of both major suffrage organisations as well as the Women's Liberal Federation, the Primrose League, the Women's Liberal Unionist Association, the World's Women's Christian Temperance Union, and the British Women's Temperance Association.

Frances was a member of the Special Appeal Committee established to coordinate the work of the 3,500 collectors,[438] and she served as a representative in England and in Scotland.[439] Writing to Fawcett in December, Frances reported that she had enjoyed a positive reception among women in Dunbar, which she 'had not thought to find'.[440] On the same holiday, she visited three women, whom she had earlier written for an appointment, to enlist them in the suffrage effort. Recounting the experience to Betty, she wrote, 'I . . . found them all sitting in their best bib and tuckers before blazing fires waiting to receive me. Bless them all. They took up the idea so quickly, said they would do what was wanted at once . . . and I could have kissed them all around'. . . . She continued, 'They asked me if I would address a meeting of women if they thought it advisable and I said I would . . . . I think I can chatter suffrage for about an hour'.[441]

By summer 1894, Scotland was only 6,000 short of their goal of a quarter million signatures.[442] Possessed of good political instincts, Frances wrote to Fawcett, 'Surely tho', we must hold our appeal over till after an election'.[443] Since Gladstone's fourth (and last) Government had 'the distinction of being the only Parliament elected since the women's suffrage agitation began in the 1860s in which no debate took place on the measure',[444] Frances's suggestion was insightful; the women's Appeal was withheld for the time being.

Factions within the suffrage movement created difficulties in 1895. Mary Cozens, now leader of a group called the Parliamentary Committee for Women's Suffrage, pursued her own tactics for getting a bill before the Commons, irrespective of the efforts of other suffrage organisations, which had always presented a unified front when dealing with Members of Parliament. When the best date for a private Member's bill in 1895 proved to be 12 May (drawn by J C H Macdona), the suffragists opted to present a resolution instead, for which their long-time supporter, W S McLaren, secured the early date of 22 February 1895 for debate. Cozens, however, rejected a resolution, even though Frances spoke with 'the little reptile' and 'point[ed] out the error of her ways'.[445] Before the session concluded, 'factionalism within the movement resulted in . . . three different women's suffrage bills and a resolution compet[ing] for Parliamentary time',[446] a source of great embarrassment to the suffragists.

Shortly after the debacle caused by Cozens, Frances assisted the suffragists' effort to find another Parliamentary leader to replace Lord Wolmer, who moved to the House of Lords in 1885 when he succeeded his father, Lord Selborne. Frances informed Fawcett on 9 May that she had secured George Wyndham,[447] who remained the women's leader in the Commons until 1899, when he accepted office in Salisbury's third ministry.

By 1895, however, Arthur Balfour, heretofore a reasonably strong supporter of the women's efforts, wanted to retreat from his prominence in the women's Cause,[448]most probably because of the unpleasant conflict into which he had been drawn in 1894 by Fawcett.

At this critical time in the women's struggle, Fawcett had embarked on a prolonged campaign against Harry Cust, Conservative MP for Stamford and editor of the *Pall Mall Gazette*, whose moral history she found repugnant. When Cust, a philanderer, impregnated his cousin, Nina Welby-Gregory, Arthur pressured Cust to marry Nina, which he did in 1893. Shortly thereafter, Cust was adopted by the Unionists/Conservatives in North Manchester. Incensed by his sexual misdeeds, Fawcett wrote Unionist supporters in North Manchester, appealing to them to oppose him as 'immoral' and unfit for parliamentary office.[449]

Frances was among those who did not support Fawcett's efforts here; she noted that Arthur was 'very angry and will do nothing for W[omen's] S[uffage]',[450] and that 'a great reaction has set in for Cust, as being the victim of a personal persecution'.[451] Undeterred, Fawcett eventually succeeded in making matters so untenable for Cust that he withdrew his candidacy 'for reasons of ill-health'[452] in September 1894.

The Cust matter did not end there, however. With a general election coming in 1895, unidentified Unionist/Conservative leaders inquired of Frances whether Fawcett would still oppose Cust if he were adopted by another constituency. In her letter of inquiry to Fawcett, Frances asserted, '[I]f you cannot say you will leave Cust alone, if he stands, there will be the devil to pay as far as Suffrage goes'.[453] Fawcett remained unmoved. As a last resort, Frances threatened to resign her suffrage post if Fawcett did not desist.[454] Frances did not have to make good on her threat because Cust did not stand for another seat until 1900 at which time Fawcett, inexplicably, did not oppose his candidacy.

It is difficult to know how much damage Fawcett inflicted on the women's movement with her campaign to discredit Cust, but there is no doubt that the leading Conservatives, Salisbury ('I should like to do that woman an injury'[455]) and Balfour, were greatly angered by her actions. Arthur is reputed to have never forgiven Fawcett,[456] and this experience may be the chief reason for his lack of enthusiasm for the women's measure thereafter.[457]

CHAPTER SIX

'Can it get right with Alice?' [458]
(1890-1900)

'You are to an election
what . . . salt is to food'. [459]

R B Finlay to Frances

'I mean to thole [endure] it'. [460]

The death of W H Smith, Leader of the House of Commons on 6 September 1891 brought much change to the Balfour households. Quickly, Salisbury chose Arthur to succeed Smith, bringing Balfour back from Ireland. Frances was delighted to have him home again, but for Alice, it was a wrenching experience; she declared to Betty that 'the best part of her life was over'. [461] The General Election in 1892 brought the Liberal Party back to power, though they were again dependent on the 81 Irish Nationalists. Gerald and Arthur were returned, but Frances's brother Lorne, Robert Finlay, and James Cecil were defeated; Salisbury, according to Frances, believed 'Labour [had] beaten [the Conservatives] not H[ome] R[ule]'. [462]

Gladstone made yet another attempt to settle the Irish question with Home Rule, and Frances broke her holiday in Scotland to return to London to see Home Rule for Ireland pass the Commons only to be thrown out by the Lords in September. The 84-year old Gladstone, increasingly worn out by his political exertions, resigned on 3 March 1894, and the Queen chose the Imperialist Lord Rosebery to succeed him. A handsome man of great wealth and eloquence from whom much was expected, Rosebery proved a disappointment once in office, and his tenure was short. In truth, Rosebery's Government was stymied by the Lords, which refused to pass almost all Liberal legislation sent to the upper chamber. With Rosebery's resignation, Salisbury came into office again, with the Unionists firmly embed in his administration.

In the General Election which followed in 1895, the Unionists/Conservatives were victorious (411 seats to the Liberal-Irish's 259). Frances's chief efforts were expended for her friend Robert Finlay, now standing as a Liberal Unionist for Inverness Burghs. One of her best efforts was made at a meeting of approximately 450 women (they had expected only 50-100 to attend).[463] Frances spoke for a half hour and 'was considered a success'. At a campaign meeting in Inverness, she had the pleasure of hearing him pledge himself to women's suffrage.

The morning of polling day was 'divine [and] peaceful', but the pace quickened in the afternoon when Frances was sent with some urgency to 'fetch a voter' over whom there had been 'a newspaper war'. Afterward, Frances declared, 'This is a day's work you will not regret Roderick Fraser'. Later, she fetched an 85-year-old who refused to vote unless transported to the polls, and then declined to vote till given the opportunity to speak with the Baillie. 'It was 7.20. . . . The Baillie and the old man met. The vote was recorded at 7.50!' Finlay won by 250 votes, and he readily acknowledged Frances's assistance, saying 'You are to an election what . . . salt is to food',[464] adding 'You made a profound impression in these parts . . . '.[465]

An article Frances wrote about the Unionists' success in Scotland may have been the first for which she earned a fee. The *National Review*, owned by Leo Maxse, **paid £4** for 'Some Lessons from Scotland', part of its coverage of 'The Election of 1895'.[466] Noting in her article that there had been only ten Conservative members in Parliament after the 1885 election, she boasted that now 33 of 72 Scottish Members were Unionists. She credited this increase to better organization.[467]

Finlay did more than thank Frances for her assistance to his political campaign and career; he appointed her his Parliamentary Private Secretary, surely a unique honour.[468] This position carried with it a level of responsibility that was remarkable to be delegated to a woman at this time. According to Betty, Finlay trusted her to handle his Parliamentary correspondence and to write letters to his constituents.[469] Moreover, he 'dictated to her and talked over all his speeches with her.' Betty added that it was not the work in and of itself, that interested Frances, but the 'stimulus of working for another'. Her work for Finlay, now Solicitor-General, immediately proved interesting and educational: in October, she assisted him on the Venezuela-British Guiana boundary dispute, for which the United States was demanding arbitration.

This period saw more births, and one particularly sad loss for Frances. Betty and Gerald's second child, Eleanor – or 'Nell'- was born on 2 November 1890. Four months later, on 7 March 1891, Alison Catherine Campbell, the last daughter of Frances and Eustace and the final member of 'Us Four', was born. Lord Lytton, whom Frances called **'the kindest of my dearest of friends',** died on 24

November 1891. He left Frances his 'blood-stone ring . . . as a tiny token of the love and gratitude and reverent esteem of one to whom she has ever been a stirling, unselfish, tender, upright, wise and honest friend'.[470]

Early in her married life, Frances had settled into a routine for writing: she arose at 6 am and wrote until 8-8:30 am, thus answering letters or writing articles before her children were up and before breakfast was served. She also wrote when she travelled on trains. Frances, who enjoyed writing, now began to publish articles: this was probably a natural extension of her interest in politics.

To her friends, Frances Balfour was a study in contrasts. On the one hand, she could be a considerate friend who extended great kindness and thoughtfulness to those she loved; on the other, she had a pen and tongue that often yielded up words that deeply wounded those for whom she cared. Once, when a servant named McLean left Whittingehame in 1891, Betty encouraged Baffy and the other children to let McLean know they were aware she would be leaving, which they did by inviting her to join them for tea. When Betty related the children's kindness to Frances, who disliked departure scenes such as this, she was venomous. 'I fundamentally differ from you in all these matters. You have that strain of your Mother strongly in you, a morbid desire to excite and watch the symptoms of suffering'.[471] Despite her personal history, it is difficult to believe that Frances would not have realized that Betty would be greatly wounded by such cruel criticism of her efforts, which were kind and thoughtful and obviously meant to teach the children to cultivate these same virtues.

Her lifelong friendship with Betty is fascinating. The relationship survived mostly due to Betty's diligent efforts to understand and tolerate Frances's occasionally outrageous outbursts and opinions. As part of this effort, Betty often 'talked as if Frances did everything best' when speaking about her to others.[472] But Betty also stood up to Frances. When chastised for not being absorbed in the day's political events, Betty responded, 'When you begin to take an interest in poetry, in the drama, or in French literature, perhaps I shall become as exclusively engrossed in politics as you are now. Speeches and sermons are your two manias. All well and good, but you have no business to be indignant with everyone else for not agreeing with you'.[473]

Frances's writing was not always well received. Once, after Frances complained about Betty's not doing enough to keep the flow of good conversation going at mealtimes at Whittingehame,[474] Betty retorted, '. . . if you desire conversation so keenly I think you should try to avoid shutting up all efforts at it so often with a rude remark. To be told that what one says is idiotic, or a damned lie, or revoltingly indecent . . . does not tend to the increase of a flow of conversation. . .'.[475] Frances seemed often to speak and to write sometimes on the spur of the moment, saying or writing whatever came into her head without regard for the effect it would have on the recipients.

In truth, Frances's words were often more harsh than she intended. She loved sarcasm, exaggeration, and chaffing, but these can, on paper, seem sharper than intended. A friend observed, '[Frances] was always delicate and often suffering, and perhaps pain sometimes set a sharper edge on her comments than she herself knew, though they were frequently accompanied by a look curiously compounded of exultation in her own wickedness, amusement, and remorse, which took half the sting from her most flagrant sallies'.[476] Reduced to black and white on a page, however, her words often appeared insensitive and harshly judgmental. And they cost her friendships. Baffy wrote about the effect her mother's writing had on people:

> My mother loved writing letters, and few people have ever written better
> ones of their kind. . . . In them she could reveal depths of sympathy
> and feeling which she could rarely bring to the surface in talk. In them
> she could scorch and scathe as even she might hesitate to do face to
> face. Yet she could never understand why the written word bit deeper
> than the spoken. She lived on her friendships, she nourished them by
> letter-writing, and by letter-writing she killed them more than once.[477]

All testimonies to Frances acknowledge her ability to extend profound sympathy to those who were ill or dying and to those who were bereaved. She particularly helped those on the Balfour or Campbell estates. In 1893, she 'did all she could to alleviate the suffering'[478] of Mrs Sked, a Balfour-estate shepherd's wife, who lingered for many months. Frances arranged for mosquito netting to be placed around her to protect her from the flies, she read *Kidnapped* to her, and she took time to confer with Mrs Sked's sister and husband.[479] In times such as these, Frances noted, she always spoke 'bravely', for 'Dr Robertson said it is both a moral and a religious duty to be hopeful'.[480] During this same year, Frances lost one of her favourite Aunts. On 30 May 1893, Lady Emma NcNeill, Aunt 'Dot' and her father's only sister, died following a **'sudden illness'** while visiting Bournemouth. Frances was Executrix of her estate, a task which she had completed by autumn.

At the end of 1893, all the Balfours, again at Whittingehame for the holidays, were awaiting the birth of Betty and Gerald's third child. Frances's New Year's wish was that Betty '[would have] the joy of saying "Unto us a son is born". It is the greatest thrill of a Mother's life'.[481] On 21 January 1894, Betty gave birth to her third daughter, Mary Edith. In September, Frances gave birth to her second son and last child, Oswald Herbert Campbell Balfour.

Just as she was preparing to return to London in early January 1894, Frances learned from Dr McGregor, whom she was visiting, of the death of the 2nd Duchess of Argyll, who finally succumbed to the chronic asthma which had made her 'an invalid for many years'.[482] Frances immediately went to Inveraray, where she found her father **'very crushed, but calm'**.[483] The Duchess, age 50, was buried beside her first husband at Cannes.[484] **'The sun blessed her as she left us'**.[485] Shortly before the funeral, the Duke gave Frances one of Duchess Mimi's jewels saying, "**You are the only one who has helped me**".[486] In this instance, as in many others, Frances evinced her loyalty and commitment to family – traits that seem stronger in her than in any of the rest of her family. She kept in touch with other family members and came to their aid whenever she believed they needed or could use her assistance. The isolated, lonely child, confined to her room and bed so often as she grew up, came to be the most family-driven of them all.

Frances was a discerning judge of intellect and character, and many of her political and religious friends went on to high office, assisted in part by her. Nor did she labour without recognition from those whom she aided. Finlay, now a QC, was named Solicitor General in the new government and knighted by Salisbury in 1895. Finlay recognized his debt to her saying, 'If I ever do anything politically I know it will be your doing. . .'.[487] She was also of assistance to George Saintsbury, who was named Professor of English Literature at Edinburgh University in 1895. She related to Betty that '[Saintsbury said] his getting the chair was indirectly my doing, for without G[erald] and A[rthur] he would never have got it, and he would never have known them except through me'.[488] That same year, Arthur wrote his *Foundations of Belief*, which Frances prepared for publication. He dedicated the book, published in March 1895, to her.

Frances's father, much exercised by Rosebery's autumn 1894 speeches urging reform of the House of Lords,[489] was anxious to answer the Prime Minister at the West of Scotland Unionists' meeting at Glasgow on 15 January 1895. Frances was present for the event. Twenty minutes into his talk, the 71-year old Duke collapsed.[490] Death from syncope was averted, although Frances declared, '[T]wice I thought him gone'.[491] Before the evening was over, however, the Duke teased that 'at 71, I must give up public meetings'.[492] The Duke's great political career was, in fact, effectively over.

Success arrived for Eustace in February 1890 when he was named Surveyor of the 1st Duke of Westminster's London estate[493] and given an office on Davies Street in Mayfair with an initial salary of £500 a year.[494] As the Duke's Architect, he was responsible for designing alterations which the Duke made on his London estate, and since 'the rebuilding of Mayfair owed much to the active patronage of the

[1st] Duke of Westminster',[495] Eustace became a 'crucial contributor' to the Duke's transformation of this fashionable part of central London.[496] In fact, Eustace was responsible for the 'overall town planning of Mayfair'.[497]

It is, unfortunately, impossible to see architectural renditions of all that Balfour designed for the Dukes: only one drawing is extant, that of 23 Wilton Crescent in Belgravia.[498] Specific works on which Eustace was involved (out of 36) included 28 Grosvenor Gardens; Edinburgh House in Eaton Gate; Aldford House at 1 Park Lane; the southwest wing of Bourdon House in Davies Street, and all the buildings in Balfour Place, which 'constitute one of the finest groups of Arts and Crafts town houses in London'.[499] In Belgravia, his most impressive achievement was in 'the stone-faced rebuilding of the northern side of Wilton Crescent'.[500]

Eustace and Thackeray Turner both worked on St Anselm's Church and Parsonage on Davies Street, built in 1894-96 for the 1st Duke; it has been deemed their 'best' work.[501] Some have attributed the design mostly to Turner, but it is instructive that Eustace's obituary carried in the *RIBA Journal* called St Anselm's 'probably the most complete and instructive example of Balfour's work'.[502] St Anselm's was also controversial. The building, with its 'plain brick exterior' and 'light and graceful interior' was also 'audacious and idiosyncratic'.[503] *The Builder's Journal,* however, deemed it 'not only one of the most interesting of modern Churches, but the best Church raised in London of late years'.[504] That he both foresaw possible controversy and that he was intimately involved in the design can be seen from Eustace's comments to Frances: 'The Church is in a very interesting stage. We are considering the staining of the stone work inside as a contrast to the colour of the plaster [white]. My three little flame windows at the East End are already producing their effect, although the inside scaffolding is still up'. He mused, 'I wonder what the public will say! My own conception has been fairly realized but it is strong meat for "Babes"'.[505] Eustace was highly pleased, therefore, when the artist Sir W B Richmond congratulated the Duke of Westminster: '[H]ow warm is my admiration for Eustace Balfour's church. . . . I was deeply struck by its nobility. . . . Indeed I cannot but look upon his work as a new departure upon lines of great dignity and restraint'.[506] Unfortunately, the 'little loved' church never enjoyed widespread support with the congregation and was demolished in 1939, though parts of the church were re-used in a new St Anselm's built in Belmont, Stanmore.[507] In recognition of his important architectural contributions to London, Eustace was elected a Fellow of the Royal Institute of British Architects (FRIBA) in January 1892.

When Lord Salisbury formed his third government (1895), he chose Gerald Balfour to be Chief Secretary for Ireland. Arthur continued as First Lord of the Treasury and Conservative leader of the House of Commons, and Joseph

Chamberlain, who chose the Colonial Office, now led the Unionists in the Commons. Gerald and Betty, whose purchase of 24 Addison Road in March 1895 had pleased Frances, now moved to Ireland. The first summer holiday at Whittingehame without Gerald and Betty was somewhat lonely for Frances: '**I missed Betty**', she admitted.[508]

There had been much speculation in the Campbell family about whether the Duke of Argyll would remarry, but his 27 May 1895 announcement of his betrothal to Ina McNeill, spinster niece by marriage of Aunt 'Dot' McNeill, was nevertheless a surprise. The future Duchess Ina's airs, together with her lack of interest in her prospective step-family, caused the Campbells to distance themselves from the Duke even before the wedding. 'Duchess Ina set about smartening up everything', Princess Louise wrote. 'Now the family coachman and footman had cockades put on their hats, knee breeches were introduced and hair powdered. The old Duke was made to wear the Order of the Garter and pumps, which was unheard of since he was notoriously uninterested in dress'.[509] Frances's reaction to the 'pomp' was similar to that of the rest of the family: after one visit, she noted that she had '**dined with my father. Eheu!**'

By 1896, Frances was going almost daily to the House of Commons – Asquith called her 'the Doyenne of the Ladies Gallery'.[510] After dinner with her children, she went to Parliament and often stayed until the end of the session, which was sometimes late at night. During one session which lasted into the next day, Frances wrote Betty that she had 'stayed to the very end of that all night sitting' and that '[a]bout 6 a.m. a dishevelled Linky, Maxwell and Warkworth came up to sit with me and administered tea and ham sandwiches, which I did not in the least feel the want of as my bod was sustained by the amusement of life'.[511]

The tension between Frances and Alice had grown steadily throughout the late 1880s and the 1890s. Frances's impatience with Alice increased in 1894 because of Alice's focus on the picayune. At one point, alarmed by the pronunciation of 'Whitten-hame' by the local School Board,[512] Alice changed the spelling of the family house to 'Whittingehame' to insure that it would be pronounced 'Whitten-Jum.' When some of the bedrooms – heretofore identified by the hues on the walls – were repainted, Alice agonised for days about what the rooms should now be called. It was pettiness over such issues as these that spurred Frances's annoyance – and even greater tactlessness – with Alice. Returning to Whittingehame from a day trip to Edinburgh in early November 1896, Frances learned that Alice had taken Cro, the '**best beloved**' family dog, out during the day and lost him. Despite extensive searches over many days, Cro's body was not found in Luggate Burn until 8 December, a '**day marked with black**'.

The hostility between Frances and Alice came to a head in 1897 over the issue of Eustace's drinking. As the food and beverage expenses grew at Whittingehame, Alice complained more and more – often tactlessly. Alice was thus the first to make an issue of the amount of alcohol Eustace imbibed.

Frances was finally forced to confront the issue of Eustace's drinking and its contribution to his health problems (including heart troubles) when she 'found him in London', apparently passed out, in early March 1897.[513] On 12 March, after a lengthy discussion with Arthur – who informed her that she had been either 'wilfully or stupidly blind' to Eustace's 'problem'[514] – she confronted Eustace, who admitted his addiction, declaring, however, that he imbibed little or no alcohol at home, except with food, and absolutely none 'at HeadQuarters',[515] an assertion which Frances questioned, since he admitted that his heavy drinking began in 1882, when he joined the Volunteers, many of whom liked a drink after their military exercises.

Determined to learn the truth about Eustace's assertion that he did not drink at Headquarters, Frances summoned Hugh Sutton, a Volunteer friend of Eustace's, to lunch in order to discuss the matter. Amazingly, shortly thereafter,[516] Alice also sought out Sutton for discussion of Eustace's 'habits',[517] a discussion about which Frances soon learned from Sutton himself. Livid at such overstepping, Frances fired off a letter to Alice about her 'disgusting conduct' and warned her to stay out of the matter. Frances ended with the observation that 'tho' I cannot say I am surprised by the lack of breeding, I am surprised at the total absence of all proper family feeling and loyalty'.[518] Certainly, given the animosity which already existed between the two women, Alice was unwise to have meddled in the matter. Eustace's addiction was an extremely painful issue with which Frances indeed needed to come to terms; nonetheless, her words need not have been cruel. Alice, however, was not intimidated by Frances's letter nor sympathetic with her demands to desist: astonishingly, she sought and had another conversation with Sutton a few days later.[519]

Eventually, Frances admitted to Arthur that she had indeed been 'stupidly blind' to Eustace's addiction. In Frances's defence, there is evidence that Eustace was a binge drinker, capable of abstaining for long periods of time – thus creating in those around him a sense that all was normal – and then drinking himself into a stupor over several days. This could explain some of Frances's ambivalence about his addiction in the early years, but by the mid-1890s, she was probably avoiding the obvious. When under the influence, Eustace – who was usually kind, gentle, and urbane – became pompous, boastful, and effusive with his gestures.[520]

In the meantime, Arthur was made aware of Frances's letter to Alice (which had gone unanswered). He was so angered that he apparently prohibited Frances from discussing the matter any further either with Alice or with him and, given that she does not appear to have been a guest at either 10 Downing Street (where Salisbury had asked him to live) or Whittingehame from 18 March to 27 August 1897, he may also have indicated that Frances was no longer welcome at his residences. During this interval, Frances was depressed and saddened by what she had brought on herself**,** recording, **'How worse than foolish I am'** (19 March). While visiting Wimbledon in April to see Arthur and Gerald play Finlay and Clough-Taylor, she noted that **'Arthur was very good to me under the regulations laid down. But how depressing it all is. I mean to thole [endure] it'**.[521]

Three months after the painful incident, Frances wrote Arthur an apology for her intemperate letter to Alice. Arthur waited a month before replying, now spelling out 'what [was] to be our policy for the future':

> I have striven to the best of my means and ability, for these many years to make Whittingehame a home centre for my brothers, my sisters-in-law, and their children. It has been a great pleasure to me; I believe it to have been no inconsiderable advantage to them and at one time I cherished the hope that I might ask in return that the inmates of my house should live in mutual affection. This demand I withdraw: I perceive with grief that it is impossible of accomplishment . . . . But if I cannot have affection I will at any rate have peace: and unless some kind of security for this can be obtained, I am afraid I must insist that henceforth you come to Whittingehame as an occasional guest and no longer as an habitual inmate. By 'peace' it must be distinctly understood that I do not mean 'armed neutrality.' Alice is your hostess: it is partly by her money that the Whittingehame life is rendered possible. For both reasons she has a right to cordial civility: and that right must be respected.[522]

Frances agreed to these conditions – she had no choice – and gradually resumed 'normal' relations with Arthur and Alice. She was apparently successful in restoring good will with Alice in a fairly short period, because she reported to Lady Salisbury at the end of the year that she had received 'a testimonial of character from Arthur lately' and that she had 'tried to earn it.'[523]

Most people familiar with the tension between the two women blamed Frances for the fissure.[524] It is not known what efforts, if any, Alice made, since the assumption is always that Frances was the chief disturber of the peace – obviously a mistaken assumption, as can be seen in the Sutton episode. One important factor in the Alice-Frances tension that was apparently unknown to some was that Alice had forbidden her brothers Eustace and Gerald and their wives to invite guests to Whittingehame.[525] It must have been embarrassing for Frances not to be able to invite friends to Whittingehame when they knew she was in Scotland.

In June 1897, Frances was delighted as the British nation celebrated Queen Victoria's Diamond Jubilee, the focus of which was on the Queen and her Empire with honours and emphasis going to the Imperial Prime Ministers. Frances watched the great procession on this occasion from the Rothschilds' residence in Piccadilly. On 14 July, she attended the Jubilee women's dinner, which she deemed a '**great success**'.

The Balfours also celebrated the Queen's Diamond Jubilee. On August 30, some 500 estate workers were treated to an evening of 'drinking, eating and dancing' at the Home Farm, after which 'pyrotechnists from London mounted a breathtaking display which culminated in a piece consisting of a crown and the words 'God Bless Her 1837-1897'.[526] The next day, also 'blessed by fine weather', the largest garden party ever hosted at the House was held for 530 attendees, which included the Lord Mayor of London. Successful though it was, Alice learned an important lesson from the event. After viewing the 55 by 30 foot tent for the lower terrace, Alice recorded: 'Note: When hiring a tent ascertain if it is clean.'

The mid- to late-1890s were marked by the deaths or illnesses of several relatives and friends of Frances and Eustace. On 18 June 1895, the Campbells were shocked and saddened to learn that Colin had died suddenly of pneumonia in Bombay. The next year, Libby, now living at Dalchenna House at Inveraray, died of pneumonia on 24 September 1896 and, because Duchess Ina was presiding over Inveraray,[527] was buried at Rosneath. Libby was the first member of 'The Sisterhood' to die. In 1897, Lady Salisbury began experiencing health problems and in May underwent two unsuccessful operations to drain fluid to relieve dropsy (edema). Frances spent many days with Aunt Georgy during this illness. Lady Salisbury 'told Uncle R[obert] that I was a comfort to her, as I was as unreasonable as herself . . . '.[528] More sadness came on 17 June 1898, when Sir Edward Burne-Jones, a dear friend of both Frances and Eustace, died of a heart attack. It was '**a day of heavy blues**', she recorded.

Health problems also plagued Frances in November 1898. While climbing on his mother, the four-year old Oswald accidentally kicked Frances in her left breast, causing considerable pain and the development of an abscess, which was finally drained on 15 November, in her home. During the crisis, Frances noted that Eustace was very thoughtful and 'delightful'[529] and Arthur Balfour stayed with her until the preparations for the operation began.[530] Unfortunately, a second operation was required before Frances was completely healed. In her benediction for 1898, Frances acknowledged that she had '**Much to be thankful for** . . . .'

The year 1899 brought no respite from illnesses and deaths for the Campbell family. On 2 January, the 6th Duke of Northumberland died; Frances's eldest sister Edith and her husband Lord Percy were now the 7th Duke and Duchess of Northumberland. In July, Lady Salisbury, whose health had continued unsure, suffered a stroke – her second – and failed to rally.[531] On 20 November, the beloved Aunt Georgy died.[532] Frances mourned the passing of Lady Salisbury as '**the end of a great center in my life**'.[533] Cecil family members invited only Frances and Arthur to join them for a private Communion Service held before the funeral of Lady Georgina Salisbury, which took place at Hatfield on 25 November. In the letter of invitation to Frances, Gwendolen averred, 'I shall always have grateful memories of your love and tenderness with her'.[534]

In 1898, Baffy was 18 years old and ready to make her debut. On 1 February, at Devonshire House, Baffy attended her first ball, her mother accompanying her as chaperone. As the number of Baffy's partners increased, 'so did Mamma's sufferings, for when she saw me dancing she got into a panic lest I should be unwilling to come away. So the more I enjoyed myself the earlier we went home'.[535] Frances presented her to the Queen on 25 February, '**a great success all around**', according to Frances. It would be the last drawing room over which Queen Victoria presided.

This same year, in September, Frank left Wixenford for Eton, which he entered having successfully taken Remove.[536] In 1900, he won the Remove Science prize. Also important in 1898 was the birth on 16 July of another girl to Betty and Gerald; they named her Evelyn Barbara.

Though foreign affairs held less interest for Frances than domestic matters, the 1897-1898 tension in China, where Germany, Russia, and France as well as Britain were scrambling for ports and commercial influence, held great interest for her. With the British press regularly reporting the disquieting revelations of *L'Affaire*, Frances was also 'much concerned with the Dreyfus trial, espousing the cause of that much-injured French Jew'.[537]

The 1899 Ritualist debate in Parliament deeply interested Frances; many believed that the Anglican Church, controlled by Parliament, had been drifting toward practices that too closely resembled those of the Catholic Church. Frances was present for much of the debate and praised Arthur's speech in which he asked the MPs to 'trust the bishops'.[538] After the debate, though the issue was not settled, the bishops appear to have been 'more active in spotting' departures from the law.[539] For Frances, the issue reinforced her preference for the Church of Scotland, with its greater emphasis on simplicity of services. She wrote, 'The greatest preacher that ever spoke, St Paul, was not cumbered with rainbow vestments, nor was his mind on Eucharistic services'.[540]

Frances, like her countrymen, was preoccupied with the unfolding drama of the Boer War throughout late 1899. Salisbury was committed to British 'paramountcy' in South Africa,[541] and rejected the Boers' demand that British troops withdraw from the Transvaal and its ally, the Orange Free State. British Commander-in-Chief Sir Redvers Buller's strategy to relieve the besieged troops at Ladysmith, Kimberley, and Mafeking was disastrous, and British troops lost the three battles of Stromberg, Magersfontein, and Colenso during 'Black Week', 9-15 December. Frances observed, 'Every second friend is in anxiety, every third in mourning'.[542]

Eustace Balfour was the first Volunteer commander to offer the services of 'a complete company of *selected* officers, non-commissioned officers and men'[543] for action in South Africa. Initially opposed to the offer, the British government changed its mind following the disasters of 'Black Week'.[544] In truth, since Field Marshall Lord Frederick Robert, who was to replace Bullers, was not yet in South Africa, the 19th century ended for Britons on a bleak note.

War news was not the only cloud for the Balfour family in December 1899. Eustace's employer and uncle by marriage, the 1st Duke of Westminster, died unexpectedly on 22 December of complications from bronchitis. His death came just one day after Eustace had volunteered for military service in South Africa, for which the Duke had given Eustace permission, even agreeing to pay his salary while he was gone.[545] The Duke's death, however, '[made] the whole difference to the Estate management and [Eustace] felt that he had no right to leave his post in such a crisis',[546] especially since the 2nd Duke of Westminster wished to retain Eustace as Surveyor of his London estate. It was, according to Frances, one of life's greatest disappointments for Eustace.

For Frances, the year, and the century, ended with another great blow. Betty and Gerald, having been offered £1,100 for their home, sold 24 Addison Road and moved to the country, eventually settling in Woking, Hertfordshire. Amidst these traumas of life, Frances closed her 1899 diary with the acknowledgement that it had been **'A momentous year in public and private'**.

CHAPTER SEVEN

'No one had dreamt of such a Success' [547]
(1895-1905)

'[I] enjoyed waiting in [Westminster] Hall [in spite of the] rumpus over our being there'. [548]

'The power of women in politics is increasing daily'. [549]

With the Conservatives back in power, the suffragists' hopes rose again in 1896-97. One of their first concerns involved presenting the Special Appeal for perusal by Members of Parliament.[550] When Speaker Gully 'found he could not lend us a room',[551] Lady Frances Balfour appealed to Lord Salisbury, who suggested that the suffragists obtain a permit to display the document – which now boasted 257,796 signatures – in Westminster Hall.[552] On 19 May, one day before the date drawn for the 1896 women's suffrage bill to be debated, the women exhibited their Appeal. "'Thanks to the actions of those Members who complained [about the women's right to use the Hall[553]], we had soon a fair number of visitors desirous of seeing the signatures from their constituencies'", Frances reported.[554] She noted in her diary that she **'enjoyed waiting in the Hall [in spite of the] rumpus over our being there'.**

Meantime, suffragist leaders determined to bring together the various suffrage societies so that a more unified effort could be made to advance the Cause.[555] In anticipation of this move, Frances was elected President of the Central Committee of the NSWS and presided at its annual meeting held on 2 July 1896. Referring to Frances at the annual meeting, Fawcett – who as chairman of the executive committee remained the dominant power in the Central Committee – spoke to how essential Frances was to the Cause, saying Frances had been "'helpful beyond anything I can describe to you today. Over and over again when we have been in difficulty, Lady Frances has helped . . . '''.[556]

The two London-based suffrage societies and the Manchester National Society had formed a 'Combined Sub-Committee' in late 1895 to liaise with Members of Parliament,[557] especially the Parliamentary committee of supporters which met yearly to discuss tactics for passing their bill. As representatives of the Combined Sub-Committee, Frances and the other women now attended these meetings,[558] and they secured a first place for a women's suffrage bill on 20 May 1896. The day, however, was subsequently absorbed by Government business.

The official establishment of one central suffrage society dates to 17 June 1897, with the creation of the National Union of Women's Suffrage Societies (hereafter NUWSS or National Union).[559] At this meeting, Fawcett moved that there should be no president, and at its next meeting (14 October), the National Union created an executive committee to handle the business of the organization, chief of which was to liaise with Parliament. It was also decided that local societies (such as Cambridge, Leeds, and Birmingham) could, like the large regional societies, also apply for affiliation with the National Union; thus, the NUWSS had 17 affiliated societies at its launch. The chair rotated among the various regional societies.[560] At the beginning of its existence, the NUWSS 'was hardly more . . . than a liaison committee', lacking not only a president but adequate funding.[561] Fawcett again led the executive committee, and thus directed the NUWSS as well as the Central and East of England Society (the new name for Frances's Central Committee when the various names were changed to reflect their regional reach). Local societies handled any work which needed to be done for the NUWSS in their community, and since most of the National Union's work was done in London, where Parliament sat, most work of the NUWSS fell to the Central Society, and therefore under Frances's purview.

Frances was a member of the executive committee of the NUWSS from the beginning: her role – as envisioned by Fawcett – seems again to have been that of political adviser, liaison with Parliament, and Fawcett's 'first lieutenant'.[562] In sharp contrast to her attendance at executive committee meetings in other organizations in which she had a leadership position, Frances did not attend many of the meetings of the NUWSS Executive in the pre-1907 period. In fact, she appears to have gone only when Fawcett asked her to or when issues which particularly concerned her – such as supporting the Scottish Graduate Women's demand for inclusion on the Parliamentary register – were debated. However, she regularly discussed National Union affairs and policy with Fawcett, usually at the latter's home.

United and ready for action, the suffragists finally secured an early date, 3 February 1897, for their franchise bill. The women's usual efforts – holding strategy sessions, sending letters to sympathetic MPs asking for their support, and scheduling meetings and social affairs to promote the Cause – were supplemented by a breakfast meeting (which Frances undoubtedly arranged) with Arthur Balfour, leader of the Conservative Party in the Commons, on 30 January. With Mrs. Fawcett in Egypt, Frances led the suffragists on this occasion.

The women's bill surprised even its strongest supporters by passing the Commons with a victorious margin of 71 and a majority in every political group – Conservatives, Liberals, and Irish – except the Liberal Unionists.[563] Frances, who was suffering from laryngitis at the time, recounted to Baffy her experiences sitting in the Gallery:

> I had a bad headache . . . and listened to the debate shivering, and was much bored by all the bad arguments. . . . The crowd of friends coming back from the 'Aye' lobby seemed to us so great we thought it could not be and the 'Nos' had got mixed. . . . Then the tellers ranged up in front of the table, our tellers on the right, and we knew we had won . . . [her ellipsis] We heard Faithful[l] Begg in a loud voice give the numbers and we heard of a majority of 71. We were left without words [-] 'incredible' one woman said in my ear, then I was shaking hands with a dozen, also being kissed, and I saw 2 sobbing! . . . . No one had dreamt of such a success. . . . [Afterwards] I was determined to go to Mrs Gully's [the Speaker's] party, where Aunt Betty said my reception and congrat[ulation]s was [sic] as if I was going to be married.[564]

It was Lady Frances Balfour who was responsible for this victory, the suffragists' first successful passage of a bill to give women the vote since the movement began in 1866.

From this heady success, unfortunately, the suffragists' fortunes declined. Before the suffrage measure left the Commons – and it had only passed the Second Reading – Lord Templeton, at the instigation of Mary Cozens and her Parliamentary Committee, presented their own women's suffrage bill to the Lords.[565] When she heard of Cozens's plans, Frances, furious, fumed to Salisbury: 'We of "the pure faith" are much troubled by a freelance of the name of Miss Cozens. I believe her to be slightly cracked . . . . [S]he has apparently persuaded Lord Templeton to introduce a [different suffrage] Bill into the Lords. . . . Miss Cozens is unlicensed, and so is her Parliamentary Committee!'[566] When the Cozens bill came before the Lords, Devonshire, speaking on behalf of Salisbury, who was at Windsor, convinced the Lords not to deal with the question until the Bill had been sent up from the Commons. Cozens's intrusion into the matter could only have distracted the public and hurt the Cause.

The women were denied the Committee phase for their bill when Members, led by Henry Labouchere, managed to use up all the time on 6 July, the last date available, on a bill about 'vermin'. When asked what she thought of the Commons's action, Frances, identified as 'a leader with whom the men must reckon', took the higher road, proclaiming that 'the very unworthiness of the tactics employed will serve to strengthen, rather than weaken, our Cause'.[567]

At the annual meeting of the Central and East of England Society held in July 1897, Frances, as President, put recent events in perspective and tried to boost members' spirits:

> We had a great success early in the year, and a majority for the Second Reading of our Bill so great that it startled even the House of Commons itself. This Parliament has, by that vote, affirmed the principle of women's suffrage. . . . . [W]e have only to be of good heart, and work earnestly, and with a strong resolution not to leave off till we get the measure through. The power of women in politics is increasing daily.[568]

Frances was correct: the women's success in 1897 was 'the real breakthrough'[569] in the women's struggle for the vote, a breakthrough which she helped engineer and which occurred several years before the Pankhurst-led Women's Social and Political Union began its work.

Except for the suffragists' success in the Commons in 1897, 'the work of the member societies was actually far more interesting – and more important – than that of the central organization'.[570] In 1897, Frances's organisation – the Central and East of England Women's Suffrage Society – created an associate scheme of membership for the purpose of extending their work into every Parliamentary constituency in their region. Enrolling all sympathizers in the work of the Society, whether or not they were subscribers, a Local Honorary Secretary created a list of all Friends of the Cause in each constituency (those not making a financial commitment to the society were enrolled as associate members). The first Local Hon Secretary was appointed in May 1897 in South Kensington and within three months' time had enrolled 240 Associates.[571] With Local Hon Secretaries in eight constituencies by 1899, Frances's Central and East of England Society gained 1,828 new supporters.[572] The suffrage societies virtually suspended their work for the duration of the Boer War, but the associate scheme had been quickly copied by many of the other regional societies, and these groups provided the womanpower for the resurgence of the women's Cause after 1902.[573]

The London Government Bill, which came before the Commons in 1899, raised the women's hopes of enlarging their sphere of influence in London politics. When first proposed, the bill did not include women, but on 6 June, Leonard Courtney moved an amendment, subsequently carried, which made women eligible to become councilors and aldermen.[574] Previous efforts to elect women to the London County Council in 1889 had ended in failure when the two women elected, Lady Sandhurst and Jane Cobden, were barred from sitting by lawsuits brought by anti-suffrage politicians. The new legislation for London called for borough councils to be created throughout the metropolitan districts, replacing the old system of vestries on which women had been eligible to serve.

Frances immediately sprang into action to assure passage of the bill in the Commons and in the Lords, but when it came to the latter body, she had less confidence of success. She wrote letters to Members of the Lords and spoke with them in the halls of Parliament and at social gatherings asking for their support. In a letter to Fawcett, she reported, 'Dufferin is safe. . . . I had a good talk with the Arch[bishop] and he is safe, but no certainty of being pressed'.[575] She also reported that she had 'told Lady Cross to look after her Lord. She had never heard of the Bill, these women sh[ould] be strangled'. Continuing, she noted, 'Kimberly voted for Lord Meath's Bill, so if he is well worked I have hopes of him'. She lamented, 'I hear Lord James says he looks to the Turf Club to turn us out! The Archbishop told me there were strong whips against us. . . . It is anxious work, the quantity is so unknown'. The response in the Lords to Frances's work was quite discouraging. At one point in the campaign, she wrote to Salisbury that the women, 'who had worked the Commons systematically, hesitated whether to pursue this course with the Peers. We think too much whipping may rouse and bring up the wrong men. . . '.[576] She herself was 'writing or speaking personally to some thirty' . . . . Her frustration showed, however: 'I am, at this moment, inclined to the abolition of the House of Lords!'

In spite of a strong speech from Salisbury, the women's work was in vain. By a vote of 182-68, the Lords passed the Earl of Dunraven's amendment excluding women from the Bill.[577] When, at the urging of Arthur, the House of Commons concurred with the Lords on 6 July 1899,[578] Frances declared, '**I keep a stiff upper lip but am desperately low and cross**!' It is worth noting that Frances's father voted to retain the Commons' inclusion of women in the bill,[579] demonstrating that he had been converted to the women's Cause, no doubt through Frances's influence.

At the same time that she was working to secure the passage of the London Government Bill, Frances and her colleagues in the women's movement entertained the International Congress of Women, which met in the British capitol from 26 June to 4 July. The press treated international gatherings more respectfully, and extensively reported the conference. The congress, whose president was the Countess of Aberdeen, divided its work into various committees: political, educational, legislative and industrial, and social (which discussed such topics as the 'Double Standard of Morality').

During the morning session of 29 July, Frances took the chair of the political section which discussed 'Women's *status* in Local Government'. Her opening remarks, which led off *The Times'* report of the day, included the statement that she had hoped to report that the status of women in local government in London was favourable; however, 'though beaten in one place, the present was not an altogether discouraging situation'.[580]

In 1900, the Central and Western Society merged with the Central and Eastern Society, forming a new organization simply called the Central Society for Women's Suffrage (Central Society or CS)., and again, Frances was elected President, with Fawcett again serving as Chairman of the Executive Committee.

Chart 7.1
Precursors of the London Society for Women's Suffrage
National Society for Women's Suffrage (1877-1888)
Central Committee of the National Society for Women's Suffrage (1888-1897)
Central and East of England Women's Suffrage Society (1897-1900)
Central Society for Women's Suffrage (1900-1907)
London Society for Women's Suffrage (1907-1919)

In 1897, Frances joined the Queen's Club, one of the newly-formed social clubs for women then developing in Britain to provide food and short-term accommodation for women as well as opportunities for meetings and fellowship. The club was a godsend to Frances, who now had a place in Edinburgh to entertain friends and visitors.

By 1903, Frances had become a nationally-known figure, as can be seen by the *Woman's Realm's* report on 22 October: 'Lady Frances Balfour is a woman of brilliant attainments, which, however, she never parades before the world. . . . She writes cleverly, [and] makes a fluent platform speaker . . . '.[581] Her younger children were now all of school age, and Frances was ready to accelerate her work for the Cause.

From the beginning of her association with the suffragists, Lady Frances Balfour was urged by supporters – especially Mrs Fawcett – to speak on the subject of votes for women to citizens all over Britain. Not only was Frances a persuasive speaker, but her name and title alone would draw crowds from whom suffragists could be recruited. During the 1890s, with all of her family obligations and responsibilities, Frances only occasionally accepted these invitations, but the speeches she did make on women's behalf earned her praise from many prominent individuals, one of whom was the women's staunch opponent, Herbert Asquith, who lauded her as one of the suffragists' 'advocates who could hold [her] own on the platform with the best male speakers'.[582]

Frances was 'speaking a lot' for the Cause by 1901.[583] Any estimate of the number of suffrage speeches Frances made is at best an estimate, and undoubtedly an undercount. The main source of information about her speeches is her diaries, where they were commonly rendered only as 'Balham', 'Colchester', or 'Plymouth', etc., but it is likely that she spoke on some occasions she did not record; moreover, she often gave more than one speech per day. It is difficult to know how many of her speeches were on women's suffrage, though the majority of her speeches 1901-1919 were for the Cause. Regardless of its stated topic, however, she worked votes for women into every speech that she made.

The only source of Frances's particular arguments for women's enfranchisement is her speeches: she did not specify her positions in her autobiography, and in the early years of the women's campaign, the national press did not usually report the suffragists' speeches. Thus, local newspapers, which occasionally covered the events, are almost the only sources for this information. The *Fulham Observer*, for instance, reported on a drawing room on 16 July 1901 at which Frances was the main speaker. Asserting that she 'had never yet heard a good argument against the extension of the Parliamentary vote to women', Frances began with an historical reminder:

> People seemed to have forgotten what an important part [women] took in politics in former times, when the Chatelaine was responsible for affairs when her husband was away at the wars. [Women] were in a lower position now . . . . She knew of a lady who had no less than 30 livings in her gift, and it seemed an extraordinary thing that she should be voteless, while her gardener and gamekeeper, and even the dustman, had the privilege. Some important towns were largely disenfranchised because the bulk of the property belonged to women. Bath and Bedford occurred to her as instances of this. A Bill was now before Parliament which vitally concerned the working women of the country, and yet not one of them had a voice in it. They were being legislated for over their heads in the Factory Bill, and it seemed as if they were going to be improved off the face of the earth.[584]

Perhaps the most remarkable aspect of this particular speech was the clear implication that all women *needed* the vote in order to have a voice in legislation which affected them. Of course, she knew what she was talking about, having spent so much time listening as Members – all males – debated proposed legislation, much of which affected women's lives.

Ever the political strategist, she suggested to her audience that '[W]omen could refuse to work for any man who would not vote for the Suffrage Bill'.[585] When in their effort to enroll more working class women in their ranks, the suffragists later began to emphasize women's need for a voice in legislation, Frances did not have to change the thrust of her speeches, since it had been an element of her argument all along.[586] Her advocacy of these two ideas – women's ability to refuse to work for male opponents and their right to a voice – pre-dated not only the NUWSS efforts but also the Pankhursts' advice in 1906.

In this same speech, she declared that the bane of the suffragists was the woman who had the vote in local elections and did not exercise it. She assured her audience that 'if women would wake up to their own interests some progress might be made'.[587] Frances concluded her Fulham remarks by asserting that the only forcible method of advancing the women's Cause was 'continual agitation', but that '[n]oisy methods did not commend themselves to her'; nevertheless, 'there must be constant and persistent pressing for this much-needed reform'.

Later that year, speaking to the Ealing Women's Association about women's suffrage, Frances was again in advance of official suffragist policy when she said that she 'saw no reason why married women with separate property should not have a separate vote'.[588] Despite this opinion, Frances accepted Fawcett's goal of securing votes on the same terms as men because both women believed that this was an easier goal to achieve.

Frances noted that one tactic that could be used effectively to influence MPs was being generated by working class women. Female textile workers in Lancashire (who outnumbered males working in the industry 648,987 to 387,583[589]) had begun in 1900 to collect signatures on a petition asking for votes for women – an action which certainly undermined the assertion that working women did not want the vote. In 1901, women textile workers in Yorkshire and Cheshire joined the effort. Finally, on 18 February 1902, the petition, 'so ponderous [with approximately 68,000 signatures] that it could hardly be carried into the Houses of Parliament',[590] was presented to Parliament by two Labour MPs.[591] The same evening, London suffragists joined the working class women at a public meeting convened in the Chelsea Town Hall.[592]

It was a heady evening for the working class women. First, the Central Society hosted a tea at the Town Hall for them. After the meeting, Mrs Fawcett treated them to a dinner of 'sole a la ravigoté and pigeon en casserole'; Frances and Fawcett dined with them.[593] For Selina Cooper, it was her first dinner with an aristocrat, an honour she never forgot. The textile workers' hard work came to fruition in 1902, when the Trade Union Congress, after a lapse of 17 years, 'again affirmed its support of the extension of the franchise to women, doubtless a result of the great Petition from the Lancashire Factory Workers . . . '.[594]

Frances frequently suffered from 'train headaches' (likely a form of motion sickness), and speaking after a rail trip was often difficult. Regardless of the discomfort, however, she continued to address audiences for the Cause, sometimes demonstrating considerable courage and spunk. In March 1902, she agreed to talk to shop girls; she wrote that 'the shopwalkers are coming to jeer, they think! I have never been jeered at any meeting and I don't intend to be at this'.[595] Suffragist speakers occasionally took their message to the employees of corporations; Frances spoke at John Barker and Company on 18 March.[596] By this time, she was also giving speeches in Scotland, where on 13 December, she and her close friend Flora Stevenson addressed the first public meeting held by the newly re-formed Glasgow and West of Scotland Association for Women's Suffrage. The meeting was quite successful, '"over 200 ladies and gentlemen being present"'.[597] Frances spoke at least 20 times in 1902.

Frances's success as a speaker can be attributed to three characteristics of her talks. They were always short, probably no more than 10-15 minutes; they were always varied; and they always contained some humour, which, other than her voice, was perhaps her greatest asset as a speaker. Newspapers frequently mentioned this talent; at Canford Cliffs, 'Lady Frances Balfour, in an informal speech, interspersed with much humour and playful satire, spoke of the change that had taken place in the education of women . . . '.[598]

The more Frances spoke, the more requests rolled in. She was soon complaining, 'I am so bothered with requests to speak. I have been asked to speak 3 times in London, to go to Malvern, Clifton, & York. I hate refusing for they are all causes I care about but I really can't become a travelling talker . . . '.[599] She spoke at least 27 times during 1905. It is both remarkable and revealing that some 800 people filled the hall in Govan to hear her speak in November.[600]

Speechmaking was not the only way Frances communicated her views. Her letters to various newspapers were also effective. In July 1899, she wrote to the Editor of *The Times* about the Shop Seats Bill, which would force employers to provide seats for women who had to stand for long hours in their work. Frances did not oppose seats for women workers but warned, 'Let our legislators take care that such Bills as those for shop seats do not make [the women's] conditions yet harder'.[601] Workers believed the employers would take the cost of the seats out of the women's pay. In 1904, she wrote to *The Times* concerning *Warp and Woof* by D D Lyttelton, addressing the author's views regarding the evils of sweated labour. 'Overwork is the curse of all women workers whatsoever, and the restrictions that lessen women's values in the labour market and limit the scope of their work are largely responsible for this',[602] she asserted. 'The remedy is obvious. . . .[W]hat is wanted is, not more inspectors and stricter rules, but the removal of regulations that restrict, harass, and penalize the employment of women . . . '.

Frances's fight for women labourers usually focused on expanding their opportunities in the workplace, not on combating the evils of their employment, however sympathetic she may have been about such conditions. At this time trade unions, whose strength was growing, were attempting to restrict women's work and thus lessen the competition for the predominantly male workforce (women were usually paid only half the wages men received). Of special concern to feminists was the proposal that individuals could not be given work to do at home unless the employers 'produced a certificate stating that the rooms in which the work was to be done were perfectly sanitary'.[603] Noting that such sanitary work ought to be undertaken by the landlord, the women had balked.

On this issue, Frances joined forces with Helen Blackburn, her closest friend in the suffrage fight.[604] Blackburn was so convinced of the need to monitor the threat from the trade unions that she and Jessie Boucherett had, in October 1899, been the prime movers behind the founding in London of the Freedom of Labour Defence (FLD) organisation. Frances was in the chair at the founding and was made President of the FLD. The object of the organisation was 'to protect industrial workers, especially women workers, from the imposition of legal restrictions which would diminish their wage-earning capacity, limit their personal freedom, and inconvenience them in their work'.[605] During the first decade of the FLD's existence, an additional goal was added: 'to maintain the right of women to the same amount of liberty as is enjoyed by men, in regard to the nature, hours, and conditions of their employment'.[606]

The work of the FLD was not very popular, a fact noted by the organisation itself in its early years.[607] At a time when legislation was being enacted to *improve* the conditions of work for all labourers, the FLD's actions seemed in opposition to such efforts. The fact, though, was that much 'improving' legislation put women, some of whom had no other options for employment, out of work. The FLD did *not* seek to prevent legislation from being enacted; it attempted to alter the factory bills to lessen their negative impact on women workers.

The perennial suffragists' bills in Parliament did not fare any better at the beginning of the new century than at the close of the old, even though after the election of 1900 the women had 274 supporters in the Commons.[608] While the suffragists' legislative efforts languished, Frances and her suffrage colleagues did their best to popularize the Cause outside of Parliament. Women's suffrage had been more successful in some of the colonies: New Zealand gave women the vote in 1893; South Australia and Western Australia followed suit in 1894 and 1896 respectively. The Australian Confederation gave women the vote in federal elections virtually without debate in 1902. When colonial premiers were in London in 1902 to attend the Fourth Colonial Conference, convened to coincide with the Coronation of King Edward VII, a deputation of British suffragists from the Central Society, led by Frances and Fawcett, called on the future Australian Prime Minister Sir Edmund Barton and the Rt Hon Mr Richard John Seddon, New Zealand, to congratulate them and their countrymen for enfranchising women. Sir Edmund acknowledged in his speech to the women that he had formerly been opposed to votes for women but 'had been converted' because 'he had not found one of the evils which it had been *predicted* would attend its adoption'.[609] Responses such as these were published in newspapers and in pamphlets by the NUWSS and became their 'most useful' publications.[610]

In spite of her busy schedule, Frances found time to add yet another activity to her string of obligations. In 1901, a group of British women, including Alice Balfour and D D Lyttleton, had conceived the idea of 'giving colonial visitors to London for the Coronation some of the lavish hospitality shown to Englishmen and women in the Colonies'.[611] From this inspiration came the Victoria League.[612] Frances agreed to assist with the organisation's work in the earliest phase, serving as Hon Secretary and Social Organiser.[613] In all, League members hosted some 40 parties during the Coronation festivities held in May, June, and July 1902, to which 4,600 visitors were invited.[614] '[S]ingularly unfitted for anything that means thinking of society except in a most spasmodic way' and hating 'lists' and 'cards', Frances persisted only through July 1902, conceding after she left that the League was a 'great conception',[615] but that its activities were just not her cup of tea: 'a slight shudder comes over me, when I hear the name "Victoria League!"'[616] Her title and her reputation as a speaker, however, continued to be used by suffragists to impress visitors to London; in July 1904, she gave the welcome for a group of American delegates stopping in London on their way home from the Berlin International Congress of Women.[617]

The expansion of local suffrage committees in London continued steadily throughout the 1898-1914 period. By 1903, the Central Society had 32 local committees, mostly in Central London.[618] Nowhere is Frances's presence seen more clearly than in the launching of both local Committees and new branches outside London, for which she was often asked to welcome members into the society and speak about votes for women.

In the early years of the 20th century came a death in the ranks of the suffragists which was especially sorrowful to Frances. Helen Blackburn, long-time suffrage leader and Frances's closest associate in the women's movement to this point, died on 11 January 1903. Frances wrote to Fawcett, 'I feel very peculiarly sad about Miss Blackburn. I had learnt to love her . . . '.[619]

In 1903, Frances became deeply involved in one particular aspect of the Freedom of Labour Defense's work: the issue of barmaids. The previous year, magistrates of the Glasgow Licensing Court had attempted to use their licensing power to bar women from working as barmaids in ordinary public-houses and other establishments where drinks were served.[620] It was estimated that some 1,500-2,000 women would be thrown out of work in Glasgow if this policy were put into effect.[621]

Inspired by the magistrates' effort, a concerted campaign by temperance workers and the Church of England was now launched to terminate the employment of all women as barmaids in pubs. To the Freedom of Labour Defence associates, the issue at stake was the right of women to 'make the best of the opportunities and powers they have of earning an honest living'.[622] The FLD believed that if men were not excluded from an occupation, women should not be – whether it was barmaids, pit-brow women, or nail and chain makers. It was necessary for women to be equal with men not only for justice's sake but also because many companies would replace women with men if women were not allowed to perform the same labour and work the same hours.

Once more, Frances took to the podiums. Her feminism, 'rooted in nineteenth century concepts of freedom and democracy',[623] demanded equal rights for all women, including those who wished to work in pubs. In perhaps her most courageous speech, delivered to the Church of England Women's Conference at Temple Church House on 28 April 1904, Frances's job was to answer a young man who advocated that barmaids be excluded from pubs. To symbolize the intemperance and immorality of women, he used the cliché of the weak young man seduced to drink by a barmaid. Calling the man's statements 'unproved assertions', Frances assessed her experience: 'I had some good figures collected in Glasgow and I spoke with ease, made them laugh, and did carry the meeting with me and a strong temperance woman got up and backed me more or less, so I went out with colours flying'.[624] Thereafter, one newspaper called Frances 'the Barmaids['] "titled friend"'.[625]

Responding to moves to preclude women from working at home because of supposedly unsafe environments, the FLD undertook to inspect the actual conditions of the homes of some of these women workers. They were 'pleased' to report that 'so far the evidence of the sanitary authorities has been absolutely unanimous in maintaining that – home for home – that of the homeworkers is superior in cleanliness and comfort to that of the idler or factory worker'.[626]

In 1903, Frances became a founding member of the Lyceum Club, which rendered services to professional women and 'those who [had] in any way distinguished themselves'.[627] That a *grand* club for professional women – like the more famous clubs for men which were common in central London – was sorely needed had become obvious to Constance Smedley, the founder, by the turn of the 20th century. She explained that 'women were just entering the professions', and, as their salaries were not commensurate with men's, women found that most clubs available to them 'did not afford sufficiently impressive hospitality' by means of which working women could return social obligations and meet with potential employers.[628]

After she had secured enough supporters to launch her endeavour, Smedley faced the ultimate challenge:

> Finally, we came to a place where the need of one supreme name as Head or Leader forced itself upon us. . . . I can see the little ring of girls discussing the most impregnable public reputation that existed. It must not be anyone who could be suspected of being impractical. We were very opposed to 'cranks'. Nor must it be anyone who gave her name easily; anyone associated with many 'movements'. Nor must it be anyone on whom the faintest shadow of self-seeking, self-advertisement or desire for popularity rested. . . . Suddenly one of them flashed out with 'Lady Frances Balfour' and the decision was made without further question. Ardently sincere, keen as a sword, perfectly poised, *sans peur et sans reproche*, an incisive penetrating intellectuality that commanded respect from men and women alike – here was someone worthy of the great empire.[629]

Frances eventually agreed to become Chairman of the Provisional Committee, and when the Lyceum Club was officially launched in March 1903, she became the club's first President and Chairman of its Executive Committee.

The Lyceum Club formally opened its permanent headquarters on 20 June 1904[630] at 128 Piccadilly, and 'for twenty-five years . . . held its ground there as the only woman's club in that most favoured spot in Club-land. . .'.[631] Speaking to members on the first anniversary of the club (with her trade mark humour), Frances asserted that "'Here we have started in Piccadilly a city set on a hill among the clubs of our weaker brethren. I believe we shall always be an example to all of them'".[632] The club was quickly successful and, by 1905, had some 2,000 members and was 'international'.[633] Early supporters of the venture included the Duchess of Sutherland, Lady Aberdeen, Mrs G Bernard Shaw, and Mrs Humphry Ward.[634]

Smedley attributed much of the club's success, especially in the early years, to Frances, of whom she wrote,

. . . [T]here was a flawless crystalline sincerity in everything she said or did . . . . Not only was there a tingling exhilaration in the air when she was present, but one was transported to a height from which one saw everything in proportion. . . . At the same time, there was a natural, homely intimacy . . . . The same sense of proportion was upheld in Lady Frances's relations with the Committee as their Chair: she was there to see that the desire of the majority was executed and the laws of the Club maintained; never to enforce her own ideas or to espouse the ideas of any one faction of the Committee. She ruled with a legal impartiality that was never divorced from the soundest commonsense.

Lady Frances was Scottish in every fibre of her being. She had their full measure of humour and many a time tension would be relaxed and problems fall into a right perspective by some 'canny crumb' of wit and humour.

. . . . [W]hatever she undertook to do was done with calm, dignity, and perfect control. There was time to attend to everything essential but no time to waste.[635]

As the necessity became apparent, the organisation broadened its membership to include many more professions, eventually boasting an Art Gallery, where members' paintings were displayed; 'monthly concerts, when original compositions were performed'; and 'a book gallery where members' books were sold.[636]

Valuable as was her advice, Frances did not always get her way with those making the decisions. In 1905, members of the Executive Committee rejected Ellen Terry, one of the best-known and most respected actresses in Britain, for membership. Frances had sponsored Terry, but she was **'piked [blackballed]'**. Frances was **'vexed'**.[637] Terry was not rejected for her character, apparently, but for 'the nature of the guests [she was] likely to bring to the Club'.[638] 'How marvelously hard women can be . . . ', Frances declared. At a subsequent meeting of the Executive Committee, members spent two hours discussing Terry, in what Frances called 'a triumph for the views of the minority.'[639] Frances did not initially plan to retain the leadership of the Society for more than two or three years. However, in 1907, 'all the Professions in their different Boards signed a petition' asking her to remain in the chair, and she 'could not resist' their entreaties.[640]

The controversy over Protection *v.* Free Trade also made an impact on the women's political organisations. When the General Council of the Women's Liberal Unionist Association voted overwhelmingly to embrace Protection on 14 March 1904, Frances, who spoke for Free Trade, left the WLUA, as did Millicent Garrett Fawcett, Flora Stevenson, and Alice Westlake.[641]

With the Boer war over and the prospect of a general election looming, a more aggressive campaign for women's suffrage began in 1903. The National Union, 'at the prodding of [W T] Stead and Elizabeth Wolstenholme Elmy',[642] agreed to sponsor 'a National Convention in Defense of the Civic Rights of Women',[643] a meeting at which all organisations sympathetic with women's suffrage, not just those allied with the NUWSS, would be welcome.[644] In the absence of Fawcett, Frances presided over the meetings held during the summer which preceded the national caucus. Finally, on 16-17 October, two hundred delegates from all the suffrage societies as well as many other women's organizations attended the National Convention, meeting in London 'for the purpose of concerting energetic action throughout the country' for votes for women.[645] The Convention approved several resolutions, the most important of which called for women's suffrage to be made a test question for candidates in the next election.[646]

The NUWSS, utilizing the Associate Scheme of the Central Society, now became the chief organizer of local branches throughout Britain, causing the Society to 'shift its focus away from Parliament to the parliamentary constituencies and pay greater attention to the activities of the affiliated societies'.[647] As a result, 133 new local committees were formed by 1906. It was in this manner that the NUWSS gradually gained power and became more than a liaison between Parliament and the member societies.[648]

Strangely enough, during the 1904-1905 period of increased activity for the NUWSS, neither Fawcett nor Frances attended any of the meetings of the Executive Committee. Frances's absence is not surprising; after all, she rarely attended unless asked by Fawcett to do so. But historians have left Fawcett's absences largely unexplained, her biographer dismissing it as evidence that she was not yet 'the indispensable leader' of a movement which was 'decentralized and relatively leisurely'.[649] Considering how closely she kept the suffrage leadership in her own hands, it seems unlikely that Fawcett would have held back, awaiting evidence of being 'indispensable' to the Cause. It is more likely that she and Frances feared the influence of the increasingly Radical Stead. Both Frances and Fawcett wrote the Executive Committee of the NUWSS stating that 'they were not in favour of taking part in anything in which Mr Stead was concerned'.[650] Moreover, during this time many of the representatives of the affiliated societies on the Executive Committee of the NUWSS were Labour sympathizers, including Miss Isabella Ford and Mrs Ramsay MacDonald. In all likelihood, Frances and Fawcett, while generally approving the action of the Executive, may have waited to see the direction the National Union would take.

The long Parliamentary drought for women's suffrage ended in 1904 when a debate on a resolution offered by Sir Charles McLaren was held on 16 March, the first debate since the suffragists' success in 1897. The women's supporters – again a Conservative Government, now headed by Arthur Balfour – won by a healthy margin (114 votes).[651] It is especially important that more Conservative (81) and Unionist (11) Members voted for this resolution than opposed it.[652] (The following year, a women's bill was talked out.[653])

With her youngest child, Oswald, now almost ready for public school, Frances involved herself in even more political activities, declaring to Sir Arthur Mitchell in early 1904 that her life was 'immersed in committees'[654] and noting in a 1905 diary entry that she had endured '**6½ hours of committees**' that day.[655] Meanwhile, Frances's popularity and stature were increasing, thus helping the Cause, as seen in a newspaper report: 'We are honoured to have with us in the city this week one whose name is a household word among readers of the *Bailie*. This is Lady Frances Balfour. McCaillean Mhor is a title to conjure with in Scotland, and when we link it with the fame of the Balfours of Whittingehame, we seem to come into touch with the fountain-head of national life and history'. The *Bailie* also observed, 'In the gentler sphere of woman's work and woman's sympathy no kindlier heart or more practical hand seeks to further the national welfare'.[656]

In late September 1905, Frances was greatly saddened by the death of Flora Stevenson, feminist pioneer on the Edinburgh School Board and long-time suffragist colleague and friend. In an eloquent eulogy written for *The Scotsman*, Frances wrote movingly about her friend and her contributions. Mindful of Stevenson's dedication, Frances wrote that Stevenson 'was ever wont to say that such success as had crowned her labours . . . came through the movement which aimed at removing sex from being a barrier to the suffrage'.[657]

CHAPTER EIGHT

'It Is *a changed Place*' [658]
(1900-1910)

'. . . I never respect weakness'. [659]

'I early abandoned the hope that anything liberal
would proceed from [Asquith's] Government'. [660]

'1900 Strange to write! It is awful to begin the year with the knowledge that we are
at war'. [661] Lady Frances Balfour's greeting of the new century no doubt echoed
the sentiments of many of her countrymen. But war concerns were combined, for
Frances, with personal anxiety: visiting Inveraray Castle in January, she found her
father very ill, unable to recover from a long bout with gout, the seriousness of
which Duchess Ina had not relayed to the family. Over the next few months, the
Duke's condition worsened; family members began gathering at the castle by April.
He finally succumbed to gout and edema on 24 April. [662]

The preparations for the Duke's funeral and interment brought additional
trauma for the grieving family. The Duke had left the funeral arrangements to
Duchess Ina, who, disregarding his wishes, refused to have the Duke cremated;
moreover, she refused to set a date for the funeral unless Lorne, executor, agreed to
bury the Duke at Iona, which by the terms of the Duke's will, Lorne could not do. [663]
Eventually, Queen Victoria ordered Duchess Ina to set a date for the funeral, and
she finally chose 11 May – seventeen days after the Duke's death – 'on the condition
that none of the family attended the Kilmun burial service'. [664] Only six immediate
family were present for the funeral service; Princess Louise, Eustace, and Archie
secreted themselves in the mausoleum until the commitment service. Urged by
Princess Louise, the minister began the service, and when he refused Ina's request
to stop, Ina left.

Edith, Evelyn, Frances, and all of Frances's children attended the memorial service held at St Columba's simultaneously with the funeral in Scotland. Though she thought the service 'very beautiful, nothing relieves the "aching void"'.[665] The Queen sent Frances a letter of condolence, assuring Frances that she would 'ever cherish the memory of your dear Father who was a kind and loyal friend of mine these 50 years!'[666] Another letter of condolence came from Mrs Fawcett, who spoke of the 'particularly strong tie' between Frances and her father.[667] It was a relationship much in Frances's thoughts; she wrote to Dr Robertson, 'Many children have had greater intimacy with their parents but I think none could have cared more for his utterances and opinions than I did'.[668] The Duke's death and its aftermath were nothing short of a tragedy for all the Campbells, but especially for Frances, the Duke's kindred spirit. 'It is trying to have foolish troubles put on the top of real heart pain', she wrote.[669]

Unfortunately, the Campbells' turmoil and distress were not yet over. When he reviewed his father's financial affairs, Lorne discovered that the estate was encumbered by bank loans and personal debts of £53,000, which family members believed had been incurred because of Duchess Ina, who also carried off 'a tremendous amount of family memorabilia, furniture, pictures, guns and flags'.[670] Despite an expected annual income from the estate of £7,000, Lorne faced an annual deficit of £3,300 for several years,[671] and he was forced to let Inveraray Castle for the next three years.

Frances did not soon recover from her grief. Throughout 1900, she fought depression and 'the blues',[672] and in 1901, she recorded that '**these anniversary days are hard to live through**'.[673] Later that year, she resumed a limited intercourse with the Dowager Duchess, whom other family members shunned for the rest of her life: Frances was keeping faith with her father.

Though she was grieving, Frances followed the news from South Africa with growing interest. British fortunes in the Boer War turned dramatically upward once British forces under Lord Roberts's offensive began to be successful. When the news of the victory at Mafeking arrived in the British capital on 18 May 1900, Frances took all the children by omnibus to witness the rowdy rejoicing ('mafficking') in central London. She declared that the '**excitement [was] without parallel**'. The Orange Free State was officially annexed by Britain on 28 May, and on 25 October, the Transvaal was finally annexed.

To capitalize on the British military successes in South Africa, Parliament was dissolved on 25 September, and Britain prepared for what would be called the 'Khaki Election'. Gerald allied himself with the successful war effort, declaring that 'To Vote For A Liberal Is A Vote To The Boer'.[674] He was returned by a majority of 1,300 votes.

This time, Frances spent the entire campaign period in the Inverness Burghs, working for Finlay's re-election. On polling day, 5 October, she again made the rounds of the polling places during the day and then waited with the Finlays until the results – a victory for Finlay over J B Duncan – were announced. After writing Finlay's address of thanks the following morning, she wistfully recorded in her diary that she '**missed the wire [of congratulations] from her father . . .**'.[675] With the Liberals badly divided over the war, the Conservatives rode the patriotic wave to an impressive victory and a 134-seat majority.

After the election, Salisbury significantly re-shuffled his cabinet, acknowledging that this was necessary, given the early reverses and errors in the Boer War.[676] Salisbury chose his son-in-law, the Earl of Selborne, First Lord of the Admiralty, and moved Gerald to the Board of Trade (regarded as the lowest-ranking seat in the cabinet, it was a great disappointment to Gerald). Arthur remained Leader of the Commons. In all, six family members now had places in the new government; Liberal critics labeled it 'the Hotel Cecil'.

In 1901, close friends and associates began to notice indications that their beloved monarch was in declining health.[677] Frances kept a record of this period of Queen Victoria's life, beginning with 18 January, when she saw a broadsheet which proclaimed the 'illness of the Queen'.[678] It was 'a newspaper inscription which had never been seen by two generations', she asserted. While driving '[Arthur] to Victoria [Station for his journey to Osborne] in Argyll's carriage', Frances shared with him her brother's belief that 'the future king could be "guided" if consulted and considered in all constitutional matters but would feel it deeply if neglected'. On the evening of the 22nd, Frances dined with Finlay, from whom she heard of the Queen's death. 'I found voice to say "God save the King", as she would wish all her loyal subjects to do'. Accompanied by her son Frank, Frances went to the House of Commons the next day to hear 'His Majesty Edward VII' take the oath of office. The feminist in Frances was offended, however, when a Scottish citizen reported to her that 'many feel a man will do things better'.[679]

Frances was given tickets to attend the burial service of the Queen at St George's Chapel on 2 February 1901 but chose instead to watch the funeral procession at Surrey House, the London residence of Lord and Lady Battersea, to which she took all her children except Frank. Thereafter Frances and her family would see a bit more of Princess Louise, whose routine was considerably altered by the loss of her mother.

Though defeated on the battlefield, the Boers did not go quietly, opting for guerilla warfare to prolong their resistance to British rule. The pressure applied by the British military over the next two years, finally wore down the Boers, and the

Peace of Vereeniging, which promised self-government to the South Africans in the near future, officially concluded the war on 31 May 1902. Frances and Baffy were present in the crowded galleries of the House of Commons on 2 June 'to hear peace announced'.

Two years after she was 'out', Baffy met her future husband, Edgar Trevelyan Stratford Dugdale, younger son of the late Sir William Stratford Dugdale. Deemed an 'excellent' man and 'a gentleman' by the Balfours,[680] Dugdale proposed in March 1902. Baffy's marriage, conducted by the Rev Lord William Cecil, took place on 18 November 1902, at St Mary Abbott's Church, Kensington. Never fashion conscious, Frances archly confided to a friend that 'Everybody asks me what I am going to wear and there is a nervous suspicion that I am coming in old clothes. . . . I don't enlighten them.'[681] At least six police on private duty were present to maintain crowd control.[682] Princess Louise and Argyll gave the wedding breakfast at Kensington Palace. After a wedding trip to Fisher's Hill and Tangiers, the Dugdales settled in Surrey, but country life was simply not agreeable to Baffy,[683] who by 1904 had a home in London.

  With peace at hand by mid-1902, the aging Salisbury, disconsolate since the death of Lady Salisbury and his energy waning, finally retired from office, delivering up his seals to the King on 11 July. The 'Victorian Titan' easily secured the Premiership for Arthur, his nephew and choice for successor (hence, 'Bob's your uncle'). Frances was in place to see Arthur received by the House on 14 July.

  The coronation of Edward VII was scheduled for 26 June 1902, shortly after peace was declared in South Africa, but the King's sudden illness on 24 June and subsequent surgery postponed the coronation until 9 August. Through the good offices of Canon Wilberforce, Frances had a place in the Bishops' seats. She '[s]aw the crowning and the dais' and was pleased to say that the 'Scene [was] most wonderful'.

  The chief legislative challenge of 1902 for Arthur and the Conservatives was the passage of the Education Act, which brought all elementary, secondary, and technical education under county or county borough councils. At least one woman now had to be co-opted onto the educational committees which would be created; 'female representation rose from 270 on the old school boards to over six hundred on the new committees'.[684] Women and their voices were more and more to be heard in Britain, though progress toward the vote was still slow.

  The elevation of Arthur to Prime Minister brought a flood of visitors to Whittingehame during the autumn holiday of 1902. Frances recorded that on 13 September there were '59 persons in the house'. During this holiday, General

Viscount Kitchener (on 19 September) and the King (on 10 October) each visited Whittingehame.

The last day of 1902 was dominated by yet another of the bittersweet juxtapositions of events which seemed to run through Frances's life. On 31 December, the Balfours learned that Eustace, who had retired as Commanding Officer of the London Scottish at the end of 1902, had been made an Aide-de-Camp to King Edward VII.[685] Just as Frances was celebrating this honour, news arrived that Betty had given birth to a son, Robert Arthur Lytton Balfour, nicknamed RAL. She knew how much the Gerald Balfours wanted a son, but RAL's birth meant that Frank, her own first-born son, would be displaced as Arthur's and Gerald's heir. It was a blow. Family lore holds that Frances 'spat' at RAL when she first viewed him in his cradle; it is more likely, however, that she simply dismissed the infant with a 'Pffft', which onlookers interpreted as spitting at him.[686] She did not, however, disguise her disappointment at his birth.

The unity and good fortune that the Unionist Party had enjoyed for eight years ended in 1903, when Chamberlain, as Colonial Secretary, began to advocate tariffs for all but colonial products. British businessmen had also been urging the Government to embrace protection to offset the high tariffs imposed by industrial competitors such as Germany and the United States. Of course, duties collected from such tariffs could provide funds for expanded governmental services and social programs.

Increasingly unhappy with Balfour's leadership and determined to promote Protection for Britain, Chamberlain now came down strongly on the side of Imperial Preference and against repeal of the corn duty (imposed during the Boer War) except for colonials. While she often admired his speaking abilities, Frances – betraying her class prejudices – had little real respect for him, believing long before his assault on Free Trade that he was too much 'the smug tradesman' and 'not a gentleman', too much a politician and not a statesman.[687] Arthur, who was not a staunch free trader, spent the summer of 1903 trying to keep his Government from splitting apart.

Frances visited the now-retired Salisbury several times during 1903, always enjoying their discussions but frequently recording after these visits that she thought the 'Tory Titan' **'rather tired'**[688] and **'feeble'**[689] and that 'the brain was not always clear'.[690] The elder statesman's health declined rapidly in the summer, and he died on 22 August. Salisbury was buried at Hatfield. Much moved, Frances **'walked with Evelyn till 3.30 when in glorious hot sun we followed him to his grave. R.I.P'.**

In August, Arthur finally presented the cabinet with a report on tariffs which suggested that a policy of tariff retaliation rather than imperial preference, which would tax food, would be a workable compromise. Unfortunately, Arthur did not come down strongly on the side of his own report. In no mood to wait, Chamberlain offered his resignation on 9 September. Even with Chamberlain's resignation behind him and the cabinet re-shuffled, Balfour still refused to provide strong leadership on the tariff question. Much as she loved her brother-in-law, Frances believed that Arthur made a fatal mistake in not checking Chamberlain while Chamberlain was in the cabinet.[691] However, her major denunciation was for Arthur's vacillation: 'I wish I could respect A.J.[B.]'s action in all this'.[692] 'I pity it, but I never respect weakness'.[693]

It was a great affront to British Labour when the Balfour government allowed the use of Chinese workers in the mines of South Africa and then consented to the separation of the 'slaves' from the rest of the population, thus denying the Chinese labourers their civil liberties. In her autobiography, Frances related that the issues of protection and 'imported oriental labour' drove her out of the Unionist party and back into the Liberal fold in 1904, but this is an exaggeration at best. The touchstone of her political philosophy was her opposition to Home Rule for Ireland, and this did not change after 1904. She may have temporarily re-aligned herself with the Liberals on some issues after 1904, but as her grandchildren remembered,[694] she remained a Unionist.

Though Frances's disappointment with Arthur's leadership was the immediate cause of her supposed flight from the Conservatives, it was only a symptom of a larger difficulty. The deaths of so many of her old political allies – her father, Queen Victoria, Lord and Lady Salisbury – and the removal of Betty and Gerald from Addison Road (they now lived in a new home, Fisher's Hill, designed by Emily Lytton's husband, Edward Lutyens, in Woking) had left her politically isolated. She could, and did, count on these friends for clear, definite statements on the issues of the day, which helped her better define her own political views. Arthur's ambivalence, therefore, was disappointing.

Arthur was playing a waiting game in 1903-1904 to enable himself to address foreign concerns on which he did not believe the Liberals could be trusted.[695] At least as early as 1895, Arthur had been concerned about Britain's isolation, a fact reflected in Frances's summary at the closing of that year. '**All looks stormy. Now Africa, America and Turkey are at war with us**', she wrote, adding that Arthur said, '**we [have] no friends, no one who would fight for us**'.[696]

With Europe already divided between the Triple Alliance and the Dual Alliance by the early 20th century, Arthur finally determined to take Britain 'down from the fence' and onto the side of the French. The forging of this alliance was not speedy, however. Frances closely followed the results of Edward VII's visit to France in the spring of 1903 and the return visit by President Émile Loubet to London in July that year. Ultimately, it was the king who won the French over. 'I hear the Germans don't at all like it', Frances wrote to Dr Arthur Mitchell, adding, 'They are wonderfully stupid with regard to the reasons why they are not popular with us at present.'[697] These visits eventually led to the Anglo-French Entente Cordiale of 1904. Arthur also achieved a renewal of the Japanese Alliance before leaving office.[698]

The conviction that the Unionists had over-stayed their tenure in office, especially since they had passed much legislation for which they had no mandate, had grown steadily by 1904, but Arthur held onto office for another two years, which did little to strengthen his party's standing with the electorate.

A downturn in the economy in 1904 and the accompanying labour unrest inspired Frances to educate herself about the problems of the unemployed by attending some of their demonstrations.[699] Thereafter, Frances wrote several articles about the issue. 'The problem of relief', she observed, 'is one that ought to occupy a prominent place in the attention of the nation',[700] but she was particularly anxious that the discussions of the problem be kept 'out of the arena of party'. Frances believed, though, that plunging into relief work without waiting for the results of experiments would result in great 'loss and failure', which would hurt the unemployed more than it would help them.[701] However sympathetic she was with the truly needy, Frances nonetheless was not supportive of their demands to '[t]ake from the Capitalist'.[702]

By late 1905, the Conservatives' luck had run out. Arthur resigned and the dissolution followed on 4 December. Liberal Leader Sir Henry Campbell-Bannerman took office on 5 December and almost immediately called for new elections to be held in January. On 30 December, Arthur began his campaign for re-election in London, Frances noting that '**his resignation [had] made it a memorable [year] . . .** '.

Frances and Eustace became grandparents in 1903 when Baffy's first child, Louise Frances Balfour Stratford Dugdale, called 'Frances', was born. Princess Louise was her godmother. The Eustace Balfours greeted a second grandchild in September 1905, when Baffy produced a son, who was named Michael Arthur Stratford Dugdale.

Money problems became an even more pressing concern for the Eustace Balfours as the first decade of the twentieth century progressed. In addition to his salary as a Surveyor, Eustace had an income from a directorship of an electric light company, apparently the St James Electric Company (Pall Mall).[703] Unfortunately, the 2nd Duke of Westminster expected him to be at his 'beck and call' – Eustace sometimes even acted as his personal assistant and deputized in the

Duke's absence.[704] Frances attempted to supplement the family's income by writing articles, but this 'brought in very little'.[705] Moreover, Eustace's health was steadily deteriorating, causing much concern for Frances and the family. With two daughters still at home and Oswald yet to be educated (though he had finished his work at the Norland school), finances and Eustace's health would be gnawing worries for Frances for several years.

Sir Arthur Mitchell, whom Frances nicknamed 'the Lord Hi', had been a long-time friend of her father, and the prominent thinker became one of her friends in 1901. Mitchell is noted for giving Scotland 'the system of caring for the insane in private dwellings'.[706] (Scotland was the only country to treat mental patients in this enlightened manner at this time.) Frances's keen enjoyment of Parliamentary debates can be seen in her assertion to Mitchell that, during an uninspiring week, she had 'done little . . . but write letters, going down to the House after dinner most nights for a little spiritual refreshment'.[707] Many citizens go to sporting events to be entertained; Frances went to Parliament.

The Conservative Party suffered a devastating defeat in the election of 1906, and all the 'Hotel Cecil', including Arthur and Gerald, were defeated.[708] Arthur was subsequently returned on 27 February for The City of London,[709] but Gerald never sought political office again. The Liberal Party won 377 seats, giving them a majority of 84 over all other parties. In what was possibly the most surprising aspect of the election, the Labour Representation Committee returned 53 Labour members, thanks to its pact with the Liberal Party not to split their votes with three-way contests. Arthur retained the leadership of the Conservative Party, and Protection was defeated for the time being: Chamberlain suffered a debilitating stroke in July 1906, effectively ending his political career.

Frances's enthusiasm for politics did not wane with the Liberals in power, but she was not as closely involved in political affairs as she had been when Salisbury and Arthur were the Government leaders. In truth, Frances was not overly enamoured of the Liberal agenda, and by the time her friend Asquith became Prime Minister after the death of Campbell-Bannerman in 1908, there was very little of the Liberal agenda that she supported, recording that 'I early abandoned the hope that anything liberal would proceed from his Government'.[710] Frances was an early nineteenth-century Liberal who favoured individual rights and the *laissez-faire* economic philosophy; she was not a 20th century, collectivist Liberal.

By 1906, Frances had been exposed for 25-30 years to the political philosophy and values of Conservatism from men she held in high regard: Lord Salisbury and Arthur Balfour. In *Ne Obliviscaris*, she noted that during this time she 'was undoubtedly broadening and possibly improving under the genial influences of this light hearted [Salisbury/Balfour] circle'.[711] Frances not only missed Arthur's leadership of the House, but with so many new faces now in Parliament, she also missed many of the old orators, those whom she deemed 'statesmen'. To Frances, there were a formidable number of Socialists in the House, almost all with working class backgrounds. She bemoaned this circumstance to Betty in 1909: '[The] Labour members in our "Navy" are a curious element. One feels they have no history, or tradition . . . in their blood. It is like children talking . . . . It <u>is</u> a changed place since old days. . . '.[712] In reality, what she missed was the leadership of the country by the aristocratic class.

Among the Liberals' earliest bills was the Dangerous Performances bill (1906), which proposed to allow magistrates to decide what constituted a 'dangerous performance'. Of special concern to young female acrobats was the proposal to add the word 'woman' to the legislation; they feared that employers would refuse to hire them in order to avoid hassles with law officers. Frances, always ready to speak for the rights of women, wrote a letter to the *Westminster Gazette*, asserting that such work 'was only dangerous to the unskilled and untrained man or woman'.[713] The Bill was blocked and did not become law.

In many ways, Frances was treated like a fellow politician by her friends in Parliament. It was not unusual for her to be invited to dinners held by Members in chambers. In June 1907, as the guest of Liberal MP 'Charlie' Masterman, she had dinner in the Strangers' Dining Room with the Dean of Westminster, the Augustus Birrells, John Seely, and George Trevelyan, after which the party adjourned to Masterman's room for further discussion. Frances was also hostess for an end of Parliamentary session dinner each summer.

One of the most important pieces of legislation enacted in 1907 was the long-awaited army reform bill, proposed by Secretary of War R B Haldane. Among other provisions, it abolished the Militia and combined the Volunteers and the Yeomanry into a new Territorial Force, which was responsible for home defence and would now serve as an adjunct to the regular army. Eustace had been concerned about the subject for years and generally approved the legislation. In truth, it is quite likely that the knowledge of weapons and military matters for which Arthur Balfour has been praised had its origin in his brother Eustace, always an informed and knowledgeable military man.

Asquith's ascension to the Premiership upon the death of Campbell-Bannerman in 1908 meant that Frances was once again able to visit 10 Downing Street on a fairly regular basis. She advised him to 'Never forget Scotland is the best half of the Kingdom, and must not be neglected. Leave it alone, it is doing well'.[714] Frances's friendship with Asquith was severely tested by his opposition to women's suffrage. She acknowledged in her autobiography that she had first believed he was 'the ideal Liberal, holding the "tradition of the elders", and yet capable of fresh impressions, and proceeding cautiously on the path of progress'.[715] His determined and calculated opposition to the Cause, however, 'removed one of my "Heroes" from his pedestal'.[716]

Frances's attendance at the debates on the Licensing Bill (April 1908) revealed not only her love of politics, but her compassion – in this case, toward the wife of a new Member, George Cave, who moved the rejection of the bill. After the speech, Ann Cave turned to 'the sweet-faced lady on my left' and said: "'Please tell me, did you think it was a good speech'"? The lady replied, "'It was too technical for me, but I am sure I understand the Bill more clearly than I did before'". Then, looking at me, she said, "But why are you so anxious about Mr. Cave's speech?" I said, "He is my husband". She got up at once saying: "I am going down to have tea with Robert Cecil and he will tell me what he thinks of your husband's speech". It was less than 10 minutes when the dear lame lady was back again. "My dear", she said, "Bob says your husband's speech has made his name". When Anne asked the lady's name, she found she had been chatting with Lady Frances Balfour. 'From that day', Ann Cave noted, 'she was always our friend, and she will ever live in my heart.'[717]

The chief Parliamentary excitement of 1909 was the debate over the budget, presented by Lloyd George on 29 April. With old-age pensions to pay for, the Government was already looking for ways to raise additional money when public opinion, worried that Britain would lose its naval advantage over Germany, demanded eight Dreadnoughts be built instead of the six proposed by First Lord of the Admiralty McKenna. To raise an additional £16 million, Lloyd George proposed to increase death duties and the income tax, and to add a new tax of 20 percent on unearned increment in land (payable at death or sale of the property). This was strongly denounced by the Unionists/Conservatives, many of whom wanted to raise the funds needed by the imposition of tariff duties.

Passage of the budget was assisted by the oratorical talents of Lloyd George, who was vehemently anti-aristocracy. In denouncing the landed class, Lloyd George asserted that the present political situation had not '. . . undermined economic confidence. Only one stock has gone down badly. There has been a great slump in dukes. They used to stand rather higher in the market, especially the Tory market. But the Tory press has just discovered that they are of no real value'.[718] Having made the wound, Lloyd George turned the knife with his observation a short time later that 'a fully-equipped duke costs as much to keep up as two Dreadnoughts; and dukes are just as great a terror and they last longer'.[719]

Shortly after this attack, Frances made her first suffrage visit to Wales, where she was the guest of Mary Drew, daughter of Gladstone and wife of the Bishop of Llandaff. Lloyd George, invited to dinner one night, 'advanced saying he was sorry I should hear him in Welsh'.[720] Frances replied with her accustomed candour (and courage), 'I understood two words – and as they were the name of a friend, I shuddered . . . [but] on reflection I remembered that he was not a Duke, so you were probably not abusing him.' She added, 'On the whole, I tho[ugh]t it would be well if you spoke in Welsh in the House'.

With Arthur's authority diminished by the tariff controversy, the Unionists rushed headlong into a Constitutional crisis. After passing the Commons on 4 November 1909, the budget went to the Lords, which defied 250 years of tradition and rejected the measure by a huge margin (350 to 75). Balfour, desperate to keep his party united, had threatened to resign if the Lords did not reject the Budget: he believed that it was one issue around which the faithful could rally.[721] Since the Lords' action meant a dissolution of the Government, a General Election would be held in January 1910. Thanks to Balfour, the election was fought not so much on the budget as on the House of Lords' veto power.

There were numerous changes and losses in Frances's life in this period. With Finlay out of office, Frances was no longer his Parliamentary Private Secretary. The continued poor health of Dr Story, her religious mentor and confidant since her youth, also concerned her. Diagnosed with 'generalized arterial degeneration and cardiac disease',[722] Story struggled throughout 1906 but failed to regain his health. Story **'said his farewell'** to Frances on 11 January 1907; the beloved 'Chimes' died two days later of cardiac failure and bronchitis.[723] His death was one of the great losses of Frances's life: '[he] was probably the single most influential person in her life' after her father, according to her biographer and eulogist, Dr Norman Maclean, another leading Church of Scotland minister (whose acquaintance she made shortly after Story's death).[724] For the rest of her life, Frances continued to see much of Janet Story and her daughters, Helen and Elma; her personal reminiscences of Story became the last chapter of their *Memoir of Robert Herbert Story*, published in 1909.

Frank received a Commission in the Northumberland Fusiliers Volunteers in 1904, and, having completed an engineering apprenticeship at Armstrong's, began his professional career in 1906 as an Engineer for the Public Works Department at Port Sudan. Family connections helped secure this post: Frances reported that Arthur had spoken with Sir Reginald Wingate, Sirdar and Governor-General of the Sudan, who 'implied that [Frank would] certainly be offered an early vacancy'.[725] While he waited, Frances suggested that he study Arabic, 'one of the necessities'.[726]

Frank was one of the mechanical engineers[727] who helped construct the new seaport, Port Sudan, on the Red Sea from 1905-1909. Despite his interest in engineering, Frank began qualifying sometime in 1907 for the Sudan Political Service,[728] and in 1908 learned that he would be given a political post in the Sudan in the near future. By this time, he could speak French, Arabic, and a little Italian.

Violet Bonham Carter, eldest daughter of Herbert Asquith and his first wife, provided a glimpse into the Balfour family dynamic from a visit to Whittingehame in October 1906:

> [We] were met by Ly Elcho & Miss Alice Balfour who has a roofless mouth and not much brain power. The relations between her and Ly Frances were disappointingly mild & friendly . . . . The atmosphere of the house is quite unparalleled. Miss Alice clinging doggedly to her little official rights – Ly Frances with flamingo hair . . . talking crisply & at times brilliantly I thought. I admire her mind – it's so powerful & clean cut like a man's. . . .[729]

Sir Arthur Conan Doyle, a fellow Scot, visited Whittingehame in September 1906, where Frances, who met and usually got to know almost every famous Briton of her day, made his acquaintance. After returning home, Doyle sent the Balfours a Collected Edition of his works, recording in his accompanying note that he hoped Frances would 'find some niche' in the library where it might be placed.[730] Doyle added, '[I]f I could feel that I had diverted Mr Balfour's thoughts for one day I should feel my existence justified. I should like to think that he had read 'The White Company' and knew me by something better than 'Sherlock Holmes'. His wish was probably not granted: Arthur was keen on detective novels.

Frances had begun to enjoy some success with her writing ventures (she made £100 from articles in 1906[731]) not only because she was well-connected to the leading statesmen and to the media, but also because she possessed talents which few women journalists had. E A Bennett (Arnold Bennett), editor of *Woman* and author of *Journalism for Women* (1898), asserted that 'few women were capable of writing a leading article about politics'.[732] Frances was, of course, the exception. Even with her party biases, she was knowledgeable about politics, and was encouraged by J A Spender, editor, to make contributions to the *Westminster Gazette*.

Finances were now particularly vexatious: 'Us four' were making their debuts into Society and needed gowns for balls and dinner parties as well as presentations at Court.[733] Frances presented Joan, age 18, at Court on 15 May 1908.[734] Travelling in Arthur's motor car, Frances noted, '[W]e fare forth in feathers and furs'.[735] The daughter most interested in Society, Joan would later explain to her mother why she liked wealth: 'I know I love [money] and what it brings tremendously. . . . I . . . have never quite forgiven Elizabeth [Asquith] for saying, "Joan, darling, what you suffer from is being the stupidest of a very clever family", but deep down I know it is so'.[736] Some motivation for her later behavior is indicated in her next statement: 'If I can't be as good as others in brains at least I can be good in other things, and that is partly why I love clothes and luxury and all it brings (female family members often consulted Joan about their clothing choices). Riding is the one thing I love away from people and that needs more money than anything'. Joan, whose letter is insightful and demonstrates intellectual talents of her own, became an avid hunter and an accomplished equestrian, though she was the child who most hurt Frances's heart.

Frances's limited 'friendship' with Duchess Ina brought a storm of difficulties down on her in 1907, even though Frances's relationship with the Duchess had been merely 'a civil exchange of courtesies'.[737] Midway through the year, on a visit out of London, she received a telegram from her 35-year old nephew Niall Campbell, son of her brother Archie: 'Surprised to hear that you communicate with Dowager in willful and open defiance of all that has happened. Stop such proceedings henceforth'.[738] When she returned home, Frances found an even more insolent letter from Niall in which he forbade her from any further contact with Ina and went so far as to say there would be those who would report her actions to him.[739] For once not writing in the heat of the moment, she waited a month, finally telling him that his letter's effect 'was to remind me I had not called on Duchess Ina, an omission I had at once put straight and then genially I told him not to make an ass of himself'.[740] It was an obvious attempt to be lighthearted and to jolly her nephew away from his adamant stance, but it was unsuccessful. Their relations remained strained for the rest of her life.

In 1908, Frances met Dr Arthur Milne, the son of another new friend in the clergy, Dr Andrew Milne, who had died while serving as Moderator in 1906. Milne was on leave from Nairobi, where he had served as Principal Medical Officer, East African Protectorate (Uganda and Kenya), since 1898.[741] He gave the Balfours a gift of a grey parrot from Kenya, which Frances soon trained to say 'Votes for Women' to astonished visitors in her home. "'It is only by surprise that you can get at the Philistines'", Frances explained.[742] However, family members apparently tired of the propaganda, and Frances enjoyed relating to amused audiences that someone in the household had also taught the parrot to say, 'No Votes for Women'.

On 22 February 1908, Frances celebrated her 50th birthday, noting that **'the years which the locusts have eaten are many'.** Unimpressed with new technology, Frances only now had a telephone in her home – when Frank had one installed, perhaps as a birthday gift. Eustace's health, which had troubled Frances intermittently for several years, took a turn for the worse in 1908, and Frances had 'very few days free of anxiety'.[743] She reported that he would not see a doctor, and even though his heart was apparently weakening, he continued to maintain a fairly busy pace as Surveyor for the 2nd Duke of Westminster. The following year brought Frances more 'private worry and sadness'[744] when, in January, Eustace again became ill; this time he recovered very slowly.[745] A new medicine, prescribed by Dr Mills, enabled him to rally by mid-February.

In August 1909, Prime Minister Herbert Asquith appointed Frances to the Royal Commission on Divorce and Matrimonial Causes, formed to inquire into the divorce laws, with special emphasis on how they affected poorer citizens and women. The only other woman named to the commission was May Tennant, the first woman factory inspector in England. King Edward VII strongly objected to the appointment of any women, saying that he believed it a 'most unusual and dangerous innovation' for women to serve in such a capacity. 'Apart from the principle involved, The King says that the nature of the subject is one which cannot be discussed openly, in all its aspects, with any delicacy or even decency, before ladies. . . . The King looks on the present submission as a Suffragette move'.[746] (It would appear that the King, like most British citizens, did not distinguish between the militant *suffragettes* and the constitutional *suffragists*, though he obviously knew that Frances was a prominent leader of the women's Cause).

Asquith overcame the King's objection – but not his 'extreme repugnance'[747] – partly by reminding him that women had sat on royal commissions before (Beatrice Webb had just completed her service on the Poor Commission) and by asserting that women's views on divorce needed to be heard as well as men's.[748] For Frances, service on the commission, which sat for three years, offered a much-needed respite from her heavy travelling schedule (though not her work) in 1911 and enabled her to remain in London when Eustace was ill. Frances's appointment to the Divorce Commission acknowledged her ability to deal with the complex issues surrounding reform of the divorce laws in Britain and recognized that at least some women understood legislation and law-making.

CHAPTER NINE

"'[N]ot playing the Game'"[749]
(1905-1910)

'I did not believe that any law breaking would show that women were fit to take part in law making'.[750]

'[A]ll parties should be made to realize that women are working for political freedom, not for party purposes'.[751]

True to the plan conceived at their National Convention three years earlier, suffragists made votes for women an important issue in the General Election of 1906 by canvassing each contestant regarding his support for the Cause, assisting their long-time champions and those whose opponents were anti-suffragists, and working against their most 'prominent opponents' regardless of the views of their challengers on the subject.

Tired of the 'pray, plead, and petition' method of advancing their cause, a former member of the NUWSS, Christabel Pankhurst, in a 'calculated maneuver',[752] took a more dramatic course of action than the National Union advocated. Fighting under the banner of the Women's Social and Political Union (WSPU), organized by her mother, Mrs Emmeline Pankhurst, in Manchester in 1903, Christabel determined to secure a satisfactory answer to the question of one Liberal MP's support for women's suffrage or go to gaol. In October 1905, at a Liberal meeting in Manchester addressed by Sir Edward Grey, an erstwhile supporter, Annie Kenney, a working class girl, and she asked from the floor, 'Will the Liberal Government give women the vote?' When their query went unanswered, the women raised a ruckus both inside and outside the hall. They were forcibly removed from the hall, charged with disorderly conduct, and hauled off to gaol. Refusing to pay any fines, Christabel was sentenced to seven days' incarceration, Annie Kenney to three. Their action heralded a new, more militant phase in the women's fight to secure the vote; or as Lady Frances Balfour put it, '[T]he importunate widow [Mrs Pankhurst] had come to stay . . . '.[753] The coming of militancy posed a dilemma for the constitutionalists, many of whom rejoiced at the brazenness of the WSPU attacks while refraining from endorsing their actions.

The overwhelming victory of the Liberals in 1906 greatly energized the Cause, and plans were made for a large deputation to Prime Minister Campbell-Bannerman, a sympathizer, who promised the suffragists a meeting on 19 May 1906. On that same date, when Keir Hardie's women's suffrage resolution was running out of time in the Commons, militants in the Ladies Gallery shouted 'Vote, Vote, Vote', disrupting the debate and leading to the first resignations from the Central Society by those who worried that the suffragists were becoming more radical and less ladylike.[754] Nevertheless, Fawcett did not at this time distance herself from the agitators of the WSPU, choosing instead to "'stand by them'" for "'doing more during the last twelve months . . . than [the constitutionalists had] been able to accomplish in the same number of years'".[755] Thinking strategically, Frances advised Fawcett not to repudiate the militants in public.[756]

When some 350-400 women from 25 organizations, together with several of their Parliamentary supporters, met with Campbell-Bannerman (a first for a British Prime Minister), they were told that it would not be politically realistic to expect the Liberals to enact women's suffrage since there was no unanimity on the issue within the country or the party.[757] It was a stunning statement: 415 supposed supporters sat in the Commons.[758] Advising them in words interpreted as 'go on pestering',[759] the Prime Minister once more urged patience, a commodity in increasingly short supply. Frances spoke at the Great Meeting at Exeter Hall, held to welcome the deputation returning from the meeting. Reminding them that 'Prime Ministers' Promises [are] made of Pie crust',[760] Frances strongly challenged the Liberals: 'It was largely the Liberal women who fought the General Election, and three-quarters of the members on the Government side are pledged to support Women's Suffrage – a majority sufficient to pass any Bill. To quietly shelve the whole matter was not playing the game . . . '.[761]

Frances remained understanding of the 'militants' not only after the incident in the Commons but also after WSPU members attempted to make speeches in the Central Hall at Westminster on 23 October 1906, when eleven women were arrested and imprisoned. When the women refused to agree to keep the peace for six months, they were sentenced to Second Division (for felons) for two months.[762] One of the few women leaders who chose to answer a request by *The Daily Graphic* regarding 'the methods adopted by the imprisoned ladies and the measures taken to restrain them',[763] Frances said that she admired their 'zeal', their 'courage', and their 'constancy', and she saw the state's treatment of them as 'ordinary criminals' not only to have been wrong-headed but also to have actually aided the women in their cause. She did not fault the police, who she said 'did their duty', showing 'neither fear nor favour', but she did pointedly note that these 'servants of the public' were being paid by the taxes of the very unrepresented women whom they arrested.[764]

Frances agreed to be 'on the plinth' on 3 November 1906[765] at a demonstration convened at Trafalgar Square by women textile workers from the Midlands, who wanted the 'right of political power and the right of combination'.[766] The Central Society co-sponsored the event. Frances explained to Betty, 'On Saturday, I go to Trafalgar Square to stand or sit on a lion, I hope not to speak, I don't like it but I feel we must stick together'.[767] Following the event, she reported to Betty that there had been nearly 3,000 women present, and that the textile workers 'held the people well'.[768] At this mass demonstration, the first in which the Central Society participated, the police removed 'one or two men' for chaffing the women. Frances was obviously not opposed to the event's taking place, but rather did believe that, as an aristocrat, she should not put herself forward this much.

In November, Frances spoke at the Great Demonstration held at Wandsworth Town Hall and at a large public meeting in the Kensington Town Hall on 3 December, where she was her practical political self. 'She did not want to say anything disparagingly of the men'.[769] 'She believed they were the women's good friends – occasionally misguided friends, perhaps – but,' she added, 'as [the women] would have to receive [their] emancipation at the hands of the men it was not politic for women to quarrel with them'.[770] Her understanding of the importance of not antagonizing the Members of Parliament who held the passage of women's suffrage in their hands clearly and succinctly spelled out one of the chief differences between the constitutionalists – the 'suffragists' – and the militant 'suffragettes'. She could appreciate the services the militants rendered in shaking off the lethargy of the 'Old Guard', but she was unwilling to follow them into militancy, which she found repugnant and believed was politically disadvantageous.

In her speeches, Frances took particular delight in excoriating the Press, which had generally ignored the constitutionalists but now avidly covered the militants' actions. In a moment of candour, she also admitted that 'the Old Guard' cannot help feeling that it is a little bit disheartening . . . that the serious, dignified, quiet efforts of forty years should actually have had less effect on public opinion than half a dozen scenes at Westminster'.[771] '[T]here is little wonder that the women's patience and faith have failed them . . .'.[772]

On the same day that the militant women were released from prison after their skirmish with the police, Frances gave one of her only interviews to a female journalist, who noted that 'Lady Frances is one of the few persons who, really and sincerely, dislike being "interviewed". She says nothing of the kind, she is much too careful of other people's feelings – but you intuitively gather her intense reluctance to talk about herself, and her silence is more disarming than any protest could be'.[773]

Speaking outdoors was difficult for Frances, who never raised her low voice;[774] thus, she always had little enthusiasm for the large demonstrations in which she participated (she also 'hated this Appeal to the mob'[775]). She did, however, force herself to participate in them because she realized the women needed to 'stick together'. Frances did not object to speaking indoors for the Cause, of course, and with women's suffrage garnering more press attention after 1905, she was even more in demand than before. In both 1906 and 1907, she spoke, at a minimum, 23 times. The increase in speaking was not without its strains. On one occasion, she was so fatigued that she complained – dramatically, of course – to Philippa Strachey, Hon Secretary of the NUWSS, that 'if I don't get away for a bit, I shall hang myself'.[776]

Frances was not just speaking in England but also in Scotland, where in December 1907 she spoke at least five times. Some 300 neighbours turned out to hear her in the Court House at Inveraray, a village of roughly 600 people at this time.[777] Travel again presented problems: 'three lectures in one week and four days of journey were too much'.[778]

Convinced that they could demonstrate to the Liberal Party that British women wanted the vote, the NUWSS began to press its case more actively, especially in parliamentary constituencies, where they now promised to vigorously oppose Liberal opponents of women's suffrage in the cabinet. Those targeted included Sidney Buxton in Poplar; Lewis Harcourt, Rossendale; and Herbert Asquith, Fife – all friends or acquaintances of Frances. The suffragists' political strategy paid dividends. Mrs Sidney Buxton told them that '"her husband would give the question his serious consideration"'.[779] By 1908, Buxton, as Postmaster-General, had voted for Stanger's Bill for women's enfranchisement. Unfortunately, the suffragists did not win over every opponent, the most important of whom was Herbert Asquith, future leader of the Party.

The new constitution of the NUWSS, adopted January 1907, greatly strengthened the organizational structure. While decisions would be made by a General Council, the Executive Committee, now elected annually (not appointed), would handle the day-to-day working of the National Union. Remaining non-party, the new structure included a President, a Treasurer, two Honorary Secretaries, and a 12-member Executive Committee, and could collect subscriptions annually.[780] The National Union had earlier created an Advisory Committee to be consulted in emergencies (that is, when there was insufficient time to convene the Executive Committee) about matters of policy and tactics. Mrs Fawcett, Lady Frances Balfour, and Mrs Broadley Reid were the only women on the Advisory Committee. The men were 'Walter McLaren, Corrie Grant, MP; Mr Fletcher, MP; and the three Parliamentary Secretaries: Cameron Corbett, George Howard, and Philip Snowden'.[781] The NUWSS's new Constitution had the effect of separating the National Union from the Central Society, which changed its name late in the same year to the London Society for Women's Suffrage, the title by which it is best known (members were confused by the names 'National Union' and 'Central Society').

The election of the first President of the newly-reorganized NUWSS was 'rather exciting'[782]: both Frances and Fawcett were nominated by several local societies for the honour. Fawcett won the election, but not before one of the Hon Secretaries informed Frances that, as the official representative of the Central Society, Frances would have to cast her vote for Fawcett![783] There are no records of this vote for the Presidency nor of the decision by the Central Society to give its vote to Fawcett; since Fawcett was one of her heroines, it is extremely unlikely that Frances encouraged her supporters or that she campaigned to win the office.

The London Society, which carried out all NUWSS activities in London, began the year 1907 by arranging for 'a monster procession of women'[784] from Hyde Park to Exeter Hall, staged on 9 February immediately before Parliament convened. Lady Frances Balfour, as President of the London Society, and Mrs Fawcett, President of the National Union, 'walking side by side', led the procession.[785] Rain that morning turned the streets to mud; hence, the 'Mud March'. Nearly 100 carriages and motor cars followed the 3,000 marching women representing 29 societies.[786] The procession 'was the largest public demonstration in support of women's suffrage that had ever been organized'[787] to that date and received full press coverage, even by the unsympathetic *Times*.

The militant WSPU, disappointed that the King's Speech did not mention votes for women, staged a 'raid' on the Commons on 14 February. At St Margaret's Church, police informed the women they could go no further and backed their horses onto the pavement to obstruct the women, who nevertheless tried to go forward. In the subsequent clash, some of the women were thrown to the ground and hurt. When the police were accused of using 'undue roughness' in handling the women, Frances again came to the defence of the police. In a letter to *The Times*, published on 15 February 1907, Frances observed, 'Women cannot use physical force and expect to meet a snowdrift in the persons of the police. . . . Neither do I believe this is their wish'.[788] Her further analysis was acute: 'They have settled their policy and, were they to lose life and limb as well as suffer imprisonment, they would only be "filling up the cup" and furthering their object. . . '. When a women's enfranchisement bill came up for a second reading on 8 March 1907, the bill was talked out once again, but not before several speakers, including its sponsor, Willoughby Dickinson, asserted that the militants had 'done great damage to the cause'.[789]

A notable piece of legislation for which many suffragists had been asking was finally enacted during 1907 and may have been one positive result of the women's agitation. The Qualifications of Women (County and Borough) Act finally gave all women, whether married or single, the right to sit 'as councillors or aldermen, mayors or chairman, on county or borough councils'.[790]

Another great procession of women's suffrage supporters was held in Edinburgh in October.[791] Both the NUWSS and the WSPU participated in the peaceful demonstration,[792] with Frances, Christabel Pankhurst, and – in spite of a just-concluded split with the WSPU – Charlotte Despard and Teresa Billington-Grieg (now leaders of the new Women's Freedom League), sharing the same platform. It was estimated that some 2,000-3,000 women marched (this time 'under delightful weather conditions') from Holyrood Park to Synod Hall, and many thousands more watched the demonstration, which even the unsympathetic *The Scotsman* called a 'success'.[793]

On 18 November 1907, Frances and Christabel Pankhurst participated in a debate sponsored by the West London Parliament, which was held in the Marylebone Town Hall. It was **'a coarse bad debate'** lasting 3 hours, during which she and her fellow 'Suffragettes' (as they were all labelled except those 'who spoke for the Socialist point of view') heard one male opponent, E S Barstowe, First Lord of the Admiralty, assert that '[i]t would be admitted that there was a generally lower intelligence in women than in men'[794] and that '[i]gnorance should not be recognized as a qualification for the franchise'.[795] Christabel Pankhurst roundly rebutted this challenge, citing, among other things, the university records of women (the sub-title of a subsequent news article was 'Miss Pankhurst Trounces Men').

Barstowe was not the most offensive opponent of the evening, however. That honour went to H Crouch Batchelor, the appropriately-styled Secretary of War, who declared that 'he regarded the Suffragettes as being sublime freaks'[796] and that if a woman were 'a decent person', she would 'find her home and her duties quite sufficient to occupy her time and attention'. Moreover, he asserted, 'If a woman, having a vote, voted against her husband, she would turn her home into a hell'.[797]

With only 10-12 minutes to sum up and 'raging internally' after listening to the 'Minister for War' make his 'brutally stupid speech',[798] Frances held forth, saying she would not 'insult the intelligence of the House by replying to his attack. He had said to give us the vote would be to coarsen and vulgarize our natures, and had I ever argued that we should have it for its refining influence [,] that argument he had forever taken from me'.[799] She then asked, 'Why, if it was only intelligent women who should be enfranchised, had the most illiterate men received the franchise?'[800]

In November, Frances welcomed the Richmond branch of the London Society into existence.[801] While such beginnings were functions over which she often presided, on this occasion, she was elected President of the branch. It may only have been an honorary title: with all her other responsibilities for the Cause, it is unlikely that she attended many meetings of the branch (there are few records). Frances's presence on the platform made it easier for 'prominent' and 'influential' ladies to join the ranks of the suffragists and thus made the effort more popular. The new Society got off to a good start: by 1908, *Women's Franchise* indicated that it already had 50 members, who included 'some of the most influential ladies of the neighbourhood'.[802]

As the National Union debated the methods and the merits of the militants, differences occasionally emerged between Frances and Fawcett. Following lunch with Fawcett in 1907, Frances provided an informative glimpse into Fawcett's personality: 'What a clever mind it is. She is the most extraordinary mixture of emotion with steel control. Not a really sympathetic nature, and if I don't see eye to eye with her, I never feel she understands my view'. Frances added this insight: 'She will do nothing to criticize the extreme party. Admires their pluck, and won't criticize methods she does not approve of'.[803] As was evident in the Harry Cust affair, Fawcett always refused to 'understand' any view with which she disagreed, which was one of the secrets to Fawcett's success in her leadership of the women's movement. By refusing to argue, she often kept disagreements from spreading and thus determined the actions that the suffragists would pursue. Threatening to resign was also a method by which she sometimes got her way.

The Frances Balfour-Millicent Garrett Fawcett relationship also revealed the kind of colleague Frances was and the type of politician she might have been. While she might differ with Fawcett on questions of tactics or policy, she never carried any such disagreements to the point of endangering the unity of the movement. If she did not win a particular argument, she always deferred to Fawcett, as the leader.

Moreover, Frances appears never to have used her rank to attempt to get her way with her mostly middle class colleagues. And Frances was a suffrage leader with whom colleagues could differ without forfeiting her friendship. The same could not be said of Fawcett, who could be extremely unkind to those who differed with her.[804]

In February 1908, Henry Yorke Stanger and eleven other Liberal MPs succeeded in getting a debate and successful vote (271 to 92) on yet another Women's Suffrage Bill in the Commons. Unfortunately, Stanger had succeeded by promising his colleagues that he would move that the bill be referred to a Committee of the whole House, thus assuring that the measure would go no further during the session. It was a vote on the principle of women's enfranchisement and not a promise of legislation. Still, to the suffragists, a positive vote by MPs was better than no vote.

In 1908, Asquith's response to Stanger's deputation was that a woman's suffrage amendment to the Government's upcoming reform measure would not be opposed 'if framed on democratic lines'.[805] Frances and Fawcett, suspecting that 'democratic' meant 'adult suffrage' (votes for **all** men and women), believed that the measure would surely be defeated and indeed harm the Cause.[806] As they feared, when the Parliamentary Committee of women's supporters in the Commons met in 1909, it refused to introduce the usual women's suffrage bill, opting instead to support Geoffrey Howard's bill for Adult Suffrage. After the debate on 19 March, it passed its Second Reading with greatly diminished support (a majority of only 35 votes).[807] It was, nevertheless, a victory for votes for women and might have been expected to impress Frances and Fawcett more than it did.[808] Frances spoke in Kensington Town Hall shortly after the debate and, with her characteristic political acuity, explained why the vote was not cause for celebration. The House of Lords, she said, would never 'permit' adult suffrage at this point in the struggle.[809] She also observed that a paradox was evolving: the more success the women had in making suffrage a popular issue in political campaigns, 'the more difficult [it became] to distinguish and settle among the candidates. Their forms of adhesion to the Cause are getting more and more dodgy'.[810]

The changes made by both the National Union and the London Society in 1907 were probably responsible for an increase in Frances's work for the Cause. When the new NUWSS constitution was adopted, an issue was made of attendance at the Executive Committee meetings. Thereafter, Frances was present for 39 suffrage executive meetings in London in 1908, and she spoke or presided over 36 other meetings, most of which were in other parts of the country.

A 1908 event in Frances's suffrage career has been misinterpreted by some historians. She agreed in March to debate at the prestigious Hardwicke Society's

Ladies' Night[811] on the resolution, 'That the grant of suffrage to women has been indefinitely postponed by the violent methods of its supporters'.[812] Christabel Pankhurst was also one of the disputants. It is not clear whether the Hardwicke Society, in inviting Frances to debate, expected her to support the resolution or not, but the two women took the same side: against the resolution.

Frances made it clear that while she 'deprecated interruptions to meetings', she believed that 'an awakened conscience, a reformed and interested Press, and much financial support had come from Militancy'.[813] (One wonders if Frances contemplated militant action herself when she learned that a young male lawyer had been provided to assist her with points she should make in the debate.) For her part, Christabel asserted that militancy had been successful judged by the financial test – 'which generally appeals to men' – and by the number of new converts.[814]

The resolution, which forced the disputants to argue against the motion instead of arguing in favour of women's suffrage, was expected to be carried. It lost: '[W]e won by 199 to 161!!'[815] Frances exclaimed. She gave most of the credit to Christabel, 'I think the honours of that debate remain with Christabel';[816] it is this magnanimous statement, combined with the fact that they were indeed opponents during most of the women's struggle, which has caused many to believe that Christabel was her opponent in this debate,[817] but she was not.

The first great activity of 1908 for the constitutional suffragists was the grand procession on 13 June in London. Feeding off the success of their 'Mud March', the London Society and the NUWSS staged another 'mammoth march' of women, this time 10,000 strong. Countering the assertion that women were all alike and would all vote '"one way"', the procession presented the diversity of professional women in a 'visual panorama'. [818] University women in caps and gowns, nurses in uniform, doctors, lawyers, authors, playwrights, music teachers, actresses, journalists, gardeners, farmers, artists, and other working women marched, each group identified by a colorful embroidered banner. The demonstration concluded at Albert Hall with a large, enthusiastic meeting. The trek, which went at Mrs Fawcett's 'uncomfortably brisk pace', was especially trying for Frances,[819] who nevertheless made the entire march to Albert Hall.

The press waxed lyrical about the procession, noting the absolute decorum of the participants and the beauty of the spectacle. *The Standard* was especially eloquent, noting that it was 'a complete success. It was spectacular, it was impressive, and above all, it was convincing'.[820] It also asserted, 'This dignified walk of ladies . . . was a much more imposing and convincing spectacle than the sight of a quartette of frail female disturbers of the peace (self-made martyrs!) being escorted to the Westminster Police Station by a squad of burly policemen'.

In the concluding speech, Frances recalled, in 'rolling cadences',[821] the long line of women who had preceded the suffragists' work for women. Of course, Frances left the suffragists laughing. Characterizing Asquith as a Prime Minister who was made of 'that material of which motor tyres are made', she urged the women to 'continue the process of peaceful squeezing. Every omen was with them. They had won the Derby as well as the Oaks [in 1908]. [Laughter]'[822]

The suffragists followed their successful march with a travelling exhibition of at least some if not all of the 76 banners carried by the participants. Once more, Frances was enlisted, this time to launch the exhibits. She opened the 'banner show' at Glasgow on 1 December 1908; in Edinburgh on 4 December 1908; Brighton, 26 January 1909; and Fulham, 20 March 1909. Of course, the 'local societies made the most of these occasions'.[823]

By 1908, it was common for Frances to address large groups in prominent venues. For instance, she spoke to 1,500 people at a suffrage meeting in Aberdeen in October 1908,[824] and on 11 November 1908, she addressed 'more than 2,000' citizens in Portsmouth. In her speech at Portsmouth, Frances reminded the audience, 'There was no by-election nowadays at which women did not speak and often spoke better than the candidates'. After the laughter died down, she continued, 'Thus, they were placed in the extraordinary position that though women were capable of working and speaking on behalf of the candidates, and arguing upon their merits, yet they were incapable of entering the polling booth and putting a cross on a piece of paper to show their belief in the cause they had been advocating. . .'.[825] The increasing interest on the part of the press in the suffrage struggle can be seen in the coverage of Frances's Portsmouth speech: reports of the event spanned two columns on page 8 of the *Portsmouth Times* and generated letters to the editor which took up another two columns of page 9. Of course, reports of the outrages of the militant suffragettes received even more publicity.

Frances's work for the Cause in 1909 eclipsed all her previous efforts. She attended meetings or councils 32 times and spoke at least 66 times, often more than once a day. At Bournemouth on 9 March, she addressed '700 women in a room meant to hold 500'[826] in the afternoon, and then debated Anti-suffragists in the evening. On 6 December that year, after speaking in the afternoon at the residence of the Local President, Mrs James Stuart, Frances and Walter McLaren were the featured speakers at the first public meeting held by the Norwich Women's Suffrage Society in the evening. *Common Cause* reported that 'The Press devoted three and a half columns to the speeches'.[827] Just three days later, she spoke in the Co-operative Hall in Rugby in the afternoon and then debated Anti-Suffragists in the same hall in the evening. In speaking several days per week and more than once a day, Frances far exceeded what Fawcett would do. Working only on votes for women, Fawcett limited her speaking to once a day, no more than four times a week, and during only four months of the year (February, March, October, November).[828] In her autobiography, Frances recalled speaking an average of three times a week for the Cause during the period of greatest activity in the suffrage struggle. This hectic schedule continued, with one exception (1911), into 1914. Unlike the other suffrage leaders, she was also still quite active in all her other organizations such as the Travellers' Aid Society, the Lyceum Club, and the Freedom of Labour Defence.

As a leader of more than one organisation, Frances often attempted to address meetings of more than one society when speaking out of town, and her schedule became quite complicated at times. Invited by Eleanor Rathbone to address suffragists while she was in Liverpool to speak on behalf of the Travellers' Aid Society in 1909, Frances explained: 'I go to Liverpool on the 1st [February], arriving about 6.30. After lunching with the Lady Mayoress, I have my T[ravellers'] A[id] meeting at 3 p.m. on the 2nd'. After stating that she had 'an engagement at tea after it that could be abandoned', she suggested, 'I could be at a meeting (drawing room) at 6 p.m. or I could sacrifice a peaceful evening I intended to spend with Miss Milne, the friend I am to stay with, on the night of the 2nd. By preference the latter. I hope not evening dress. I must leave early on the 3rd.'[829] Frances, now in her 50s, also warned her hostess that there were limits to her energy: 'I cannot work all day and all night'. Despite such protestation, Frances spoke to the Liverpool suffragists on the evening of February 2, and, after returning home on the 3rd, journeyed to Blackheath on the 4th and to Reading on the 5th to speak for the Cause.

Frances was frequently asked to debate Antis and was pitted more than once against one of their strongest debaters, Gladys Pott.[830] Frances had little good to say about Antis: 'Their colours were "black and blue", which lent themselves to ribald jests. They were late in the field, badly organized and full of class distinction; in argument the Suffragists were veterans', and, in Frances's inimitable words, 'rode through the Antis like standing corn, they were always defeated, horse and foot, bag and baggage'.[831]

One of Frances's favorite colleagues in the suffrage fight was Ethel Snowden, whose husband was Labour MP for Blackburn. Frances shared platforms with Ethel at least five times in 1909. They were particularly suited to speak in tandem: Ethel generally discussed economic issues, while Frances took the political approach to their subject. In Penrith, Ethel observed that if women had the vote, the Government would probably have to pay equal wages to women inspectors.[832] Observing that trade unionism could not effect this change, she noted that Labourites had turned to Parliament to get the factory legislation and political power they needed to achieve additional legislative assistance. For her part, Frances powerfully challenged the charge that women were incapable of understanding political questions. Noting that men now asked women to work quite hard during elections, she made her point with light but effective sarcasm: 'I have known women who have given their whole time during elections, helping party organisations, and during that time – it is very remarkable – they were never told to go home and mind the baby. (Laughter)' Savoring the laughter, she finished her point. 'It was only after the candidate was safely landed in Parliament that they discovered that women were better employed . . . in the kitchen, or rocking the cradle (laughter)'.[833]

Frances's work for the Cause was so well known by 1909 that Dr Marion Phillips, responding to a request for information about Lady Frances, asserted that Frances 'has made more suffragists perhaps than any other leader[,] for her pointed witty tongue and charm of manner are irresistible' (this was four years *after* the Pankhursts were on the scene).[834] The Very Rev Dr Norman Maclean, too, praised her oratorical powers, averring that '[s]he had a great gift of rhetoric and could rouse an audience of women to white-heat'.[835]

Frances's stature as one of the best-known suffragists can also be seen in the response of the editor of the *National Review* to an anti-suffrage letter written by a Scottish woman, Mrs Parker Smith of Jordanhill, published in the magazine's December 1909 issue. Leo Maxse wrote, 'I am not surprised to hear that you have had many approving letters . . . and it is to your credit that it should anger people of the type of Lady Frances Balfour, who are really almost demented on the question'.[836] He added, 'In fact one of the things which most puts me off Woman Suffrage is the extraordinary inability of women to keep their temper when discussing it. Men's political controversies are bad enough, what would it be with women'. While he may well have considered her 'demented' on the subject, Maxse clearly betrayed his own anti-suffrage bias when he likened Frances, whose speeches were models of decorum, to those of the more strident suffragettes. Frances was never known to show any temper when discussing women's suffrage in public, nor did she have a high, screeching voice, a fact she used to her advantage. 'When the meetings were rowdy, there were always a set of boys and men who imitated what they thought must be the female voice, it began on a high note[;] my voice when raised was always deep, and in their silenced astonishment, I got leave to hold forth'.[837]

Frances became involved in an exciting bit of suffragist strategy while visiting Aberdeen in October 1908. She apparently attended a meeting of women suffragists (an Aberdeen University Woman Suffrage Association had been formed in 1908[838]) where it was proposed that she stand as the Women Graduates' candidate for Lord Rector against Herbert Asquith and Edward Carson. The object, she declared, was 'not to put me in, but to defeat Asquith, and show the suffrage strength'.[839] Declaring that 'the whole incident was full of excitement', Frances was enthusiastic about the prospect of the fight.[840] The *Aberdeen Daily Journal* acknowledged that there were three parties campaigning for the Rectorial election, 'the Asquithians, Carsonians, and Suffragists'. The women eventually abandoned the idea, no doubt because they learned that they did not have enough time to properly establish their candidate for the election, but it was a heady and delightful interlude for Frances.

It was not long after this that Frances was asked whether women would soon be made eligible to stand for Parliament if women got the vote. She responded with a dose of her signature honesty:

> . . . everybody seemed to think [women] could rush down and take their seats in the House of Commons. First of all, they had to elected, and be voted for by men, and she would let them in on a little secret. Men were curiously unwilling to elect them on the bodies for which they were eligible, and also women voters were very much inclined to vote for men candidates for these bodies. She would like to sit in Parliament, and would give them fair warning that if ever she got the opportunity she would stand. (Laughter and applause.) But she could not go into Parliament until she was elected, and she did not honestly believe that she was going to be elected.[841]

Judging by Aberdeen, Frances would have enjoyed 'stumping'!

In the midst of a busy year of suffrage work, Frances was deflected once more by the question of the employment not just of barmaids but of all women working in pubs, restaurants, and hotels. The Licensing Bill of 1908 proposed to allow justices to 'attach to the renewal of a license any condition they thought fit in respect of . . . the employment of women on licensed premises'.[842] It was estimated that some 100,000 women might be thrown out of work if this legislation passed. In her Opening Address of the Freedom of Labour Defence's Annual Meeting in 1908, Frances argued, 'We may be of opinion that certain professions are more dangerous than others, but there is no profession as dangerous as unemployment, and where there is a question of a woman being on the street or behind a bar, there is no question as to where the greatest [sic] danger lies'.[843] On 2 November, the Commons agreed to strike out that part of Clause 20 which adversely affected women working in the hospitality trade. Arthur's note to her in the Ladies Gallery after the offending section was omitted substantiates her influence on politicians: **'The Barmaids are saved'**.[844]

By 1909, the London Society had 37 local committees; the NUWSS now boasted of 130 affiliated societies.[845] In spite of their public success, however, the suffragists were finally forced to concede by late 1908 – early 1909 that all their efforts – processions, deputations, public meetings – had failed. No party would commit itself to their Cause. Moreover, public opposition to the as yet relatively mild militancy of the suffragettes adversely affected the constitutionalists: most residents of Britain did not (or could not) distinguish between the two groups[846] – at least in part because the newspapers seldom made the correct distinction.

In the face of government obstinacy, vandalism – even of the most timid kind – was the natural next step for the militants. In the summer of 1908, a WSPU rock-throwing incident reduced the constitutionalists' support for the suffragettes.[847] Frances and other non-militant leaders realized that militancy gave Members another excuse to reject votes for women.

In November 1908, relations between the suffragists and the WSPU were seriously strained when four women who had membership in both the WSPU and the London Society attempted to get the Society to adopt the militants' Anti-Government policy at by-elections.[848] The Society, convinced that the WSPU was trying to capture its organization, rejected this proposal but was now on alert. At its next Annual Meeting, 5 November 1909, the Society added to its Constitution the requirement that members *pledge* themselves 'to adhere solely to lawful and constitutional methods of agitation' and to support financially *only* non-militant societies.[849] This motion was only narrowly passed, 197-172 (several new shilling members joined the Society shortly before the meeting[850]), and the dissidents, undeterred, again presented a resolution urging the National Union to adopt the anti-Government policy of the WSPU at by-elections. The lateness of the hour caused this meeting to be adjourned.

Two more meetings were held, during which Fawcett and the Executive Committee succeeded in codifying members' obligation to accept the National Union's election policy. Mrs Fawcett added for emphasis that 'if members differed on matters of principle it was best [for them] to withdraw'.[851] On 18 December, she reported to Frances that '51 of the malcontents have resigned', and that she believed 'it will greatly strengthen us to finally get rid of the militants within our gates'.[852] Frances ruefully wrote to Fawcett, 'I begin to understand what Parnell felt when his followers murdered Lord Frederick'.[853]

The friction between the NUWSS and the WSPU continued to grow, causing the NUWSS to expend much energy making a clear distinction between itself and the militants. Frances herself rejected all militancy in connection with women's suffrage: 'I did not believe that any law breaking would show that women were fit to take part in law making'.[854]

It is not surprising that Frances's sympathy with the militants was short-lived. She was a product of aristocratic, Victorian Britain, and her propriety predisposed her against militancy. Also, Frances would not have welcomed the press attention that would have come to her – as it did to, say, Lady Constance Lytton – if she participated in raids, and more so if she were imprisoned for the Cause. Importantly, she was convinced that militancy was not only improper but also not the most effective means to achieve votes for women. Frances's chief objection to militancy was that it 'distracted the attention of the public from the cause to the methods. They spent their time discussing whether militant methods were right, and they forgot that the real thing was to speak about the Cause for which both' were working.[855]

Frances said little about her own personal safety though she was exposed more than once to dangerous situations. One benefit of her rank, however, and another boon to the suffragists, was that Frances usually received a polite hearing from her audience. In March 1908, for example, she knew ahead of time that she faced the likely prospect of violence at a suffrage meeting in Corstorphine, Scotland. The Scottish Women Graduates' Parliamentary Franchise Committee, desirous of countering the bad press from two earlier suffrage meetings and of sponsoring a successful meeting, enlisted Frances's services. Two of her nephews, Eric Clough-Taylor and Ralph Glyn, accompanied Frances to the meeting, offering her their protection. 'The nerves of all the people concerned in the former meetings were much ajar. . . . The Police had orders to arrest anyone I pointed out as likely to damage us – or the Hall'. Onto the platform Frances went, where she 'was greeted by a yell', but she saw that 'the hooligans' were well at the back. 'I was very firm – said I expected to have a courteous and fair hearing and I had come from London to take the chair. It was very frightening but to Ralph's disappointment, no actual violence, much to Eric's relief'.[856]

Nor did Frances make much out of the assault she did experience in 1909. On 29 June, she and Betty decided to attend the WSPU's 'Women's Parliament' held at Caxton Hall, after which both joined the procession to Parliament. Immediately after the experience, Frances wrote to Mrs Fawcett:

> I am just back from a night with the militants. . . . The speeches were of
> a very serious nature, almost like a service of dedication. There was no
> excitement. We were all asked not to move as the deputation [of nine
> led by Mrs Pankhurst] left the Hall, 'to remain seated in silent thought
> for three minutes, and then to follow and cheer on comrades on the
> Square'. . . . The police in solid lines turned us into Victoria Street. We
> slowly battled our way to the West side of Parliament Square and up

to Whitehall[.] [H]ere we saw several arrests, the women all showing extraordinary courage in the rough rushes of the crowd round them. . . . The police kept us all moving . . . . We were finally driven up to the north end of Whitehall. B[etty] and I stood on the Treasury steps watching the crowd slowly driven up by a wedge of police. The police on the pavement asked us to come down, and as we did so, two women exactly in front of us threw stones at the windows. . . . A policeman flew on them, and had his arms round their necks before one could wink. Crowd and police made a rush together, and B[etty] and I were both knocked flat, falling in a rather ignominious heap! I was afraid the crowd would fall over on us, but we were quickly picked up and walled in by the police and kept moving. The two women were swept away with incredible speed. . . . The courage that dares this handling, I do admire. . . I wonder much as I write what has happened to them all.[857]

Frances does not appear to have participated in by-election work, a major thrust of the National Union after 1907. If she were going to have any effectiveness with Members of Parliament, she would wish not to appear allied with any particular politician or party (a position which was consistent with the suffragists' policy). As she put it, '[A]ll parties should be made to realize that women are working for political freedom, not for party purposes'.[858]

The annual Congress of the International Women's Suffrage Alliance (IWSA) was held in London from 26 April to 3 May 1909. The President and presiding officer was Mrs Carrie Chapman Catt, an American; 23 nations were represented at the Conference. Two days into the Congress, *The Daily News* carried on its cover pictures of eight women whom it labelled 'Leaders of the International Congress'. The only British women depicted were Lady Frances Balfour and Mrs Fawcett.[859]

Two major questions dominated the procedural discussions at the meetings of the International. By a vote of 59-27, the International decided to allow membership only by national, not individual, committees, thus thwarting the WSPU.[860] The National Union had been a member since its inception. Secondly, it decided that women's suffrage should be the member organisation's sole object.

As one of its leaders, Frances of course attended the sessions of the Conference every day, she helped Mrs Fawcett greet the delegates at the dinner/reception on 28 April, and she spoke to the delegates once. At the end of the conference, Frances reported to Betty that the Congress was very interesting, 'but exhausting was not the word for it'; she added her admiration of the President: 'My enthusiasm for Mrs Catt as chair knows no bounds'.[861]

The non-militant suffragists could only for so long prevent disorder in their meetings. As related in the Prologue, Frances only ever had one meeting broken up (at Aylesbury in 1909), and that incident provides some insight on her ability to hold an audience, despite the fact that she was, only on this one occasion, ultimately unsuccessful.

On 15 April 1909 – rather late in the day – the NUWSS finally launched its own newspaper, *The Common Cause*. For the second issue, Frances provided an article entitled 'Our Chances for the Future', which dealt mostly with the women's prospects in the next election. 'To the Suffragists it matters little which party is in power';[862] she predicted that the Unionists/Conservatives would emerge with a slight majority over the Liberals and therein 'lies the best hope of the Franchise' for the women. Frances believed that if women convinced the politicians that they meant to have the vote, the Unionists/Conservatives would not oppose it, especially since they feared Adult Suffrage more than a limited women's bill. She ended her article with some political posturing of her own by predicting that the Unionists/Conservatives would 'anticipate the Liberals by introducing a Women's Enfranchisement Bill in the near future'.

This article is important in terms of indicating Frances's political instincts and her working relationship with Mrs Fawcett. Frances understood better than most women that the *only* entity that posed a real threat to the Liberals was the Unionist/Conservative Party, and that if the suffragists would consider approaching them, the women might be successful. Unfortunately, Fawcett never really considered that any but the Liberal Party could achieve women's suffrage. In truth, even if the suffragists did not get an agreement with the Unionists/Conservatives, just negotiating with them would likely have put greater pressure on the Liberal Party than had all deputations, petitions, and raids. With a major election coming up soon, Frances went about as far as she could to nudge Fawcett toward the Conservatives, a party which had passed the women's bill on two previous occasions (1897 and 1904) and which at least was led by a friend of the suffragists (Arthur Balfour). Regardless of her understanding of the politics involved, though, Frances was not going to challenge Fawcett's leadership, and Fawcett ignored her hints. In this same period, Frances became an active member of the editorial board of *The Englishwoman* (launched 1909).

Perhaps the biggest family news regarding work for the Cause in 1909-1910 was the imprisonment of Betty's sister, Lady Constance Lytton. A shy, reclusive woman, Con, as she was called by her family, had joined the WSPU in 1909.[863] By this date, imprisoned suffragettes had begun to hunger strike, which had the effect of dramatically shortening their imprisonment, since no Government wanted any woman's death on its hands. To counter the women's success, the Government introduced forcible feeding, wherein hunger strikers were pinned down, a hose inserted up their nostrils or down their throats into their stomachs, and a concoction of milk, egg, and brandy poured down the tube. The uproar over forcible feeding was tremendous, and Lady Constance Lytton was at the center of the furor. When she was not force-fed during her first or second imprisonments in 1909 (London in March; Newcastle in October), it became clear to Con that she was being treated differently because she was a member of the aristocracy and linked by marriage to several Members of Parliament. In disguise and calling herself 'Jane Wharton', Con got herself arrested on 14 January 1910 in Liverpool, was sentenced to 14 days in Third Division, and refused to eat. After a cursory medical examination failed to reveal her heart problems – about which she said nothing[864] – she was force-fed eight times. When she was released, Con became a national celebrity. Seeing her in a large WSPU procession in June 1910, Frances observed, 'Con was a wonderful figure . . . . I was impressed with the youth of the Procession. The great mass under 30-35. I felt the <u>torch</u> was handed on . . . but Con's face is the thing that remains to me. I don't feel she is to be long amid the waves of this troublesome world'.[865] As Frances predicted, Con's health had been damaged by the forcible feeding, and she suffered a 'heart seizure' in autumn 1910. She nevertheless resumed some of her efforts for the Cause in 1911,[866] but a stroke in May 1912 prevented Con from participating in the suffragettes' activities thereafter.[867]

Her admiration for Con aside, Frances strongly objected to Con's personal references in speeches and interviews, and, when Frances was asked for an interview, she was unequivocal to Betty: 'A man wants to interview me on my public work. No thank you. Con is a lesson'.[868] Thereafter, Frances made herself unavailable to the press, and thus created yet another factor in her being less well-known to posterity than the other leaders of the movement.

In spite of Frances's work of nearly twenty years for women's suffrage, Alice and Betty, long-time sympathisers with the Cause, had both steadfastly refused to join any suffrage societies because of Arthur and Gerald's political careers.[869] This changed for Alice, however, in 1908. With support for women's suffrage increasing in Britain, Anti-Suffrage Leagues were formed by both women and men in 1908-1910 and by 1911 combined to form the National League for Opposing Women's Suffrage. Lord Cromer was its first President; he was succeeded by Lord Curzon, perhaps the best-known male Anti. A Men's League for Women's Suffrage had been created in 1907; its President was Lord Victor Lytton, Betty's brother. Alice informed Fawcett in August 1908 that she had decided to join the NUWSS because '"This new anti-suffrage league has roused my indignation and makes me feel one must rise up against it"'.[870]

In 1909, Betty also committed herself to work for the Cause, joining the Conservative and Unionist Women's Franchise Association, founded in 1908 and supported and later led by Lady Maude Selborne. It was probably Con's decision to join the militants which caused Betty to more clearly define her own support for the Cause. Though she usually defended the actions of her sister, Betty could not follow Con into the ranks of the militants. Once involved, however, Betty became, if anything, more outspoken and determined on the subject than Frances. She even went so far as to refrain from undertaking all other political work 'till the vote is won'.[871] Alice also joined the Conservative and Unionists Women's Franchise Association. In 1909, Betty became the President of this organization in Edinburgh.[872]

CHAPTER 10

'The Kirk of the Crown of Scotland'
(1885-1915)

'I never once have been bored'.[873]

'Could any work be more important?'[874]

B esides politics, the other major passion of Lady Frances Balfour's life was the Church of Scotland, and here, too, her father's influence was greatest. Having grown up listening to discussions about Church dogma and religious matters between family members and the numerous clergy who visited her homes, Frances gradually began to attend the General Assembly of the Church of Scotland as an adult, and by the mid-1890s, was a fixture in the Throne Gallery during the late-May event. Technically, she had no right to attend, much less sit in the Throne Gallery (provided for the Queen[1] or her representatives), but her interest in the Church, together with the stature of her family and her supporters, meant that her presence was not only tolerated by Church officials but generally welcomed.

Frances's first visit to the General Assembly was in 1885, when her Church faced the threat of Disestablishment (the Liberal Party wished to end the National status of the Church). When Disestablishment legislation was before the House of Commons in 1885, church members answered: between 7 April and 11 May, 1,192 petitions bearing the signatures of 649,881 opponents of the bill were presented to Parliament.[875] Disestablishment was therefore one of the first subjects broached by the General Assembly when it met on 27 May 1885. Frances recounted the day to Arthur: 'Proceedings were dull till [Dr John] Tulloch got up. . . '. After

---

1 The Church of Scotland is the National Church north of the Border, but the British monarch is not its head, though she or her representative, the Lord High Commissioner, is present at the meetings of its General Assembly.

describing how conciliatory the Church had been, Tulloch 'proceeded to say that there were limits to this and that they must remember it was *the Establishment* of the Church they must stick to. "Moderator, we must take our stand somewhere and we will take it here"'. The house positively shrieked with enthusiasm.' Then Dr Story rose and 'made a most brilliantly clever speech'. Referring to a commentator who had said the Church would die hard, '[Story] said in a voice which was like a trumpet for clearness, "but it shall not die" and the scene was such that if I live to a hundred I shall never forget it. I believe I was holding on to Lady Aberdeen's chair, it might have been her hair for all I knew'. [876] Ultimately, Church of Scotland disestablishment was averted in the late nineteenth and early twentieth centuries largely because Scottish Liberals were 'divided on the issue'. [877] The Church of Scotland still enjoys its National status.

While Frances's initial interest in the affairs of the Church might have come from her father, her attendance at the General Assembly was due to her close association with Dr Story, who by the 1880s was playing a significant role. In fact, Story was one of the Church leaders credited with helping to re-establish the dominance of the Church of Scotland in the late nineteenth century. [878]

Story was most likely responsible for liberalizing the theological views of Frances, a traditionalist. In 1865, he had been one of the founders of the Church Service Society, one of whose objects was to make the worship 'more seemly and liturgical'. [879] In doctrine, Story rejected the infallibility of the Bible, 'substitutionary atonement', and election, [880] thus placing him 'at the opposite pole in theological thinking to Knox and Calvin'. [881] At Rosneath, Story added 'a choir, an organ, stained glass windows and Christmas Day service'. [882] Despite Frances's early reservations, her positions regarding these things evolved.

In 1886, Story was elected Junior Clerk of the Assembly by an impressive majority (195). [883] During the same year, he succeeded Dr John Caird as Chaplain-in-ordinary to Queen Victoria (renewed by King Edward VII); and on 9 November, Arthur, as Secretary for Scotland, chose Story to be Professor of Church History at Glasgow University, [884] no doubt in part through Frances's influence. In 1893, Story was elected Moderator, a position 'none could hold till after they had been in orders 25 years', [885] and Frances asserted that she would be 'with them thro' it all'. [886]

Frances **'saw the beloved Chimes'** inducted as Moderator in 1894. Of course, the remaining meetings were mostly filled with reports from various Church committees, but Frances attended these sessions, sitting through the dull as well as the interesting in order to 'really make a study of the Assembly. I never once have been bored'. [887] As Moderator, Story gave the closing address. Arthur, who had suggested before the event that 'things so anticipated never come off', learned from Frances that she 'enjoy[ed herself] as [she] had never done before'.[888] '[I] feel stronger and brighter than I have done for months. I find in the strength of such meat as the Assembly affords, I require little food and less sleep, & I have a sensation of being thoroughly alive every minute'.[889]

At the 1895 General Assembly, with Dr Story completing his year as Moderator, Frances, lodged at Holyrood Palace, was even more intimately involved in the activities. Following the levee and procession to St Giles, she heard Story deliver the out-going Moderator's sermon, which – not surprisingly – focused on unity in the Church.

Frances's engrossment in Church affairs in 1894-95 coincided with the decision of the High Kirk of St Giles to install in the cathedral a permanent memorial to her ancestor, the 1st Marquess of Argyll, who, as the Commander of the Covenanter army and upholder of Presbyterianism, was executed for treason in 1661 by Charles II. On 27 May 1895, the anniversary of the execution, the Argyll memorial and window were unveiled and dedicated. Substituting for her father and her eldest brother, Frances **'laid a wreath [of immortelles and laurels] on it',** handed to her by Lord Breadalbane, Lord High Commissioner. 'There was not a dry eye in St Giles', she proclaimed.[890]

Though few General Assemblies after this date held the personal appeal of the 1894-95 sessions, Frances never faltered in her support or attendance at the meetings. She once mused, 'Curious how I love this Scottish manse and Church world'.[891]

Frances also took part in other special Church events. In June 1897, she travelled to Iona, an island owned by her father, to celebrate the thirteen-hundredth anniversary of the death of St Columba (c. 521-597), who 'laid the foundations for the establishment of Christianity in Pictland [Scotland]'.[892] The celebration featured four special services held at the church on Iona; Frances declared 9 June 1897 **'a day to be had in remembrance'.**

The Catholic Church also wanted to hold a commemorative service in the church. The Duke acceded. However, to be sure that the properties would always be associated with the Church of Scotland, he presented the ruins of the Abbey, nunnery, and St Oran's chapel to the Church of Scotland in 1899-1900.[893] As a condition of his donation, the Duke required that the Cathedral be restored.[894]

Dr Story's success as Moderator was followed by his appointment in 1898 as Principal of Glasgow University. On 20 October, Frances attended his inaugural lecture to the assembled students, but Story's reception by the student body, whose clamour prevented him from delivering his speech, was not as successful as his welcomes at the General Assemblies.

Story's reforming instincts did not lag, and nowhere can they be better seen than in his opinion about the Church's Confession of Faith and in his 'desire for liberalization of the Church's doctrine and government'.[895] Story believed that the Confession contained statements 'not in strict accord with modern thought and . . . statements disproved by advancing knowledge'.[896] The latter charge led the Church of Scotland to appoint a committee in 1900 to 'examine the whole question of the Church's relation to its Confession'.[897] Eventually, the General Assembly decided that the Church did not alone have the power 'to modify or abandon the Confession of Faith on its own initiative' but must secure the agreement of Parliament.[898]

Though there was little movement toward reunion with the Church of Scotland in the late 1890s, one union did occur on 31 October 1900, when the United Presbyterian Church joined with the Free Church of Scotland to form the United Free Church, an event which Frances – who was good friends with several Free Church ministers – attended. Unfortunately for the new venture, some 27 Free Church ministers[899] (out of 1,095 congregations[900]) refused to join the new Church and commenced a lengthy legal and political struggle to retain the property of the pre-1900 Free Church. When the House of Lords ruled in favour of the 'Wee Free' minority in 1904, Parliament was forced to resolve the issue. In 1905, it passed the Scottish Churches Act, which created a Royal Commission to determine how best to divide the church property between the two churches and gave the General Assembly (via Clause V, for whose passage Frances worked) 'the right to alter the formula for Confessional subscription'.[901] As Prime Minister, Arthur Balfour played a key role in settling these issues.

Frances learned of the Lords' decision before it was officially announced. 'We have in our party here [at Terling] the Lord Chancellor's secretary [Kenneth Muir-MacKenzie]. Not only has he made no secret about the judgment but he has brought many of the judgments with him as "he thought I might be here"'. Frances added, 'All he stipulates is that I should not write to *The Scotsman* in time for them to have the right article on Monday morning!! The judges are 5 to 2 in favour of the wee Kirk'.[902]

The Rev Archibald Fleming came into Frances's life in 1902 when he was appointed minister of St Columba's in Pont Street, the church in which Frances now worshipped on most Sundays. At Fleming's induction service on 31 January, Frances presented his robes. She also presented him a gown and hood when he received a Doctor of Divinity degree from the University of Edinburgh in April 1906. Relations between Frances and Fleming were not, however, as smooth as were those with most of her minister-friends. Over the years, Fleming took offence at many of Frances's comments and pronouncements and, rather than overlooking them or chiding her for her declarations, would not speak to Frances for long periods of time.

Frances was also friends with most of the ministers' wives, Dr Story's wife being a good example. This is not to say that Frances had a high opinion of all ministers' wives, however. On one occasion, she invited 'several bishops to lunch, one of whom mistakenly brought his wife'. Pointing to a chair, Frances instructed the woman to sit, "'but don't open your mouth or you will spoil the whole thing"'.[903]

Nowhere is Frances's love of the Church of Scotland and its traditions more obvious than in her defense of Holyrood in 1903. The physical condition of this historic site was so dire that the Earl of Leven, Lord High Commissioner in 1903, announced that he would stay in a hotel during the annual meeting of the General Assembly. Always a woman of strong sentiments and even stronger statements, Frances quickly dispatched letters to *The Scotsman* and to *The Times*,[904] condemning the decision. 'The Presence of the King's Commissioner is necessary to the proper constitution of the General Assembly. But to have a Commissioner who, instead of driving in state from venerable Holyrood, makes his way from the door of a brand-new hotel in a noisy and bustling street is hardly consistent with the dignity of the office and of the assembly over which he presides'. She then pointedly asked, 'What would Londoners say if the King were to come to open Parliament from the Hotel Metropole, or even the Hotel Cecil?'[905]

This time, Frances's righteous indignation was matched by that of her countrymen, whose letters of support poured into the country's newspapers. 'Finding [myself] suddenly a popular national saint', she declared, was 'a new sensation'.[906] The day after her letter appeared, Scottish members of the House of Commons began debate on the Civil Service Estimates with questions about the condition of the palace. The Government quickly assured citizens that the necessary repairs would be made, prompting Frances to assert that 'Holyrood will not again be neglected'.[907] The king stayed at Dalkeith Palace during his visit in May 1903, but held a levee at Holyrood.[908]

Frances began her great work for the Church of Scotland in 1905, when she agreed to assist the effort to save Crown Court Church, a Scottish National Church in London.[909] The rich history and tradition of the Church undoubtedly proved an irresistible combination for Frances, and ultimately Frances carried the lion's share of the work that saved the church. Members believe that their Presbyterian church was given its first English home by the first Stuart monarch of England, who is purported to have allowed Scottish Presbyterians to use a chapel which he had built near his London residence. After James's chapel was destroyed by fire in January 1698, members eventually made their home on Russell Street. The 'Kirk of the Crown of Scotland', as Frances christened it, was officially opened as Crown Court Church in Covent Garden in 24 March 1719.

Between 1719 and 1905, the Church had a 'chequered career'.[910] The high point in its extended history occurred during the ministry of the Rev Dr John Cumming, one of London's most popular preachers, who served from 1832-1879. Following the ministry of Dr Cumming, however, the decision was made to build a new church closer to where most members lived. When St Columba's was opened in Knightsbridge in 1884, it attracted most of the membership away from Crown Court. Indeed, Frances herself primarily attended St Columba's when she was in London; she later credited her sister, Victoria, with keeping her interest in Crown Court Church alive.[911]

Although dedicated divines saved the Church from dissolution, they were not in a position to preserve the building, which, by the turn of the twentieth century, was in such 'ruinous repair'[912] that some members needed umbrellas in church on rainy Sundays, and it was feared that local government officials would soon require that the building be pulled down for reasons of safety. The congregation, now quite small, was 'entirely destitute of wealthy members'.[913] Having sought assistance for 15 years, the Rev Alexander Macrae, who became minister of Crown Court in 1890, finally had success when he enlisted Frances's help on the project. She possessed the enthusiasm, dedication, and influence to resuscitate the 'Ragged Kirk', as Dr Cumming had called it.[914]

Frances was the only woman on the nine-member Renovation Committee, which held its first meeting on 19 June 1905. The Committee's first task was to decide whether the decaying church should be renovated, rebuilt, or abandoned. Several issues had to be considered before a decision could be made. These included the remaining 41 years on the leasehold, held by the Duke of Bedford, and the ground rental for the church, which, at £127 per year, represented more than one-third of the church's annual income.[915] There were also the questions of membership (there were only 309 members on the communion roll) and church attendance (only 113 persons at the morning service and 170 at the evening service on a recent Sunday), both of which had been steadily declining.[916] (St Columba's listed 928 members on its communion roll in 1907.[917])

Of all the issues confronting the Renovation Committee, only the question of need could be resolved immediately. Frances made the moving and strongly persuasive argument that Crown Court Church still rendered invaluable service to Church of Scotland members:

At the usual evening service, . . . there is a most interesting gathering
of young Scotsmen and Scotswomen, in the anxious beginnings of
London careers and therefore as yet far from affluent, ardently attached
to the Church of their native land, and in circumstances particularly
calling for its aid, its counsel, and its protection. The number on the
Communion Roll is 309; but this is no adequate measure of the extent
to which the ordinances offered are made use of; for the elements of
the congregation almost entirely change from year to year: the young
Scottish residents of Bloomsbury pass on to the preferable life of the
suburbs whenever they can; and others swarm in, fresh from Scotland,
to take their places. Can any work be more important? . . . Motor
omnibuses now approach the Church from every side: two of the new
'tube' stations are to be near it; and the means of access are therefore
more, rather than less easy than in Dr. Cumming's time. . . . The Sunday
and Night Schools are well attended and energetically conducted; and
the classes in connection with the Church of Scotland Young Men's and
Women's Guild, and the athletic, rambling and other Clubs connected
with the Church, serve the useful purpose of supplying wholesome
recreation and instruction to the young – and for the most part lonely –
Scotsmen and Scotswomen who form the bulk of the congregation.[918]

One by one, the committee tackled the remaining issues. Frances was asked to
approach the Duke of Bedford about the leasehold issue, and by June 1906, the
Duke had agreed to extend the lease for 99 years at an annual fee of £50 for an
area approximately 70 feet by 50 feet with an entrance on Russell Street.[919] About
all the committee now needed to know, before beginning its fund-raising campaign,
was whether the proposed site was adequate. Even though there was an architect
on the committee, it chose to consult Balfour and Turner and, at its meeting of
18 June 1906, in the firm's offices, Eustace assured the committee that the site was
adequate if the church were built on the upper floor with schools and/or hall on the
ground floor of the new edifice. He estimated that the structure could be erected
for £12,132.

The Renovation Committee now turned its attention to the task of soliciting
funds for the construction of a new church. Here most especially it looked to
Frances, who declared that Mr Macrae simply 'could not beg'.[920] First, Frances
drafted 'A Statement concerning the Position of Crown Court Church' to send out
to 250 potential contributors to the building fund. The committee had voted to seek
financial assistance in the amount of £2,000 from Bedford for the new building,
'in consideration of the importance of the portion of the original site to be given

up'. When the Committee reconvened on 29 November 1906, Macrae was able to report that the Duke had pledged £1,000 for the rebuilding effort.

Support for the project was not unanimous, though opposition came from only one member of the committee, George Christison, who refused to support the decision to construct a new church because he believed that £12,132 was an 'unwarrantable extravagance', and because he thought that an endowment should be created sufficient to assure an adequate salary for a full-time minister (Macrae supplemented his income with his other employment as a chaplain in the armed services). Since the Renovation Committee's proposal did not include such a plan, Christison could not support the project.

Once more, Frances was called upon to help. In a carefully reasoned response to Christison's objections, she conceded that 'we should all like to have ministers fashioned according to our ideals of the perfect minister', but that increasing Macrae's stipend would not change him into 'an organizing force' and that '[W]hat he does now, he will always do'. [921] Frances asserted that Macrae performed a valuable service at Crown Court because '[He] has a considerable gift of preaching, and he has the power of touching the springs of inherited national and religious life in a simple and moving way'. She added, 'Endow and rebuild Crown Court Church, as you may, you will not alter Mr Macrae'.

In its final decision (made in January 1907) before proceeding to dismantle the old church and construct a modern replacement, the Renovation Committee selected Balfour and Turner as architects and appointed Frances's brother, Lord George Campbell, as treasurer of the building fund. [922] The committee made these decisions at the only meeting which Frances did not attend.

It was at this point that Frances began her most important work for Crown Court: soliciting contributions for the rebuilding. In her autobiography, she revealed the way she went about her fund-raising: 'One of the Church Records, revealed a list of original donors in 1718. I conceived the design of asking their descendants, as near as I could trace them or impose on them, and also the forty-five Scottish Ministers past and present of the Crown, five Scottish Prime Ministers among them, to become subscribers. For two whole years, I wrote two letters a day'. [923]

In seeking donations, she went to great lengths to establish connections between those she was soliciting and their ancestors. On one occasion, she contacted Lewis Harcourt because she 'had discovered Admiral Vernon Harcourt had been a great supporter of Cummings in 1850 in the Protestant rows. Harcourt wrote back it was the worst piece of Scotch blackmailing he had ever known . . . . All the same I got my £5 and a laugh'. [924]

Frances also prevailed upon a large number of the politicians whom she knew.[925] In all, 35 Scottish Ministers helped her cause, and these included, of course, the five past and future Scottish Prime Ministers (Lord Rosebery, Balfour, Sir Henry Campbell-Bannerman, Herbert Asquith [representing the Scottish constituency of Fife], and Andrew Bonar Law). Even the Liberal/Socialist John Burns contributed.[926] Betty Balfour later averred that the money for the rebuilding of Crown Court Church was raised 'by Frances Balfour's untiring and unflagging begging'.[927]

Frances did not limit her appeals for contributions to letter-writing. Soon after joining the Renovation Committee, she launched a publicity campaign for the church by writing articles about it which she persuaded the major British newspapers to publish. In much of what she wrote, she tried to 'raise the consciousness' of Scots to the importance of 'the oldest Scottish possession in London'.[928]

Except for fund-raising, most of the Committee's work should have been completed by 1908. The Committee was forced to meet regularly thereafter, however, to deal with unexpected difficulties and problems which required deliberation and resolution. At its meeting of 13 April 1908, Eustace informed the Committee that the estimate for a new organ was £1,250, with an extra £250 for its case, increasing the total expense of rebuilding to £13,632 at a time when Frances was having difficulty raising even £12,000. Fortunately, the organ problem was resolved when Andrew Carnegie, the Scottish-American philanthropist who had emigrated with his family from Scotland to the US in 1848, responded to Frances's personal appeal with a generous donation for the organ.[929] Carnegie did not initially agree, however, to give Crown Court all Frances requested. His private secretary, James Bertram, informed the committee in June 1908: 'Mr. Carnegie desires me to say that according to our standard the amount allowed for an Organ for a Church of the size [of Crown Court] would be, say 500 to 550 pounds, and I am to say that Mr. Carnegie is willing to add 50% to this and to provide 750 pounds for the purchase of an instrument'. He added, 'For him to spend more than this he does not think would be a wise use of money'.[930] Nevertheless, Frances persisted in her efforts and eventually persuaded Carnegie to contribute £856, the entire cost of a less-expensive organ and its case.[931]

Crown Court Church held its last services in the old building on 28 June 1908, after which the congregation used Newton Hall on Fetter Lane. Frances was accorded the privilege of locking the old church's doors for the last time.[932] The foundation stone for the new church was laid by Arthur Balfour. The stone reads: 'To the glory of God. This stone in remembrance was placed by the Rt. Hon Arthur James Balfour, M.P., 12 May 1909, to record the raising of the Kirk of the Crown of Scotland. Built by the Scottish people in 1718. Rebuilt in 1909'.[933] *The Times, The Scotsman,* the *Westminster Gazette,* and the *Scots Pictorial* accorded prominent publicity to the laying of the stone.

The new church was officially dedicated on 30 October 1909 by Lord Kinnard, the Lord High Commissioner to the General Assembly of the Church of Scotland; the Rev Dr John Campbell Gibson of Swatow, China, Moderator of the Synod of the Presbyterian Church of England; and the Rt Rev Dr James Robertson, Moderator of the General Assembly of the Church of Scotland this year as well as minister of the parish church at Whittingehame. Frances, to whom Lord Balfour of Burleigh presented a gold-plated key, officially opened the door, saying simply, 'The Kirk of the Crown of Scotland is now open'.[934]

Eustace Balfour, whose style was characterized by 'simplicity of surface' and a sense of spaciousness,[935] had been a good choice as architect for the project. The architectural difficulties resulting from the diminished site were exacerbated by the fact that the church had light only from the east, and, of course, the pulpit and communion table had to be made visible to the entire congregation. Eustace solved the light and space problems by constructing a clerestory and gallery (which held 213 persons) above the main sanctuary. The main floor seated 275 (the old church could seat 1,000).[936]

The most arresting feature in the Neo-Elizabethan church is the colourful coat-of-arms emblazoned on the wall above the dark-oak panelled area of the communion table. The arms were those of the Hanoverians, who held the crown when the former church was built in 1718. Below the arms is the St Andrew's cross, 'intertwined with thistles' and red roses to 'denote the English connection'.[937] The carving was done by Laurence Turner, brother of Eustace's partner Thackeray, who also provided the ornamentation on the organ case, the communion table, the baptismal font, and the Burning Bush emblem at the rear of the church. The pulpit was given by the granddaughters of Dr Cumming.

On 8 March 1912, the Renovation Committee convened its last meeting, held to discuss means of clearing the remaining debt. Frances had recently secured pledges amounting to £1,500, leaving the debt at £1,700. After an appeal 'to the friends of the Church of Scotland', the debt was reduced to £550. In 1914, it still stood at £250, when Frances made her most outrageous effort to help reduce the debt: she bet Sir Robert Finlay that there would be no general election within the year. She won, thanks to the war, and Finlay's money went to the rebuilding fund.[938] The debt was finally satisfied in 1915 when Frances' sister-in-law Sybil 'paid the last hundred pounds owing' as a memorial to her husband, Lord George Campbell, the building fund treasurer, who died that year.[939]

It is unlikely that Crown Court Church would still exist were it not for Frances's efforts. She not only raised most of the funds for the reconstruction but also personally launched and wrote all the appeals, persuaded recalcitrant committee members to accept the majority opinion, wrote reports of the proceedings for the press, secured the free services of the architects and the treasurer, and served as an advisor to Macrae. Moreover, after her sister Victoria died, Frances succeeded her as Crown Court Church's Woman's Guild President; she served in this capacity for the rest of her life. In a eulogy rendered in her honour after her death, the Rev Dr Norman Maclean confirmed the importance of Frances's work on behalf of Crown Court: 'I do not know any other instance of a Scots church being built south of the border by the exertions of one woman. In Edinburgh there are Lady Glenorchy's Church and Lady Yester's Church, and Crown Court Church is, in fact, Lady Frances' Church'.[940] The Church bears one special testimony to its female patron: it has one stained glass window entirely devoted to women of the Bible.

Frances made her last rebuilding gift to Crown Court Church in 1924. In memory of her beloved Eustace, she presented to the Church 'the Jacobean oak chair made from the beams of the demolished church',[941] which had been given by the builders to the architect shortly after the church's completion. For its part, the kirk session assigned to Frances and her family the front pew 'in perpetuity'. In her memoirs, Frances later wrote: 'My Lines[942] may lie elsewhere, but my heart lies in the Kirk of the Crown of Scotland'.[943] In all, she had devoted ten years to restoring this 'National Zion' to its former glory. During this decade, she gave much more than her time and her money to Crown Court Church: she gave her love and her tireless energy to preserve this 'wee bit' of Scotland in the heart of London.

CHAPTER 11

'[T]he complete victory of Redmond' [944]
(1910-1914)

'The London Scottish never had such a friend'.[945]

Lord Haldane to Frances

'Parliament is getting <u>hot</u>, no mistake'.[946]

In the General Election of 1910, Arthur was reelected for the city of London, and Sir Robert Finlay now sat for Edinburgh and St Andrews Universities. Gerald had declined to stand. Lord Robert Cecil was defeated, but his brother, Lord Hugh Cecil, would represent Oxford University. In the final tally, the Liberals had held on to 275 seats, while the Unionists/Conservatives increased their numbers to 273, the Irish Nationalists had 82, and Labour only 40. Unfortunately for the Unionists, the Liberal Party was now dependent on the Irish and Labour Members for the enactment of its programme, which meant that Home Rule for Ireland and a curb on the veto powers of the House of Lords would be issues for this Parliament. Pressed by the Irish to pass the latter legislation first, the Liberals presented their Parliament Bill on 14 April.

Since meetings of the Divorce Commission, which began in February, were held in London, Frances was free to attend many of the evening sittings of the House of Commons during this eventful period. She was at dinner with the Asquiths on 14 April when she **'heard his surrender to the Irish'**, now led by John Redmond. Two days later she witnessed the **'complete victory of Redmond'**.

King Edward VII, stricken with bronchitis contracted on holiday[947], died on 6 May, shocking the nation, which had only one warning of his illness. The new King, George V, whom Frances believed 'a moral man, but a terrible fool',[948] called a round-table conference to work out compromises to assure passage of the Parliament Bill, but it failed. '**Asquith [announced] dissolution**' for 28 November, and the country faced a second ballot in December 1910.

The beginning of the second decade of the new century was pivotal in Frances Balfour's personal life. On 2 July 1910, Frances, having learned her sister Victoria was quite ill, hastened to Edinburgh. Vi died of influenza and pneumonia four days later.[949] After helping to clear up Victoria's personal effects, a weary and depressed Frances returned to London in time to be home when Eustace, who had struggled with a bad ankle during the year, resigned his surveyorship with the 2nd Duke of Westminster on 15 July. The Duke awarded him a pension of £300 a year.[950]

About Eustace's architectural career there are lingering questions, which must be addressed. One topic must be how much of the architectural work done for the Dukes from 1890 to 1910 was the work of Thackeray Turner, to whom most of the best work done by the two partners has often been attributed (obituaries of Turner, who died in 1937, contributed to this belief[951]). The few extant letters from Eustace in which he discussed his architectural work indicate that he had quite definite ideas about architecture, as illustrated by his refusal to compromise on the design for the windows at No 17 Upper Grosvenor Street – a refusal which in 1908 lost the sale of that property to the Countess of Wilton.[952]

It is difficult to imagine that the vast majority of the designs attributed to Eustace on the Grosvenors' London estate, especially the exteriors, were not by Eustace. On occasion, other architects, including his partner Turner, were hired to design some of the buildings, but as the *Survey of London* noted, '[b]y far the most prolific architect of private houses was . . . the new estate surveyor appointed in 1890, Eustace Balfour, who seems to have been able to get whatever work he wanted . . .'.[953] Since it appears that the Estate Surveyor received additional pay if he served as architect of any of the buildings on the estate, commissions given to Turner would reduce Eustace's income – something Eustace would not have welcomed.

Since an architect must design what his client wishes to build, Eustace's work on the estate clearly reflects the tastes of the Dukes. The 1st Duke was especially 'arbitrary', opinionated, and particular.[954] He liked Queen Anne revival and '"the more red brick the better"';[955] he also preferred 'stucco to be painted bright orange, and railings either chocolate or red'.[956] Eustace, who was 'on terms almost of social equality with the Duke', would have spent more time discussing the architectural projects with the Dukes than most surveyors would have been allowed.[957] It is therefore likely that the designs were worked out in the discussions between the two men, with Eustace reflecting the results in his sketches.

It is known that Eustace wished not to be architect for Nos 2-8 Green Street because he wished to focus his attention on the Portugal Street site;[958] this was his first work for the Duke, so it is probable that Eustace worked out the designs in the Duke's presence. Westminster was so pleased with Eustace's work on Portugal Street that two years later (1892), he renamed the street as well as the mews at the end of it for Balfour.[959]

Of course, the 'fastidious'[960] Eustace was also responsible – with ducal approval – for choosing the contractors, designing the sewage plans and the electricity mains, securing the permits, inspecting the work, 'vetting and controlling the designs of the various developers',[961] and fielding occupants' complaints about their property.[962] The workload was great, and to help him, Eustace had in his office only two or three assistant surveyors and a draughtsman.[963]

It should also be noted that the least significant work – usually characterized as the most eccentric – which the firm produced dates to the last two or three years of Eustace's surveyorship,[964] years when Eustace was in declining health. Turner may well have produced more of the firm's output during this time, but it is known that, at the Duke's request, Eustace planned the addition to Bourdon House in 1909-1910; that Sir William Cuthbert Quilter agreed to the redesign of the front of 74 S Audley Street 'in a Georgian manner', provided Eustace was the architect for the project;[965] and that Eustace 'improved' the plans for the Duke Street electricity sub-station. It is especially revealing that when Grosvenor House was 'let to the Government for war work', the 2nd Duke took Bourdon House as his residence in 1917 and liked it so much that he stayed there until his death in 1953.[966] An additional important contribution made by Eustace to Mayfair, though not carried out until 1914, was the plan for the Green Street Garden, 'a large private garden shared by the residents of the houses which backed on to it'.[967]

There is no indication in the actions of the Dukes that Eustace's work suffered from his alcoholism. The 1st Duke was a 'firm temperance man' (his campaign against 'demon drink' reduced the number of pubs in Mayfair from 47 in 1869 to eight in 1891[968]); he would not have tolerated any truancy for drunkenness. The 2nd Duke, reputed to be even more demanding of his surveyor's time, would certainly not have retained the services of one who might not be always available at his 'beck and call'.[969]

In August 1910, Frances travelled to Tiree to complete the clearing up of Victoria's effects. After completing her work, Frances informed the residents of the island that she intended to continue her sister's work on Tiree, and thereafter spent a portion of each summer -- usually August and September -- on the island working out of The Lodge, lent to her by her brother Argyll. Meanwhile, the pier, for which Victoria had worked for twenty years, was finally being built.

Dr James MacGregor, long-time minister of St Cuthbert's Parish Church in Edinburgh, died in November. The recently-retired 78-year-old was the last of her clerical friends from her childhood, and Frances lamented, '**With Hamish goes a long chapter in life . . .**'.[970]

In December, Frances and Eustace were at Whittingehame for the usual family holidays. Battling heart problems as well as alcoholism, Eustace spent more and more time in a 'dreamy sleep',[971] and on 7 January 1911, his physician began 'tapping' to lessen the effects of edema. (Photographs indicate that Eustace was a large but not heavy man until shortly before his death.) Eustace still spent some part of the day out of bed, but fought depression at times, at one point saying, '**I wish I could die**'.[972] He was given morphine on 20 January, and he finally had a good night's sleep and no suffering when he awoke. The next day, 'Teddy', the Balfours' favourite cleric, arrived and, on Sunday, administered Communion to Eustace. '**God be thanked for his Peace**. . . ', Frances recorded. When it was time for some of the rest of the Balfours to return to London, Alice made arrangements for Joan, Alison, and Frances to be given every comfort and consideration in her absence. Thereafter, family members came and went as they could. Though patient, helpful, and considerate with Eustace and Arthur – to whom she always 'showed her best side'[973] – Frances was so protective now of Eustace that family members, particularly Alice, were often forbidden to see him.

Eustace continued to experience periods of sleep alternating with periods of lucidity and calm. When Frances was bothered with toothache, he sang to her. Following a quiet night, '**Eustace gave me such a warm kiss**,' she confided to her diary; and on the following day, another quiet one, he kissed her again. When Eustace began refusing food and requiring ever-stronger doses of morphine, all the family were called back to Whittingehame. Early in the morning of 14 February, Eustace died, surrounded by all his children except Frank, who was still en route home. His death was attributed to 'Cirrhosis of [the] liver and Dilation of [the] Heart'.[974]

Frances delayed the funeral until Frank could be present. In his sermon, Dr Robertson noted Eustace's 'eminent courtesy. Of noble figure, fine voice and charming smile, his manner was . . . the disclosure of a very fine nature'.[975] Accompanied by Arthur, Gerald, Betty and all of her sons and daughters on the one-and-a-half-mile journey to the graveside, Frances followed the casket, draped with the Union Jack and the Scottish Standard. Pipers from the London Scottish played the lament. Colonel Balfour, as he was called, was the first Commander of the London Scottish to die.[976]

Memorial services were held in London at St Columba's and Crown Court Churches on 19 February and 20 February respectively. Dr Archibald Fleming, Chaplain of the London Scottish, conducted the one at St Columba's, where some 600 members of the London Scottish paraded. At Crown Court Church, mourners heard the Rev Alexander Macrae pray, "'We thank thee for his child-like heart, his able mind, and this Church which he has built to Thy Service'".[977] Lord Haldane, one of those who made a contribution toward the debt on Crown Court Church in memory of Eustace, enclosed with the contribution a note saying, 'We miss your husband. He was an institution in his part of the military organization. The London Scottish never had such a friend'.[978]

Judging from her diary and her letters, it would seem that Frances coped reasonably well following Eustace's death, but comments by Frank and Betty in the Balfour Papers indicate that it was a difficult time for Frances as well as for her children. On and off for the next couple of months, Frances apparently suffered from delusions similar to those she had experienced following her brother Walter's death in 1889, when she had been given bromide, which can cause hallucinations. This time one of the drugs she was given to help her sleep was veronal, a barbital, some of the side effects of which are mental confusion and delirium.[979] Compounding the stress and strain of Eustace's illness and death, Frances was now experiencing menopause.[980] Frances's children initially attempted to be around her in case she became delusional, but she wanted to be left alone to come and go as she wished, and Dr Mills agreed that this should be allowed. Ultimately, Frances found her salvation in work and, keeping herself busy, gradually succeeded in overcoming her mental distress.

Besides her mental turmoil, the main difficulty which she faced was the challenge of clearing up the debts on the estate. In addition to any current bills due, she had to settle Eustace's debts of about £4,400. Eustace's life insurance policy was only worth £1,560.[981] Arthur provided the money to settle Eustace's affairs and helped some of Frances's children as well. Arthur was always extremely generous to all his family members.

For several years, Frances experienced waves of depression and loneliness on the anniversaries of Eustace's death. In her summary of the year 1913, Frances wrote, '**I miss Eustace more not less**'. For the rest of her life, she visited '**my grave**' every time she returned to Whittingehame.

Frances remained aware and informed of political events, even in her concern and grief for Eustace. The Unionists/Conservatives, who could ill afford to fight a second election in 1910 on the House of Lords, argued against Home Rule for Ireland this time around, but with no more success: the Liberals and Conservatives each garnered the same number of seats (272), meaning that the Irish (with 84) and Labour (42) would still control the legislative agenda.

The Parliament Bill, originally planned for introduction on 20 February, the day of Eustace's funeral, was presented on the 21st in order to allow Arthur to be there.[982] With every Member given ample time to speak on it, the Bill passed its third reading by a majority of 121. The tension produced by the speeches caused Frances to exclaim to a friend, 'Parliament is getting <u>hot</u>, no mistake'.[983]

Once the bill reached the Upper Chamber, the amount of political manoeuvering was considerable, but, informed that the Prime Minister had the King's consent to create enough new peers to accept the bill, the Lords eventually capitulated, passing it on 10 August, 131 votes to 114, thus limiting once and for all the Lords' power in the upper chamber; the Lords could now only delay legislation for two years.

Arthur's role in the Parliamentary drama of 1909-1911, particularly his 'refusal to take a narrow view of his duty in the crisis'[984] as well as his lack of resolute leadership, alienated many Conservatives.[985] Now, with his Unionist/Conservative opponents organizing the Halsbury Club and Leo Maxse crafting their 'die-hard motto' – 'B M G', or 'Balfour Must Go', which he popularized through his *National Review* – Arthur increasingly felt himself 'badly treated' and began to think about resigning the party leadership.[986] Convinced that the timing was good for a successor, Arthur informed the nation of his resignation in a speech to the City of London Conservative Club on 18 November 1911. Bonar Law, "'another Scot'",[987] was chosen to succeed him. Frances was quoted as saying thereafter that she did not believe Arthur would return to political office 'unless the Conservative Party or the country [was] visited with some great crisis'.[988]

Though exercised about the Parliament Bill, Frances came to admire the Insurance Bill, which passed in 1911. She described it as 'a really great idea. [The bill would provide insurance against sickness for all workers and against unemployment for some labourers in fluctuating trades. Rev Norman] Maclean says it is nearest to the ideal for a Christian State that we have ever got'.[989] When Arthur had complained about the mechanics of it, Frances told him 'if it raises the sweated industries perhaps we should not complain'.[990]

Against the background of political fireworks and the unsettling loss of Eustace, Frances was also serving on the Royal Commission on Divorce and Matrimonial Causes (it sat from 25 February 1910 to 17 May 1911, hearing witnesses and taking evidence; its report was issued in 1912). The key questions for the Commissioners included whether any additional courts would have jurisdiction in divorce matters, whether women would be on an equal footing with men in seeking divorce, whether any grounds other than adultery would be reasons for divorce (as opposed to separation), whether the press should be limited in reporting divorce proceedings, and what laws would be needed to accommodate their recommendations.

British laws regarding divorce had changed little since 1857, when divorce was taken away from ecclesiastical courts and eventually given to the Probate, Divorce, and Admiralty Court of the High Court of Justice, which sits in London. Half of the fourteen Commissioners were lawyers and judges, including the chair, Lord Gorell, retired President of the High Court and prime mover for the Commission.

Two Scots served on the Commission: Lord Guthrie, a Senator of the College of Justice, and Frances. Scotland's divorce laws were more progressive than those in the rest of the British Isles: Scottish women were equal with men in divorce proceedings, and poorer citizens could get a divorce free of charge.[991] In the rest of Britain, wives had to prove adultery *and* an additional offence such as 'cruelty, incest, bigamy, or [willful] desertion'[992] on the part of their husbands, and that offence must have been ongoing for two years or more. A husband, on the other hand, only had to prove his wife was an adulteress.

Frances asked the witnesses her share of questions, but she was especially vigilant when they insulted the intelligence of women or minimised women's rights in a marriage. When Sir John Bigham – who had succeeded Gorell as president of the Division – was asked whether a wife should have grounds for divorce if her husband committed adultery which resulted in the birth of a child, he answered, 'No'. When he further asserted, 'A wise wife, in my opinion, shuts her eyes to her husband's mistakes',[993] Frances asked, 'Her price would be above rubies, I suppose, to him?'[994]

After J H Watts, a barrister and member of the Central Legal Aid Society, held that he would not give relief to the wife for what had been called by Sir John Bigham 'accidental'[995] acts of adultery by her husband, Frances asked if he did not think the adultery inflicted injury on the mind and body of the wife. 'I think naturally for the moment, certainly it inflicts mental cruelty but I think it passes away in the case of most women',[996] Watts replied. When she asked if it passed away when it was a question of physical health, Watts said, 'I do not think the effect of the knowledge does cause the loss of physical health in most cases. . . '. Frances pursued the issue, asking, 'A wife's capacity for forgetting, prevents her suffering?'[997] 'For forgiving', he countered. Mental cruelty was not accepted as grounds for divorce by English judges (though by the early 20th century, divorce court judges had become increasingly willing to broaden what constituted 'cruelty').[998]

The commission had to make recommendations on whether 'incurable lunacy' and 'habitual drunkenness' were grounds for divorce. Most of the testimony, however, concerned incurable insanity and little was heard about habitual drunkenness, though this issue was believed by the majority to be the more difficult one.[999] Only two 'Inebriate Experts' – both men – testified. As a result, the commission modified very little about the definition of an habitual drunkard defined in the Licensing Act of 1902.

Despite her intimate knowledge of alcoholism, Frances did not believe that habitual drunkenness should be grounds for divorce. However, she only expressed this opinion during the discussions which the commissioners held in private in 1911 to arrive at their final recommendations.[1000] She asked no questions about the subject when the two witnesses spoke about the issue (she was one of only six commissioners present when they testified), and she made no objection to the commission's recommendation to include habitual drunkenness as grounds for divorce.[1001]

Frances enjoyed the experience of serving on the Divorce Commission, but she was not very sympathetic with the Church of England's representatives; she declared that she was 'getting positively to detest "The Church"'.[1002] It was, of course, the opposition of the Church that was the primary impediment to all divorce law reform, both before and after this date.[1003]

The Majority Report, signed in November 1912, 'was a remarkable document for its day'[1004] and is a good example of the progressive attitude of Frances and the majority of the Commission members on this pressing social issue. First, the report recommended the decentralization of sittings for the hearing of divorce cases for those with assets less than £250 whose incomes were £300 or less per year. Secondly, it proposed that men and women be on an equal footing with regard to the grounds for divorce. Finally, in addition to adultery, grounds for divorce would include desertion for three years and upwards, incurable insanity after five years' confinement, habitual drunkenness found incurable after three years, and imprisonment under a commuted death sentence. The commissioners also recommended that judges be allowed to close portions of the divorce proceedings if 'the interests of decency, morality, humanity and justice required it'.[1005]

The report was not, however, enacted in a timely manner. There was much resistance to reforming the divorce laws. As Mrs Steinthal reported to the Commission members in 1910, some '85,491 working women at Mother's Union meetings had voted against extending divorce facilities'.[1006] And World War I soon took the nation's attention.

Frances found peace and solace in Tiree. She journeyed there in mid-July 1911 and remained there through August, assisting victims of influenza and tuberculosis while trying to complete a biography of Victoria. During this visit, Frances arranged teas and treats for the children of Tiree and was a judge of the home industry, dairy, and home-baked breads sections[1007] in a competition of livestock and home industries by crofters and cottars, the first such competition since before the crofters' disturbances in the 1880s.[1008]

Her brother Archie joined Frances and, on 29 July, they gave a dinner for 29 employees of the Gott Bay pier contractors.[1009] Frances admitted that on this occasion she 'supplied cigarettes [for the men]! Against my principles, but I thought it was festive'.[1010] Sometime between 1906 and 1911, she herself gave up smoking, and thereafter was remembered as offering money or chocolates to young men to quit the vice.[1011] (Frank, Joan, Alison, and Oswald all smoked.)

Just months after Eustace's death, Frances faced another loss: Finlay's wife Rosemary (nicknamed 'Biba') had been failing since suffering a 'serious heart attack' in 1908.[1012] She had retired to Nairn in spring 1911 and died there of heart failure in June.[1013] It was a **'devastating blow'** for Frances.[1014] She would continue her friendship with Finlay and have the usual political conversations and occasional dinners with him, but Frances did not see as much of him as she had before Biba's death, perhaps because propriety dictated otherwise.[1015]

Oswald, only 16 years old in summer 1911 and deemed to 'lack perseverance'[1016] with his studies at Westminster School, began cramming for the entrance exam to Sandhurst. He passed the exam but, presumably because of his age, did not enter the prestigious military academy until February 1913.[1017] Upon the successful completion of his work there, the Balfours learned that Princess Louise had convinced the King to include Oswald's name on the list of the King's Royal Rifle Corps, into which he was commissioned in February 1914.[1018] *The Scotsman* reported that he was 20th in his division.[1019] 'How pleased Father would have been, and how proud', Frances wrote to Frank.[1020]

Ruth Balfour – the first female Balfour to attend University – finished her first year at Newnham, passed her exam in August 1911, and entered the London (Royal Free Hospital) School of Medicine in October 1912.[1021] She wanted to be a researcher, not a medical doctor.[1022] 'It will please Uncle who does not like Balfours to fail', Frances observed.[1023]

The great political event of 1912 for Frances was the introduction of the Home Rule Bill for Ireland on 11 April 1912. Frances said little about the detested legislation, and when debate on the bill occurred in October-November 1912, Frances was away from London on another speaking trip. Home Rule for Ireland eventually passed the House of Commons twice, in 1912 and in 1913, but was rejected by the House of Lords each time.

Almost simultaneously with the political crises of 1910-1912, Britain endured a period of labour unrest, which indicated, in part, that the working class was turning to direct action in light of the inability of the fledgling Labour Party in Parliament to meet its needs. Strikes occupied Frances's thoughts often in 1912. On 28 February, having had lunch with the Asquiths, she noted that the Prime Minister was **'in the midst of the [miners'] strike conference'**. Mine owners in Scotland and Wales, as well as the Miners' Federation, rejected the offer of a proposed minimum wage for each district, and by early March, 1.3 million miners were on strike. Frances, again lunching at Downing Street on 10 March, **'talked about Italy, Suffrage, and the strike'** with Asquith, who she believed showed **'signs of strain'**. Meanwhile, Frances and the nation were enduring considerable inconvenience: 'We have all learnt economy in coal and no house is burning fires as they did before . . . '.[1024]

The Home Rule Bill finally passed the Commons for the third time on 26 May 1914; determined to get Home Rule on the Statute Books, the Liberals took their final vote on 15 September, and on 18 September Home Rule for Ireland received the Royal Assent. It would not, however, go into effect until after the war, at which time an amending bill would deal with the question of Ulster.

In October 1912, the Balkan nations of Serbia, Bulgaria, and Greece declared war on Moslem Turkey, whose massacres of Christians were a recurring challenge. In less than a month, the Christian nations had pushed the Turks back to Constantinople and were soon victorious on every front. Frances enthused to Frank, 'The Balkans have done it this time!'[1025]

The success of the Christian states was not, however, welcomed by Austria-Hungary and her ally Germany, who were adamant that Russia not be assisted as a result of this success. A conference to work out the post-war settlement was convened in London in December, presided over by Britain's foreign minister, Sir Edward Grey. To Linky, Frances wrote, 'I hope that the Powers . . . will have enough wit not to spoil this undreamt of solution of the old Eastern Question.' If Bulgaria could be 'settled in Constantinople[,] the centre of a federation of Slavs and Greeks', and 'the Turk over the way in Bursa to prowl the menaces of Islam and Russia', she believed, 'Austria & Germany hemming in the obstreperous youth of the new Federal States is really ideal for the poor Christians'.[1026] As it worked out, Bulgaria did not get Constantinople, the Serbs did not gain a coast on the Adriatic except for Montenegro, and Albania declared her independence, but otherwise, the Balkan states got to keep much of what they had secured by warfare, even after two further skirmishes on the battlefield. Frances rejoiced.

Working in London on the biography of Victoria rather than at Whittingehame, where 'my spirit and my memories are too much for me now',[1027] Frances finished the work by October 1911. In April 1912, Frances began a biography of the 'mighty orator',[1028] the Very Rev Dr James Macgregor. Frances undoubtedly turned to writing not only to commemorate the lives of her subjects and to assuage her grief, but also to earn money She was not old enough to receive a pension, and she did not inherit any money. She chose to write biography because it was one of her favourite reading choices. Hodder and Stoughton editor Robertson Nicoll offered her '£300 for an edition of 2,000 plus royalties' for the book on Macgregor,[1029] which was published on 26 November 1912. This same month, Frances recorded that her biography of her sister, also published by Hodder and Stoughton, was selling well in Scotland.[1030] It went through at least three editions. That Frances managed to pen two books in two years is remarkable, considering her depression following Eustace's illness and death, her work for the Divorce Commission – which lasted until November 1912 – and her speaking for the Cause (49 times in 1911 and 84 in 1912). The next year, she would sell Eustace's books to supplement her income.

The year 1912 brought the final addition to the Balfour extended family. On 4 June, Betty gave birth to her last child, Kathleen Constance Blanche, who was almost ten years younger than RAL. On 24 June, Frances presented her youngest daughter, Alison, at Court.[1031] Some of the financial difficulty of providing for the daughters was eased by Nora Sidgwick, who began the tradition of giving each niece £1,000 at age 21.[1032]

To honour the debuts of 'Us Four', Arthur held a ball at Carlton Gardens the day after Alison was presented. The event was so rare for Arthur that the *Sunday Times* opined that for Balfour to give a Ball was '"like the Archbishop dancing a hornpipe in Piccadilly"'.[1033] However, with eight girls in the two families, all the Balfours, including Arthur, spent much time 'trying to get some young men for the nieces!'[1034]

Soon after she was 'Out', Alison received a marriage proposal: on 10 July, she informed her mother that Arthur Milne (called the Savage – there was already an Arthur in the family) had proposed and that she had accepted. Frances, who greatly admired Milne and valued his friendship, was pleased but had a few concerns about this marriage. Alison was considerably younger than Milne (who was 44), and Frances wished 'he had some small fortune'.[1035] Otherwise, however, she thought her daughter could have no better husband.

From his post in Africa, Milne corresponded regularly with Frances and provided good insight into his work. Conversant in Arabic and Swahili, he worked as far afield as Zanzibar, where he toiled among the 500 cholera cases which had erupted there in only two months in 1912; and in 'Nubia', where an outbreak of beriberi raged.[1036] While at Zanzibar, he met an ardent British suffragist and affectionately relayed her compliment to Frances: 'I asked her if she'd ever heard you speak. She got quite enthusiastic, "Heaps of times" and always went whenever you were on the platform. She liked your voice so, and you had such a delightful dry humour. . . This from Zanzibar, my dear!'[1037]

On the last day of 1912, Frances's benediction for the fading year included, **'Tonight I am again alone in my room. . . . It will be best tonight to note the blessings of the year, not to forecast my fears. . . . Feel very lonely and so puzzled how my future should be spent'.** Frances went on, though, to ponder the future, wondering how she would continue to provide for herself and her family, whether she could write a book a year for the rest of her life, and whether this was the best use of her talents. With Eustace gone, she was alone, even when surrounded by family and servants. Always, when she was down, she fastened on her fears, but also as always, this focus led to renewed energy and forward progress.

The wedding of Alison Balfour and Arthur Milne, conducted by Dr Fleming and Dr Robertson, took place at Crown Court Church on 29 April 1913.[1038] Arthur gave the bride away. The wedding breakfast was held at Arthur's London home in Carlton Gardens.[1039] Since they were paying for the wedding breakfast, Alice had insisted on putting only her and Arthur's names on the invitations. Hurt and offended, Frances left the honor of receiving the guests to Alice and Arthur.[1040]

Frances had lost only four of her eleven brothers and sisters by 1913. Now, though, she lost two in one year; the first was Archie. Stricken with influenza in mid-March 1913, he succumbed on 29 March. Since his brother Argyll had no children, Archie, age 66, had been heir to the dukedom. He was buried at Kilmun, the family burial place on the Holy Loch. A writer of verse and a published author, Archie had been 'a great favourite on the ducal estate'.[1041]

Shortly after Alison's wedding, Frances's eldest sister, Edith, Duchess of Northumberland, became ill with gallstones. Doctors advised surgery, which initially seemed successful. A few hours later, Edith began hemorrhaging, and the doctors – operating in haste without chloroform – could not stop the bleeding in time to save her life.[1042] After her funeral at Alnwick, Edith was buried 'at the feet of her five children in Lesbury Churchyard'.[1043]

Though Frances often corrected Betty's children, she was capable of seeing their best sides as well. When Ruth made the decision to become a doctor, Frances eloquently defended her to Frank, who had criticized Ruth for pursuing such a career path. 'Ruth has by direct inheritance got the gift of scientific research. She is your Uncle Frank in her generation.' She further observed, 'The student life and the life of scientific knowledge is [sic] born within her. The desire for research and exact knowledge is as strong in her as the desire for military research and practice was in your father, as born with her as his gifts as an architect and artist. The gift will out. . . '.[1044]

With Alison's marriage to Milne, Frances now had two children in Africa who regularly kept her informed of their lives. Alison appears to have quickly adapted to her new environment and was soon in the swing of Nairobi's social scene. One of the Savage's closest friends in the colony was Reginald Berkley Cole, a son of Lord and Lady Enniskillen, a brother-in-law of Lord Delamere, and a member of the Legislative Council of Kenya.[1045] On 2 July, Alison reported that Cole had asked her to be hostess in Lady Delamere's box on the occasion of the July races.[1046]

Lady Delamere was the first wife of Hugh Cholmondeley, 3rd Baron Delamere, the most influential settler in Kenya in the early 20th century.[1047] All of these individuals were friends with Isak Dinesen (Karen Blixen) of *Out of Africa* fame.[1048] It is highly likely that it was the Savage who diagnosed Dinesen's venereal disease in 1914.[1049] In May 1914, the first Lady Delamere died 'in Alison's house'.[1050]

Frances had an opportunity to meet Lord Delamere at a dinner in London in 1922, where East African celebrities, who were attempting to keep the Indian community in Kenya from gaining 'full equality of citizenship',[1051] spoke. Her report to Nell was typically discerning: 'The upshot of it all was the Indians were not to have [East Africa]. It was to be a white settlement'. 'I could not help feeling', she added, that 'the "native" was trotted out with new friends. Not a man there but had oppressed and driven them out of their lands, and now when the Indians had come in they were full of the native'. . . .[1052]

Although the year 1914 is significant in modern world history, it opened with little change of routine for most Britons, including Frances and her family. During the week of 11 January, she went to Glasgow to hear Arthur deliver three Gifford Lectures: Arthur entitled his offerings 'Theism and Humanism'. After the first, attended by a large audience, Frances noted that she '**was struck afresh by the man**'.[1053] Also in early 1914, good news arrived from Africa: Alison gave birth to a daughter on 13 February. She was named Evelyn Elizabeth Milne, but called Elizabeth.

With her suffrage work having fallen into a routine, Frances was once again at loose ends. Relief from boredom came in Lord Aberdeen's request that Frances 'edit the papers and write the biography of his Grandfather', 4th Earl Aberdeen.[1054] Lord Aberdeen offered her £500 for the manuscript, which would become his property.[1055] Frances was predisposed to like her subject: as Prime Minister from 1852 to 1855, Aberdeen was the British political leader who first acknowledged her father's talents with cabinet office. That Frances was aware of Aberdeen's shortcomings is evidenced by her observation to Frank: 'He was a very good man, but not a very great one'.[1056]

Not all the family news in early 1914 was good. She learned on 28 April that her eldest brother, the 9th Duke of Argyll, was seriously ill of double pneumonia[1057] at Kent House, East Cowes, where he and Princess Louise were visiting. Princess Louise sent for Frances, who arrived at her brother's side with two nurses to assist with his care.[1058] She remained at Kent House until his death on 2 May. **'So goes the elder brother, very dear to us all. God rest his pure soul . . . '.**

Foreign diplomats, Members of Parliament, and many royals, including the King and Queen, attended the memorial service for Argyll in Westminster Abbey, as did Frances and Joan. From London, the Duke's casket was taken to Rosneath Church, where, after another service, it remained until the funeral at Kilmun. That service, held on **'a day of glory unspeakable and great beauty'**, according to Frances, was conducted by 'Teddy' Glyn. Frances wrote at least two eulogies of her brother, whom she admitted that she hero-worshipped. She noted that '"Enthusiasm" was the note of everything he did'[1059] and that 'No man ever received an unkind word from him . . . '.[1060] Her nephew Niall now took up residence in Inveraray Castle as 10th Duke of Argyll.

The assassination of the heir to the throne of Austria-Hungary and his wife by a Serbian Nationalist from Bosnia triggered a chain of events which eventually led to the Great War. Arthur Balfour noted at this time that '"If Germany <u>wants</u> to go to war, there is no doubt the Irish situation will make her feel this is the moment to choose"'.[1061] When Germany, expecting a sustained struggle against Russia on the eastern front, decided to cut through Luxembourg (1 August) and Belgium (3 August) in order to knock France out of the war before the Russians could fully mobilize (the Schlieffen Plan), Britain – pledged to uphold Belgium's neutrality – declared **'War with Germany'** (4 August). With this pronouncement, Frances's life changed dramatically – as did those of her countrymen and -women.

CHAPTER 12

"No Votes for Women"' [1062]
(1910-1914)

'We are not afraid of the Antis. No one need be afraid
of anyone who is trying to prove a negative'.[1063]

'. . . [I]f women legislated for men do you think
men's interests would get proper notice?'[1064]

Convinced that their enfranchisement was at stake, British women who were members of various suffrage organizations worked tirelessly during the General Election of January 1910. No fewer than 345 candidates included women's enfranchisement in their election addresses.[1065] Since Asquith and other Liberal leaders had 'implied that the new Parliament should have a mandate to act on the question' of votes for women,[1066] the National Union adopted a new tactic to advance their Cause: they collected voters' signatures on petitions asking that the House of Commons pass legislation giving women votes 'without delay'.[1067] Working in 'snow, hail, and sleet' in more than 290 constituencies, the suffragists collected 290,498 signatures during the short campaign.[1068] The women's efforts resulted in the election to the House of Commons of 407 sympathetic Members. Though in a minority, approximately one-third of the Conservative Members were supporters.

Convinced that the women's Cause had become something of an embarrassment to the Liberals and an issue all parties wished to see resolved, supporters in the Commons sought a way to make women's suffrage a non-partisan effort. A Conciliation Committee, led by Lord Lytton as Chair and Henry Brailsford as Hon Secretary, was formed to settle the question. The women's Bill that proved to be most acceptable to all parties called for extending the franchise to women householders, as these women already had the municipal vote. If passed, the measure would enfranchise approximately one million women.[1069] The militants, believing that milder militancy was "'played out'", declared a truce on 31 January 1910, after much urging from Lytton and Brailsford.[1070]

The various suffrage organizations mounted a vigorous campaign for the bill. They wrote letters, made deputations to some of the Members, sent whips to the MPs, and 'lobbied energetically'.[1071] Frances, true to form, certainly worked hard to secure the bill's passage. In late May, she reported her results to Fawcett: '[Alfred] Lyttelton will back the bill from the front bench, [Augustine] Birrell, and Winston [Churchill] on the Government side. Arthur has refused to ask for time for it, but promised if there was a division to vote for it'.[1072]

Though the Conciliation Bill passed its first reading on 14 June, the suffragists were worried that further facilities for the bill would not be readily forthcoming, since Asquith refused to guarantee the time. To keep up the pressure on the Government, the London Society held a large, 'enthusiastic' meeting presided over by Frances in Queen's Hall on 28 June, raising £1,500 for the women's demonstration and campaign.[1073] Two days after the meeting, Asquith announced that the Government would allow a debate and division on the Conciliation Bill on 11-12 July 1910.

Meanwhile, Fawcett, hoping to demonstrate women's unity behind the Bill (even though she was wary that any association with the militants would confuse the public), attempted to get the WSPU leaders to join the National Union in a major demonstration at Trafalgar Square in support of the bill. WSPU leaders, however, refused despite their truce to agree to abstain from violence during the demonstration, and the effort failed. According to at least one who has written about the events during this period, the tensions within the women's movement were caused not only by the different tactics pursued by the NUWSS and the WSPU but also by 'a lack of rapport between the leadership' and 'a lack of communication' between the rival groups[1074] – although all the suffrage societies in Scotland, militant and non-militant, cooperated in the mass meeting on Calton Hill in Edinburgh on 23 July.[1075] One wonders if the situation in London would have been any different if the London Society, which was in charge of NUWSS events in the city, had been represented at this meeting not by Fawcett but by Frances (President of the London Society and friend of Christabel) or Edith Palliser (Hon Secretary). (In 1910, Fawcett had relinquished the Chairmanship of the Executive Committee to Palliser.) It was just as the date for the women's massive demonstration at Trafalgar Square neared that Frances's sister Vi became ill and died, and Frances missed this great event, which was attended by at least 10,000 people.[1076]

The outcome of the debate on Shackleton's Conciliation Bill, when it finally arrived, was positive for women, but the speeches – especially by some Members who were supposed to be supporters of the Cause – were disappointing for many. Not only did Asquith make an impressive speech against it,[1077] but Churchill and Lloyd George, erstwhile supporters, opposed the bill because it was 'anti-Democratic' and could not be amended. *Common Cause* drily observed,

'Lloyd George and Winston Churchill are our faithful friends, we know;
We did not notice it ourselves, they kindly told us so. . .'.[1078]

The best speakers for the women on this occasion were Arthur Balfour and Philip Snowden, Snowden being considered 'brilliant in his defense' of the bill.[1079]

When the vote was taken, the women's measure passed 299-189 – a good result, but it could have fared better: there were, supposedly, 407 supporters in the House, and the bill was considered a non-partisan effort. The true extent of their problem could be seen when the House voted 320-175 to commit the bill to a Committee of the Whole House, thereby effectively killing the bill unless the Government gave it facilities in the autumn. Frances gave Fawcett the bad news: '[Arthur] thought the best speaking was against us. . . . He understood the cabinet had taken the matter very seriously, all the more that they were so divided. . . . [T]he talk implied the bill was dead'.[1080] The greatest disappointment for Frances personally, though she made no reference to it, was probably the vote against the bill by Finlay, a former supporter of the Cause. It is not clear why Finlay became an opponent, but he was probably offended by the militants.

The Suffragists, believing that they had no other choice than to continue the agitation for facilities, campaigned throughout the summer for 'the Government to carry the Bill through its further stages during the autumn session',[1081] but all efforts were to no avail. The Liberals were now struggling with the House of Lords, a conflict that ended with a dissolution on 28 November 1910.

Possibly as an election ploy, Asquith answered a query in the Commons on 22 November 1910 saying, 'The Government will, if they are still in power, give facilities in the next Parliament for effectively proceeding with the Bill if so framed as to permit of free amendment'.[1082] That same day, the militants went on another rampage, this time mobbing Asquith and Birrell, whose knee was injured in the melee. Having spoken with Birrell after the attack, Frances reported that he 'spoke with extreme disgust of the senselessness of their conduct and said it had cooled him to the Cause', petulantly asserting, "'I was their best friend in this beastly Cabinet . . .'".[1083]

Suffragists worked the second election of 1910 knowing that the new Government, whether Liberal or Conservative, would have a mandate on women's suffrage.[1084] The results of the General Election were fairly favourable to the women. Each of the two major parties won 272 seats, and, though the number of declared supporters of suffrage was reduced, 323 Members were 'prepared to vote for a woman's suffrage bill on the lines of the Conciliation Bill'.[1085] The first task, however, was to alter the Bill to silence its critics. Therefore, an 'improved' Conciliation Bill was crafted, omitting the £10 qualification, allowing the Bill to be amended, and '[prohibiting] a husband and wife from registering in the same parliamentary borough or county constituency'.[1086]

To garner the greatest support in the Commons for their Bill, the NUWSS asked their affiliates to secure as many resolutions in favour of the women's Bill as possible from towns, counties, and district councils. The affiliates eventually got 146 councils to support their Bill,[1087] including those in Glasgow and Edinburgh in Scotland, and Manchester, Liverpool, Birmingham, and Newcastle in England. In London, nine borough councils also followed suit.

When the vote on a second reading of the Bill finally came up on 5 May 1911, it was almost a non-event: the vote was 255 to 88, giving the suffragists a majority of 167 votes. The suffragists were jubilant; Mrs Fawcett wrote to Frances: 'Yes, it really is quite glorious and I feel we are nearing the end of our long fight'.[1088]

But, as the women already knew too well, a favorable vote did not mean that Parliament would enfranchise women in a timely fashion, and indeed, the Government announced on 29 May that no additional facilities would be made available during the rest of the year but that 'a week' would be given the women's Bill in 1912. Once more, the women burned while Asquith fiddled!

To keep their Cause before the public and Parliament, the suffragists planned another massive demonstration in London on 17 June 1911, timed to coincide with the presence of large numbers of visitors in the city for the Coronation, scheduled for 22 June. In an unusual demonstration of unity, 'all the Societies working for Women's Suffrage for the first time took part' in what was labeled 'the largest procession of women ever seen' in London.[1089] *The Scotsman* declared that 'The National Union of Women's Suffrage Societies had the largest contingent of all, the numbers running into thousands',[1090] and Frances was again one of its three leaders (with Fawcett and Lady Beatrice Kemp, wife of the Member in charge of the women's bill). It was a strenuous event for her, but she found humour in the undertaking: 'It was a long march for me, and many doubted if I could win through. . . . One daughter followed in a carriage. . . . I believe the carriage was meant to pick up my pieces'.[1091] Frances too was optimistic about the women's chances at this point. **'I think [the procession] is our last and that we are to get [the vote]'.**

Despite all their optimism, the suffragists' leaders still faced numerous challenges in late 1911. Lloyd George disliked the Conciliation Bill and began promoting a more generous women's measure (many politicians believed that the current bill would mainly assist the Conservative Party). With many Liberals still urging substantial electoral reform, Asquith announced on 17 November that the Government would introduce a Franchise Reform bill in 1912 that would end plural voting and give all adult males the vote. He also asserted that the bill could be amended to include women. Disappointed that women were not included in the legislation to begin with, the NUWSS managed to get Asquith's pledge that if such amendments were carried, 'the government would regard it as an integral part of the bill'.[1092]

The WSPU, however, incensed that the new Franchise Bill did not include women, ended their truce and, on 21 November 1911, broke a large number of windows in Government offices and some business premises; 220 women were arrested. The militants followed the window-smashing by heckling Lloyd George so badly when he spoke to the National Liberal Federation that he angrily bragged about having "'torpedoed the Conciliation Bill'".[1093] On 29 November, they continued their aggressive heckling, preventing Asquith from delivering a speech. These actions were the last thing the constitutionalists needed. Dismayed and irate, the NUWSS quickly issued a manifesto denouncing the actions of the WSPU. Fortunately, its energy spent, the WSPU suspended its militancy again in December.

The constitutional suffragists' success during this period [1910-1914] was reflected in the growth of the NUWSS and its affiliates. At the end of 1910, the National Union had 207 affiliated groups, and its membership stood at 21,571;[1094] by the end of 1911, it had 30,408 members.[1095] The National Union now sponsored the creation of federations of affiliated suffrage societies in various areas of the country as a more effective way to coordinate the work for women's enfranchisement in their regions. By the year's end, 15 federations had been created. The NUWSS gave the London Society federation status in 1912.[1096]

Frances took on yet another responsibility during these hectic years when she agreed in 1910 to become President of the Girls' Guildry, a forerunner of the Girls' Brigade. Very little is known about Frances's service to this organization because the archives of the organization do not cover her administration.[1097] She appears to have held the office of President at least until 1915, when Lady Tullibardine succeeded her.[1098]

Frances continued to address audiences on behalf of the women's Cause, but she did not speak as often in 1910 as she had in 1909. Still, considering the 56 times she was in London for meetings of the Divorce Commission and the obligations she shouldered following the death of her sister, her work for women's suffrage is impressive. She spoke for the Cause at least 39 times during the year; most of these speeches were delivered outside of London. She also attended at least 17 suffrage meetings during the year.

The lengthy *Coventry Standard's* coverage of Lady Frances's speech to the 'recently-formed' Coventry Branch on 3 May 1910 illustrates both her stature and the power of her name. Under the general heading 'Women and the Suffrage', a sub-head, also in large print, read, 'Lady Frances Balfour and the Coventry Branch'.[1099] The newspaper reported at length on her speech, in which Frances took aim at 'those who were against them' who said that 'woman's place was in the home'. Statistics and figures are always persuasive, as she knew; she argued that there were 'from two to five million women whose homes were made by their own hands and their own brain work, who had to labour long hours . . . to keep a decent home over their heads. . .'. It was 'mere irony and cruelty to say to them, "Stay at home". . . . [I]t was an injustice that women should live under laws and bear the burdens of a country in which they had neither voice nor power. . . '. After she addressed three drawing room meetings sponsored by the Glasgow and West of Scotland Association for Women's Suffrage in 1910, one hundred new members signed up.[1100]

In October, Frances delivered a particularly successful speech at Guilford, following a demonstration in favour of the Conciliation Bill. She noted that the Antis were in reality assisting the suffrage cause. Particularly useful, she said, was spokesman Lord Cromer's recent speech, which was 'the richest treat they had ever received'.[1101] Pointing out his hypocrisy, she said, '[i]t must have been very pleasant to the women who organized Lord Cromer's meeting to listen to him saying that they could not have any part in government because they were given to vague generalization and weak sentimentality and everything which unfitted them for making the platform upon which he himself was standing. [Laughter]' She concluded that 'His cries . . . were those of a beaten man.'

Even with all the personal tragedy in 1911 that sidelined her for almost four months, Frances still managed to attend 15 suffrage meetings and give at least 49 speeches. Together with Mrs Fawcett and George Lansbury, she spoke on suffrage to 'about 1,000' working women on 2 June, when she reminded them that 'Our bill is before the Nation. . . . We are not afraid of the Antis. No one need be afraid of anyone who is trying to prove a negative. . . '. She went on to assure them that 'Before [your] excellent babies are many months older, we are going to get the vote. . . . Let every woman here lay it on the conscience of her man to use his influence as a voter with his Member of Parliament'.[1102] The *Annual Report* of the London Society for 1911 identified this meeting as 'the most noteworthy' of the Society's meetings during the year, and reported that the audience 'rose to their feet to carry the Resolution with acclamation'.

Not only did Frances often speak at the launching of new suffrage committees, she was also asked to help with the formation of some branches. For example, she gave a speech to 'a large and influential gathering assembled at Coombe House' who were trying, with the help of Lady Edith Fox Pitt (who had offered to 'mother' it) to form a suffrage society in East Grinstead.[1103] In Oban, Scotland, she spoke at the founding meeting of a branch of the NUWSS. She also helped launch the first branch of the NUWSS on the Isle of Wight in October.[1104]

With her sister's biography completed in October, she began a hectic speaking schedule, the intensity of which exceeded her previous record. During the week of 24 through 31 October, she spoke at Talgarth, Kensington Town Hall, the Isle of Wight, Fareham, Newport, Brandon, and Colchester. Between 13 November and 5 December, she presided over the Annual Meeting of the London Society, spoke at 'Mrs Booth's meeting', and addressed audiences at Wandsworth, Winchester, Epsom, Kings Lynn, Goole, Perth, Glasgow, Lenzie, Ambrose, Blackburn, Beeston Castle, Chester, Frodsham, Blackpool, St Helens, Chorley, Gourock, and Kirkcaldy, speaking at least 20 times in 23 days. At the last meeting, in Kirkcaldy, she helped the suffragists win a debate with Antis by a vote of 161-131. Frances noted in her diary on 25 November that she was '**very tired and [in] pain**'. One might have expected her to be exhausted after such a tiring speaking schedule; yet her audiences heard a speaker who was always vigorous and fresh.

The first three months of 1912, which initially augured well for the women, instead became a period of conflict and uncertainty. First, Churchill began a campaign to settle the votes for women issue with a national referendum, which the suffragists bitterly opposed. There was too much uncertainty about who would vote and what would be voted on; the National Union feared that women would not win such a vote, even though their Cause was becoming increasingly popular. Irish Nationalists were also backing off their commitment to the women because they feared that time taken for the women's measure might adversely affect the passage of Home Rule in 1912. However, a referendum appealed to many Liberals, who saw it as a way to prevent a split in the cabinet and to remove the issue from national politics.

In the midst of all these threats, the Government announced in early February that it was postponing the Franchise and Registration Bill, which meant that the Conciliation Bill would precede the Government's electoral reform efforts. Disappointed, the suffragists nevertheless worked hard on behalf of the Conciliation Bill, holding numerous meetings (the London Society held 199 meetings in the first three months of 1912[1105]) and a procession at Richmond, where Lady Frances Balfour, Ethel Snowden, and John Cockburn spoke, 'all in their best form and that is saying much'.[1106]

But their efforts were not enough. On 1 March, the WSPU resumed its militancy, this time attacking private property as well as Government buildings. The suffragettes shattered windows of business establishments in the West End and, three days later, 'went on rampages in Knightsbridge and Kensington'.[1107] The constitutionalists could do little more than watch as their hopes, so high just a few months earlier, went down with the glass shards. Frances was furious with the militants. Seeking out Constance Lytton in St Stephen's Hall, she asked Con if she 'was now happy?'[1108] Frances heatedly wrote to Betty, 'I think they are all drunk with vanity and the love of going a-warring. . . . Selborne came to me in the House exclaiming their madness'.[1109]

On February 23, the constitutionalists had sponsored what one newspaper called '"the most impressive meeting held in London"'[1110]. Lloyd George was the principal speaker at this assembly, held in Albert Hall; £7,000 was collected.[1111] Once the WSPU's militancy began, however, defections from the Cause were many and damaging. Writing to Fawcett, Frances reported that the Archbishop of Canterbury, Haldane, Grey, and Asquith 'all agreed nothing more could be done this session for suffrage'.[1112] Some sympathetic MPs, like Sidney Buxton, did not want to be perceived as being intimidated by women,[1113] nor did they wish to appear to condone the efforts of the militants;[1114] they therefore either voted against the women's bill or abstained. Frances acknowledged to Fawcett, 'I don't believe we could be worse off than we are just now. There is a regular stampede'.[1115]

In answer to Margot Asquith, who apparently expressed anger at the actions of the militants, Frances penned a 16-page letter explaining the role of the militants in the fight for the vote. This statement is one of the most complete comments she ever made about the women's claims and the issue of militancy, and deserves review.

> . . . [W]e are very sensitive to our troubles just now. . . . Forty years of peaceful persuasion, and not one of our section of citizens to represent us in the Constitution. You said, [']the Reform Riots were caused by men having no vote.['] You can't have thought for a minute. The Commons have existed since the Middle Ages, and some men have always had the vote. When the Reform Bill [of 1832] came, those in the Commons fought for the class of voters who were desiring it; outside now, another class of voters, persons – citizens, are claiming it. They deny that men do or can represent them. They are taxed as individuals, let them have the representation of individuals. . . . Women help pay Members of Parliament, but have no voice in their election. Women pay insurance money, and have no power to dictate terms, as the doctors have with their votes, for instance. The laws which protect women are

inadequate. Divorce laws are unjust. Factory legislation presses on the voteless woman, and they <u>need</u> the vote, as much as the male citizens, even more because they are handicapped in many ways.

In 1832, the great manufacturing towns had no representation. I dare say Parliament said to them as you did to me, 'Every woman has a man to vote for her'. So, no doubt it was said to Birmingham, 'Old Sarum has two members and no population, consider yourselves as represented by the members of Old Sarum'. Oddly eno', they were not content to take that advice. They burnt Bristol, and stoned Wellington's House, and even Downing Street. 'These people are unfit to have the vote, they are revolutionists', shouted Parliament. But the country said, ['T]heir claim is just, though their methods of asserting it, are wrong.['] Of course, it is wrong, but unfortunately every revolution has come with the surface of the waters troubled. The Reformation had its iconoclastic mobs. The Commonwealth had its wars. The Reform Bill, its riots, the reform of S. Africa, its Jamieson's Raid, Home Rule has had its course 'tracked in blood', and the Reform Bill for the women citizens is coming to us, not as we would have wished it, but because the people will no longer be patient under injustice. I wish it had come otherwise, this wave of turbulence may make it more difficult to attain . . . . [1116]

Frances trenchantly and succinctly summed up her point: '. . . [I]f women legislated for men, do you think men's interests would get proper notice?' Margot later wrote in her autobiography that 'Lady Frances Balfour [was] one of the few women of outstanding intellect that she had known. . . '.[1117]

When the vote was finally taken on the Second Reading of the Conciliation Bill on 28 March 1912, the women's measure lost by 14 votes. The women's disappointment was profound, and virtually everyone blamed the militants – who were, indeed, probably the greatest contributors to the bill's rejection, but they were not the only guilty parties. Forty-one Irish Nationalists, usually faithful to the women, voted against the bill 'to avoid the possibility of Asquith's resigning'.[1118] Moreover, strikes in the North caused 16 Labour MPs to be absent when the vote was taken; these Labour Members alone could have saved the bill. And with 10 more Unionists voting for the Conciliation Bill in 1912 than had supported it in 1911, the bill's failure must be attributed to the militants and to the Liberal/Labour/Nationalist camp. In retrospect, it seems that this check on the women's Cause probably emboldened those Members who were somewhat reluctant supporters to move permanently into the ranks of opponents.

In Worcester, where she was speaking for the Cause, Frances learned of the women's loss from a newspaper headline: 'No Votes for Women'. She declared, 'It turned me rather green. I had not really expected it. . .' . In quite an understatement, she went on, '[T]he check is a considerable one'.[1119] The women's predicament was reflected in a limerick contest, which was apparently about Frances.

> *There's a lady whose name's in Debrett*
> *She became a great suffragette*
> *She walked and she talked*
> *She wrote and she spoke*
> *But Adam is adamant yet.[1120]*

The winning line – the last line – was among two thousand answers.

Given her great interest in religion, it was inevitable that Frances would be one of those instrumental in enrolling Scottish Churches in the women's Cause. During the 1912 General Assembly, the Scottish Churches League for Woman's Suffrage was formed, with Lady Frances Balfour appointed President. The object of the League was 'to unite on a non-party basis members or adherents of any of the Scottish Churches who are in favour of woman suffrage, in order to secure for women the Parliamentary vote on the same conditions as men'.[1121] Church suffragists in Scotland, however, found it was not easy to sway the Establishment in any of the nation's churches.

The women's setback of 1912 not only ended the possibility of a non-party solution to the suffrage issue, but for the NUWSS necessitated a new political approach to women's enfranchisement.[1122] With the Franchise Bill pending in the Commons, the suffragists had to take steps to prevent another failure like the previous one, in which 42 'best friends' had voted against the Conciliation Bill and 91 had abstained.[1123] Fawcett, who noted that the Labour Party was the only party officially committed to women's suffrage, now decided it was time to let the Liberals know the extent of the suffragists' disappointment by concluding a pact with the Labour Party. On 14 May 1912, the day that the Government's Franchise and Registration Bill was introduced, the Executive Council voted to create the Election Fighting Fund (EFF), which the National Union would use to 'vigorously' support individual Labour candidates 'against Liberals whose records on Women's Suffrage were unsatisfactory'.[1124] The NUWSS did not work against all Liberals, as the WSPU advocated, but only those who proved to be Antis. Fawcett believed that only in this manner could women put pressure on the Liberal Party to put its votes where its pledges were. Of course, this tactic meant three-sided contests – a prospect which the Liberals, whose hold on the

Commons was already tenuous, could not welcome. The suffragists believed that this policy would also put pressure on the Irish, who feared that the loss of Liberal seats would jeopardize Home Rule.

Initially, Frances was not impressed with this new policy. A staunch opponent of Socialism, Frances would not have been pleased about any plan to assist Socialists politically, and she was not alone in the NUWSS. Unlike those loyal Liberals who were publicly unenthusiastic about the plan, like Eleanor Rathbone,[1125] or others who resigned (144 members of the London Society, including Miss Emily Davies, resigned between January 1913 and October 1913[1126]), she said little against it at the time – though she may have thought that the suffragists were again ignoring the Conservative Party – 'and continued to speak' (19 times in the six weeks after it was adopted) and otherwise to work for women's enfranchisement. The NUWSS had some success using the Fund: in three of four by-elections in 1912, the results were undoubtedly influenced by their work. In Crewe and Midlothian, both Liberal candidates lost their seats as a result of Labour's contesting the race.[1127]

The major hurdle was, of course, the Franchise Bill, and again the women made every effort to secure the passage of one of four amendments proposed to secure votes for some women. The suffragists hoped that the Dickinson Amendment, which would give votes to all women over age 25 who were householders or wives of householders, would be passed: it would enfranchise approximately six million women. If it failed, however, the women were willing to fall back on the Conciliation Amendment (now the Lyttleton Amendment), which would qualify only women householders – approximately 1 million women. (Frances noted that Arthur was prepared to vote for the Dickinson Amendment.[1128])

In Scotland, Betty and Frances were actively working to counter a large anti-suffrage meeting held in St Andrew's Hall, Glasgow, in November. On 9 December, '[t]he Scottish Federation, the Conservative and Unionist Women's Franchise Association, and the Glasgow and West of Scotland Association worked together to make a pro-suffrage demonstration a success'.[1129]

In the midst of the suffragists' preparations to secure passage of one of the women's suffrage amendments, the WSPU again upstaged them, injecting a new dimension into their militancy: they began an arson campaign. Once more the suffragists' leaders asked the militants to call a truce, and once more the militants spurned them, until they were finally prevailed upon to desist in January 1913.[1130]

Though the NUWSS sponsored an impressive rally at Albert Hall and held 137 meetings during one week in October 1912,[1131] all their efforts went down to defeat when the Speaker of the House, James Lowther, ruled on 27 January 1913 that a women's amendment would alter the Bill so much that the Government would have to withdraw the Bill and re-introduce it in another form. In the uproar which followed, the Liberals not only withdrew their Franchise Bill but offered the women time for a private bill, which the women refused, knowing that any bill which was not sponsored or supported by the Government would never pass. The women may have been betrayed again – but there was recompense. As Frances succinctly put it, 'The Speaker's ruling made the Government withdraw their Franchise Bill and proved they will never be able to touch that subject again without dealing with the women'.[1132] The Asquith Government never did get its much-desired franchise reform.

In past analyses of how the Labour Party came to replace the Liberal Party in the early 20th century, most of the attention has been given to the grievances of male workers. Few have acknowledged the role that suffragists played in changing the political climate. However, as Martin Pugh noted, 'thousands of women were recruited' into the Labour Party's women's organizations in the post-war period.[1133] Not only was this a 'long-term benefit of the 1912 pact'[1134], it was also a by-product of the Liberal Party's betrayal of the suffragists.

The militants grabbed the headlines again on Derby Day, 4 June 1913, this time through an independent effort by one individual. During the home stretch of the Derby race, Emily Wilding Davison rushed onto the course, placing herself in front of the King's horse, Anmer.[1135] The jockey was unable to avoid her, and Davison, seriously injured, died on 8 June. On a speaking tour with Victor Lytton the next day after the race, Frances referred to the incident: 'I said a word as to her courage at one of my meetings which made people say I agreed with the militants. I don't but I think they teach us the old story that what people will die for has behind it ultimate success'.[1136]

Frances had the satisfaction in 1913 of seeing one of the committees on which she laboured conclude its work. On 3 June, 'the recommendation of the Executive Committee [of the Freedom of Labour Defence] that the active work of the society should cease'[1137] was accepted because it was believed that the committee's work was no longer needed. There was 'a note of triumph' in Frances's address at the final meeting. Noting that the FLD's success had left it without scope for further work, she asserted that this 'was the greatest justification of its existence'.[1138]

The National Union further energized the Cause by sponsoring pilgrimages from all over the country to London for a massive demonstration that suffrage for women was popular with the nation's women. Beginning 'at distant points'[1139] on 18 June 1913, bands of suffrage 'pilgrims' reached London on or before Saturday, 26 July, when some 70,000 women demonstrated in Hyde Park; 19 platforms (for 19 Federations) were provided. The pilgrimages were so successful that they have been declared the 'most spectacular single piece of propaganda undertaken by the NUWSS . . . '.[1140] The demonstration so affected Asquith that he consented to receive a deputation from the NUWSS, but 'nothing came of the effort, of course'.[1141]

The Richmond branch, of which Frances was President, was among those playing a prominent role in the pilgrimage. Two of the pilgrims' routes converged on 24 July on Richmond, where an open air meeting was held in the evening. The crowd was so large that the Society had to erect three platforms for the speakers. The following morning, Mrs Nott-Bower, one of their members, spoke from one of the 19 platforms in Hyde Park.[1142]

The NUWSS also began a shift in its arguments for women's enfranchisement, which heretofore emphasized individual rights and equality for women with men. Now the organization turned to arguments which stressed how women's lives would be helped by having the vote. Of course, Frances did not have to be re-programmed. A long-time student of Parliament, she was well aware of how much legislation there was on which women should have a say.

Frances understood that it would help the Cause if women used the votes and the political rights they already had. She often spoke about this problem and, in 1913, added her name and stature to a new organization, the Women's Municipal Party, formed to encourage women to stand and to vote in municipal, parish, and borough elections. The first chairman of the WMP, as the organization was called, was Consuelo, Duchess of Marlborough, nee Vanderbilt, who enlisted Frances as the Party's Vice President and also for its Executive Committee.[1143] WMP candidates were pledged to promote women's 'interests and . . . needs' at the local level but were non-party, meaning that they could 'vote according to their own political views' on all other questions.[1144] The same year the party was formed, the WMP put forward a Mrs Cassidy for a London City Council seat in Battersea. Cassidy polled twice as many votes as the Labour candidate, though she did not win the election, which went to a Moderate.[1145]

Frances had long been friends with the American-born Consuelo, and was, according to the Duchess, one of her favourite guests. Consuelo said that Frances had inherited 'a superior intelligence and an easy flow of talk' from her father, 'the eloquent Duke of Argyll'.[1146] Frances herself 'was a stimulating person' with whom 'it was my fortune to work . . . on several committees, and at meetings to share the honours of public speaking. Invariably she was amusing, shrewd and witty, leaving the boring marshalling of facts to my patient chairmanship'.[1147] On the issue of militancy, the Duchess broke rank with her mother Alva, a supporter of Mrs Pankhurst: "'[Frances] held my views on women's suffrage . . . believing in the more conservative approach rather than in the distressing exhibitions of martyrdom which were shocking society. . . '".[1148]

The suffragists, working harder than ever before (the London Society held 351 meetings between 20 December 1912 and October 1913[1149]), focused on politics for the rest of the 1913-1914 period. One of the main objects of their attention was now the Conservative Party. In 1914, Frances's long-time colleague and relative, Selborne, agreed to introduce in the House of Lords a woman's suffrage bill giving votes to women based on the municipal register,[1150] and the measure - essentially the Conciliation Bill - was successful beyond the expectations of the suffragists. Expected to be roundly defeated, it lost by only a 104 to 60 vote. Most importantly, 30 Conservatives had voted for the measure, as had six bishops. With this encouragement, the suffragists set out to convince the Conservative Party to promise a women's suffrage bill if they were returned to power in the next General Election. By August 1914, however, the Conservative Party had not endorsed any of the plans, all of which called for some type of referendum. In truth, the suffragists' efforts were probably too late.

Militancy in Scotland did not begin until 1913, but one incident perpetrated by the suffragettes in 1914 was particularly upsetting to Frances, who otherwise wrote little about the audacious attacks on property made by the suffragettes as they escalated their militancy. In the early morning of 26 February 1914, suffragettes ignited two bombs in Whitekirk Church in East Lothian, destroying all of the building except the stone walls and one porch. '[T]he suffragettes made it clear that the act was a response to the first case of forcible feeding [of Ethel Moorhead] in Scotland'.[1151] A reward of £100 was offered for information about the identities of the suffragettes who burned the church and for 'the identification of their motor car'.[1152] However, the perpetrators remained unknown. (Since imprisonment and forcible feeding were taking a considerable toll, the suffragettes now engaged in 'hit and run' acts of violence. Very few were apprehended.)

Frances and Betty immediately sprang into action.[1153] As constitutionalists, they were determined to counter the bad press of the militants by leading the campaign to restore the 'Lantern of Lothian'. In a Letter to the Editor of *The Scotsman*, published on 2 March 1914, Frances declared that 'Whitekirk will be rebuilt'. She asserted that '"To call a halt" to its restoration [which had been suggested by a friend] would be to acknowledge defeat at the hands of those whose works and ways are evil and covered by the night of darkness'. Whitekirk was eventually rebuilt but, due to war-time constraints, not until 1917. Frances attended the re-dedication of Whitekirk Church with Alice on 18 October 1917.

Somewhat ironically, the chief beneficiaries of the press's obsession with the militants, and to a lesser extent, the Antis, were the constitutional women's suffrage societies, notably the NUWSS, whose numbers of societies and members grew significantly (411 societies and 42,438 members in 1912; 478 affiliated societies with 52,336 members in 1913; and 602 societies by August 1914).[1154] When the Friends of Women's Suffrage was added, the membership total of the NUWSS was 98,998.[1155] The WSPU, now declining in membership, had only 90 branches in 1913[1156]. Of course, the war interrupted the women's work the next year.

Frances's popularity among the suffragists is evident in her success in elections to the NUWSS Executive Committee. At least once between 1907-1909 (the vote count for some of these elections is unknown), she headed the polls, as she did again in 1910 and 1912, even though she could only attend six meetings in 1912.[1157] When she offered to go off the Executive,[1158] Mrs Fawcett assured her that 'We all feel you have been quite splendid in the great amount of work you have done for W[omen's] S[uffrage] during this last 12 months'.[1159] Not everyone agreed with Fawcett. The Cambridge Women's Suffrage Association had recorded in its Minutes of 1911 that it would not vote for Frances's re-election to the Executive Committee 'because she had so rarely attended the meetings'.[1160] The Society did, however, remark that 'if she were not re-elected, she should be named a Vice President'.

Fawcett had no trouble flattering Frances and probably wanted to have her name among the members of the Executive. However, it appears that the more popular Frances became, the more Fawcett began to marginalize her in the inner councils of the suffragists. When an NUWSS deputation met with Asquith, a friend, on 27 November 1911 to discuss the proposed Reform Bill, Frances '**was not on it**'. Frances was also not on the platform or in attendance at either of the large meetings held in Albert Hall in 1912 (February and November). By this time, of course, Arthur Balfour was no longer head of the Unionist/Conservative Party, and this may have been the major reason Fawcett began to disregard Frances in the suffragists' work. Some proof of the cooling of the relationship may also be found in the considerable decrease of correspondence between the two women. (If the holdings of the letters which passed between the two women are reasonably complete in The Women's Library, there was a dearth of letters after early 1912).

It is not surprising that Frances wrote more letters to Fawcett than Fawcett did to her from 1889 through 1918 (106 from Frances to Fawcett; 23 from Fawcett to Frances, though some of Fawcett's were apparently not preserved); after all, one of Frances's chief duties was to liaise with Members of Parliament and report to Fawcett. It is also possible that some of the decline was due to Fawcett's championing of the NUWSS-Labour Pact during 1912. However, considering that 44 letters passed between the two women between 1907 and 1911, it is a bit shocking that the women corresponded *only three times* between 19 March 1912 (during the lead-up to the Conciliation Bill debacle) and January 1918.

The suffrage Cause often enjoyed great success when Frances spoke. In 1913, Frances participated in the winter campaign of the Scottish Federation of the NUWSS, which began in September. With Nell Hunter and Helen Fraser, Frances joined in a tour of the Highlands from Inverness to Kirkwall on Orkney. On 11 September 1913, she gave a 'witty speech' which 'delighted the audience' and 'added many new members' to the Dornoch Society for Women's Suffrage.[1161] In October, at Dingwall, the constitutionalists in the city 'witnessed [their] largest ever suffrage meeting – an assembly of 500 – with Frances Balfour as the speaker'.[1162]

On 20 February 1914, Frances found herself again debating Pott, this time at Bournemouth, where the coverage was extensive. Pott argued that those who elected the legislators needed to put the community before the individual. She also asserted that 'what was most necessary in the good voter was that they should be mixing mostly in the business side of life and this could not be said of women who were in the home'.[1163] Frances answered Pott by asking whether male voters put the community first when they cast a vote? She declared that 'the mass of the democracy need the vote to improve themselves',[1164] and that 'a good housewife was as good a business woman as a man was a good business man in his work'.

When the vote was taken – and one audience member asked if women could vote – Frances won the debate 240-115. (In fact, Frances won every debate she entered when a vote was taken.) She recorded in her diary that she **'was popular'**, a fact which appeared to surprise her. After the debate, Frances was 'much distressed' by the 'bad manners' of the organizers, who gave her a large bouquet of flowers but did not give one to Pott.[1165] Frances did not have to wait long to see Pott join the National Union, to which in 1916 she reported on women's work in agriculture in her district for the Women's Interest Committee.[1166]

Frances took a leave of absence from the Travellers' Aid Society from 1912-1914 in order to be free to concentrate on votes for women. Out of 84 speeches delivered in 1912, she spoke on 43 occasions between October 3 and December 14. In 1913, she spoke at least 59 times, and in 1914, she spoke 35 times between 28 January and 11 July, when she went to Tiree. By the time she had returned from Tiree, however, Britain was at war, and the whole scheme of work for the suffragists changed.

CHAPTER 13

'We go from shock to Shock' [1167]
(1914-1918)

'Every name connected with ours now
has representatives in both services'. [1168]

'[Women] can face what war means. . . '. [1169]

World War I took Britain by surprise.

Lady Frances Balfour's chief anxiety was, of course, Oswald, who shipped out on 11 August, the first day that British Expeditionary Forces (BEF) crossed the English Channel. He was in the 2nd Battalion, King's Royal Rifle Corps (60th Rifles), serving in the 2nd Infantry Brigade, 1st Division, BEF.[1170] Ruth's fiancé, Bill Balfour, shipped out on 12 August; both young men would take part in some of the earliest fighting on the Western front. 'The Great War', as World War I is usually called in Britain, had an immense impact on the nation, and particularly on the aristocracy, which lost a disproportionate number of its young men. 'Every name connected with ours now has representatives in both services',[1171] she wrote in September; ultimately, at least 22 family members served in the conflict.

In the early days of the war, Frances did her bit on Tiree, first consulting with the factor Hugh MacDiarmid about a recruiting party. Later, she spoke about the war at meetings held at two of the island's churches, all the while awaiting word from Oswald, from whom she finally received two letters at the end of August. **'Laus Deo'**, she wrote in her diary.

On 17 September, Frances received news she had dreaded: Oswald had been wounded in the fighting at the Aisne River, to which the Germans had retreated after being halted at the Battle of the Marne. Unprepared for war or casualties, wounded British soldiers were initially at a great disadvantage. Oswald, who was mentioned in the dispatches, related that, after taking a bullet in the jaw, he had

> . . . stayed in the firing line for over an hour with [my jaw bone] constantly slipping right out of my mouth. Another officer came up finally, and that enabled me to crawl away before I was too weak. I crawled and walked . . . to a village about a mile behind the firing line. Half way to the village I met a doctor who shoved the bone back into my mouth . . . . I walked on to the village, and there I sat on the ground in the garden of a house all day . . . . We were helped into the house which contained 60 wounded, and we lay on the bare boards all night. By that time we were . . . so weak that we could not move; my throat was so swollen that I could not swallow at all. By some oversight there was not a single doctor, or R.A.M.C. Orderly in that house . . . . At about noon the next day, the ambulances began to arrive, but there was only room for the cases that could not possibly walk, so I refused the seat they offered me, and hung on to the flap of the ambulance for the four mile walk, . . . a most unpleasant walk . . . . The German guns . . . searching the road . . . . [Then we were put into lorries] and carried . . . 25 miles. . . . We were all night, next day, next night in the [hospital] train, and also a bit of next morning going 50 miles to Versailles. . . . [At] the hospital . . . even I was not worried about for another 24 hours, ... I have lost a wedge of bone and a tooth, but they have pulled it together . . . .[1172]

On 17 November 1914, Frances reported to Frank that Oswald, who was mentioned in General French's dispatch of 21 October, was 'one of only 20 2nd Lieutenants in the list'.[1173]

British losses were considerable: between 12 September and 8 October, they lost 561 officers and 12,980 men.[1174] Among the officers serving in the fighting under Col Eric Serocold, only Oswald had survived the onslaught.[1175] Family members killed included George Cecil, only son of Violet and Edward Cecil, on 1 September 1914[1176;] Aymer Maxwell, Mary Percy's husband, in October; and John Balfour, elder brother of Bill ('shot through the head while speaking to the Adjutant'[1177]) on 8 October.

When Secretary of War Kitchener, who disliked the Territorial armies, was pressured by Field Marshall French to utilize soldiers who at least had some training, he finally agreed to 'select two Territorial Divisions composed of the best units'.[1178] In September 1914, 'the first Territorial Infantry battalion in France' was the London Scottish.[1179] Eustace would have been proud.

The now-elder statesman Arthur Balfour also served, accepting Asquith's invitation in early October 1914 to join the Committee of Imperial Defence, which Arthur himself had created in 1902. This body shortly evolved into a smaller War Council to direct the war planning; Arthur was again a member.

As part of an effort by the suffragists to encourage women to do their duty,[1180] Frances published an article in the *Daily Mail* on 'What Women Can Do' to assist the struggle. Her main message was that 'Women should hold nothing back'. Their sons, she said, were 'given to the Mother, and she in her turn must give them to the country in time of adversity'.[1181] She also encouraged women to take up their own roles: 'the place that women fill has been altered' since the Crimean War. '[Women] have now trained heads and educated minds. . . . They can face what war means . . .'. She also acknowledged that British women, who would have 'the glorious duty of succouring the wounded in body and . . . in spirit', would fulfill this traditional role as well in support of their country.

In April 1915, Oswald, having recuperated, returned to France, where the deadly conflict had settled into trench warfare, and there was stalemate on the Western Front. Nevertheless, commanders on both sides believed that they could still overwhelm their enemy and achieve victory, and launched repeated campaigns to try to end the war.

Like families all over the British Isles, the Balfours regularly received from their soldier-sons letters conveying some of the desperation of the fighting men. In his 15 May 1915 letter, Oswald, now in a command position, gave this heart-rending description: 'We have gone 26 days in the trenches [fighting for Aubers Ridge], which means no night sleep and you rarely . . . get more than 2 hours consecutively by day. The men . . . need refitting terribly as their feet are so swelled up with never getting their boots off that they have cut them. . . .'.[1182] He further added, 'This is the second day's pouring rain and the place resembles a London Sewer'.

The Germans used chlorine gas for the first time on the Western Front in the Second Battle of Ypres (on 22 April 1915). Arthur and Alice sent Oswald a respirator, one which he asserted had 'the most excellent pattern [he] had yet seen'.[1183] Fighting in this battle, Oswald was 'hit [in the upper chest[1184] on the last day] during a so-called counter-attack, was bandaged by a stretcher-bearer and, with his help, walked a little over a mile into Ypres, bleeding a lot'.[1185] He was eventually treated in Hasebrouck, in northern France.[1186] Again mentioned in the dispatches, Oswald finally got to London on 18 June to finish his recuperation.

Low supplies and poor quality ammunition plagued the British Army in the early days of 1915. Thus, British forces had to conserve or ration their supplies until manufacturers back home could produce the millions of shells needed for both the artillery bombardments – which preceded the frontal attacks – and the attacks themselves. Bill Balfour's words on the subject were harsh: '[T]he 8000 we lost the first day unavailingly should be written on Asquith's tombstone for saying we had plenty of ammunition. . . '.[1187] 'You simply can't think how infernally helpless one is without ammunition.'[1188] Quality was also on the soldier's minds. Noting that '8 out of 10 shells did not explode', Oswald fumed to Baffy, 'our artillery is rotten [underlined 3 times]'.[1189] Criticisms such as these must have been part of the fodder for Lord Northcliffe, 'the Napoleon of Fleet Street',[1190] in his launch of the 'Shells Scandal' in the *Daily Mail* and *The Times*, which helped bring about a Coalition Government in 1915.

In the new National Government partnership announced on 26 May 1915, Arthur Balfour replaced Churchill at the Admiralty, and Lloyd George held the newly-created position of Minister for Munitions. Frances diagnosed the chief political problem of the nation as a lack of leadership. 'There is no born leader amongst any of the men. . . . The best men are too balanced, the young men too rash'.[1191]

With higher wages and overtime pay due to war needs, allegations soon surfaced that some workers were spending part of their increased income on alcohol, to the presumed detriment of the nation's industrial productivity. In response, licensing laws limited the hours for serving alcohol in pubs, forbade treating, raised prices, and diluted beer. The Central Control Board's efforts were so successful that drunkenness was diminished by one-half within 18 months and by more than 80 percent by the end of the war.[1192]

The deaths of close friends of the Balfours and Campbells were a constant heartache throughout the war. In 1915, Frances noted that the Desboroughs were 'the 1st of our immediate circle to lose two' sons.[1193] In a letter of sympathy to Etty, Frances noted that, traveling down the Clyde, she had read Etty's son Julian's verses in *The Times* while

> the sunset light was everywhere – light at eventide. So it will be with you. Thro' the grave and gate of this death you will pass into the peace and light with him and for him. There is something very wonderful in motherhood today. We were given our children at a time when they would be ready to fight the good fight. Their half day's march is done, and it is given to us to know that what we have given of ourselves, has done its duty . . . .[1194]

Ruth, who wed Bill during a short Christmas leave in 1914, was not the only member of 'Us Four' to be married during the war. On 8 March 1915, Joan informed her mother that Edward Lascelles, second son of the Earl and Countess of Harewood, wanted to marry her **'before next Monday'**. A Lieutenant in the Rifle Brigade,

Eddy visited Frances on 10 March, and afterward she declared, '**I liked him**'. Joan and Eddy were married in St Columba's on 11 March. Arthur gave the bride away and hosted a luncheon for the couple, but there was 'no large reception'.[1195]

Because German East Africa shared a border with Kenya and Uganda, war also came to British East Africa, where Alison and the Savage lived. The campaign was severe, and the Milnes sent their young daughter, Elizabeth, to England to live with Frances for the child's safety. Elizabeth and her nanny, Bertha Barrett, arrived in London in September 1915. Elizabeth quickly won her grandmother over. Though she found Elizabeth to be 'the strongest willed child' she had ever come across,[1196] Frances fondly recorded while at Tiree that '[s]he grows in height, notably in vigour, and in good looks'; 'she is an amazing piece of iniquity'.[1197]

Frank Balfour was now in the Sudan Political Service (SPS); as one of the few civilian officials in the Sudan, he was not eligible for service in World War I. Frank had been a good candidate for the SPS, 'the elite among British African administrations'.[1198] An 'active young man, endowed with good health, high character and fair abilities',[1199] he could also 'withstand the essential loneliness of the bush D[istrict] C[ommissioner]'s life',[1200] accommodating himself, for instance, to a great variety of lodgings and placements. He described Tendik, where his accommodations were 'planted about all over the landscape', as 'a lonely place . . . 4 days to the nearest white man and 3 to the railway . . . '.[1201] His first posting was as 2nd Inspector of Berber Province, an Intelligence position.

Despite the general loneliness of his job, Frank had his share of excitement while serving as 2nd Inspector to the newly-created Nuba Mountains Province in 1915. He was tasked with bringing in Fiki Ali, the Mek (or chief) of the Miri Nuba, who were planning an attack on the British;[1202] Fiki Ali fled to avoid being hanged. When it appeared that he had 'lost prestige by bolting',[1203] and after a peaceful meeting designed by Frank, Ali finally surrendered. For his essential role in this venture, Frank was subsequently awarded the Sultan's new Nile decoration. Sir Reginald Wingate, Governor-General of the Sudan, praised Frank's courage and congratulated Frances on 'having a very capable and gallant son . . . who should go far'.[1204] The next year he was posted to Gedaref, near the Abyssinian border, where civil war was raging between Emperor Haile Selasse, supported by the British, and Lij Yasu (Scottice MacJesus), 'a pretender' backed 'by the Germans'.

In 1915, Frances's brother George, to whom she was closest, succumbed to pneumonia, and 1916 opened with more sad news. Her nephew Ivar Campbell, only son of George and Sybil, was killed at the ineptly-fought battle of Kut al Amarna in Mesopotamia on 8 January.

Oswald, at last recovered, returned to the fighting on 29 January 1916. He was now deployed to Salonika in the eastern area of Macedonia near Stavros. Despite punishingly cold or scorching hot weather and difficult terrain, on balance conditions were better for Oswald and his troops in the Sturma zone than in France, because they saw only 'limited' action.[1205] Oswald shared Frances's love of flowers and at one point sent her 'iris roots which just poked their glorious blue flowers through one fall of snow'.[1206] He noted that it was 'a rotten present [for her birthday] . . . with one merit[:] that you can't ask its price and offer to pay it!' Frances called them her 'blue regiment of soldiers'.[1207]

On 7 March 1916, just four days after Frances learned that Alison was expecting her second child in August, Savage wired that Alison needed to have her appendix removed. Unfortunately, the fetus was placenta-deprived during Alison's appendectomy, and daughter Catriona Margaret Balfour Milne, born on 9 September, suffered physical difficulties throughout her life.[1208]

Now on Tiree, Frances began to record the results of food scarcity caused by German submarine attacks on British shipping. 'We adhere to one dish for each meal, and try not to have afternoon tea, but often "fall"'.[1209] That summer and autumn, she took up fishing. Once, she caught 14 saithe, declaring that she enjoyed 'the excitement'.[1210]

From 24-30 April 1916, the attention of most British citizens was diverted from the war to the Easter Rising in Ireland, when Irish rebels attempted to win the independence of Ireland while British troops were preoccupied by the war effort. Some 16,000 British troops were rushed to Ireland and routed the 1,600 rebels in five days. As this excitement wound down, the Battle of Jutland – the largest naval battle in history – ended with the German fleet retreating under the cover of night. Thereafter, the German military concentrated on submarines to attack and destroy British vessels. British citizens, who had no idea that Secretary of War Kitchener was at sea, were stunned on 6 June to learn that he had died when the ship on which he was sailing to Russia struck a mine and went down. Frances, writing to Frank, declared, 'We go from shock to shock . . .'.[1211] Lloyd George replaced Kitchener, and shortly thereafter, Arthur – knowledgeable but cautious – was replaced by Sir Eric Geddes as First Lord of the Admiralty.

Frances would have been reminded continually of what was going on in the war: the distressing letters from family members serving on almost every front were circulated among family members at home. Writing to Ruth about the Somme on 24 July 1916, Bill Balfour asserted, 'One can read about the guns at Verdun but until you see a really big lot one simply cannot imagine it . . . '.[1212] He tellingly added, '[Y]ou can have no idea what absolute hell a modern big battle is'.

Inveraray Castle in Spring
By kind permission of the Duke of Argyll.

Photo by Nick McCann

Elizabeth, Duchess of Argyll
By kind permission of the Duke of Argyll
Photo by Nick McCann

George, 8th Duke of Argyll
By kind permission of the Duke of Argyll
Photo by Nick McCann

Princess Louise, daughter of Queen Victoria
By kind permission of the Duke of Argyll
Photo by Nick McCann

Lady Mary Campbell and Lady Frances Campbell
Portrait by W B Richmond
By kind permission of the Duke of Argyll
Photo by Nick McCann

Lady Victoria Campbell

Lord George Campbell

VIII

1865 or 1866 Photo of some Campbell family members at the Rose Arch in the Garden at Inverary Castle

By kind permission of the Duke of Argyll. Faded detail digitally retrieved by David Cockeroft.

Top row: Lord Shaftesbury, Lady Archibald Campbell, and Elizabeth, Duchess of Argyll
Second row: Lady Frances Campbell and Edith, Countess Percy
Third row: Lady Mary Campbell (side view), Lord Archibald Campbell, and Lady Constance Campbell
Fourth row: Duke of Leinster and the Marquis of Lorne, afterwards 9th Duke of Argyll

Frances and Eustace in Canada

'F. B.' photography by Lord Battersea

XI

Eustace Balfour and Cromach

Oswald Balfour

Frank Balfour

Baffy with Frances and Michael

Lady Frances Balfour 1906
By kind permission of Andrew Michael Brander

1908 Suffrage Procession led by Lady Frances Balfour and Mrs Millicent Garrett Fawcett
'By kind permission of the British Library Board,
Illustrated London News, June 1908

15th March. 1907.

National Union of Women's Suffrage Societies.

WOMEN'S SUFFRAGE.

GREAT MEETING,
QUEEN'S HALL, Tuesday, March 26th,
at 8 p.m.

Chair.—MRS. FAWCETT, LL.D.

Speakers.—THE LADY FRANCES BALFOUR.
MR. CAMERON CORBETT, M.P.
MR. GEORGE BERNARD SHAW.
LADY BAMFORD SLACK.
MR. PHILIP SNOWDEN, M.P.
MISS FRANCES STERLING.
MR. W. H. DICKINSON, M.P.
And others.

TICKETS—5s., 3s., 2s., 1s., and 6d.,
to be obtained at
WOMEN'S SUFFRAGE OFFICES,
25, VICTORIA STREET, WESTMINSTER, S.W.

From the Daily Graphic, 15 March 1907

EPH XXXIII. 2.32

CHURCH LEAGUE FOR WOMEN'S SUFFRAGE

(WIMBLEDON BRANCH).

A Public Meeting

will be held on

TUESDAY, JULY 2nd, 1918,

At 5.30, in the

"Home Field," No. 30 Arterberry Road

(By kind permission of Mrs. Finlay).

ADDRESSES on

"The Responsibility of the Vote"

will be given by

LADY FRANCES BALFOUR

. . and . .

The Rev. JOHN DREW ROBERTS

(Vicar of St. Andrew's, Wimbledon).

ALL ARE WELCOME.   WOMEN VOTERS ESPECIALLY INVITED.

(Note.—If wet the Meeting will be held indoors).

S.Y.   W. H. STOAKLEY AND CO., TYPS., WIMBLEDON.

Lady Frances in Vogue Magazine, published in early February 1921
By the kind permission of the British Library Board

Lady Frances and Dame Millicent Garrett Fawcett 1925
By kind permission of The Women's Library

17 Upper Grosvenor

Balfour Place

Wilton Crescent

Crown Court Church interior © David Cockroft

Women of Bible window

Whittingehame House
By kind permission of Paul Harris

Arthur Balfour
By kind permission of Mrs Alexander Lindsay

Gerald Balfour

George Frederic Watts   The Right Honourable Gerald William Balfour

oil on canvas   c.1898-99   Watts Gallery Trust

Alison Balfour
By kind permission of Mrs Alexander Lindsay

Joan, the Hon. Mrs. Edward Lascelles
Portrait by Philip de Laszlo
By the kind permission of the Trustees of the 7th Earl of Harewood Will Trust
and the Trustees of the Harewood House Trust.

Four generations of Lady Betty Balfour's family: Lady Edith Lytton, Lady Betty Balfour, Ruth Balfour, and Nora Balfour
By kind permission of Lord Henry Lytton Cobbold

The Savage, Nell, Kathleen, and Elizabeth, Fisher's Hill
By kind permission of Andrew Michael Brander

Aunt Evelyn, Nunkie, Ral, Joan and Eddy
By kind permission of Andrew Michael Brander

Frances wrote to Frank about the first use of 'caterpillar armoured motors', called 'tanks' by the British, which occurred on 15 September 1916 during the Battle of the Somme.[1213] Shortly thereafter, Frances learned that 'trials [of the tanks] were carried out with great secrecy and under close guard in Hatfield Park'.[1214] Also in September, Oswald, his luck running thin, was one of 162,000 soldiers[1215] who contracted malaria in marshy, eastern Macedonia; he was sent to Malta to recuperate.

The change of Government consumed Frances in late 1916. As military losses continued to mount, British citizens became more and more insistent that someone be put in charge who could bring the war to a victorious conclusion. The common sentiment was that Lloyd George had solved the munitions problems and had handled Labour, so why not let him lead the country? He quickly got the support of Labour and of key Unionists, including Arthur, whose support was probably 'the biggest part played in the crisis'.[1216] Balfour's reward was being made Foreign Secretary.

The change in the Government was awkward for Frances: Asquith, one of her close friends, was furious at the way he was ousted from power. Frances finally wrote directly to him, both with sympathy and political insight:

> My mind is constantly with you . . . . As between you and Lloyd George, there is no question which [Arthur] would rather serve with, but the question of the moment was ["]shall we back Lloyd George in forming a Government or shall we be without one", for [the Unionists] were convinced that in the state of feeling, you could not carry on as Prime Minister. . . [because there was] a growing conviction that your methods of governing could never end the war.[1217]

The year 1916 ended on a positive note for Frances. Lloyd George chose Finlay to be Lord Chancellor; thus, Frances saw one of her oldest friends 'established [on the Woolsack], . .'.[1218]

To counter the effects of the British naval blockade of their ports and to starve Britain out of the war, Germany resumed unrestricted submarine warfare 1 February 1917, and the US broke off relations with the country. In March, the Germans, now turning also on the US, sank seven American ships, and on 6 April, the US declared war. Almost immediately, the British cabinet decided to send to Washington DC '"someone of the highest status"' with '"entrée to all circles"'; and Arthur was that someone.[1219] His task was to win friends in the former colony and continue the dialogue begun with Wilson regarding war aims. Frances wrote to her son: 'The news of the week is the arrival of America. Now the greatest English-speaking race is one with the Allies'.[1220] Arthur's legendary charm served him well in the United States, and he was roundly praised for his work there. He '"established good rapport with Wilson"', and he was '"well received"' when he addressed the

House of Representatives, where the President of the United States joined the line to shake hands with him.[1221]

Though the war dominated the attention of British citizens at this time, their everyday lives went on. In 1916, Teddy Glyn retired as Bishop of Peterborough, and Frances travelled to the Bishop's seat to commemorate his last day in the city. January 1917 brought the safe return of the Milnes from Africa; Elizabeth was now reunited with her parents after having lived for almost a year and a half with her grandmother, time which was quite formative for her. To only this one grandchild did Frances show 'a side of gentleness and lovability'.[1222] There is no mystery as to why Elizabeth was her favourite: she had lived with her grandmother, and Frances had a role in rearing her. She was also a great comfort to Frances, who disliked living alone and enjoyed her companionship; Elizabeth was, Frances touchingly remarked, **'the child of my old age'**.[1223] It was after this year's trip to Tiree that Catriona, at last introduced to her British relatives, was christened, **'in glorious weather and by the Cross'**, in the Cathedral at Iona.[1224]

In 1916-1917, the casualty lists continued to contain names of friends and family members. The 1916 casualties included Bobby Palmer, son of the Selbornes, and Rupert Cecil, a second son of the William Cecils to die. In February 1917, Jim Balfour, younger brother of Bill, fell.

By this point in the war, the food crisis had become severe. It was estimated that in April 1917 Britain had only a six weeks' supply of food left. In answer to Germany's accelerated submarine attacks designed to starve Britain out of the war, Lloyd George ordered convoys to be attempted – an action the Admiralty had opposed. Fewer than one percent of the ships convoyed were destroyed; indeed, this action enabled Britain to survive and helped Lloyd George carry great political power into the post-war era.

In March, in their first major success in the war, British forces had finally captured Baghdad from the Turks.[1225] Four months later, Arthur informed Frances that Frank had been appointed to Mesopotamia (modern-day Iraq). It was an appointment, Arthur said, of 'high distinction'.[1226] Frank's immediate concern was his Arabic, but, once in Mesopotamia, he found that it 'goes down here very much better than I expected'.[1227] Frank was Assistant to the Oriental Secretary, 'the key Intelligence post'.[1228] Here he would work with the premier Iraqi 'expert', Major Gertrude Bell, the only woman with rank in the British army.[1229] Bell now included Frank in the political-social dinners she arranged at her home in Baghdad.[1230]

Frank's diplomatic talents and patience were tested in late March-early April 1918 by uprisings in the holy city of Nijf,[1231] which had resulted in the death of Capt W M Marshall, the Political Officer there. In April, for his work in pacifying the city,

Frank was awarded the Military Cross for his "'conspicuous gallantry'";[1232] later that year, he was made Military Governor of Baghdad.

Some mention must be made of the Balfour Declaration, suggested by Arthur Balfour, which was issued by the British Government on 2 November 1917. Arthur sccms always to have been 'an admirer of the Jews',[1233] and he had been converted to the Zionist aspirations of some British Jews by Chaim Weizmann. With the war situation dire in 1917, the British Government agreed to support Arthur's call for a homeland for the Jews in Palestine in return for the support of the international Jewish community and their help in settling Palestine for the British. The Declaration itself was in the form of a letter, which Arthur personally delivered to the President of the Zionist Federation in Britain, Lord Lionel Walter Rothschild, 2nd Baron:

> His Majesty's Government view with favour the establishment in Palestine of a national home for the Jewish people and will use their best endeavours to facilitate the achievement of this object, it being clearly understood that nothing shall be done which may prejudice the civil and existing religious rights of non-Jewish communities in Palestine, or the rights and political status enjoyed by Jews in any other country.[1234]

The residence of the Prime Minister of Israel in Jerusalem is located on Balfour Street.

The war's cost in human life again came home to Frances and her family in 1918 when the William Cecils lost a third son, Jack, on 27 September. Compounding the loss of life from the war, an influenza epidemic during summer 1918 took the lives of some 150,000 citizens, including Frances's beloved cook and **very faithful servant of 15 years**',[1235] Mary Macfarlane. Frances Dugdale, first-born grandchild of Frances, was also quite ill with the flu but survived.

The shortage of farm hands during the war was considerable, and Frances made at least one small effort to enlist young women in the work. At Sunderland House, Frances spoke in 1916 on behalf of the Country and Colonial Training School for Ladies. Noting that if women 'took up work to which they were unaccustomed they would fail', Frances urged the audience to give money for scholarships for needy girls 'with a love of agriculture'.[1236] This was a subject close to Frances's family: Eve Balfour, who read Agriculture at Reading University, was Bailiff on a farm in Monmouthshire which was run by women for the war effort.

On 15 February 1918, Elizabeth returned with her family to Kenya, and Frances lost her beloved companion for the time being. Just as soon as she believed that Elizabeth might be back home, Frances began sending letters to her 'darling' in which she attempted to teach her proper behavior and good manners. In one letter, she offered this bit of advice, 'You can never be too Forward running to do things for other people. You can never be too Backward in making other people do things for you'.[1237] Frances frequently corrected Elizabeth's spelling, and in one of her most remarkable lessons, included in her birthday presents to Elizabeth in 1919 some gifts *for her to give away,* asserting that it was better to give than to receive.[1238] In the same vein, Frances also urged that her chocolates, which were the chief treats she sent to Elizabeth and Catriona, be 'hand[ed] round'.[1239]

The British lines held in spring 1918, though they were pushed back to within sight - or sound - of Paris. Now desperate, the Allies belatedly achieved a unified command, with General Ferdinand Foch as the Supreme Commander of the Allied forces on the Western Front.

Frances, who by 1916 had ceased to write very much in her diary about the war, began to record much more about it in 1918. On 22 March, she noted that the Germans' **'[o]ffensive had begun'**; later, she recorded that they had gained 15 miles by 25 March. It was not until July that the Allied forces finally succeeded in stopping the German advance; on 8 August, the Allies began their counteroffensive and in September broke through the Hindenberg Line. On 25 September, she recorded the resignation of the Chancellor of Germany. She also wrote that that day, Oswald's birthday, was **'signalized by great success in Macedonia',** when the Austrians and Bulgarians were expelled from Greece. On 28 September, Palestine was **'free of the Turk',** and on 7 October the **'Germans [had] asked for an Armistice'.** When Armistice day finally arrived, Frances wrote only one word in her diary: **'Peace!'** The end of the 'Great War' had finally come. In response to Betty, who asked 'how London took the Armistice', she wrote, 'There is only one quotation which fitted it. "And with one start and with one roar, the royal city woke". Never shall I forget the instant rush of feet to the Palace and the surge-like cheers.'[1240]

On 15 December 1918, a Peace Thanksgiving was held at Albert Hall; Arthur read the verses from Ecclesiastes on the 'Praise of Famous Men'. Frances, who was in the audience, noted that when the list of Divisions was read, 'the best cheer was for the nurses mentioned in the 7th Division',[1241] many of whom were present. At the New Year's Church Service at Whittingehame, with all the Balfours now back from the war, the Whittingehame Roll of Honour was read.

CHAPTER 14

'The triumphant Feminist' [1242]
(1914-1924)

'I must not desert Mrs Fawcett'.[1243]

'[W]omen had not failed' their nation.[1244]

War necessitated a change of work by the women's suffrage organizations, which suspended their suffrage activities and vowed to support the war effort. In the case of the WSPU, work for women's enfranchisement never effectually resumed. The National Union, however, only put votes for women on hold. As Mrs Fawcett explained in *Common Cause*: 'Now is the time for resolute effort and self-sacrifice on the part of every one of us to help our country. Let us show ourselves worthy of citizenship, whether our claim to it be recognized or not'.[1245]

It was easier to decide to suspend their suffrage work, however, than it was to agree on what the suffragists should think – and do – about the war. A majority believed that the NUWSS should pronounce in favour of peace and a negotiated settlement, and against war. Lady Frances Balfour recorded her exasperation with the peace faction in a meeting on 4 December 1914: "**Suffrage in Parliament Street. Long and worrying**'. Love of country and loyalty were two of Frances's strongest virtues, and when her country was at war, she supported it wholeheartedly, however much she regretted the war. Like Fawcett, she also believed that an anti-war stance would ultimately hurt the Cause.

At Fawcett's urging, the National Union refused to send representatives – or to allow constituent societies to send delegates – to an international congress of women at The Hague in March, when discussions regarding a peace settlement were to be held.[1246] Frances was present for the Special Council held in Birmingham 14-17 June to finally decide the peace issue: 'I must not desert Mrs Fawcett', she declared,[1247] and wrote elatedly on 17 June, that it had been **'a success for Mrs F[awcett]'**. Ten members of the Executive Committee of the National Union eventually resigned.

It was mostly left to the local societies to inaugurate specific schemes of work to assist the war effort. The London Society, now dedicated to providing relief for the women and families left at home, matched women with work – voluntary or paid – or with relief organizations needing assistance.[1248] All this was possible because of the 62 branches of the London Society.[1249] Frances, on Tiree at the time, was not involved in setting up the London Society's scheme of work, which was just as well, since her talents did not really lie in the area of administration. However, when she returned to London, Frances was nearly as busy as she had been before, delivering ten speeches and attending 14 long NUWSS Executive Committee meetings before the close of 1914.

But British suffragists also wanted to assist wounded soldiers in the war zone. Especially the Scottish physician, Dr Elsie Inglis, who offered her services as a surgeon to the War Office, where she was peremptorily told, 'My good lady, go home and sit still'.[1250] Inglis then turned to the Scottish Federation, of which she was Hon Secretary. At its September meeting, the Federation offered to supply the Allies with hospitals for the wounded, staffed entirely by women (the National Union endorsed their efforts).[1251] Eventually, they established 14 hospitals, called Scottish Women's Hospitals (SWH), in France, Serbia, Russia, and Macedonia (Salonika).[1252] In February 1915, the London Society, probably through Frances's initiative, agreed to act as the London agents of the SWH and to support two London Hospital Units of the SWH abroad. [1253]

Frances's role in supporting the Scottish Women's Hospitals was significant. Not only was she a member of the Executive Committee of the London SWH, but she held Drawing Room meetings and gave speeches promoting the scheme. Her April 1915 Drawing Room at her home, where Dr Inglis spoke, raised £28 to benefit the hospitals. Among other places, Frances went to **'Manchester to speak for Women's hospitals'**. Moreover, Frances probably recruited the majority of the supporters of the SWH in the London effort, including, on its Executive Committee, Arthur, Robert Cecil, Louise Creighton, D D Lyttelton, Victor Lytton, Mrs Leopold Rothschild, Alice Salisbury, and Maude Selborne. The Society, which held 82 meetings to benefit this charity, raised over £7,000 in this effort in 1915.[1254] Frances continued to speak for the SWH throughout the war, eventually incorporating lantern slides into her talks.[1255]

By 1915, most of the dislocation difficulties and distress brought on by the war had been addressed, and the London Society now turned its attention to another need. With so many men serving their nation on the battlefields, manufacturers were in desperate need of trained workers, and the London Society urged the Government to employ women to fill some of these jobs. As the London Society put it, '[T]he need last winter was for work, this winter it is for workers'.[1256] Arguing that women were prepared for this responsibility, Frances reminded the Wandsworth Committee of the London Society that, for the first time in any great war, women had been called into the great factories where ammunition and explosives were being manufactured',[1257] and that 'women had not failed' their nation.

Both the London Society and the National Union were at this same time urging the Government to guarantee women the same wages men were paid if women replaced the men. This was apparently the first time the issue of equal pay for equal work had been promoted by the suffragists and other women's organizations like the National Union of Women Workers.[1258] Throughout the war, British feminists continued their work to expand women's role in British life and to seek equal treatment for women with men.

When it became obvious that munitions and aircraft workers were needed, the Society began offering classes in acetylene welding, micrometer and vernier viewing, and engineering tracing in July 1916; all of these classes were taught by women and were well-attended. Of course, the Society noted that much more could be done if it had more money. It was precisely for this reason that the women appealed to the Government for assistance.

In 1915, the Government again called upon Frances to serve her country. When the Central Control Board (Liquor Traffic) heard accusations of excessive drinking by working women, who were now filling new jobs in both agriculture and industry, the Control Board decided to create a Women's Advisory Committee to study the issue and 'suggest action if required'.[1259] Louise Creighton, President of the National Union of Women Workers, was appointed chair of the committee, and, on 8 September, Frances was asked to be a member.[1260]

Having listened to 21 'experts' and received reports from special inquiries conducted in 28 towns and districts, the committee issued its preliminary report on 18 February 1916.[1261] The women concluded from the evidence that, while 'drinking amongst women had increased since the beginning of the war, . . . there was no considerable increase of drinking amongst women who did not drink before'[1262] nor any 'evidence of extensive drinking by women munition[s] workers', and that 'the charge of drinking amongst women has been exaggerated and is a great injustice to the great mass of women of the working class, who are sober, [and] steady . . . '.[1263] Shocked by the women's conclusions, the Control Board declined to publish their report![1264] It took a Special Investigation Committee – with men in its number – which came to the same conclusion to vindicate the women's findings.[1265]

On the whole, women's employment during the war was encouraging. So many new occupations were opened to women that the London Society could not even name in its *Annual Reports* all of those in which it had found employment for women. Their placements included ambulance drivers, lamplighters, policewomen, power station operators, painters, chemists, and librarians. The Society was especially proud of its Munitions and Aircraft Department. In 1915, employment had been found for some 3,000 women workers, 170 of whom were 'employed as supervisors at Woolwich Arsenal at wages that sometimes reached £5 per week'.[1266] In late 1916, the Ministry of Munitions took over the training of women engineers.[1267] It also agreed to subsidize the Society's welding classes, making it possible for the London Society to provide free training to more students. The government still refused, however, to guarantee women equal wages.

Several dramatic events occurred in the history of the Scottish Women's Hospitals during 1915-1916.[1268] The women's hospital at Royaumont, France, where the London committee maintained a ward of twenty-five beds, was honoured by French authorities, including the President of the French Republic and Generals Joffre and Petain. In Serbia, the SWH maintained five hospitals. When the German-Austrian-Bulgarian invasion began in October 1915, hospital personnel were forced to make repeated rapid moves, culminating in retreat with the Serbian army across the mountains into Montenegro. Drs Inglis and Hutchison courageously stayed behind and continued to minister to the Serbian wounded until the doctors were taken prisoner. Finally allowed to cross the border into Switzerland, these medical professionals returned home in February 1916 to much acclaim. The Serbian Government decorated both women.

Dr Inglis and her colleagues soon decided to assist displaced Serbs. To this end, the London Society sent two hospitals, with a staff of 75 women, to the Serbian Division of the Russian Army in August 1916.[1269] In addition, the SWH continued to administer hospitals for the Serbs who were now in Macedonia. Oswald wrote to his mother that the SWH doctors – nicknamed the 'skittish' doctors – did admirable work in Salonika.[1270]

The Society undertook numerous money-raising efforts in 1916 to support this work, including three large meetings at Bedford College and an evening performance at Criterion Theater, at which Frances shared a stage with the actor Forbes Robertson. The scope of the Society's war work was so great that the Society received permission to hold a Lamp Day sale for the Women's Service Fund. The date chosen, 12 May 1916, was the birthday of Florence Nightingale and, in her memory, badges featuring small lamps were sold to the public. This sale raised £2,856;[1271] the Society was given permission to hold a second Lamp Day in 1917, raising £2,636.[1272]

Eventually, much of the money for the Scottish Women's Hospitals came from the New World. A paid organizer, Kathleen Burke, Hon Organising Secretary of the London Units, visited Canada and the US in 1916 and 1917 to promote the scheme. During her first trip, Burke, who even spoke with President Wilson, raised over £11,000 for the hospitals.[1273] On her second tour, Burke raised £52,000 and inspired the American Red Cross to donate $50,000 for soldiers in France.[1274] Before the war was over, British suffragists raised £428,905 for the SWH.[1275]

The work of the Travellers' Aid-Society, which 'was completely disorganized by the war',[1276] diminished dramatically at first, but as the war wore on, the services of the TAS were required on several fronts. In 1917, the Ministry of Munitions asked the TAS to protect young women as they traveled to their work in munitions factories.[1277] In 1918, the Society helped 9,346 young women in London, which exceeded the number assisted by the organization in the pre-war period.[1278]

In November 1916, a Special Register Bill was introduced in the House of Commons to correct the problems posed by a new Electoral Register. With over two and a half million men serving in the war effort and therefore not qualified to vote due to the residence requirements, the new bill would give combatants the vote, but the issue of franchise reform was so contentious that an all-party electoral reform conference, chaired by the Speaker, was convened to make recommendations on the subject.

The National Union, anticipating such a move, had in March created a Consultative Committee of Constitutional Women's Suffrage Societies (CCCWSS – no organizational name was too long for Fawcett) to urge that any legislation *expanding* votes for men should include votes for women as well. Some 33 organizations eventually had membership on the Consultative Committee.

While heeding the advice to avoid lobbying Members of Parliament, the Consultative Committee exerted its main influence through a special committee of 25 suffragists who met with a comparable number of MPs under the leadership of Sir John Simon. When the NUWSS held its election for 17 of the committee members, Frances was, of course, an early selectee.[1279] One of the tactics discussed for getting the women's bill passed included Simon's suggestion that suffragists promise to wait at least ten years before asking for any further extension of the vote.

By February 1917, the suffragists had the support of the Liberals and Asquith, their former nemesis.[1280] The major question confronting the Speaker's Committee was which women would be enfranchised. To prevent the enfranchised women from outnumbering men voters, the Conference ultimately recommended that women householders or householders' wives over the age of 30 be given the vote.

With the support of Lord Northcliffe, proprietor of the *Daily Mail* and *The Times*, Fawcett arranged a 'united deputation' to the Prime Minister for 29 March 1917. When the constitutional suffragists learned that Mrs Pankhurst wished to be part of their deputation, they suggested that she 'arrive at the same time' as the suffragists and that she 'be asked by Mr Lloyd George to speak'.[1281] Frances does not appear to have been part of the group. Lloyd George informed the women that a draft bill along the lines of the Speaker's Conference had been prepared that very morning.

In the days before 19 June 1917, the crucial date for debate in the Commons on the much-desired legislation,[1282] the NUWSS mobilized its womanpower once more. A demonstration of women war workers was held in Queen's Hall on 20 February, the 'first suffrage meeting held since the war by the NUWSS';[1283] Frances was present but she **'did not speak'**. A mass meeting in support of the women's clause was also held in Edinburgh.

Finally, in June 1917 – 50 years after the suffrage struggle began – the Commons voted in a free vote 214-17 to accept the Speaker's Conference Report as a whole, meaning that some women over 30 would get the vote. It was appropriate, given his long support for the Cause, that on 19 June – just in time to vote for women's enfranchisement – Arthur Balfour made his first appearance in the House of Commons since his highly successful visit to the United States. In August 1917, the Grille in front of the Ladies' Gallery was removed.[1284]

Ray Strachey said that the suffragists' one-sided success was due to the 'new atmosphere' in which women now laboured for the vote. '[T]he response of women to the call for [war] service had worked a marvelous change. Old enemies had become new friends'.[1285] Frances pointed out a more political reason for the lop-sided vote, informing Fawcett that Lord Balfour of Burleigh had asserted to her that many Members were afraid 'to vote against possible new voters'.[1286]

After the Representation of the People Act passed the Commons, the Bill still had to go to the House of Lords. The suffragists held their collective breaths until their arch-enemy, Lord Curzon, asked his fellow peers if they were 'prepared to embark on a conflict with a majority of 350 in the House of Commons of whom nearly 150 belong to the party to which most of [the] Lordships belong?'[1287] The Lords ultimately enfranchised women by a vote of 134-71.[1288] Frances, still in Scotland on holiday, was not present when the Lords voted .

When she finally appeared in the Lords' chambers on 21 January 1918, she 'had a great reception . . . , all sorts of Peers coming to speak to me. . . .Talking it over with A.J., he said the whole thing was settled by the country. "As Asquith explained to us in the Cabinet, the <u>War</u> had changed his whole view as to the position of women and their claims." "There", said Arthur, "lay the whole thing'".[1289] The Bill received the Royal Assent on 6 February 1918. Shortly after the Representation of the People Act of 1918 was finally passed, women were given the right to sit in Parliament.

Sadly, just as the Lords had been preparing to debate votes for women, Dr Elsie Inglis, whose courage and leadership of the Scottish Women's Hospitals had earned much political capital for the suffragists, died. Inglis had managed to return home from Russia following its Revolution but was so ill from cancer when she arrived at Newcastle on 25 November 1917 that she could not be moved from her hotel; she died the next day.[1290] Frances, who helped make some of the arrangements, attended her funeral service at St Giles Cathedral in Edinburgh on 29 November, declaring it a **'[g]reat and moving'** event.

Frances was determined to memorialize Inglis, and she immediately settled on writing a biography of the courageous physician. With her usual speed, Frances wrote *Dr. Elsie Inglis* and got it published by Hodder and Stoughton by October 1918. *The Scotsman* praised the book's author, saying, 'If Dr. Elsie Inglis was fortunate in her life, she has also been fortunate in her biographer'.[1291] In a deeply moving tribute to Inglis, Frances noted that she was buried in "the faded ribbons" of the orders bestowed on her by France, Russia, and Serbia. It has often been asked at home and abroad why she had received no decorations at the hands of her Sovereign. It is not an easy question to answer'.[1292] Frances then quoted a shawl-draped woman in the massed crowd viewing Inglis's coffin as saying, "'Why did they no gie her the V.C.?'"[1293]

Since 1918, students of history have argued over whether it was women's work for the Cause undertaken before the war – including the militancy which some politicians may have feared would be resumed after the conflict – or women's work during the war that earned them the vote. The war certainly dispelled one argument that the Antis made before the hostilities: women finally had the opportunity to demonstrate that they could and would undertake many tasks which before the war had been deemed unsuitable or even impossible for them to perform. Women drove ambulances, flew airplanes, plowed fields, and worked in munitions plants. The women's work in the Scottish Hospitals – many of which were in war zones – as well as their work in the Women's Army Auxiliary Corps, the Women's Royal Naval Service, and the Women's Royal Air Force Service (about ten percent of whose members served in France) removed the physical-force argument which had previously been employed so successfully against them. It would appear, therefore, that British suffragists may have popularized the Cause during the pre-war years, but it was British women's work during the war that tipped the balance in their favour.

The suffragists held one more great meeting after they obtained the vote in order to offer Thanksgiving for their Parliamentary success. Deciding that 'music alone could really convey what they [felt]', Fawcett secured the services of Sir Hubert Parry for a concert, which was heard by an overflow audience of suffragists at the Queen's Hall on 13 March 1918.[1294] Lady Betty reported on the event to Nell:

> The Queen's Hall was packed, right up to the ceiling. . . . The music part of the programme was perfect. Vic [Victor Lytton] came in after the Bach [Double violin concerts] and was well received. . . . Maud and Frances were in the front row. The moment of Mrs Fawcett's rising to speak was a thrilling one. The audience all rose and cheered so long she had at last to motion to them to sit down. . . . [After thanking Sir Hubert] she turned to us, and made her noble, short victory speech. Then she introduced Vic, saying she had seen him first at the wedding of Lady Frances Balfour's daughter, and as she looked at his face she wondered who he was, and said to herself, 'I wish he were on our side', afterwards she was introduced to him and found he <u>was</u> on our side! Vic['s] opening sentences made me want to cry. . . . When he referred with regret to those who had dropped out of the fight before victory, who had given their lives, or their health to the Cause, and could not be with us tonight, it was understood he had Con [Constance Lytton] in mind, and a great burst of cheering came, a real glowing tribute.[1295]

Though her talks were not directly about votes for women during the war, Frances had continued to attend meetings and give speeches for women's causes and to work for women's organisations, all of which were doing some kind of war work. As the years progressed, her speaking and attendance at meetings increased. In 1917, she attended 88 meetings, in addition to her speeches; and in 1918, she spoke 51 times in a wide range of venues, including Harrods. Having kept so busy, Frances was still popular with suffragists even though most of her efforts were not the service-oriented work in which they were engaged: in elections for the Executive Committee of the NUWSS during the war, she received the sixth highest number of votes in 1915[1296]; third in 1916[1297]; and second in 1917[1298].

The National Union's work was not completed with the passage of the Representation of the People Act of 1918. When Lloyd George called for elections to be held on 14 December 1918, the former suffragists were confronted with the question of whether to run candidates of their own or not. By a narrow margin, the National Union (endorsed by the London Society) elected to do so. Since legislation to allow women to sit in Parliament had not been passed until November 1918, women candidates for a seat in the House of Commons had only three weeks to campaign, and party acceptance would be a problem since official candidates were already in the field. It was probably for these reasons that Frances disagreed with the NUWSS decision to run candidates.

In the event, Frances was asked to stand for a seat in the House of Commons. A deputation of women from Hillhead, 'a better-class residential district'[1299] of Glasgow in the heart of the West End, sought her out on 16 November while she was still in Scotland. It was a difficult decision for her: she very much wanted to be among the first women elected to Parliament, and the offer to stand for a well-to-do section of Glasgow must have been tantalizing. However, Arthur answered the question of her standing when he told her that there was not enough money available to assist her in her campaign because he – and Gerald – had invested unwisely, and by 1918, the money was gone.[1300] She, of course, did not have the resources herself.

What would her chances of victory have been? No women were returned to Parliament in this election,[1301] and she, too, might have failed. However, Hillhead was a new constituency created by the re-distribution scheme, and therefore had no incumbent as a candidate. Though only about a third of the 25,335 electors in Hillhead were women,[1302] in a field with three candidates, Frances might have had a statistical chance. The eventual winner, Sir Robert Horne, endorsed by the Coalition, was opposed by Councillor Izett, representing Labour. Horne, though a strong candidate, was a political neophyte who had lost the two elections in which he had stood before this race. Despite his strength, Frances would have matched him.

Moreover, Frances was well-known by this time, and her title would probably have helped her (the first woman to sit in Parliament, who was not even born in Britain, was titled). She likely would have been able to counter the lack of endorsement by the Coalition party with speeches by Arthur and other Unionist/Conservative political figures. The novelty of her being a woman candidate might also have helped, and her chances were probably better than those of any of the other women candidates, including Christabel Pankhurst. Frances already had a large female following in Scotland, and she might well have had the support of some Glasgow University officials and professors. Her years of 'stumping' would have made her comfortable in speaking to the electors, male or female, and her humour in her speeches would probably have won many converts. There is no doubt that Frances would have had an up-hill battle, the other two candidates having had a three-week head start, but she very well might have been successful. On the day of the election, 14 December 1918, Frances began her diary entry for the day with the words, '**My first vote!!**'

When it was revealed that no women had been elected to the House of Commons in 1918, the feminists knew that they still had much political work to do. For Lady Frances Balfour and Mrs Fawcett, however, the work continued outside the National Union of Women's Suffrage Societies, now re-titled the National Union of Societies for Equal Citizenship (NUSEC). With their work essentially done, both women, who opposed an immediate campaign to extend the vote to more women, resigned the NUWSS in 1919 and continued their feminist activities through other organizations.[1303]

Frances also yielded up the Presidency of the London Society for Women's Suffrage at its Annual Meeting on 24 February 1919 – '**a milestone**', she asserted. As the first order of business, Mrs Fawcett moved a resolution, seconded by Lady Strachey, which was carried unanimously:

> That this meeting expresses its deep regret at the resignation as President after over 17 years of office of the Lady Frances Balfour, to whose staunch and loyal support the women's cause owed so much of its advancement during the strenuous years of labour for political recognition. It recalls with sincere gratitude Lady Frances Balfour's share in the education of public opinion, her eloquent advocacy of the cause both in the Press and on the public platform, and her readiness whenever the question came before Parliament to give to the Society the invaluable benefit of her special political knowledge.[1304]

Thus did Frances bow out of her long campaign to give women the vote.

Though she never criticized Fawcett, it must have been a disappointment to Frances to hear that her service to the London Society was 'over 17 years', since she and Fawcett had served in tandem as leaders of the London Society (and its predecessors) and of the National Union respectively for exactly the same length of time: 23 years, starting in 1896. This was a fact which Fawcett would not have had to research since she was the one who had suggested, prior to the creation of the National Union, that Frances be named President of the Society which would eventually be known as the London Society. Moreover, Frances had been a member of the Executive Committee of the national society since 1892 (27 years) and had assisted the Cause as Parliamentary liaison from 1889, meaning that, in fact, she worked for the Cause 30 years.[1305]

The contrast in the treatment accorded these two leaders at the end of their suffrage service was considerable. Fawcett, who served the Cause for 50 years, was lauded or celebrated almost every time she spoke or presided over a major suffrage event *after 1907*. Nor did the accolades for Fawcett end when the vote was attained. In 1920, former suffragists raised £500 as a New Year's present to her, and many of the same women contributed to Bedford College, which raised £2,000 for the Millicent Garrett Fawcett Scholarships.[1306] Frances, whose loyalty to Fawcett continued, was Treasurer of that Fund.[1307]

Fawcett undoubtedly deserved the applause she received, and her service certainly should have been lauded more than Frances's or that of any other leader in the campaign to secure votes for women, including the Pankhursts, whose major suffrage service occurred 1906-1914. There is a statue outside Parliament of Mrs Pankhurst but none for Fawcett, who is more deserving, nor of Frances. The only acknowledgement of her 30 years of valuable service was this inaccurate London Society resolution. It is eminently unfair to Frances's legacy that students of history are left with the impression that her work was of a much shorter duration than it was.

Unfortunately, Frances's own words fed this notion. Her upbringing had taught her that one in her position did not brag about her work for others, so she most commonly made light of her efforts for the Cause. Declaring that she 'was by no means one of the hardest workers in the Cause',[1308] she implied that her efforts were not as extensive as those of others. In fact, her contribution must have been among the greatest made by British women in the campaign for the vote: she traveled to the far corners of England, Scotland, and Wales, met frequently with MPs, and made innumerable speeches and meetings, all while continuing her other work for women.

Of course, many other veterans of the suffrage 'war' also served without special recognition, but Frances's position was unique. She had served as President of the London Society for Women's Suffrage for the entire time that the organization existed under its various names. This body was the largest women's suffrage society in Britain and was the hardest working, having the responsibility for carrying out all the work that the National Union did in London. In fact, the National Union was mainly a national coordinating body. Of course, Frances herself did not perform all the work that the London Society did; she was nevertheless the hard-working public face of the Society.

The very fact that she was the only member of the aristocracy who held a sustained leadership position in the suffrage ranks beginning in the 19th century also made her exceptional. No other suffragist had such direct contact with the leading political figures of the day, and her relationships were not limited to just a few Members of Parliament, all of whom she knew, but included five Prime Ministers.

Several of Frances's activities came to an end around this time. She gave up the Presidency and Chairmanship of the Executive Committee of the Lyceum Club at this time. 'Lady Frances had been a superb choice' for the Presidency, according to one historian of the society.[1309] As there are no further references to the Lyceum Club in Frances's diary after this date, she probably also gave up her membership as well at this time. The work of the Scottish Churches' League for Woman's Suffrage was also concluded in 1919, during the General Assembly of the Church of Scotland. The Women's Municipal Party did not continue its work for long in the post-war era either. Apparently, 'independent local government women were regarded as a nuisance by the main political parties' and the WMP simply 'faded away' by 1920.[1310]

Further evidence of Frances's stature in the British women's movement is found in the fact that, in June 1919, she was asked to come to New York for a speaking tour; Frances, who loathed ocean voyages, refused the offer. Her renown was also such that, on 16 December 1920, she was photographed at the Ritz Hotel for *Vogue* magazine: her picture appeared as the Frontispiece in the Early February 1921 issue.

Having foreseen the end of her work for women's suffrage, Frances now acquired a new Cause, transferring her efforts and energy to the National Council of Women of Great Britain. Before 1917, this society – which she had helped launch in 1895 – was known as the National Union of Women Workers (NUWW). A member of several organizations which were affiliated with the NUWW, Frances had attended many of the annual meetings between 1895 and 1917 but does not appear to have had any other involvement in the work of the society. At its annual meeting in the autumn of 1917, she was elected to the NCW's Executive Committee, and then was re-elected in 1919. During 1917, the organization changed its name to the National Council of Women of Great Britain (NCW), by which name it is still known. One reason for the name change was that the society was not an organization of or for working-class women but rather middle class women. Those served were described as women who 'look upon their work [whether paid or not] as a vocation'.[1311] The organization, while not only promoting 'the social, moral and religious welfare' of its members, was a federation of women's organizations 'dealing with industrial, philanthropic and educational matters'.[1312]

Over the years, the NCW examined virtually all aspects of women's lives. For example, in 1910-1911, it conducted investigations into lodging houses and examined the National Insurance Bill of 1911, positioning itself on the latter as 'an authoritative source of information for Members of Parliament'.[1313] In affiliating with the NCW, Frances was again involving herself with an organization which had a strong political component but also, like the NUWSS, was affiliated with no party.

Meanwhile, Frances' life was in transition. She was not as busy in the months immediately following the war, but she did speak several times – once at 10 Downing Street – on behalf of the YWCA, which was launching an Appeal to provide more hostels and clubs for women away from home, a goal begun during the war.

Frances got the first acknowledgement of her contributions to women in May 1919 when Durham University awarded her the honorary degree Doctor of Letters, or D. Litt., ostensibly for her written publications but probably also because of her efforts for women. Frances was the only female among the Chancellor's selectees for a doctorate (one woman received an Honorary MA). She was only the third woman to be honored with a doctorate from Durham University.[1314]

Frances had long believed that women should have a voice in the affairs of the Church and seems never to have hesitated to instruct the learned divines in the Church of Scotland regarding the status of women in the Church. In 1919, she challenged the Moderator during the General Assembly. When moving the adoption of the report of the Women's Home Missions, she asserted that 'no minister had ever been able to give her an adequate reason why women should not be admitted to kirk-sessions'.[1315] She wondered about the wisdom of this prohibition because, she asserted, women 'were better administrators of money than men'. Frances also noted that the Church of England 'was trying to reconstruct itself [the Church of England Assembly (Powers) Act 1919]', and she 'wish[ed] that our Church would enlarge its borders as to giving women greater . . . responsibility. Why have two committees for Home and Foreign Missions?' she asked. In his answer, The Right Rev Professor W P Paterson explained that women were not debarred from performing the work of elders, and '[w]hat', he asked, 'was in a name? A deaconess meant a person who served, while an elder meant one who was rather old'.[1316] Frances was no doubt used to such flippancy, and since the Churchwomen who were present were not permitted to speak, Paterson probably expected this absurdity to be accepted without challenge.

Shortly thereafter, however, Frances wrote the introduction for a book by Edith Picton-Turbervill entitled *Christ and Woman's Power;* Frances's contribution was acknowledged by an inclusion of her name on both the title page and the spine of the book. Lady Frances used the opportunity to remind the Church of its past record regarding reform:

It is sad to have to note in this little history of the struggles women have

made for the reformation of the treatment of women, that in no case
has the organized Church been a leader in their fights for emancipation,
and against the horrible injustices of legalized vice. The ecclesiastical
polity has never stood for reformation. The farther away the Church
gets from the ideal, that in Christ there is neither male nor female . . .
less living will its hold be on the Christianity of the world.

In her autobiography, Frances was even more pointed: 'In what great reforming
effort has the Church of Christ ever led?'[1317]

Despite the teachings of her Church's founder John Knox (author of *First Blast
of the Trumpet against the Monstrous Regiment of Women* [1558]), who believed in and
preached the natural inferiority of women and their rightful subjection to men,
Frances believed in the Church's teaching of equality of all believers before God. She
also was certain that 'the church . . . . could be moved by the Holy Spirit according
to the needs of the times'.[1318] Her conversations with the many ministers in her
Church, most of whom were the Church leaders, must have been strained at times.
Nevertheless, she probably helped win some of them over to reform in the Church.

Frances clearly relished the occasion in October 1923 when the Rev Maude
Royden, Unitarian minister at City Temple in London, preached at St Cuthbert's,
Edinburgh, where the Very Rev Dr James MacGregor had once presided. Frances
described the event for Betty: '[The Church] was packed from ceiling to floor and
from wall to wall. . . . She took 'Martha and Mary and Spiritual Strength' [as her
sermon topic]. . . . I was confirmed in my belief that she is among the first six
preachers in our land'.[1319] Frances also reported that '[t]here were two disapproving
elders at supper whom we steadily chaffed. The wife of one said, "When you retire
Dr Maclean, we mean to call Miss Maude Royden"'.[1320]

When the Scottish Women's Hospitals were finally disbanded, feminists in
Scotland desired to use the funds remaining for a memorial to Elise Inglis. To raise
additional funds, a Caledonia Fair was held over three days in May 1920 at Australia
House in London. Nine titled women were stallholders and chairs of the event.[1321]
Lady Frances opened the fair on its final day.

In October 1923, Frances again spoke about Dr Elsie Inglis prior to Lady
Novar's laying the corner-stone for the hospital, which was erected in Inglis's honour
at Spring Gardens, Edinburgh.[1322] The Elsie Inglis Memorial Maternity Hospital,
which boasted 20 beds, was opened in Edinburgh in July 1925. Thereafter, Frances
assisted the hospital as a vice-president. Frances had also participated in an effort
to create a memorial to Dr Inglis in Serbia. She was the main speaker at a meeting
at Mansion House in London in 1918 to establish a chair of medicine in Inglis's
honour at the University of Belgrade. The Serbian minister was in attendance at the

meeting, a fact not lost on Frances, who expressed the hope that it would be women who would occupy the Inglis chair.[1323]

In the first nine months of 1919, Frances apparently spoke only 17 times, including speeches at a Red Cross tea and dance, the Speaker's House, and '**a rotten little municipal meeting**' at Balham.[1324] The number of meetings and speeches increased as wartime receded: in 1919 she was present at 29 meetings, and in 1920, at 39. Finding her stride in the 1920s, she added attendance at meetings of the Board of Education and agreed to serve as a vice-president of the YWCA, and her attendance at meetings (52 in 1922 and 54 in 1923) and the frequency of her speeches began to approach the level of involvement she had reached before the war.

In July 1921, a university in her own country acknowledged her work for women; Edinburgh University awarded Frances an honorary degree: the LL D, or Doctor of Laws, degree. The evening before the ceremony, the honorees were feted at dinner in the Upper Library of the Old College of the University where, by custom, the Principal, Sir Alfred Ewing, 'hailed' the honorary graduands. He acclaimed Frances as 'the accomplished biographer and the triumphant feminist'.[1325]

Frances was again the only woman who received an honorary doctorate. At the awards ceremony, Sir Alfred remarked of Frances, 'In the great struggle for female emancipation she has been a prominent leader and a chivalrous fighter, and now in the hour of triumph she does not allow her sex to forget that the right to the vote has its obverse side of responsibility for the use of it'.[1326] Only four women had been given honorary degrees by the University of Edinburgh by this date.[1327]

During the National Council of Women's General Conference held at Sheffield the last week of September 1921, Frances was elected to a two-year term as president of the NCW, which both publicized women's grievances and tried to get them redressed. Frances succeeded her colleague and relative, Lady Maude Selborne, who credited Frances with having introduced her to the organization. To her diary, Frances confessed that she was '**moved by [the] evidence of affection [that members had shown for her]**'.[1328] A regular routine existed at all the conferences: after the opening speeches, the delegates met in Representative Council Meetings during the mornings (and some afternoons), and each evening they held public meetings which addressed various issues of the day. In the public meeting, Frances, not yet serving as President, spoke on 'Women in Public Service', one of the most enduring goals of the NCW, which worked to get women civil servants all the opportunities for advancement and the same pay that men enjoyed.

In 1922, Frances's first year as President, the NCW was 'the largest women's organization in the country'.[1329] With 126 branches, 145 affiliated societies, and over a million women members, it was 'the most comprehensive in its scope'.[1330] In closing her first presidential address, Frances – at one point described as 'picturesque and loveable in bright blue brocade and black satin'[1331] – noted that the time in which women were seen as curiosity was passing, 'in the accounts of juries, of whom so many were women; of electorates, of whom so many were women; of members of Parliament, of whom two were women. (Cheers)'.[1332]

The resolutions debated and voted on by the members were ranked by the Executive in order of importance; the first item discussed by the NCW members in 1922 was a resolution urging the employment of policewomen 'in thickly populated areas where offences against women and children were not infrequent'.[1333] The second resolution urged *the Government* to 'take steps' to secure 'the admission of women to membership in Cambridge University' (women could study but not take degrees), Cambridge being the lone exception among universities of the British *Empire* to withhold this right from its female students by this date.[1334] (Cambridge held out, however, until 1947.)

During her final year as President of the NCW, the annual conference was held in Edinburgh. In her Presidential address, Frances urged the women to 'take stock of the past and resolve to follow in the footsteps' of the pioneers.[1335] Asserting that 'every great movement springs from the passion and faith of one man or woman', Frances then declared that 'they looked around the world for the individuality of the present race'.

Meanwhile, Oswald regularly regaled his Mother with stories of the ineffectiveness of the temperance legislation in effect in the U S in the 1920s. When he attempted to order coffee at a cabaret in Atlantic City in 1923, he was informed by the waiters that they did not serve it there. '"What can we drink then?"' brought the response, 'Whiskey or gin. There ain't anything else'.[1336] By this date, however, the National Council of Women was keen on limiting the sale of alcoholic beverages, and Frances enthusiastically took up the cause, declaring 'America and Geneva are trying to emancipate mankind from the thraldom of drink and warfare. . . . How are we women meeting it?'[1337] She concluded, 'Can we not arise and work for the will to be sober, as we work and pray for the will to be at peace. . . ?'

Included in the resolutions passed in the 1923 representative meetings were several that pertained to children. The NCW wanted heavier fines for those accused of 'criminal and indecent assaults on young girls'[1338]; early treatment of tuberculosis in children; early diagnosis of venereal diseases in children; and pensions for 'fatherless legitimate necessitous children'. In addition, the NCW wanted an amendment to the Old Age Pensions Act which would award pensions to women without their having to reveal 'their private affairs to strangers'.[1339] The NCW noted that 'Three Lord Chancellors had recently received pensions from the State of £5,000 per year but they could be quite sure that no pensions officer would go to their houses to find out if they were receiving gifts of coal, food, or clothes, or had £50 in a War Loan'.[1340]

Before the 1923 annual Conference closed, NCW members demonstrated their appreciation of Frances's work for the organisation: 'The representatives, after prolonged applause, sang with great cordiality "For she's a jolly good fellow"'. Frances received this mark of appreciation in characteristic fashion. "Beautifully sung", she commented, "but let us recollect that the tea pot waits. We must get on". (Laughter) She then expressed the pleasure and interest which her term of the presidency had given her'.[1341] To her son Frank, Frances related that she had 'looked down on that body of women, suffrage, & Philanthropic, & Political & I hope all Christians, & felt contented that my lot had been cast with them'.[1342]

Once women had the vote, women's organizations like the NCW were surprisingly successful. The Sex Disqualification (Removal) Act of 1919 had admitted women to many professions, including the Bar; one of the goals of the NCW in the early twentieth century was to secure the appointment of women as magistrates, and in 1920, some 200 women had finally been appointed Justices of the Peace. Included in the initial female appointees to the bench were Maude Selborne, Alice Balfour, and Millicent Garrett Fawcett.[1343] One year later, 133 had joined the NCW's Justices of the Peace Sub-Committee, and in 1923, there were 1,032 women magistrates.[1344] The women did not gain all they sought, however, which is evident in the resolutions that continued to appear year after year. These included demands for equal pay for equal work for women and men, especially in the civil service; equality with men regarding the nationality of married women; and the *actual* appointment of women police throughout the country.

The primary concern indicated in Frances's 1923 Presidential address was the apparent lack of new women leaders. 'Where [are] the Elsie Inglises of today?' she asked. In truth, this debate was already ongoing in the councils of the NCW. Recruiting younger women to the organization was not easy, and the chief historian of the NCW, Dr Daphne Glick, suggested that the older members 'appeared remote and formidable to younger women'.[1345] Frances did recruit at least one younger member to the NCW: Dr Ruth Balfour.[1346]

Frances appears to have used her stature whenever she could to help women, and on one occasion – during winter 1922 – was surprisingly successful. Asked to preside over a function for a woman's hospital in Edinburgh, Frances refused on the grounds that there were no women on the Boards of the various Hospitals in the city. Frances learned a few months later that, shortly thereafter, women were appointed to 'all the city [hospital] boards except that of the Royal Infirmary [where one woman already served on the Board of Management]'.[1347] Frances herself was that year elected vice-president of the Edinburgh Hospital and Dispensary for Women (today the Bruntsfield Hospital) as well as the Elizabeth Garrett Anderson Hospital in London.[1348]

Her suffrage work effectively completed, Frances now turned her efforts to other areas where much was still to be done.

CHAPTER 15

'Everything Changes' [1349]
(1919-1929)

'If the country was not re-formed
in a Christian spirit it would be
in a revolutionary spirit . . .' .[1350]

'"I told them the fault of their
Party was vanity, ignorance
and self-centredness"'.[1351]

In the long-delayed election after World War I, Lloyd George and the Coalition received an overwhelming endorsement, and Asquith, who had represented Fife since 1886, lost his seat. When Lady Frances Balfour expressed her regrets, Margot proclaimed, 'It was your females who have voted Tory all over England . . .'[1352] Irish members, nearly all of whom were Sinn-Feiners, were almost totally absent now, having proclaimed an Irish Republic in Dublin complete with its own Parliament, the Dáil Eireann. Meanwhile, new tensions arose in the British Isles. Strikes plagued the nation, and Glasgow, or 'Red Clydeside', became a symbol of the tension and political struggle between socialists and non-socialists during the inter-war years.

At the Paris Peace Conference, Lloyd George, suspicious of professional diplomats (whom citizens blamed for the war), negotiated most of the peace with Germany, leaving Arthur largely outside the negotiations.[1353] Many now hoped that the newly-created League of Nations would represent a different, more open diplomacy. Now Lord President, Arthur would represent Britain on the Council of the League of Nations, which meant that he would continue to have a major role in foreign affairs.[1354] Baffy was also involved in the peace process, working on the boundaries and frontiers issues. She helped identify the minorities of East Galicia, which were eventually returned to Poland.

Celebrations large and noisy were held all over Britain when the Germans finally signed the Peace Treaty on 28 June 1919. On Tiree at the time, Frances relied on Baffy to describe the exhilarating parade that took place in London in July. '[P]erhaps the finest thing of the day', she said, 'was the passing of the Regimental Colours'.[1355] Then 'a distant roar was heard as General Pershing came around the corner', and behind him were 'rank on rank of Green-Grey Americans. . . ,' from whom, Baffy declared, 'little toll had been taken'. The arrival of the Belgians, however, resulted in '[a] far deeper cheer'. As the French turned into the Mall, they were greeted with cheers 'more thunderous than the guns of Jutland', according to Admiral Beattie.[1356] It seemed to Baffy that '[t]he French . . . were in tears the whole way. . . '. 'Haig's coming heralded a new roar'. The London Scottish were also there, with Pipers from the Black Watch. 'The Nurses and VAD's got as great a reception as the Navy itself'.

Women candidates for Parliament had been unsuccessful in the General Election of 1918, but one woman gained a seat in the House of Commons in 1919. When Viscount William Waldorf Astor went to the House of Lords following his father's death, his wife Nancy contested his seat as a Coalition Unionist. Assisted in a minor way by Arthur,[1357] she was elected over two other candidates and took her seat in the House of Commons on 1 December.

Frances and Nancy had been friends at least a decade or more and, following the election, Frances published an article about Nancy, entitled 'First MP for the Hearth', in the *Weekly Dispatch*. Frances praised her to Margot as 'a woman who believes in her sex and is willing and wishful to represent them rightly'.[1358] Nancy and Frances were in a rare position, as explained by Margot in a letter to Nancy: '''[Now the females are divided into butterflies and suffragettes. I can only talk [politics] to Lady Frances Balfour.'''[1359]

Frank was quite busy in Baghdad in 1919. He 'battled flood waters and the plague, helped plan the new Baghdad in the summer, and toured Nijf, Kubela and Hendiyah Barrage in the fall'.[1360] His work earned him 'a mention in [General Sir William] Marshall's Dispatch' as well as a CIE (Companion of the Order of the Indian Empire), in September 1919.

Mandates awarded to Britain and France on 25 April 1920 by the League of Nations gave Britain control over Mesopotamia and Palestine, and the French over Syria and Lebanon. Desirous of defeating the Turks, the British had encouraged Arab nationalism, and now had to live with the Arabs' heightened sense of identity. Gertrude Bell and Frank agreed with the recommendation of Sir Percy Cox (again

Commander-in-Chief in Mesopotamia) that native ministers, with British advisers, should govern Mesopotamia. Frances finally got to meet the 'Khatun' – important lady – when Bell, on a trip back to England in 1919, visited her; Bell's effusive praise of Frank – he 'did not know the meaning of fear'[1361] – prompted Frances to note that she **'[l]iked [Bell] so much'**.[1362]

The pace of Frances's life slowed a bit in 1919. She still made speeches and attended meetings, but the demands were not as numerous, at least at first. Money woes would have added to her difficulties. She still wrote articles for publication, but apparently the income from her labours was insufficient (she made only £10 'from pure journalism' in 1920[1363]). In order to raise sufficient funds for her needs, she was forced to sell some of her furniture, appraised at £177,[1364] a necessity which she **'felt it absurdly'**. No doubt some of her restlessness and depression stemmed from her inability to stand for Parliament, which would have been the ideal replacement for her suffrage and war work.

Oswald, a professional soldier, next served in Cologne, where he was part of the Army of the Rhine, the occupation army stationed in Germany. Having expressed a desire to be an attendant at Court, Joan became Lady-in-Waiting to Princess Alice, Countess of Athlone, in 1919. After the war, Joan's husband, now Maj Edward Lascelles, had become Arthur's Personal Private Secretary, thus allowing Joan plenty of access to her beloved 'Nunkie'.

When Frank's engagement was announced in early May 1920, Gertrude Bell declared herself delighted with the news. Bell had met Frank's future wife, Phyllis Goschen, daughter of the Edward Goschens, when she and her parents visited Mesopotamia in February. Bell recorded that she 'liked her', but added that she 'should like her better doubtless if I could catch a glimpse of her face through the paint'.[1365] The post-war style of make-up for women's faces was something that Frances also opposed, but aside from not cutting her hair in flapper style (probably more due to age than any fashion preference), she followed most women's style trends. A photo in the *Evening Dispatch* in 1923 shows Frances dressed in a coat of fashionable length and snugness, with fur collar and cuffs.[1366] This photograph also demonstrates that Frances was not self-conscious about her heightened shoe, which, with the shorter fashions, now showed prominently.

Phyllis and Frank were married in St Augustine's Church in the East Sussex village of Flimwell on 31 August 1920.[1367] After his wedding, Frank chose to return to the Sudan Political Service in 1921 as Assistant Director of Intelligence. Two years later, he was made Deputy Governor of Kassala, a promotion that was, because he was married, a more congenial position. Imperialist though he was, Frank was a somewhat enlightened colonial administrator: he wrote to Frances at one point, 'I am feeling glad we took the jump [to a constitutional state] and are over it. It's time we stopped putting out proclamations without consulting these local people at all!'[1368]

Frances continued writing to Elizabeth, periodically sending books, paper, notebooks, paints, and toys which she believed that Elizabeth and Catriona would like.[1369] Frances does not appear to have written any letters to Catriona – at least none have survived – but she sometimes signed her letters to Elizabeth with the initials 'E' and 'C' enclosed in hearts.

Frances may have shown more affection to Elizabeth than to her other grandchildren, but she regularly entertained these children. Almost every time she received a cake, she held a tea party for various grandchildren, cousins, nieces, and nephews. She was also involved in the lives of her older grandchildren; when Frances Dugdale turned 17, Frances had a birthday party for her and her friends.[1370]

Frances apparently got along quite well with her servants – indeed, one relative recalled that 'her servants loved her'.[1371] In March 1920, when Frances's cook, Annie Campbell, married Malcolm Macintyre at Tiree, Frances 'gave her away'.[1372]

In September 1920, the Savage retired, having 'reached the age limit',[1373] and the Milnes returned to Britain for good. Unfortunately, the Savage, having survived two bouts of Blackwater fever, was quite ill at his homecoming.[1374]

Soon after his work in Germany was completed, Oswald was appointed ADC to Canada's Governor-General, the Duke of Devonshire. (Oswald would have liked to be in a command position in the army, but, as Betty explained, he was still bothered by 'malarial fever, facial neuralgia, and trouble with his lungs'.[1375]) Oswald traveled extensively with the Governor-General; in March 1920, he visited Washington, DC, and New York City. His remarks about the American political scene must have greatly entertained his mother:

> The Senate and all its proceedings really take the cake. . . . I was in the Senators [Senate] Relations Gallery with Mrs [Alice] Longworth (Roosevelt's daughter, who was married to a Senator). She is a sort of Margot of America, if the latter had been Gladstone's daughter, if you can imagine it. She is very amusing and lives in the Senate almost. Some Senator proceeded to quote a good many speeches of Roosevelt's to prove that the latter was in favour of the League of Nations [the Senate was debating the Versailles Treaty] at the time of his death. . . . The whole House got very angry, and Mrs Longworth proceeded to converse from the Gallery with two Senators on the floor of the House telling them the exact dates of the quoted articles of her father's. Imagine this in the House of Lords.[1376]

Many of those who were links with Frances's past died during this early post-war period. Her long-time political ally, G W E Russell, MP, died in March 1919, and on 30 June, her brother-in-law John Rayleigh passed away. On 2 February 1920, she lost Lady Burne-Jones. Frances had visited her the day before her death; she later published eulogies of Georgina in three newspapers. While Frances was attending the General Assembly of the Church of Scotland in 1920, the long-time minister of Whittingehame, the Very Rev Dr James Robertson died. As the only family member around, Frances postponed her planned trip to Tiree to attend his funeral. In 1921, Frances' sister Evelyn lost her husband, James Baillie-Hamilton.

In July 1921, another long-time friend, Alexander Hugh Bruce, 6th Lord Balfour of Burleigh, died of a 'severe heart attack'.[1377] In addition to her newspaper eulogies of 'Lord B of B', as he was known, which appeared in at least two newspapers,[1378] Frances would go on to write a book-length biography of this 'large in bulk, big hearted, impetuous' Scot,[1379] whom she credited with securing passage of legislation which paved the way for re-union of the Church of Scotland. Early in February 1922, Frances received word that her youngest sister, Lady Constance Emmott, had passed away in Cannes. William Robertson Nicoll, publisher of all Frances's books through Hodder and Stoughton, died on 4 May.

The period brought happier news as well; in Scotland to attend the General Assembly on 26 May 1921, Frances learned that she was a grandmother once more: Phyllis had given birth to a son, whom she and Frank named Eustace Arthur Goschen Balfour. '**Eustace's name goes on**', Frances commented of her fifth grandchild. Despite the family's grief for the loss of Lord Rayleigh, the erection of a Memorial Brass for him in Westminster Abbey in 1921 was a source of pride. Arthur succeeded Rayleigh as Chancellor of Cambridge.

Oswald's stay in Canada was extended when in 1921 he accepted the invitation of the new Governor-General, Viscount Byng of Vimy, to continue as ADC. Oswald was therefore in the New World when Arthur represented Britain at the Washington Conference, called in November to discuss disarmament, which resulted – among other agreements – in a 5:5:3 ratio for the capital ships of Britain, the US, and Japan. Oswald lavishly praised Arthur for his work at the Conference. 'All agree that the progress of the conference must be regarded as a great personal triumph for him', he said.[1380]

Indeed, upon Arthur's return from the successful Washington Conference, the King asked him to accept a peerage for his invaluable service to his country. Though Arthur had earlier declined the honor, he accepted the distinction this time, taking the title Earl of Balfour; at the same time, he was made Viscount Traprain. Arthur did not heed Gerald's advice not to accept a heredity title. In fact, he chose Gerald to be his heir, then Gerald's male heirs, and finally the male heirs of his brother Eustace (Roderick, the 5th Earl of Balfour, is Frances's great-grandson). Later the same year, Arthur was awarded the Order of the Garter. He was back in the Foreign Office (summer 1922) after Curzon had a 'bad breakdown'.[1381]

Frances continued to work for divorce law reform long after the Commission rendered its report because the Government had been extremely slow to achieve any of the Commission's recommendations. In 1917, she had been one of only two women who joined a deputation to the Home Secretary in support of legislation which attempted only to make 'separations convertible into divorce after a lapse of five years'.[1382] This appeal and others were unsuccessful. In 1923, Britain finally equalized the grounds for divorce for men and women regarding adultery (the Matrimonial Causes Act), and again, Frances worked to assist its passage. In an article published in the *Edinburgh Review*, Frances asked, with biting humour, 'Is there any other form of justice which is so administered? If a person steals property, the State condemns him for the crime, and does not require of him that he should be a forger as well'.[1383] Most of the rest of the Commission's recommendations did not become law until 1936, when the Herbert Act was passed as a private Member's bill.[1384]

Oswald, having tired of ceremonial functions and 'the ringing telephone',[1385]left the army in autumn 1922 and took a position with the investment firm Harris, Forbes & Company in New York City. This company, which pioneered door-to-door salesmen and was the first to specialize in municipal and public utility bonds, had a branch in London (as well as Boston, Chicago, and Montreal).[1386] In recognition of his services in Canada, Oswald was given the CMG, Companion of the Order of St Michael and St George, in 1923. 'With one son CIE and the other CMG, we have sampled the Empire', declared Frances.[1387]

Since Irish representatives no longer came to Westminster after 1918, one would have expected that Irish home rule would be achieved fairly quickly. However, the issue of Ulster still remained to be settled officially, diverting much of Lloyd George's attention in the period from 1919-1922. After the creation of two Parliaments for Ireland, one in the south and one in Ulster, home rule finally appeared to be achieved when the British offered southern Ireland Dominion status, which was eventually accepted. Frances was usually present in the House of Commons during these debates and pragmatically asserted that while her 'heart was with the Diehards ... the cause of the Union is lost – better now to concentrate on Ulster and hope for the best about the [Irish] Free State'.[1388]

Until 1921, Britain's post-war prosperity seemed assured. Jobs were plentiful – especially after most women left the work force – and wages remained high. In

October 1920, however, the coal miners had gone on strike for an increase in wages. Shortly thereafter, the British economy imploded. When unemployment doubled between December 1920 and March 1921, Britain found herself in a serious depression, and the miners' effort collapsed.

In 1922, Arthur was again called upon to provide critical guidance in foreign affairs for his country's Government. The restoration and rebuilding of Europe were being stymied by the question of reparations: the defeated powers, especially Germany, were hard-pressed to pay. The next year, when the Germans were again unable to manage reparations payments, Frances made a prescient observation, 'I have no sympathy with [the Germans], but I know that the most unfruitful of passions is vengeance – and the most vindictive'.[1389] Via the Dawes Plan, the Allies eventually restructured Germany's debt, and the American government helped the Germans meet their obligations.

The wheels of political success came off for Lloyd George in 1922. Exhausted by the depressed economy, Irish affairs, and his protracted time in office, the British public turned against their war leader in the election of November 1922. Frances reflected the public will, declaring in February, 'The Government is going to its fall. The country is sick of it'.[1390]

Though the Coalition Government decided in October 1922 to fight a General Election on the Coalition ticket, Unionist/Conservative MPs meeting at the Carlton Club voted 187-87 to end the Coalition, in spite of the appeals of Chamberlain, Birkenhead, and Balfour to maintain it. With Labour rising in popularity, a three-way election had worried many political leaders, but on 15 November the Unionists/Conservatives, led by Bonar Law, triumphed overwhelmingly. Frances heard the welcome news at the Carlton Club,[1391] which, though it was 'very glum last night,' she found 'intensely interesting', not just for the politics, but also for the surroundings: women were not usually admitted. 'I was much interested in the place where the coup de grace was given [against Lloyd George]' and the '[b]usts of Dizzy [Disraeli], Salisbury, and pictures, A.J. [by] Sargent . . . .The results were announced by megaphone. . . . Derby had [said that] Labour would gain 10 seats in Lancashire. Certainly the gains seemed all Labour as they came out. . . '.[1392] The victorious Unionists/Conservatives won 344 seats, Labour 142, the Asquith-led Liberals 62, and the National Liberals, led by Lloyd George, only 53. The Unionists/Conservatives' victory was impressive, but perhaps the main sensation was the success of the Labour Party, which was now the second party, having won 142 seats to the Liberals' 115: it 'brought home to the Liberals that they had ceased to be a central force in British politics'.[1393]

During this election, Frances had spoken for Edith Picton-Turbervill, taking her onto a Labour Party election platform 'for the first time and only time'.[1394] Frances might support Picton-Turbervill, but she did not agree with her politics. Asked by Labour supporters after the meeting how she would rate Edith's speech, Frances replied, "'Very well, indeed . . . until she began her confounded nonsense about God and the Land!'"[1395] Such strong sentiments did not bother Picton-Turbervill, who asserted, 'I loved Lady Frances!'[1396]

Two women were re-elected in 1922: Nancy Astor and Margaret Wintringham, a Liberal elected for Louth in a by-election in 1921 to replace her deceased husband. In June 1923, a third woman, Mrs Mabel Philipson, a Conservative (and former Gaiety Girl who had moved into serious theatre), replaced her husband in Berwick. Frances informed Frank that the three women were called "Notoriety, Piety and Variety".[1397]

Politically speaking, Frances was a Whig/Unionist, placing her always in the middle between the stalwarts of the Liberal and Conservatives parties. This was not only her heritage, but also her instinctive leaning, especially after her marriage into the staunchly Tory Balfour family in 1879. When the Liberal Party ceased to be a viable political entity – by 1922 she was referring to them as the 'wee Liberals'[1398] – she was even more a Unionist. The one thing she apparently could not do was call herself a Conservative, no doubt out of loyalty to her father – 'I always thank Heaven that no creature belonging to our name has ever been in the Tory camp!'[1399] Regardless of such statements, Free Trade was virtually the only difference she had with the Tories.

Since the election had been more about rejecting Lloyd George than about policy, the Government that Law created was not a dynamic, innovative administration. Yet when it was time for the legislative wheels to grind once more (11 February 1923), Frances was still excited about the prospect: 'This week Parliament meets, always like the return of a friend', she wrote.

In May 1923, Frances reported that Arthur was 'gloomy' about Bonar Law; suffering from cancer of the throat, he was forced on 19 May to resign as Prime Minister. (He died in October.) When Stanley Baldwin was chosen the new leader of the Conservatives, Frances's assessment of the political surprise was blistering: 'There is no such rise in political history as that of Stanley Baldwin. He is quite unknown outside Parliament . . . . Birkenhead and Lloyd George remain . . . . It is a day of small men and small things . . .' .[1400] When the inexperienced Baldwin suggested that Protection would help solve both agricultural problems and unemployment, he was forced to call another election (6 December 1923) because Law had rejected Protection in the election of 1922.

As part of the election campaign, Frances travelled to Glasgow in October to speak for Mrs Margaret Wintringham,[1401] the first woman MP to address a Scottish audience. Eight women, including Wintringham, were elected to this Parliament; another was the Duchess of Atholl, a leading 'Anti'. Frances congratulated the Duchess but, anxious 'to point out [her] past errors', asked if she planned to wear 'a white sheet with a candle in either hand' when she appeared in the Commons.[1402]

Once more, Tariff Reform cost the Tories dearly. The Liberals, led again by Asquith, were re-united for this election, but they fared poorly compared to Labour. (And Margot bemoaned the 'anguish' of 'having to take back Lloyd George'.[1403]) The Unionist/Conservative party received the most votes in the election, but nevertheless lost over 90 seats. No party dominated the Commons, and on 21 January 1924, after a motion on the Address lost in the Commons, Baldwin was out and the Labour Party leader, Ramsey MacDonald, in as Prime Minister. Frances reminded herself that MacDonald was a Scot, though this was probably not much consolation.[1404]

On 22 January, the day MacDonald became Prime Minister, she wrote to Betty that Labour 'has come in at the 8th hour and that they will learn the difficulties of Government – and we shall learn the "Red Flag" is part of their war equipment. I hope they will remain in long enough to track both Conservative and Liberals to take the country seriously and think of its good and not the good of the party'.[1405] Frances was one of many British citizens who expected 'Bolshevism' and, if not revolution, at least strikes and other unpleasant challenges to 'law and order' in the wake of the Socialists' success. Frances had been concerned about the revolutionary aspect of Socialism for quite some time. When she spoke in support of the appeal of the YWCA at the close of the war, she had asserted that '[i]f the country was not re-formed in a Christian spirit it would be in a revolutionary spirit . . . '.[1406]

Frances may have been surprised – pleasantly so – when Labour Party leader, Ramsay MacDonald, a Socialist but also a pragmatist, chose for his cabinet not only men from the moderate spectrum of the Labour Party but also one representative of the Liberal Party, Lord Haldane. In truth, Labour Party representatives now serving in the House of Commons were no longer trade unionists but middle-class individuals, few of whom were revolutionaries.

As one of his first challenges, MacDonald faced a rail workers' strike, which Frances suggested must be 'a great embarrassment to the Government'.[1407] Her own experience with the strike is indicative of the effect on the country: it took 12 hours for her to get from Edinburgh to London on 25 January, where she found 'no porters and no taxis'.[1408] Strikes became even more vexatious when the dockers walked out in February, and this was followed by a bus strike.

At lunch with the Asquiths on 1 February 1924, Frances heard political comments about the new Government which she found both interesting and irritating from some of the Liberal Party supporters who were present, including W M R Pringle, MP, and A G Gardiner, formerly editor of the *Daily News*. The conversations included criticism of the women in Parliament. '[They were] very down on all the women's first efforts in the House. Mrs Wintringham was the only one praised. Kitty [Duchess of Atholl] with a sheaf of notes and very dull. Margaret Bondfield a complete failure, "shrill". "We have a terror on our side, Lady F". "The worst is Lady Astor" from Asquith. I spoke firmly in her defence'.[1409]

Her dislike of the Socialists did not prevent Frances from attending the debates in the Commons, where she very quickly concluded that J R Clynes, Lord Privy Seal, was 'a bad leader' of the House.[1410] Frances consoled herself with the knowledge that 'The muddles are mostly Parliamentary – otherwise "the new ministers are so respectful to their permanent officials that the offices will be better run that ever before"'.[1411]

One issue in which Frances – and the National Council of Women – showed considerable interest in the 1920s was the housing shortage, which became dire when the Liberals ended the build-at-any-cost public housing sanctioned in 1921 by Christopher Addison, Minister of Health. Writing to Gerald about her conversations with 'Jem' Salisbury, Lord President in both Law's and Baldwin's Governments, she urged solution of the issue: '[I]t is and will be the burning question of the day. Bad housing is the seedbed of everything that is revolutionary today. Every party must make it the topic'.[1412] While it did not overwhelm the country with Socialistic legislation, Labour did pass the Housing Act of 1924, providing subsidies for local authorities to construct houses which workers could *rent* at prices that the authority could regulate. The Act aimed to provide 2.5 million homes for citizens over the next 15 years.[1413]

Despite this success, Macdonald's popularity with the working class waned during his tenure in office, and the Labour Party did not remain long in power. In addition to not giving working class Britons what they wanted, it incurred political problems with its proposed treaty with the Soviet Union, which called for a loan from Britain. The accumulated evidence of the possible radicalization of the Labour Party (the J R Campbell case and the Zinoviev Letter) also doomed the treaty, which went down to defeat 368-198. Macdonald, losing this vote of confidence, promptly resigned and called for the third election in three years.

The 1924 election was not even close. The Conservatives won 414 seats, Labour was reduced from 191 to 151 seats, and the Liberals now held only 42 seats. Almost half the people in Britain had voted for the Conservatives – including the working class, which cast more votes for the Tories than for the Labour Party. Churchill, who had been defeated in his two previous Liberal election efforts, now returned to the Conservative Party representing Epping.[1414] Though Asquith had returned to Parliament in 1920, he was now defeated in a straight fight against a Labour candidate at Paisley and never returned to office thereafter. He subsequently entered the House of Lords as the Earl of Oxford and Asquith. Frances, never one to hold back forthright criticism, wrote Frank that her 'sole objection [to Asquith's earldom] was that he should enter the House [of Lords], whose powers he had maimed and whose existence he had never liked'.[1415]

Though in 1923 she had expressed little enthusiasm for the relatively unknown Baldwin as leader of the Conservative Party, Frances gradually became a convert, reporting to Frank that 'Baldwin is going up by leaps and bounds in the estimation of the party'.[1416] Arthur was asked to join the Committee of Imperial Defence, which '"exactly suits me"', he averred to Alice.[1417]

Before 1924 ended, a political crisis engulfed Egypt and the Sudan. On 19 November, a friend of Frank's, Maj Gen Sir Lee Oliver Fitzmaurice Stack, Governor-General of Anglo-Egyptian Sudan and Sirdar of the Egyptian army, was shot and killed in Cairo. The Sudan, whose status was left largely unchanged when nominal Egyptian independence[1418] was achieved in 1922, was still 'ruled' by British officers in the Egyptian army. In response to Stack's death, a British Note, or ultimatum, removed Egyptian troops from the Sudan,[1419] an action much desired by the Sudanese and their political officers. Frank felt the blow of Stack's death. In a service where 'personal relations and initiative' mattered more than 'titles and portfolios',[1420] Frank had 'lost a very good friend in Stack . . . . [H]is death has stiffened the Home Government into doing the sensible and firm thing at last. Unless we bungle incredibly now we have got the Sudan launched on a sensible basis . . . the best monument that poor old Stack could have had'.[1421]

In March 1924, Frances saw the Goschens, together with Phyllis and her children, off to India, where Lord George Goschen would serve as Governor of Madras. Shortly thereafter, Frank was seconded as Military Secretary to the Governor of Madras, and Frances sought out an authority to help her understand the political forces raging on the sub-continent. Lord Willingdon – who had just completed two terms as Governor of Bombay and then Madras – and his wife came for lunch in June. She learned that he favoured 'India for the Indians, and a definite policy, not of suppression, but "go ahead"'.[1422] Frances declared to Frank, 'What a splendid moment to be [in India]!'[1423]

The year 1924 would prove physically difficult for Frances. Though she had suffered aches and pains on a daily basis throughout her life, Frances had overall enjoyed fairly good health. Now, however, she was plagued with numerous health problems, and the activities in which she engaged appeared to tax her strength more than usual. Her friend and family physician, Dr Herbert Mills, arranged for her to see a London specialist (probably Dr Howell Gabriel Gwyn Jeffries), who diagnosed Frances with cancer in her left breast. Of course, she preferred Scottish doctors and shortly thereafter consulted an Edinburgh physician, probably Mr William James Stuart,[1424] who confirmed Jeffries's findings.

Her immediate concern was her yet unfinished biography of Balfour of Burleigh, and she worked intensely to complete it before her operation. When ordering books from the Douglas and Foulis Library to be sent to her at the nursing home, Frances proclaimed, not without a twinkle of dark humour, "'Yes, I'm going to have a severe operation but I've finished the Life of B[alfour] of B[urleigh] so it doesn't matter if I do die!'"[1425] The standard treatment for breast cancer at this time was radical mastectomy, which Stuart performed on 6 November 1924.[1426] Betty, Ruth, and all of Frances's daughters were present for the operation. Chemotherapy did not yet exist, of course, and postoperative radiotherapy was apparently either not prescribed or was not elected. Lymphedema was a painful problem for patients who had this operation during this era, and Frances did not escape the condition; she told Betty her arms 'felt like sausages' hanging by her side.[1427] Meantime, ever frugal, she asked her daughters if people were 'wasting money on telegrams'.[1428]

Now 66, Frances appears for once to have exercised a modicum of caution while recovering. Betty, no doubt attempting to allay Frank's fears, reported on Frances's post-operative activities to her nephew: 'Your Mother is beyond words wonderful. . . '. Only a few days after the procedure, she sat in a chair in the afternoon, and 'has done [so] every day since and yesterday she announced in triumph [that she had partially dressed herself unassisted]. . . . She declares she has suffered nothing she would call real pain (her standard in this region pretty high) . . .'.[1429] Stuart removed her stitches on 17 November, and ten day later, she returned to London by rail, with Betty as her travelling companion.

Frances's recovery was long, but she was persistent. She recorded on 11 January 1925 that **'the healing [was] complete'** and the nerve pain was improving,[1430] but when she attempted to resume some of her normal activities, she found that they made her 'too tired', she had 'not much energy', or she was 'exhausted'.[1431] The fatigue – and possibly even post-operative medicines – left her depressed at times, causing this strong woman to admit that she had to **'struggle and fight and pray'**.[1432] Nor did Frances regain her strength quickly. One year after the procedure, having spoken on 10 November 1925 to 300 women in a Congregational Church, she wrote, somewhat forlornly, to Frank that '[I] did not speak well, I was too tired, and I have not got back such powers as I once had'.[1433] Betty asserted that Frances continued to lead a busy and strenuous life to the end, but, for all her bravery and 'gallantry', hers was 'more and more a sedentary life' thereafter.[1434] For Frances, 1924 was '**A terrible year. God help me through the future**'.

Arthur, now Lord Balfour, went to Palestine in March 1925 for the official launching of Hebrew University in Jerusalem. He was accompanied by Dr and Mrs Chaim Weizmann and Major Edward and Joan Lascelles.[1435] The inauguration of the University, on 1 April, was witnessed by 7,000 people, many more being turned away.[1436] On rising to speak, Arthur, dressed in his red robes as Chancellor of Cambridge University, received 'a tremendous ovation, the audience rising and for a long time cheering and waving hats and handkerchiefs'.[1437] Speaking without notes, Balfour asserted that 'this marks a great epoch in the history of a people, who made this little land of Palestine the centre of great religions, whose intellectual and moral destiny is, from the national point of view, reviving, and who will look back to this day we are celebrating as one of the great milestones in their future career'.[1438] To further a reconciliation that he desired and believed was necessary, Arthur also asserted,

> I hope the Arabs will remember that in the darkest days of the Dark Ages, when Western Civilization appeared almost extinct and smothered under barbaric influence, it was Jews and Arabs together who gave the first sparks of light which illuminated a gloomy period. If in the tenth century, Jews and Arabs could work together for the illumination of Europe, cannot Jews and Arabs work in cooperation with Europe [today]?[1439]

> Arthur did not neglect the Arabs. En route to Galilee, the Balfour party had coffee at a Bedouin camp, where Arabs, many coming 'all the way from the far end of the Jordan valley', welcomed the visitors.[1440] After a Jewish ceremony of blessing at Galilee, Arthur received Sheik Muhamed Ali, the representative of the Arabs of Galilee, who assured Arthur that he and his followers had lived 'in perfect harmony' as close neighbors for 35 years, a harmony which he hoped would spread over Palestine.[1441] In reply, Arthur confirmed to the Sheik that the Balfour Declaration embodied a policy of peace. Sadly, Arthur's promise of peace remains unfulfilled in the second decade of the 21st century.

When George Nathaniel, Marquess Curzon of Kedleston, died in March, Arthur replaced Curzon as Lord President, meaning that he was back in the cabinet once more. Frances's biography of 'B of B' was published in May 1925, timed to coincide with the General Assembly of the Church of Scotland. The work received many favourable reviews, especially that of *The Scotsman*, (20 May) and *The Times (25 May)*. *The Scotsman*'s review concluded that her controversial ecclesiastical and secular political opinions '[make] the volume all the more readable and suggestive'. [1442]

Oswald returned to Britain for a visit in spring 1925 and came home for good in November as the London representative of Harris, Forbes & Company. He created an apartment for himself out of the nursery wing at 32 Addison Road, complete with a private entrance. Thus, he was available to assist his mother, could provide occasional company for her, and still had privacy for himself.

By the 1920s, most of the animosity and tension which had marked Frances's relationship with Alice had dissipated. That she had reason to be leery of Fire Practice, which Alice insisted family and staff perform yearly, can be seen in what happened during one drill in 1925. Three housemaids shooting down the fire escape hurt themselves: one broke her false teeth and two others cut their hands. It is a wonder that Frances herself, now quite frail, could survive the trip down the chute without enduring pains in her hip and palpitations of the heart, which she was now experiencing. Her participation in these drills in the 1920s says a lot about her determination to get along with Alice as well as her physical and emotional courage.

Before the end of 1925, Frances was faced with a grim task. In the 25 years following her father's death, Frances had not boycotted Ina as Niall wished, though in fact she spent little time with her. In autumn 1925, Princess Louise informed Frances that Duchess Ina's health was failing and apparently asked Frances to check on the Dowager Duchess. [1443]

Since her husband's death, the Duchess had spent considerable money and effort rebuilding and restoring some of Iona Cathedral, given by the Duke to the Church of Scotland during their short, five-year marriage. In her will, Ina directed her heirs to have her funeral at Iona and to bury her in the tomb she had built beside one she earlier had built for the Duke. [1444] Her labours were part of a pitiable effort to create the impression that she was buried beside the Duke, who, by the wishes expressed in his Will, was buried at Kilmun.

Early in her final illness, Ina asked Frances to accompany her body to Iona, and Frances said that she would go 'as it is fitting'. [1445] Ina died on Christmas Eve 1925; her funeral was to be held in Iona Cathedral on 30 December. Frances made the trip to Iona in spite of bad weather. The description of the experience published in *The Scotsman* speaks volumes to her determination, her loyalty, and the courage that marked her entire life: '[During the journey, by her insistence] she sat on the top deck on a chair lashed to the rail, with the coffin of the dead Duchess under a tarpaulin at her feet, with the wild Atlantic waves sweeping over the ship – all alone with the dead in a fury of winter wind and spray. 'That's a brave woman', said the skipper [of] the *Ross of Mull . . .* '.[1446]

That it was the association with her father which had prompted Frances to go to Iona can be seen from Frances's last recorded words in her diary of 1925: '**the last bit of my father [is] gone**'. Unhappy that Frances had participated in the funeral, Niall forbade Frances henceforth from staying at the Lodge on Tiree, her long-time island residence, and he informed her that she was no longer welcome at Inveraray Castle. Being banned from these residences must have been a blow, but Frances dealt with it as she dealt with adversity throughout her life.

Before the year 1925 closed, Dr Mills warned Frances, who had continued to tire easily, that her heart was weakening. In 1926, she began to have more heart problems, including breathlessness, fainting spells, and palpitations, but despite her age and health concerns, she did not slow down appreciably. She continued to speak, open bazaars, give prizes, and attend committee meetings, but travel was more fatiguing and difficult. She did not lose her sense of humour, however. When Mussolini was quoted in 1927 as saying that 'woman neither inspires nor creates', Lady Frances scoffed, 'It seems rather hard to abuse women for not creating when the race continues through them. One woman must have been concerned in creating even Mussolini'.[1447]

Strikes had been intermittently problematic for British citizens during the post-war period, but the General Strike of 1926 touched every life in a more comprehensive way. It began with the miners' discontent over a proposed decrease in wages, accompanied by a demand for longer work hours from owners of mines that were now losing money. When negotiations among the miners, the owners, the Trades Union Council, and the Government collapsed, the nation was confronted with a General Strike, which began on 4 May 1926.

With newspapers unavailable, Frances was forced to join the technological revolution and, on 6 May, acknowledged that 'Oswald has given me a wireless set'[1448] and noted that 'the Public are being warned three times a day not to listen to rumours'. On 9 May, Frances listened to Baldwin's evening broadcast, which she deemed 'good. He is a master of conciliatory and yet firm platitudes'. 'The good news "Strike Off" came quite unexpectedly' on 12 May, and Frances noted that it was '**my wedding day!**'

In February 1926, Frank returned to the Sudan. He was appointed Deputy Governor of the Red Sea Province in 1926, meaning he again was headquartered at Port Sudan. He served in this post for a year before becoming Governor, serving from 1927 to 1929.

Baffy began the 'important work' of sorting the Papers of Arthur Balfour this year. There were some 30 boxes of material, from which Baffy would eventually write the first major biography of her uncle. Meanwhile, Frances was still continuing her political dinners at the ends of Parliamentary sessions. In July 1926, however, because Arthur had become so deaf, she could only have six in attendance.

Britons were both engaged and enraged in 1927-1928 by the struggle in the House of Commons over a proposed New Book of Common Prayer for the Church of England. The Revised Prayer Book, a work that had long been in production, was widely supported by the Anglicans, both in the Church of England Convocations and the Church Assembly. One of the chief reasons for the alteration was to better accommodate Anglo-Catholicism, the direction in which more ordained Anglicans were inclined. Declaring that she had 'responded like an old war horse to this raging ecclesiastical crisis',[1449] Frances wrote scores of letters on the subject during the 1927-1928 period. When the Revised Prayer Book failed to pass the House of Commons in 1927, she was surprised: 'I thought it was sure to pass. [But] . . . [t]he Church has given in to the Anglo-Catholics, and must suffer'.[1450] Meanwhile, she thanked God she was a citizen of a country with a 'Church of reason and freedom from ritual'.[1451] The House of Lords approved the Revised Prayer Book, but the Commons ultimately rejected it again in 1928, even though a further compromise had been offered.

The year 1929 saw another election, the Conservatives having enjoyed five years at the helm; overall, things had moved smoothly along. Frances was still a supporter of Baldwin, saying, 'How English, and honest, and excellent, Baldwin always is'.[1452] Though the Conservatives polled more votes, Labour won 288 seats to the Conservatives' 260. The Liberals' 59 seats meant that no party had a majority. Baldwin resigned immediately, and Ramsey MacDonald became Prime Minister again.

With the defeat of Baldwin's Government, Arthur handed in his seals of office to King George V, thus ending fifty-five years (1874-1929) of public service; his record of active service in the Governments of his day has not been equaled in modern times. Afterwards, he spent part of the morning in the garden with the King and then had lunch with the monarch before leaving Bognor.

In August 1928, Frank was made Governor of Mongalla Province, the southern-most part of the Sudan (today the Republic of South Sudan) and played a role in guiding the development of the southern part of modern Sudan. Frank informed Arthur in an especially succinct manner what approach he would be taking on behalf of the British Government as Governor of the province: 'The Government is out for two things – to preserve tribal organization and to rule indirectly through the tribal chiefs and elders[,] and secondly to give as much education as will enable the natives to share in administration and commercial development and avoid the necessity of importing Arabic-speaking clerks and artisans from the North'.[1453]Arabic was to be avoided, he continued, because 'Islam always follows Arabic – Politically, and we don't want that. There are quite enough Moslems in N[orth] Africa already'.

By the late 1920s, Frances no longer attended all of the sessions of Parliament: her health would not permit it. It was touching that, when she had lunch in the House with Edith Picton-Turbervill in July 1930, '"The Headwaiter"', remembering her fondly, '"shook hands [with her] with warmth"'.[1454] Her limited attendance did not prevent her from giving her frank opinions to the Labour leaders, however. 'I told them the fault of their party was vanity, ignorance and self-centredness'.[1455] When asked of what they were ignorant, Frances replied, '"History and customs and reverence for old things"'.

In April 1927, Michael Dugdale, in his last term at Oxford, announced his decision to become an architect, thus carrying on his grandfather's profession.[1456] Frances gave him Eustace's box of instruments 'with his initials in the lid'.

In spring 1927, Frances learned that Asquith had a form of paralysis – 'The papers call it neuritis'[1457] – and was confined to a wheelchair. His health continuing to decline, Asquith resigned as Leader of the Liberal Party in October 1927; he died the next February. Frances attended the private memorial service for him at Westminster Abbey. 'Dear Henry', she wrote to Margot, 'I shall always think of him – a heart of gold, and so Trustworthy'.[1458]

Although Arthur's increasing deafness limited conversation, he had generally enjoyed good health. In 1928, however, he began to experience esophageal spasms which brought on coughing spells which made eating and talking difficult, so he began to take his meals in his bedroom. He did not return to London for the Parliamentary Session of spring 1928, but he did begin writing his memoirs, and when by summer his health had improved, he was back in London resuming some of his old life. In July, Arthur celebrated his 80th birthday. The British Academy commemorated this milestone at its public luncheon on 24 July; the Prince of Wales proposed his health. The next day, his actual birth date, Parliament, at Nancy Astor's arrangement, presented him with a Rolls-Royce automobile and a gramophone, which would become prominent features of his daily life thereafter. Twenty-two of 29 family members also celebrated with a dinner party in Arthur's honour, all of those absent being out of the country except Betty, who was ill. (To get **'the farmers'** [Eve and Mary] back to their farm New Bells in time for morning milking, Betty informed Frances that she was going to have them picked up by a 'fast Daimler', to which Frances queried, 'Is there any other kind?'[1459]) When doctors forbade him to return to London in the autumn, Arthur offered his resignation, but

Baldwin refused to accept it, requesting instead that he be available for consultation. To be closer to London, therefore, he moved in January 1929 to Fisher's Hill, home of Betty and Gerald.

Also this year, Oswald purchased Landmere, a large country estate on the Essex coast. After spending much of the year collecting furniture for the residence, he moved into his new home, called The White House, in the autumn. Declaring that it was 'all in the best taste',[1460] Frances added poignantly that '[i]t is all Eustace coming out, a little different in date'.

Quite possibly the biggest event of 1929 for Frances was the reunification of the Church of Scotland after two decades of efforts to overcome several sticking points. The Government, desiring to remove politics from the celebration, acknowledged the importance of the event by choosing the Duke of York, the future King George VI, as Lord High Commissioner.[1461] Frances recalled being with the Duke and Duchess of York at the General Assembly in May. At the dinner at Holyrood Palace, Frances went in with the Duke. They spoke of Aunt Louise and Uncle Lorne and 'talked of the pleasure Princess Elizabeth is to the King'.[1462] Of course, when the Duke expressed the sentiment that 'the Church is a wonderful thing in Scotland', Frances could not resist the temptation. '"No bishops, and no Prayer Book, Sir"', she replied. 'He smiled but said nothing'.[1463]

The official reunification was 'consummated' on 3 October 1929.[1464] Frances's pleasure at the reunion service was effusive. 'We lifted the roof with the opening Psalm'. After the devotional service,

> Dr Paterson said the Union reminded him of the history of Scotland. How we had fought England with stubborn resistance, . . .[but] when the Union became inevitable we said 'Well, we will go on with it and we will make a good thing of it, and so we have!' So – of this Union, 'We will make a good thing of it . . .'. [E]ndless hand grasps from Ministers. I am in Paradise.[1465]

At Fisher's Hill, Arthur listened on the wireless to the 2 October morning service in St Giles and to the joint Assembly meeting in the afternoon. When he read that she was 'in Paradise', Arthur poked a bit of fun at Frances, noting he had 'heard many descriptions of Heaven, but none comprised solely of ministers!'[1466]

The next day, Frances and Elma Story returned to the large Hall on Annandale Street for the main service.

> 12,000 seated in blocks. A high platform. . . . No organ or any instrument. . . . I was seated just behind Cantuar in Convocation Robes. They say his speech in the evening was really good – full of emotion

– I don't trust him! . . . All Scotland was represented. 'The Church
of Scotland engrossing the mind, talk, thoughts of the whole of my
beloved Scotland' as the King [George V] in his really fine letter said.[1467]
Frances missed the concluding meeting because the strain was apparently too much
for her – 'I gave out at the end'[1468] – and the following morning, she had breakfast
in bed at Rosneath, where she was staying with Princess Louise. Arthur made Betty
read Frances's reports of the great event to him *three times*. This was not the last
meeting of the General Assembly that Frances attended; she was also there – and in
the Throne Gallery again – for the 1930 meeting, the first since the reunion.

CHAPTER 16

'Women are looking Up' [1469]
(1924-1931)

'I think a good set of women are in.' [1470]

'[S]he will be numbered among the
greatest of [Scotland's] women'. [1471]

The Very Rev Dr Norman Maclean

By 1924, women had had the vote for six years and were using it. They were also continuing to do their part for their country – perhaps in ways not imagined before – and the 'Modern Girl' was developing and gaining much attention. In March, Lady Frances Balfour agreed to debate Viola Tree, daughter of Beerbohm Tree, on the question 'Is the young woman of the day any worse than she ever was?' at the London School of Economics (the program was one of a series arranged to raise money for the King Edward Hospital Fund). [1472] Not only could Frances draw an audience; she could be counted on to rouse a crowd with her observations and speaking style. In front of 'a large audience', Frances led off with the statement that, though young women of the past were 'more sheltered and less informed,' their lives were 'more romantic'. 'They knew less of men, and "sweet seventeen" in the past thought of men as paladins, heroic creatures with all the virtues. Old age changed that attitude. (Laughter)'. She went on to say, though, that 'this attitude had made men of that time better than men were to-day. It was good to be believed in, especially for a man'.

Frances could not let this opportunity pass without making a reference to make-up and perfume, however. She recalled that 'when she was young red hair was supposed to distinguish the professional courtesan. What do we see today?

(Laughter.) The young woman doing everything in her power to imitate the courtesan . . . !'

Viola Tree, on the other hand, focused on women's freedom, which she said 'was the best guarantee of their good behavior'. She believed that '[t]he young woman of the day seemed . . . to be an open-air, hurried, unashamed person. She had nothing to hide, and, if she had, would not hide it'.

In reply, Frances recalled 'the shame which women of her generation felt in looking at old photographs of themselves in the extraordinary garments they once "worked themselves into", and she wondered if the young women of the day would in time be ashamed of photographs of themselves with practically no clothes on at all. (Laughter.)'

Frances reported to Frank that the debate, which had been broadcast, had made her 'notorious': 'post and press raged furiously together'.[1473] Afterward, she was asked by *John Bull* magazine, *The Weekly Dispatch*, and *The Express* to write further on the subject. Frances's 'notoriety' even reached America, where Oswald was asked what his mother would do if she came to New York. He answered, 'She wouldn't get here. She would either die of shock or be deported for felling a Reporter at the quarantine station!'[1474] Indeed, there was enough interest in Frances that a New York photography company, Kadel and Herbert News Photos, carried her photograph in its portfolio.[1475] Frances undoubtedly knew that the more 'outrageous' her statements were, the more interested people would be in attending, and the more money the debate would raise. She came to realize, however, that participating in such debates had gained her the reputation of being old-fashioned, behind the times, so she began to make it clear that she was not 'hostile to the modern young woman. . . . [S]he admired the independence and athletic spirit of the girl of to-day'.[1476]

'Old suffragists' like Frances had an opportunity to gather again when the National Union of Societies for Equal Citizenship hosted a garden party at Aubrey House in honour of now Dame Millicent Fawcett, who had been recognised in the 1925 New Year's Honours List with a GBE (Dame Grand Cross of the Order of the British Empire). Frances was one of the speakers at the party,[1477] where she and Fawcett were photographed, seated together.

By 1925, women over age 30 had voted in four elections, and there was now a Bill in the House of Commons which proposed to give votes to women at the age of 21. Of course, the NUSEC had this as its object, and the suffragists succeeded in getting the Second Reading of a private Member's Bill, supported by the Government, passed by a 216-73 margin. Surprisingly, Frances wrote a letter to *The Times* in opposition to the measure. 'We have barely tested the working of the franchise that we have. It used to be said that it took ten years before the voters of 1884 used and appreciated their votes'.[1478] Frances certainly did not oppose extending the vote to women over 21; her statement probably indicated that Frances believed that the suffragists had acceded to Sir John Simon's 1917 suggestion that they promise to wait ten years before altering the franchise again on behalf of their sex. Indeed, Sir William Bull, Conservative, had insisted during the 1925 debate 'that there had been an undertaking by leading women's societies in 1918 . . . to agree to no further political agitation for a ten-year period.'[1479]

Frances assisted two new women's organizations in the 1920s – the Six Point Group and the Open Door Council, the purposes of which resembled the older Freedom of Labour Defence committee. Both were founded by Lady Rhondda, another equal rights feminist friend. In spite of the supposed guarantee under the Sex Disqualification (Removal) Act of 1919 that individuals were not disqualified '"by sex or marriage"' from '"the exercise of any public function"', women were still discriminated against (female teachers, for instance, still lost their jobs when they married).[1480] Frances was a speaker at the Six Point Group's 'most spectacular moment', a meeting in November 1922 highlighting this discrimination.[1481] With the Labour Party's influence growing and trade unions still attempting to limit women's work and competition, the Open Door Council opposed the extension of 'protective legislation' which was restricting women from better-paying jobs in some industries.

Frances's illnesses and physical problems reduced the number of speeches she made and meetings she attended in 1924: she apparently spoke only nine times and attended only 17 meetings. Both speaking and attendance at meetings increased in the next two years, but again in 1927, health problems increased and she spoke only ten times that year. Her best-known effort was her broadcast on behalf of the National Council of Women, which proposed to raise £5,000 for the lease of newer, larger office spaces. The Council especially desired a broadcast by either 'Sybil Thorndike or Lady Frances Balfour'[1482] – not bad company – to explain the situation and issue a call for contributions. It was Frances who eventually made the broadcast, but not without considerable inconvenience and irritation. The broadcast had to be made at Bournemouth on Saturday, 8 October, two days before the Annual Conference of the NCW was to open in that city and would necessitate two days' travel for Frances. Her letter to General Secretary Norah Green condemning the plans was typically Francesesque: 'I am dreadfully bothered by this tiresome broadcasting. . . . An infernal invention. . . . [Bournemouth] is an unholy arrangement and I should have chucked it when I heard what it meant, but I was in the Hebrides & hoped I might die before the date'.[1483]

Frances's objection to radio broadcasting came from the experience itself. She considered the chairs on which she had to sit electrocuting-looking, she disliked being in a windowless room (which kept out sound), and she especially loathed having to read her speech rather than deliver it extemporare, her usual form of address.[1484] Despite her objections, however, she made such radio broadcasts at least four or five times in the 1920s and early 1930s.

In her appeal for the NCW, Frances used humour and cajoling to snare her audience. After detailing the inadequacies of their present offices ('the Congested Districts Board would have condemned them'), Frances declared that the NCW only needed 'the modest sum of £5,000. If we were man-run we should need at least £15,000'.[1485] Urging the NCW branches to '"drive" in every shape and form – cards, Sales, American Teas"', she concluded her appeal with the promise that '[o]ur treasurer is a woman and therefore may be entirely trusted. . .'.

There are no diaries of Frances in the Balfour Papers after 1927. Thus, there is no way to determine the number of speeches she gave, the subjects on which she spoke, or the meetings that she attended during the last three years of her life. We do know that she continued to be present at most of the annual meetings of organizations such as the National Council of Women, and the TAS Minutes indicate she attended most of those meetings.

Frances did write about one suffrage activity in 1928 in which she was a leading participant. In what she called her last suffrage meeting (held to celebrate the Flapper vote, as the extension of the franchise to women over 21 was called), Frances presided on October 28 over a platform in which a young school teacher, representing the youngest of the new voters, spoke. Shortly thereafter, this same woman, who Frances declared had 'made a capital speech',[1486] was elected to Parliament. She was Janet Jennie Lee, future wife of Aneurin Bevan. 'Two women owners have won the first two great races of the season. Women are looking up', Frances declared.[1487] Though there is little about her feminist work that can be documented for the rest of her life, with Betty's assertion that Frances continued her normal activities down to her death, it is fair to say that she worked for women all her adult life.

On 5 August 1929, Millicent Garrett Fawcett died. Writing to Betty, Frances noted that 'no prominent leader took notice of her death', though Baldwin had unveiled a statue to Mrs Pankhurst around the same time.[1488] She again asserted that Arthur never liked Fawcett, and neither did Asquith: '"Wicked old man", [Fawcett] called [Asquith] to the end'.

In her eulogy of Fawcett, published in *Contemporary* magazine, Frances maintained that militancy had been a 'stern trial' for the veteran leader. 'Her strong sympathy with the injustice of the woman's position made her understand the movement. . . . Her emotion at their treatment, her sense of the crass stupidity that met force with superforce, her sense that we should not win the cause, neither would the opponents, almost broke her down'.[1489]

With fourteen women elected to the House of Commons, the year 1929 was an important one for women in Britain. Nine newcomers included Frances's long-time friend Edith Picton-Turbervill as well as Jennie Lee, Dr Marion Phillips, and Dr Ethel Bentham, all Labourites. In the new cabinet, the position of Minister for Labour was filled by Margaret Bondfield, the first woman cabinet member in Great Britain. Anti-Socialist that she was, Frances nevertheless lauded the women's success: 'I think a good set of women are in', she declared.[1490]

It is generally believed that organizations like the Travellers Aid Society were not as successful in the post-World War I era as they had been before the Great War. However, the number of people assisted by the Society in 1920 (6,190 in London) and 1924 (5,289 [1491]) suggests that the services of the organization were as much in demand as before the war and that the organization's work was still vital, since 'girls are more adventuresome but they are not more discerning . . . '.[1492] The TAS encountered major problems in the early 1920s: inflation, maintenance of an old building, and frequent staff changes meant that the Society struggled to acquire both funds and workers to carry on its work.

From the outset, the Travellers' Aid Society was predominantly a women's organization, with women as almost all the managing officials, officers, and staff. Earlier in the nineteenth century, women working in similar philanthropic efforts would likely have been the foot soldiers in an organization run by men. The TAS was one of the premier examples of a successful philanthropic effort launched and sustained for over a half century by women,[1493] thanks in part to Frances and an Executive Board which boasted, in 1902 for instance, 72 women and only 9 men (many of whom were clergymen). In fact, the first eleven-member Executive Committee approved for the TAS in February 1886 was entirely female.[1494]

Frances was nearly as active in the TAS in the post-war era as she had been prior to 1914. However, by the time the war ended, she was in her sixties and unable – financially and physically – to host many of the fund-raising events needed by the Society. Nevertheless, she still did what she could. When the Society had to raise £3,000 to purchase the lease of 3 Baker Street and make repairs to the building in 1920, Lady Frances wrote 'special letters' to *The Times* and *The Westminster* to solicit contributions.[1495] When radio became available, Frances made appeals for money over the airwaves on behalf of the TAS, and her appeal in 1927 raised over £100 for the Society.[1496] Frances also secured Princess Louise as a Patron, and she enlisted the services of her son-in-law, Captain Edgar Dugdale, to serve as Honorary Treasurer in 1924. Additional testimony to Frances's competent leadership of the Society can be found in the longevity of service provided by the honorary officers, some staff, and many members of the Executive and General Committees.

Frances would not live to see the end of the Travellers' Aid Society; but her importance to the existence of the Society can be seen from the subsequent history of the organization. By the 1930s, the TAS was in continual financial straits, and the number of organizations affiliating with and supporting the TAS declined. Only 14 societies were represented on the General Committee in 1920; this number had fallen to ten by 1934.[1497]

An equally serious problem for the Society during the 1930s was the death of many prominent members, the chief of whom was Lady Frances Balfour, the only president the Society had had in its 45-year history. Shortly before her death, F L Lucas died, his final gift a legacy of £1,000 given to the Society 'free of Legacy Duty'. Numerous other deaths of long-serving members in the 1930s (Lady Battersea, J B Braddon, Mrs Arnold de Grey, and Miss Lowndes) left a great vacuum in the leadership.

One major change effected by the TAS shortly after Frances's death undoubtedly had a detrimental effect on the membership of the Executive Committee and possibly on donations to the organization. At their meeting on 22 January 1932, members, desiring to make it clear that the TAS was not a department of the YWCA, voted 18 to 5 to delete the phrase 'under the auspices of the YWCA' from its literature. This action cost the Society the services of two especially valuable, long-time members, Mrs Sidney Buxton, daughter of Lady Emily Kinnard, and Mrs A F Buxton, another relative of the founder of the YWCA. Frances had carefully maintained the ties between the YWCA and the TAS ('[I]t was the last thing for the good of the TAS for it to depart from under the 'auspices' of the YWCA', she had asserted in 1893);[1498] one wonders if the decision to disaffiliate with the YWCA actually sped the demise of the TAS as an independent, viable organization. In 1939, running a deficit of £300, the TAS was absorbed by the National Vigilance Association;[1499] it was terminated in 1952.[1500]

If Frances had led and served only this one Society, she would have earned a place in the history of British women, but this was only one organization – and not the main one – to which she rendered noteworthy services.

In the late 1920s, the health of Frances's old friends was declining. By 1928, Lord Finlay was blind in one eye from a cataract. '[He] longed for the operation to remove it, but though the eye healed from the operation, his 'brain became affected shortly thereafter. [T]he iron framework gave way, and he died unconscious [on March 9[1501]]. No sadness of farewell'.[1502] Frances wrote eulogies to him, her 'oldest friend', which appeared in *The Times* and *The British Weekly*.

By February 1929, Frances too was experiencing significant health problems. She told Linky (Hugh Cecil) that she was 'a close prisoner [of home], heart and tubes both giving out, but I can still fight on paper'.[1503] She also informed Mary, Lady Wemyss in early May 1929 that she was 'rather a stationary person now', having 'a heart which won't allow walking', so '[I am] losing my temper', 'getting excited', and 'overeating'.[1504]

Arthur's health, too, was slowly deteriorating. After his visit to the King to hand over the seals of office in May 1929, Arthur returned to Fisher's Hill and dined downstairs. A few days later, he had a seizure.[1505] He gradually overcame the resulting mild paralysis, but 'never again left his two upstairs rooms'. Nevertheless, family members marveled over his good spirits. 'When a newcomer asks, "How are you?" he always says "very ill indeed", in a perfectly cheerful voice'.[1506]

Further evidence that Frances had made peace with Alice can be seen in Frances's decision to go 'mothing' with Alice in late September 1929. 'Off we went to Ravenheugh Wood. . . . Very pleasant talk for an hour, when midges set in in force'.[1507] After this outing, Frances reported to Betty what Jean Balfour had said: "'[Alice] has ceased to have any grudge against the world". It is that exactly, it is like talking to another person'.[1508]

Frances began thinking about writing her memoirs in 1925, but she did not begin until 1926. She later explained that she had had a difficult time tackling the task until she decided to focus on Eustace. Her motivation to write about Eustace, whom family members often disparaged, (unfortunately, when an individual dies of alcoholism, this is usually all one remembers of the person) was, no doubt, to remind readers of what he had accomplished in his shortened lifetime. Even so, her modesty held her back; thus, the two-volume work is mainly about the individuals and the political and religious scenes which played such a prominent role in her life and the life of the country, rather than about herself and the impacts she and Eustace had. Writing about the Church of Scotland's beliefs and its leaders, however, Frances expressed her concern about the current lack of interest in organized religion. 'A young pagan niece of mine was marveling over [Lady Frederick Cavendish's] interest in creeds and Church, . . . but why should people be astonished that religious beliefs did interest? They are interested in Christian Science, Psychic Research, Telepathy, and a dozen other signs of senile decay'.[1509] Frances sent each chapter as soon as she wrote it to her long-time friend Professor George Saintsbury for commenting and editing. Saintsbury forewarned Frances that if readers liked her, they would like the memoirs. 'If otherwise, otherwise'.[1510]

Ne Obliviscaris (Dinna Forget) was published in January 1930 to considerable praise. In a subhead entitled 'A Perfervid Scot', *The Scotsman* acknowledged that Frances was a woman who 'was singularly well placed for near-hand and first-hand observation, which, with her temperament, meant active participation, as far as sex and opportunity allowed, in the movements of her time'.[1511] Another even more positive reviewer asserted that her autobiography would 'take rank among the most valuable of its type . . . . Not all of the countless personal records published to-day can be trusted to provide authentic material for the historian, but this is one of those that will not be neglected'.[1512]

One aspect of her book was universally praised by family members. Her close friendship and love of the Salisburys – especially her memories of Lady Georgina – were evident in her chapter on Hatfield. Frances asserted that no one ever bored Lady Salisbury,[1513] and that she would have 'loved the age of motors, the only thing which today seems to match her love of movement, or open air, and of traversing space'.[1514] She also declared that 'Lord Salisbury was [Lady Georgina's] vocation and ministry and that between them there was [perfect] understanding'.[1515] Appreciative of her words, Alice Salisbury wrote to Betty: '[W]hat gratitude one feels for the picture of Her Ladyship, glowing and vital even as she was. I don't think anyone else could have done it. They had a special understanding of each other that few had, and I feel if her Ladyship were here she would not wish for any other memorial of her'. She added, 'I feel grateful to it for giving my children and their children this living portrait and also of old Hatfield days. . .' .[1516] Another Cecil was also pleased. Bob not only admired 'the freshness and vitality' of her book, but found himself 'more in agreement with' the political aspects of it than he had expected.[1517] Meanwhile, her niece Joan Campbell, who believed that she got off 'lightly', promised to visit Frances and bring her a gift of 'a bottle of new nail polish – bright green!'[1518]

Frances's decision to focus on Eustace, which meant that the book ended with his death in 1911, caused *The Scotsman* to conjecture that there would be forthcoming 'at least another volume to complete the record'.[1519] It is doubtful that Frances would ever have finished her life's story. Had she done so, she would have been forced to write about World War I and the changes that came to Society and Britain in its aftermath. As she put it, her biography stopped short of the Great War 'from which we count a new era'.[1520] Her autobiography was about the heroes and heroines in her life, and these did not include David Lloyd George or Ramsay Macdonald!

Arthur was no longer at Whittingehame, so the family gathered around him at Fisher's Hill for Christmas in December 1929. Though his mind was clear, in early 1930, he began a further physical decline. On 9 March, he had two seizures, the second of which left him unconscious. When he regained consciousness, he was for a few days able to recognize visitors, such as Dr Weizman.[1521] On 18 March, Arthur sent his love, first to Oswald, who had telephoned for news, and then to Auntie, and finally to all the Whittingehame people. Betty and Gerald were summoned at 7.15 the next morning; the end was near. Baffy, Nora, RAL, Jean, and Coleman, his long-time valet, joined them in a silent vigil while Arthur 'appeared conscious all the time, his eyes open but glazed'. Around 8 am, his 'breathing became quieter, stopped, went on again, and then silence. Baffy looked at the nurse and she nodded. He was gone'.

The Dean of Westminster Abbey offered burial or a memorial service for Arthur, and Gerald accepted the latter. Arthur had wanted a simple funeral and interment at Whittingehame; after a funeral service at the Parish church (22 March 1930), attended only by family (19 were present[1522]) and neighbours and conducted by the Rev Dr Marshall Lang, Arthur's body was carried by farm wagon to its place of final resting, next after Eustace. Frances, now unable to walk the long distance, rode to the service in the car with Alice (who now needed a wheelchair).

> The day was a benediction, flooded with sunlight from morn till eve. . ., the little quiet church packed with our own folk. . . . [At the grave site] Alice [armed with a basket of snowdrops] was wheeled to the foot of the grave. . . . [She] threw in the snowdrops . . . then everybody threw in [their flowers] and the last farewell had come. . . . Lang had given the people a perfect sermon ending with [Arthur's] last words, 'Give my love to all at Whittingehame.[1523]

One concern of family members following Arthur's death was whether the cohesiveness of the family would remain. All members were so determined, however, that this would be the case that the unity and good will continued after his death. At their next reunion, Jean noted that 'Aunt Frances was never nicer'.[1524]

Frances had one more task to complete before she would be at peace with Arthur's demise. Before taking up his post in Ireland in 1887, Arthur had instructed Frances, in the event of his death, to open a leather pouch which accompanied his letter and 'read the scrawl inside'.[1525] Therein, Frances learned that Arthur wished her to take a small gift of a brooch to Mary Elcho and tell her 'that, at the end, if I was able to think at all, I thought of her.'[1526] Arthur's 'friendship' with Mary Elcho had lasted until his death. Frances delivered his message and brooch to Mary, now Countess of Wemyss.

Alison and the Savage bought their own home, called The Cottage, Oldbury Wells, at Bridgenorth in 1930. On visiting the new house for the first time, Frances noted that Eliza, 'with her hair up', was now 'quite grown up'.[1527] When Elizabeth

Milne was 14, she was sent to St George's School in Montreaux, Switzerland, to 'finish' her education, so she was a young lady by this time. Sadly, early in 1931, the Savage was diagnosed with cancer, and concerns about the well-being of Alison and her family continued. (He died in February 1932).

Another award came to Frank in the New Year's Honours List of 1931: he was made CBE, Commander of the Order of the British Empire. Frank had resigned from the Sudan Political Service effective January 1931. Shortly thereafter, he became the Representative of the Peruvian Corporation, a British company which owned transportation facilities, such as railroads and steamers, in Peru. He and Phyllis sailed for Lima, Peru, on 8 February 1931.

Health problems continued to bedevil Frances. In fall 1930, she had developed bronchitis, which returned in the New Year. Nevertheless, she had lunch with Sybil on New Year's Day.[1528] Meanwhile, still bothered by her Church's attitude toward women, Frances focused her work on women in the Church. In an article entitled 'The Ministry of Women' and published by *The Scotsman* on 16 January 1931, Frances pondered 'Why no woman . . . however gifted with apostolic zeal, [was] ever called by the Church . . . . The real difficulty is their sex, and the belief that the ministry is a priestly office. . . . We Presbyterians have [r]ejected the idea of a priesthood . . . '. [1529] She might not be as mobile as she once was, but – as she had noted – she could still 'fight on paper'.

Frail and infirm, her lameness and general deterioration considerably more pronounced,[1530] Frances still experienced good days: in late January, she noted having 'walked around the garden three times'.[1531] She had lost none of her mental spunk, however. When Oswald, visiting Joan, became ill with a bad throat and fever and had to go into a nursing home, he did not recover and return to London until 11 February. Impressed with the good food he had had while in the Nursing Home, he lectured his mother on foods that should be avoided.[1532] She countered, 'The longer I live the more sure I am that food cranks are the silliest and St Paul right when he said, "Eat what is put before you"'.

Early in February, three members of Frances's household staff contracted the flu. Betty reported that Frances also contracted it, though she herself recorded nothing about having it. She left her sickbed, however, to broadcast on the BBC on the subject of the Western Isles, especially her '"beloved Tiree"'.[1533] Dr Mills lent her his car to make the trip to the studio, and she made the broadcast on the night of 17 February 1931. 'It was her last public act'.[1534]

After she returned home, Frances became 'acutely' ill of bronchitis and had to send for a nurse. 'Alison came up from Shropshire to be with her. Oswald was in the house and saw her daily. Joan, Baffy, and Aunt Sybil were in and out and Betty came up from Woking'.[1535]

One especially important action Frances took was to send for the Rev Dr Archibald Fleming. She made up a long-standing quarrel with him, but Betty noted that she 'left all directions for her funeral in the hands of other Ministers'. Two days later, Alison, who had just left her mother's bedside, was called back by the nurse, but it was all over. Frances died of pneumonia and heart failure on 25 February 1931.[1536]

It was her request that a Memorial Service be held in Crown Court Church, London. As *The Times*, whose headline declared her a 'Great Whig Lady', noted,

> No Scotswoman of her generation was better known or more highly thought of among the mass of her countrymen than Lady Frances, and though they did not all share her enthusiasms, there was never any doubt about her zeal and public spirit in the affairs of Church and State alike. If she had been a man she might well have been a great political leader, for she had an acute and independent intellect, she was an eloquent speaker, and she had a firm grasp of those Whig principles which she inherited and which she never abandoned.[1537]

The paper also spoke of her ability to 'give the most real consolation',[1538] and Princess Louise's remarks echoed the sentiment. "'I shall miss her too terribly, she was really just the one only friend I could go to and know I would be able to have interesting talk with, give, and get sympathy'".[1539]

Her funeral and burial were at Whittingehame on 1 March 1931. Because her death was the next in the family after Arthur's, she was buried at the foot of Arthur's grave in 'the beech cathedral' in the Whittingehame cemetery. Betty related that she did not suggest that Gerald visit Frances during her last illness, but later wished she had. When he visited 32 Addison Road following her death, he was 'overcome with emotion as he entered that paneled drawing room of many memories. Aunt Sybil saw how moved he was and left him alone . . . '.[1540]

A Memorial Service at St Giles Cathedral in Edinburgh was held at the same time as her funeral at Whittingehame. The eulogy was delivered by her long-time friend and prominent Churchman, The Very Rev Dr Norman Maclean.

> It was impossible to think of Frances Balfour as silent while a wrong was left in the world unrighted. . . . The secret of all noble living was the capacity to sink oneself in a great cause, indifferent to the pain or loss that might ensue. For fifty years Frances Balfour lived on that height. She gave herself to the service of others. . . . She did not cry aloud in vain. Fifty years ago women had no rights as citizens, and no careers open to them as workers. She, more than most, helped to place

the weapon of the vote in the hands of the women of the country.[1541]

Maclean also provided the eulogy which *The Scotsman* published when it announced her death in large headlines which read in three lines:

'Lady Frances Balfour

Death in London

A Great Scotswoman'

> There was one great, all-controlling love in her life to which everything else was subservient, and that was her love for Scotland and for the Scottish Church. And no ancestor drew sword from scabbard with fiercer zest than she seized her pen and fell on the enemy. . . . There seldom has been so courageous a spirit tabernacling a body so frail. . . . I don't think she knew what fear was. . . . She lived a life of ceaseless activity. If she was not campaigning she was writing, and if not writing she was talking. She moved all her life among those who moved the world – Cecils and Balfours and Gladstones. . . . There was a divine fire in her that kindled and flamed. There was a passion for righteousness in her that could scorch and blister the enemy, and there was a great loyalty towards her friends that grappled them to her in spite of storms and stress. . . . Scotland will not forget this eager, ardent daughter who loved her with passionate devotion, and whom she will number among the greatest of her women.[1542]

The General Assembly of the Church of Scotland did not forget Lady Frances at its next gathering in May 1931 either. In his opening remarks, the Lord High Commissioner, Mr Brown, began his comments about those the Church had lost during the year with the observation that 'Lady Frances Balfour, whose presence we miss from the Throne Gallery. . . was a great Churchwoman in every sense of the word'.[1543] More importantly, the petition by Frances for women to be ordained by the Church was finally taken up during the 1931 session of the General Assembly.[1544] Frances would have been pleased (though women did not get this right until 1936), but she would have been even prouder when, in 2002, Crown Court Church got its first woman minister, the Rev Sigrid Marten.

Frances's demise was mourned not just in Britain but in Canada and the United States, where newspapers devoted lengthy articles to her death.

Not everyone praised Frances, of course. Unlike her relationship with the middle class leaders with whom she worked for such causes as women's enfranchisement, barmaids' employment, and peace, family members had been the recipients of many of her 'improvement' efforts, which did not meet with universal acceptance or pleasure. Jean Balfour, representing the Gerald Balfour family, in comparing Frances's family status with that of Arthur, concluded that 'we didn't love Aunt Frances'.[1545] A more intriguing commentary on her was provided by Lady Gwendolen Cecil, with whose letter Betty ended the Frances Balfour Papers.

> The immediate difficulty is to reconcile her devastating outbursts with her own serenity. . . . My conclusion is that one is in danger of digging too deep. . . . It is impossible not to be convinced that the storms meant nothing to her . . . . I think another influence on her was her cult for XVIIth c. Whig-Presbyterianism. . . . [S]he was consciously 'testifying for righteousness' in the manner of the Covenant Ministers who thundered against individuals in their congregation. . . .
>
> [O]ne touches the element of greatness in her character – the invincible courage, self-dependence, readiness to take without flinching any blow or deprivation which came to her. I never heard her complain of suffering or disappointment or anything like that. . . . I verily believe that so far as her own consciousness went, she lived and died at peace with herself. . . .[1546]

Frances did not leave a will per se, but she kept a notebook in which she recorded what items she wished Oswald, whom family members chose to be the Administrator of her Estate, to give to various individuals.[1547] She left her Papers to Betty, who already had 80 boxes of Frances's letters to her (Frances had a like number from Betty). Betty spent much of the 1930s organizing and editing the letters, which today comprise a significant portion of the Balfour Papers in the National Records of Scotland. These materials provide students of history with one knowledgeable woman's observations of many of the important political events of late 19th-early 20th century Britain.

On 24 April, at its first quarterly meeting held after her death, the General Committee of the Travellers' Aid Society decided, as its first order of business, to issue a brochure 'with the President's portrait and extracts from press notices about her' with its Annual Report, as a Memorial to its late President. 'Her true worth to the Society was only known to those who looked to her for guidance for so many years . . . . Whatever she considered to be the highest good for the T A S she would urge with all the energy of her strong personality'.[1548]

Included among the comments made by eulogists from numerous British newspapers was the observation that 'There are many who believe that had Lady Frances lived in another age, she might have been Britain's first woman Prime Minister [*The Daily Telegraph*]'. *The Daily Express* reported that 'Lord Balfour once said of her that if she had been a man she would have been leader of one of the great parties'. These were remarkable tributes for one who never even sat in Parliament –

though she might have sat there for twelve years. Such statements acknowledge as little else does the impact that she made, particularly in the newspaper and political world, on those who were current on national and world events and could recognize political knowledge and talent.

Though widely respected, Frances could be an intimidating woman. A biographer of John Buchan wrote that on one occasion, 'he and his wife were asked to dinner by the formidable Lady Frances Balfour, A J Balfour's sister-in-law, who was almost as influential as the minister of St Columba's and much more feared.'[1564][9]She came to have a stature and to command a respect that many public figures only aspire to. Indeed, the regard in which Frances was held was the primary recompense for her work for women.

This does not mean that she was always consistent. Long-time friend – and foe of women's suffrage – Herbert Asquith commented upon her contradictory nature, saying that she was 'a very remarkable person, with all sorts of contradictory qualities – courage enough to win the Victoria Cross, Celtic fervor to set all the heather in the Highlands on fire, masculine interest in politics and the world of action, passionate personal prejudices. . . '.[1550]

Constance Battersea wrote about her,

I have always held her to be a remarkable woman. A telling speaker and a brilliant writer, she championed the cause of women's emancipation from an early day, and was a strong upholder of Mrs. Fawcett and her views, although opposed to the actions of the extreme suffragettes. Her sense of humour is very keen and adds a point to her speeches, whilst a somewhat combative disposition makes her enjoy a tussle of words. She excels in impromptu orations, is quick in argument and telling in retort, but she never descends to flippancy in order to be witty . . . . She has the most remarkable pluck and force of will, which enables her to control bodily fatigue and discomfort, and to dispense, if need be, with many of the amenities of life. She is a very staunch friend, but her friendship never obscures her critical faculties. She is an unmistakable little personage . . . .[1551]

Assertions that Frances was unhappy in her marriage also do not stand up to scrutiny. She appears to have talked everything over with Eustace, seeking his opinion on every issue she faced for as long as he lived. Eustace's decision not to participate in the political life of his country but rather to involve himself with the military was no doubt a disappointment for her, but his decision was likely the catalyst that propelled Frances toward championing women's rights for the rest of her life and into friendships with those whose interests dovetailed with her own. Eustace's drinking undoubtedly was a heartache for her, but she loved her husband steadfastly throughout her life and missed him deeply after his death.

Some mention must be made of Lady Frances's 'storms' (what she called her 'temper'), which she herself recognised as intense and beyond her control. Additionally, there were times when she said she did not remember writing or saying words that family members attributed to her. Jean Balfour characterized this as 'a twist to her mind' and remembered that she 'sometimes seemed transported'.[1552] Given the difficulties and pain caused by her hip (and the ineffective but rigid and often painful regimen imposed upon her in her youth to correct that condition), there is a possibility that this led to some psychiatric problems; however, no such diagnosis could have been made during her life, and it is impossible to come to any definite conclusions now. In light of these difficulties, her achievements are only more impressive.

One of Frances's biographers has, after reviewing only a small portion of her life's work, pronounced her to be – and thus reduced her to – 'a snob.'[1553] Frances did share the prejudices of her class and her age (at this time, Britain was very much a class society), but no snob would have joined the suffrage movement at all, much less played a secondary role to Mrs Fawcett – a commoner – in championing the Cause. In an age when at least one nobleman regarded his wife's 'lack of snobbishness as a personal failing'[1554] and even servants had a rigid hierarchy, Frances worked with, not above, middle and working class women for a common goal. In truth, if one believed in the class system – still a strong force in Britain during Frances's lifetime despite challenges to it – one would be classified as an elitist. This is a better description of Lady Frances and more accurately reflects her philosophy of society and government. Snobbery is an affectation; elitism is a belief that the upper class by birth, heritage, training, education, and obligation should lead their community and nation. This was what her ancestors had done, and Frances believed that this obligation was hers as well. It is also worth mentioning that Frances should be judged by the standards of her day, not by those of the 21st century.

Except for her intelligence, courage (both physical and mental) was Frances's most noted characteristic. In truth, Frances was much farther out of her comfort zone in speaking for her various causes than were women like Mrs Pankhurst, Christabel Pankhurst, and Charlotte Despard, all of whom came from a tradition of challenging authority, whereas Frances's tradition was one of ladylike self-effacement.

Frances's style of public speaking further exemplifies her mettle. She appears never to have read a speech (except on the radio), though doing so was acknowledged at that time as a 'graceful way to sidestep a public speech'.[1555] Schooled in the political oratory of Parliament, her technique and presentation made her a memorable voice for the many causes she espoused. Frances did more than just speak occasionally for women's causes, however. She was the first member of the aristocracy to have a leadership role in the votes for women campaign, and she continued in this role, working increasingly longer hours, until it was won in 1918. She was, according to historian Colin Mathew, '. . . the only prominent [aristocratic] activist before 1900. . .'.[1556] It also says a great deal about Frances that she was willing to be such a faithful lieutenant for Mrs Fawcett: most aristocratic women would have expected to be – indeed, would have been – the chief leader of *any* movement in which they worked.

Frances's life spanned an incredibly fertile era. When she was born in 1858, the House of Lords was a powerful deliberative body, and members of the aristocracy led their communities and the nation. Only upper and middle class males voted, and women usually received only the education provided by governesses or local schools. Britain had experienced no great external threat since 1815, and Ireland was snug – if not secure – within the Empire. Large and small homes were lighted by candles and heated by fireplaces, and citizens wrote or telegraphed their news and opinions to their family and friends. Travel was by foot, horse and carriage, and rail – a mode of transportation only 28 years old in 1858.

By the time Frances died, Charles Darwin, Sigmund Freud, Max Planck, and Albert Einstein had challenged the stable, predictable world of the Victorians. Natural selection, the id, and relativity had ushered in a new way of thinking about humans and their world. The Republic of Ireland without Ulster was now created and independent of Great Britain, and the House of Lords was only a delaying factor in the legislative cogs. The automobile and the airplane now made it possible not only to move faster within Great Britain but to reach the rest of the world in a relatively short time. The incandescent light was available in most homes, and radios broadcast news and entertainment instantly to all citizens. Accepting these changes did not come easily to Frances, but to the end she remained an 'optimist'[1557] who could always see the good as well as bad aspects of new developments. As she said in her last broadcast, 'Much of the modern mechanisation is destroying the old beauty of Scotland, but if I am to be fair to things new, I must say that . . . mechanisation has its uses – in the swift ambulances, . . . the swift post office service, . . . the gallant army of country doctors . . . and the trained nurses have had their lives made a little easier by the motor'.[1558]

Frances was indeed a remarkable woman. She is not considered today to have been the most prominent woman of her age, and there are many studies of women's work for the vote which do not even mention her or include her autobiography in their bibliography. However, very few of her contemporaries can match her record of selfless work and toil for women and the success that marked her efforts. As long as there were grievances to be righted and trials to be overcome, Frances wrote and spoke about them. Gifted with a voice that was low, vibrant, and pleasant and an intellect that was quick and incisive, Frances continued throughout her life to enlighten audiences throughout the British Isles to the plight of women. Nearly a century after her death, her work for women still impresses.

It seems appropriate to conclude the life story of Lady Frances Balfour with a statement about her attributed to Eustace, her husband of 32 years about whom little is known concerning their marriage. Near the end of his life, '[w]hen he was ill and befuddled, he said of her, "In spite of all her being so difficult, and the way she spoils life for herself and me [at times], still, she is the only woman in the world for me, and I'd marry her again tomorrow!"'[1559]

APPENDIX A

Lady Frances's Organisations and Work for Women

Travellers' Aid Society, President, 1885-1931 (45 years)

Central Committee of the National Society for Women's Suffrage, Member, 1889-1892 (3 years)

Executive Committee, Central Committee of the National Society for Women's Suffrage, 1892-1896 (4 years)

Executive Committee, National Union of Women's Suffrage Societies, 1896-1919 (23 years)

London Society (and precursors) for Women's Suffrage, President, 1896-1919 (23 years)

Scottish Churches' League for Women's Suffrage, President, 1912-1919 (7 years)

Women's Liberal Unionist Association, 1888-1904 (16 years)

Freedom of Labour Defence, President, 1899-1913 (14 years)

Parliamentary Private Secretary, Sir Robert Finlay, 1895-1906 (11 years)

Victoria League, Hon Secretary and Social Organiser, 1902

Swanley Horticultural College, Director, 1903-1905 (3 years)

Rebuilding Crown Court Church, 1905-1915 (10 years)

The Englishwoman, Editorial Board, 1909-1921 (12 years)

Royal Commission on Divorce, Member, 1910-1912 (3 years)

Crown Court Church Woman's Guild, President, 1910-1931 (21years)

Scottish Women's Hospital, 1914-1919, Executive Committee, London SWH (5 years)

Girls' Guildry, President, 1910-1915 (5 years)

Women's Municipal Party, Vice President and Member, Executive Committee, 1913-1919 (6 years)

Women's Advisory Committee, Liquor Control Board, Member, 1915-1919 (4 years)

National Council of Women, Member, Executive Committee, 1917-1922, President, 1922-1924 (14 years)

ENDNOTES

PROLOGUE

1 *The Bucks Advertise and Aylesbury News*, 4 December 1909, 8. All of the quotes concerning this episode were taken from this source.

CHAPTER ONE   'Emancipation was a Passion'

2. Frances Balfour, *Ne Obliviscaris,* (2 Vols, London, Hodden and Stoughton, 1930), I, 91.

3. Frances Campbell's childhood diary is cited as Gibb Diary, 24 November 1868.

4. Jehanne Wake, *Princess Louise* (London: Collins, 1988), 109 and 157.

5. Taken from the cover of the guidebook to the castle, *Inveraray Castle and Gardens*, written by Her Grace, Duchess of Argyll.

6.   *The Times*, 23 April 2001.

7. Townsend, Peter, ed., *Burke's Peerage* (105th ed., London: Burke's Peerage, Ltd., 1970), 102.

8. Ina, Dowager Duchess of Argyll, ed., Campbell, George Douglas Eighth Duke of Argyll, *Autobiography and Memoirs* (2 vols., New York: E. P. Dutton and Company, 1906), I, 4.

9. J.D. Mackie, *A History of Scotland* (2d ed., New York: Dorset Press, 1978 [1964], 285.

10. Mackie, *History*, 284-286.

11. Stuart, Denis, *Dear Duchess: Millicent Duchess of Sutherland, 1867-1955* (London: Victor Gollancz, 1982), 31.

12. John Bateman, *The Great Landowners of Great Britain and Ireland,* (4th ed New York: Augustus M Kelley, 1970 [1883]), 14. See also *The Times*, 3 January 1877.

13. Bateman, *Great Landowners*, 431.

14. Stuart, *Dear Duchess*, 30.

15. FB, *Ne*, I, 44.

16. Ibid, 32.

17. Story, J L, *Later Reminiscences* (Glasgow: James Maclehose and Sons, 1931), 92.

18. Ibid.

19. The sons and daughters of the Duke and Duchess of Argyll were: John, 6 August 1845; Archibald, 18 December 1846; Walter, 30 July 1848; George, 25 December 1850; Colin, 9 March 1853; Edith, 7 November 1849; Elisabeth, 14 February 1851; Victoria, 22 May

1854; Evelyn, 17 August 1855; Frances, 22 February 1858; Mary, 22 September 1959; Constance, 11 November 1864.

20. DSS Ina, ed., *George Douglas, 8th Duke of Argyll, (1823-1900), Autobiography and Memoirs*, I, 291.

21. Wake, *Princess Louise*, 309.

22. A G-E, 'Campbell, George Douglas eighth Duke of Argyll (1823-1900)', *DNB*, XXII Supplement, 386.

23. Ibid, 390.

24. H C G Matthew, 'George Douglas Campbell, 8th Duke of Argyll, *ODNB*, article 4500.

25. Ibid.

26. Ibid.

27. DSS Ina, George, 8th Duke, *Autobiography*, I, 372.

28. FB, *Ne*, I, 60.

29. Wake, *Princess Louise*, 157.

30. H C G Matthew, 'George Douglas Campbell, 8th Duke of Argyll, *ODNB*, article 4500.

31. 'Campbell, George Douglas 8th Duke', *DNB Supplement*, 390.

32. Aberdeen, Lord and Lady, *More Cracks with 'We Twa'* (London: Methuen and Company, 1929), 7.

33. FB, *Ne*, I, 91-92.

34. DSS to Emma Campbell, 24 November 1858, Family Correspondence, Inveraray Castle (FC, INV).

35. Duchess's Diary, 1 November 1860, FC, INV.

36. Jean Balfour stated in her unpublished 'Notes and Reflections upon the "Old Generation"', the family of James Maitland and Blanche Balfour, of Whittingehame' that Frances 'was lame, the result of a tuberculous hip wrongly treated in childhood.' The treatment – rigid immobilization – was essentially the same for either problem in the 19th century. Today, Congenital Hip Dislocation would be diagnosed at birth and corrected with the Pavlik harness or surgery. Tuberculous Hip would be treated with chemotherapy.

37. FB, *Ne*, I, 11.

38. Ibid.

39. Ibid, 11-12.

40. Ibid, 12.

41. FB, *Lady Victoria Campbell: A Memoir* (London: Hodder and Stoughton, 1911), 15.

42. Norman Maclean, "Balfour, Lady Frances (1858-1931), *Dictionary of National Biography, 1931-1940*, 34-35.

43. FB, *Lady Victoria Campbell*, 35.

44. Ibid.

45. Interviews with Frances, Lady Fergusson, 23 June 1987, and Elizabeth Gibb, 7 September 1989.
46. Wake, *Princess Louise*, 178, stated that she was 'intellectual'.
47. Wake, *Princess Louise*, 151.
48. Interview with Elizabeth Gibb, September 1991.
49. Quoted in Wake, *Princess Louise*, 178.
50. Gower, Lord Ronald Sutherland, *Records and Reminiscences* (New York: Charles Scribner's Sons, 1903), 75.
51. FC, Gibb Diary, 7 November 1868.
52. FC. Gibb Diary, 24 November 1868.
53. All quotes taken from FC, Gibb Diary, August 1867.
54. FB, *Ne*, I, 32.
55. Anita Leslie, *Edwardians in Love* (London: Hutchinson & Company, 1972), 22.
56. Quoted in Wake, *Princess Louise*, 175.
57. FC, Gibb Diary, 4 September 1867.
58. FC, Gibb Diary, 16 November 1867.
59. *The Times*, 4 November 1868.
60. *The Times,* 17 December 1868.
61. FB, *Ne*, I, 127.
62. Leonore Davidoff, *The Best Circles* (London: Croom Helm, 1973), 28.
63. Leslie, *Edwardians in Love*, 14.
64. FB, *Ne,* I, 127.
65. DSS Diary, 1869-71, FC INV.
66. Wake, *Princess Louise*, 99.
67. Ibid, 107.
68. FB, *Ne*, I, 101.
69. Mark Stocker, 'Princess Louise', *ODNB,* article 34601.
70. Blanche E C Dugdale, *Family Homespun*, (London: John Murray, 1940), 38.
71. Ibid.
72. FC Diary, 26 January 1872, 392.
73. Wake, *Princess Louise*, 181.
74. FC Diary, 6 January 1877, 392.
75. Ibid.
76. FC Diary, 7 January 1877, 392.
77. FC Diary, 15 June 1877, 392.

CHAPTER TWO   'Many Plans for the Future'
78. FC Diary, 11 June 1877, 392.

79. FC Diary, 4 July 1877, 393.

80. FB to Lord Lytton undated but November 1887 suggested by BB, 299.

81. Wake, *Princess Louise*, 66-67.

82. FB Diary, 11 June 1877, 392.

83. Aberdeens, *More Cracks with 'We Twa'*, 1-2.

84. FB Diary, 7 March 1877, 392.

85. *The Times,* 15 March 1877.

86. Jean Balfour, 'Notes and Reflections', 56.

87. FB, *Ne*, I, 149.

88. FB, *Ne*, I, 157.

89. FB Diary, 18 July 1877, 392.

90. FB, *Ne*, I, 157-158.

91. FB, *Ne*, I, 140-146.

92. Dugdale, *Family Homespun*, 3.

93. FB, *Ne,* I, 160.

94. Ibid, 160-161.

95. Ibid, 162.

96. Dugdale, *Family Homespun*, 43-44.

97. John Bailey, ed., *The Diary of Lady Frederick Cavendish (London: John Murray, 1927)*, I, 219. Death Certificate for the Duchess is No. B159905, General Register Office, London.

98. Quoted in Joan Perkin, *Women and Marriage in Nineteenth Century England (Chicago, Lyceum, 1989)*, 97.

99. *The Times*, 4 June 1878.

100. FB, *Ne*, I, 114.

101. Spelled 'Whittinghame' until 1897.

102. Blanche E C Dugdale, *Arthur James Balfour, First Earl of Balfour, 1848-1906,* (New York: G P Putnam, 1937), I, 7.

103. Rev Charles Chittendon to Lady Blanche, 5 August 1867, 237A.

104. BB to FB, 2 July 1893, 308.

105. FB, Ne, I, 218.

106. A D K Hawkyard, Archivist, Harrow School to author dated 28 July 1991.

107. [George] Faithfull to Miss Emily Faithfull, 9 November 1870, 241.

108. Letter to author from Assistant Manuscript Cataloguer, Trinity College Library, Cambridge, 1 July 1993.

109. J A Venn, *Alumni Cantabrigienses*, (Cambridge University Press, Part II, Vol I, 1940), 134.

110. 'Candidate's Separate Statement' submitted by Eustace prior to being admitted a Fellow of the Royal Institute of British Architects, dated 28 November 1891, RIBA.

111. ABB to GWB, 12 May 1878, 449.

112. Mrs Charles Sartoris, nee Callender, to Mrs Henry Sartoris, nee Clough-Taylor, 30 January 1879, FC INV.

113. FB Diary, 4 February 1879, 393.

114. FB Diary 6 January 1879, 393.

115. Dugdale, *Arthur Balfour,* I, 30.

116. Mrs Charles Sartoris to Mrs Henry Callender, 30 January 1879, FC INV.

117. EJAB to ABB, 25 December 1878, 295.

118. ABB to FB, 31 December 1878, 295.

119. FB to ABB, 31 December 1878, 295.

120. 'Settlement by Duke of Argyll', 20 June 1900, Reference RD5/3040, 395-426, National Records of Scotland.

121. Mrs Charles Sartoris Mrs Henry Sartoris, 30 January 1879, FC INV.

122. Wake, *Princess Louise*, 121.

123. Patricia Branca, *Silent Sisterhood* (London: Croom Helm, 1980), 40.

124. My thanks to Christina Mackwell, Assistant Librarian at Lambeth Palace Library, in locating St John's Presbyterian Church, which in 1975 became St Mark's Coptic Orthodox Church. Letter to Miss Ierne Grant dated 13 October 1993.

125. Davidoff, *Best Circles*, 55.

126. *The Scotsman*, 24 May 1879.

127. FB Diary, 2 March 1879, 393.

128. Ibid, 17 February 1879, 393.

129. Interview with Elizabeth Gibb, September 1995.

130. FB, *Lady Victoria Campbell*, 315.

131. FB, *Ne,* I, 219.

132. Ibid, 172-173.

133. Ibid, 179.

134. *The Times*, 14 May 1879, 7, and FB, Ne, I, 179.

135. FB, *Lady Victoria Campbell*, 120.

136. FB, *Ne*, I, 185.

137. FB Diary, 13 May 1879, 393.

138. FB, *Ne*, I, 137.

139. Ibid, 307.

140. Michael Brander, *Eve Balfour* (Haddington, Scotland: The Gleneil Press, 2003), 7.

141. FB, Ne, I, 308.

142. BB, Note, 310.

143. FB Diary, 13 June 1879, 393.

144. FB, *Ne*, I, 186. The house is no longer standing. Mrs Elizabeth Gibb to author, postmarked 14 June 1995. Also letters from Gibb to author, 22 November 1994, and

from Lady Kay Oldfield, n d but received 12 June 1995.

145. FB, *Ne*, I, 227.

146. Margaret, Duchess of Argyll, *Forget Not* (London: Wyndham Publications, 1977 [1975]), 123.

147. Dugdale, *Family Homespun*, 117-118.

148. *Survey of London: North Kensington,* Vol 37, 1973, 161.

149. Census, 1881.

150. Dugdale, *Family Homespun*, 94.

151. *Survey of London: North Kensington*, Vol 37, 1973, 161.

152. FB to Lady Elcho, 21 September [1887], Neidpath Papers.

153. Cherida Seago, 'Cards on the Table', *The Lady*, 28 May to 3 June 1991, 1139, explains the ritual in detail.

154. FB, *Ne*, I, 117.

155. Ibid, II, 125.

156. FB to Lord Lytton undated but November 1887 suggested by BB, 299.

157. FB Diary, 9 June 1879, 393.

158. Ibid, 28 July 1879, 393.

159. Ibid, 12 May 1880, 393.

160. W R Lethaby, 'Willliam Morris's SPAB: "A School of Rational Builders"', (London: Society for the Protection of Ancient Buildings, 1982), 10.

161. 'Report of the Committee', Second Annual Meeting of the Society [for the Protection of Ancient Buildings]', June 1879, 14.

162. Miele, Chris, 'The Conservationist' in Parry, Linda, editor, *William Morris* (London, Philip Wilson, 1996), 78.

163. Andrew Saint, formerly of the *Survey of London*, to author, 12 October 1988. Records of Balfour and Turner were destroyed in World War II.

164. FB Diary, 26 December 1879, 393.

165. Interview with Elizabeth Gibb, September 1993.

166. FB, *Ne*, I, 223-224.

167. The portrait, one of only five portraits he painted, now hangs in the Musée de Beaux-Arts, in Nantes, France, having been sold to the Musée by Eustace Balfour, son of Frank.

168. FB, *Ne*, I, 235.

169. Edward Burne-Jones to Eustace, undated but shortly after 23 May 1880, 295.

170. FB, *Ne*, I, 235.

171. FB to ABB, 18 September 1880, 295.

172. *The Times*, 12 April 1880.

173. FB Diary, 19 April 1881, 395.

174. Wake, *Princess Louise*, 267.

175. BB, Note, 452.

176. FB Diary, 19 December 1880, 394.

177. Egremont, *Balfour,* 17, and FB Diary, 16 September 1880, 394.

178. Robin Harcourt Williams, *ed., Salisbury-Balfour Correspondence, 1869-1892* (Cambridge: Hertfordshire Record Society, 1988)*,* 66.

CHAPTER THREE 'You are one of us now, you Know'

179. GWB to FB, 7 February 1884, 297.

180. FB to GWB, 20 March 1882, 452.

181. FB to GWB, 4 May 1882, 452.

182. FB to GWB, 21 December 1881, 452.

183. William de Morgan to EJAB, 26 November 1881, 295.

184. FB to GWB, 22 January 1882, 452.

185. *Ottawa* (Ottawa: Irving Weisdorf & Company, 1995), 24.

186. Quoted in FB to GWB, 22-23 January 1882, 452.

187. The assessment of P B Waite, 'Campbell, John George Edward Henry Douglas Sutherland, Marquess of Lorne and 9th Duke of Argyll', *Dictionary of Canadian Biography*, XIV (1911-1920), (Toronto: University of Toronto Press, 1998), 177-180, agrees with Frances.

188. FB to GWB, 31 January 1882, 452.

189. Ibid.

190. Ibid.

191. Ibid.

192. FB to GWB, 5-6 March 1882, 452.

193. FB to GWB, 31 January 1882, 452.

194. FB Diary, 4 February 1882, 396.

195. Arthur had a laburnum tree on the estate removed 'in order to get a peculiarly high and dangerous run'. See FB, *Ne,* I, 361. See also Williams, *Salisbury-Balfour Correspondence*, 94.

196. James Noonan, 'Lord Lorne Goes to the Theatre, 1878-1883', *Theatre Research in Canada (TRIC)*, Vol 11, No 1 (Spring 1990), 13, [1-15].

197. FB to GWB, 31 January 1882, 452.

198. FB to AJB, 6 February 1882, 295.

199. FB to GWB, 22 February 1882, 452.

200. Ibid.

201. FB Diary, 31 January 1882, 396.

202. FB to GWB, 31 January 1882, 452.

203. *The Daily Citizen*, 9 February 1882.

204. *The Daily Citizen*, 25 February 1882.

205. *The Ottawa Daily Free Press*, 13 February 1882.

206. FB to AJB, 28 February 1882, 295.

207. FB to GWB, 5-6 March 1882, 452.

208. FB to GWB, 20 March 1882, 452.

209. Ibid.

210. FB, *Ne*, I, 246.

211. Eustace Balfour, 'Candidate's Separate Statement', application for Fellow of the Royal Institute of British Architects, dated 28 November 1891. 5.4.2 Fellows Nomination Papers, 1834-1857, 1866-1971, RIBA.

212. FB, *Ne*, I, 330.

213. Ibid.

214. FB to ABB, 12 March 1882, 295.

215. FB to GWB dated 5-6 March 1882, 452, and FB to ABB, 12 March 1882, 295. All the quotes in the paragraph are from these sources.

216. FB to GWB, 5-6 March 1882, 452.

217. FB Diary, 7 March 1882, 396.

218. FB to GWB, 5-6 March 1882, 452.

219. [Elma and Helen Story], Daughters of Dr Story, *Memoir of Robert Herbert Story, D.D., LL.D.,* (Glasgow: James Maclehose and Sons, 1909), 26.

220. FB Diary, 8 March 1882, 396.

221. FB Diary, 27 March 1882, 396.

222. FB Diary, 25 March 1882, 396.

223. FB to GWB, 20 March 1882, 452. The National Art Gallery of Canada has no art works by either Eustace or Alice in its collection. Inquiry made by author in May 1999.

224. FB to GWB, 12 February 1882, 452.

225. FB to GWB, 30 April 1882, 452.

226. *The Times*, 27 April 1882.

227. Janet Oppenheim, 'Balfour, Gerald William, (1853-1945)', *ODNB*, article 30556.

228. FB to GWB, 14 May 1882, 452.

229. FB, *Ne*, I, 311.

230. J W Clark, 'Francis Maitland Balfour', *Saturday Review*, July 29, 1882.

231. 'Balfour', *Encyclopaedia Britannica*. See also Arabella Buckley, *Natural Science*, in a bound volume of tributes to Frank Balfour, BP, 101.

232. GWB to AJB, n d but 'Saturday morning' [29 July 1882], 477.

233. FB, *Ne*, I, 351.

234. Edward Shils and Blacker, Carmen, eds *Cambridge Women: Twelve Portraits* (Cambridge University Press, 1986), 14.

235. BB, Note, 296.

236. Dugdale, *Family Homespun*, 81.

237. Dugdale, *Family Homespun*, 79-80. Alice's face has been obliterated – by her – in the few Balfour family photos in which she appeared.

238. Ibid, 74.

239. See FB to GWB, 28 August [1881], 452.

240. GWB to FB, 13 April 1883, 296.

241. BB, Note, 297. Also GWB to FB, 8 December 1884, 297.

242. Pat Jalland, *Women, Marriage, and Politics, 1860-1914* (Oxford: Oxford University Press, 1988 [1986]), 268-269.

243. See Kenneth Young, *Arthur James Balfour* (London: Bell & Sons, 1963), 10-11, 113; and Jalland, *Women, Marriage,* 268-272.

244. Jalland, *Women, Marriage,* 269.

245. Egremont, *Balfour,* 47-48.

246. GWB to FB, 5 December 1882, 296.

247. FB, *Ne*, I, 369.

248. Egremont, *Balfour*, 47.

249. Interview with Elizabeth Gibb, September 1995. See also Peter Lord, ed., *Between Two Worlds* (Aberystwyth: National Library of Wales, 2011), 85.

250. GWB to FB, 19 January 1884, 297.

251. FB to GWB, 9 June 1882, 452.

252. BB, Notes, and GWB to FB, 10 January 1884, 297.

253. GWB to FB, 7 February 1884, 297.

254. GWB to FB, 19 January 1884, 297.

255. See Ridley and Percy, *Letters of Arthur Balfour to Lady Elcho*, 19, for this sentiment.

256. Lady Maud Wolmer to FB, 6 December 1883, H H CHE 58/30.

257. Kenneth Rose, *The Later Cecils* (London: Harper and Row, 1975), 295.

258. FB to ABB, 14 December 1882, 296. All the quotes in this paragraph were taken from this letter.

259. FB, *Ne*, I, 414-419.

260. 'Candidate's Separate Statement', submitted by Eustace prior to being admitted a Fellow of the RIBA, 28 November 1891, RIBA.

261. FB to GWB, 4 May 1882, 452.

262. *The Times*, 2 April 1883.

263. AJB to Lord Salisbury dated 25 August 1880 in Harcourt Williams, *Salisbury-Balfour Correspondence,* 49.

264. Egremont, *Balfour*, 55

265. 'Introduction' by Hugh Cecil in Williams, Robin Harcourt, *The Salisbury-Balfour*

Correspondence, ix.

266. Dugdale, *Arthur James Balfour,* I, 50.

267. Quoted in FB, *Ne,* I, 427-428.

268. *The Times,* 13 June 1884, 9. Also Millicent Garrett Fawcett, *What I Remember,* (Honolulu, Hawaii: University Press of the Pacific, 2004 [1924]), 113.

269. FB, *Ne,* I, 408.

270. Dugdale, *Family Homespun,* 113-114.

271. FB, *Ne,* I, 432.

272. Copy of article entitled 'Emigration' by Alasdair Sinclair prepared for 'Tiree: Island of Two Harvests: A Statistical Account' edited by John Holliday for An Iodhlann.

273. Article by John Holliday, 'The Crofters' War', An Iodhlann.

274. I M M MacPhail, The *Crofters' War* (Lewis, Scotland: Acair, 1989), 188.

275. See Harcourt Williams, *Salisbury-Balfour Correspondence,* 75.

276. BB to FB, 28 May 1891, 303.

277. Letter to author from Sinclair dated 8 March 2001.

278. Ibid.

CHAPTER FOUR   'What an interesting Parliament it will Be'

279. Letter from FB to Constance Flower, 3 December [1885]. British Library Add Ms 47911, f 68-69.

280. FB to ABB, 26 November 1885, 298.

281. FB Diary, 30 December 1887, 401.

282. Quoted in FB, *Ne,* II, 33.

283. FB to ABB, 26 November 1885, 298. All the remaining quotes in the paragraph are from this letter.

284. Letter from FB to Constance Flower, 3 December [1885]. British Library Add Ms 47911, f 68-69.

285. FB to Walter Pollock, 8 December 1885, Gordon N Ray Collection of Literary and Historical Letters and Documents, Rare Book & Manuscript Library, Columbia University.

286. FB, *Ne,* II, 55.

287. FB Diary, 2 July 1886, 400.

288. *Glasgow Herald,* 5 December 1922.

289. Quoted in Harcourt Williams, *Salisbury-Balfour Correspondence,* 165.

290. *The Times,* 17 February 1885.

291. Dugdale, *Family Homespun,* 117.

292. FB to Bob Cecil, 31 May 1886, H H CHE 58/7. All quotes in paragraph are from this letter.

293. G H Fleming, *Lady Colin Campbell, Victorian 'Sex Goddess'* (Gloucestershire, Windrush Press, 1989), 1. The author has relied mainly on Fleming's work and *The Times*.

294. Wake, *Princess Louise*, 274.

295. *The Times*, 4 December 1886, 4; 6 December 1886, 4; and Fleming, *Lady Colin Campbell*, 144-145.

296. Quoted in Fleming, *Lady Colin Campbell*, 38.

297. Ibid, 185.

298. Ibid, 185-186.

299. *The Times*, 10 December 1886.

300. Wake, *Princess Louise*, 275-276.

301. Ibid, 276.

302. *The Times*, 21 December 1886.

303. Most British papers found O'Neill's testimony '"unfit for publication."' Quoted in Fleming, *Lady Colin Campbell*, 107

304. *The Times*, 16 December 1886, and 18 December 1886.

305. Fleming, *Lady Colin Campbell*, 166.

306. Wake, *Princess Louise*, 285.

307. *The Times*, 21 December 1886.

308. FB to AM, 12 January 1887, 492.

309. FB to AM, 16 February 1887, 492.

310. Fleming, *Lady Colin Campbell*, 222.

311. Wake, *Princess Louise*, 313.

312. Cynthia Asquith, *Remember and Be Glad* (London, 1952), 178.

313. Comments by Betty, July 1887, 299.

314. FB Diary, 8 October 1887, 401.

315. FB to Lady Betty Lytton, 'Friday [22] July 1887', 299. All the quotes in Frances's initial letter to Betty are taken from this letter.

316. Lady Betty Lytton to FB, 27 July 1887, 299.

317. BB, Note, August 1887, 299.

318. FB to BB, 6 September 1887, 299, and FB Diary, 17 to 22 September 1887, 401.

319. Lyndsey Jenkins, *Lady Constance Lytton: Aristocrat, Suffragette, Martyr* (London: Biteback Publishing, 2015), 10.

320. BB Note appended to letter from Lytton to BB, 23 September 1888, 300.

321. GWB to FB, August 1887, 299.

322. Lutyens' *Blessed Girl, 152.*

323. Ibid, 155.

324. Dugdale, *Family Homespun*, 139.

325. Ibid, 142. Frances read some Shakespeare growing up.

326. Ibid, 141.

327. Ibid, 137.

328. Ibid, 137.

329. Ibid, 140.

330. Ibid, 143.

331. Ibid, 90.

332. FB Diary, 21 January 1886, 400.

333. Ibid, 3 March 1886, 400.

334. Dugdale, *Family Homespun*, 143 and FB Diary, 2 July 1891, 405.

335. Ibid, 149.

336. Comments made at the Opening of the 'New Dawn Women' Exhibit, Watts Gallery, 30 June 2005, by Alice, Lady Renton of Mount Harry, great-granddaughter of Lady Frances.

337. Dugdale, *Family Homespun*, 168.

338. FB, *Ne*, II, 85.

339. Ibid, 86.

340. Quoted in Roberts, *Salisbury*, 384.

341. Ibid, 449.

342. FB to Mary Elcho dated 21 September [1887].

343. Roberts, *Salisbury*, 451.

344. Quoted in FB, *Ne*, I, 190.

345. See William Knox, *Lives of Scottish Women: Women and Scottish Society, 1800-1980* (Edinburgh: Edinburgh University Press, 2006), 112.

346. Wake, *Princess Louise*, 288.

347. BB, Note labeled 'Mental Trouble', 301.

348. Ibid.

349. Dr Waddell Barnes e-mail to author. 18 October 2002.

350. Roberts, *Salisbury*, 105.

351. Ibid, 107 and 157.

352. Jane Abdy and Charlotte Gere, *The Souls: An Elite in English Society, 1885-1930* (London: Sidgwick & Jackson, 1984), 9.

353. FB, *Ne*, I, 390-391.

354. Ibid, 392.

355. Abdy and Gere, *The Souls*, 11-12.

356. Egremont, *Balfour*, 109-110.

357. Betty's sister, Lady Emily Lutyens, included both Betty and Frances in the Souls. *A Blessed Girl: Memoirs of a Victorian Girlhood Chronicled in an Exchange of Letters 1887-1896* (New York: J B Lippincott, 1954), 112.

358. See also Angela Lambert, *Unquiet Souls* (New York: Harper & Row, 1984), 101-102.

359. Officially the 15th and later 7th Middlesex V R

360. Information on Balfour's military career is taken from the lead article in the *London Scottish Regimental Gazette*, Vol I, no 5, (May, 1896), 1, and from Regimental records.

361. *The Bailie*, 19 October 1904, 2.

362. Ian Beckett, *Riflemen Form: A Study of the Rifle Volunteer Movement, 1859-1908* (Aldershot: The Ogilby Trusts, 1982), 76 and 112.

363. *LSRG*, Vol I, no 5, (May 1896), 1.

364. Beckett, *Riflemen Form*, 200.

365. *LSRG*, Vol I, no 5, (May 1896), 1.

366. Beckett, *Riflemen Form*, 199.

367. FB, *Ne*, II, 426.

368. See Mary Edgeworth David, *Passages of Time* (Adelaide, Australia, Rigby, 1978 [1975]), 77, for observations on the regular army's view of the Territorials.

369. FB to BB, 27 December 1889, 301.

370. FB to Nora Sidgwick, 1 September [1889], 301.

371. FB to BB, n d except December 1889, 301.

CHAPTER FIVE   'Our [Parliamentary] Champions are rather Pitiful'

372. FB to MGF, 9 November 1890, 9/01/0030.

373. Ibid.

374. FB to BB, 22 December 1890, 302.

375. FB, *Ne*, II, 126.

376. Annual Report (AR), 1886, TAS.

377. See AR for 1886 and 1889. See also Minutes of the Executive Committee (MEC), 10 July 1889. All statistics are taken from the Annual Reports (AR) of the appropriate year. Where there are no endnotes, the figures have been compiled from the available data (counting the number of officers, etc.)

378. Minutes of the General Committee (MGC), 28 October 1885.

379. Ibid.

380. MGC, 20 October 1885.

381. Ibid.

382. The phrase 'for girls and women' was added in 1891 in part because the Society made the decision in that year not to meet boys. MEC, 20 November 1891. In 1894, the General Committee also turned down a request from the Wandsworth Blind School to meet blind boys ages 13 to 15 years. MGC, 20 July 1894. Modern organizations with this or a similar name are not the same entity.

383. See FB Diary, 1 June, 2 June, 3 July, 27 July 1885, 399.

384. AR, 1887, 9. In 1889, the Girls' Friendly Society contracted with the TAS to meet young women members of its organization for whom the GFS agreed to defray the expense.
385. Miss Beauchamp, a member of the Executive Committee (EC), undertook the initiative in enlisting women volunteers for the TAS work in foreign countries. MEC, 7 December 1886.
386. AR, 1886, 10.
387. AR, 1893, 22.
388. Quoted in AR, 1906, 22.
389. AR, 1893, 18.
390. MEC, 20 March 1896.
391. AR, 1900, 28-29.
392. Ibid.
393. AR, 1901, 40.
394. Ibid.
395. MEC 17 July 1896.
396. MGC, 16 October 1896. The quotes around 'volunteered' are the author's!
397. MEC, 19 May 1899.
398. Ibid, 21 June 1901.
399. *'Coming of Age' Celebration*, 18-19.
400. MGC, 18 April 1902.
401. Ibid, 15 July 1904.
402. Ibid, 16 February 1894.
403. Minutes of Sub-Committee of GC, 13 November 1893.
404. FB to BB, 22 December 1890, 302.
405. FB, *Ne*, II, 128.
406. Ibid.
407. Ibid, 114.
408. The Primrose League was prevented from affiliating with organisations like the National Society for Women's Suffrage.
409. FB Diary, 11 January 1887, 401.
410. FB to Robert Cecil, 31 May 1886, H H CHE 58/7.
411. AR, Central Committee, 1892, Blackburn Papers, Girton College, Cambridge.
412. Strachey, *The Cause*, 280.
413. David Rubinstein, *A Different World for Women: The Life of Millicent Garrett Fawcett* (London: Harvester Wheatsheaf, 1991), 117, and FB Diary, 5 July 1888, 402.
414. *Women's Suffrage Journal*, 9 April 1889, 64.
415. Ibid, 1 May 1889, 66-70.

416. Pugh, *March*, 151.

417. RBF to FB 1 December 1890, 302.

418. FB to MGF, 9 November 1890, 9/01/0030.

419. FB to MGF, 28 April 1891, M50/2, 1/127, Manchester Central Library.

420. Rubinstein, *Different World*, 133.

421. See editorial and news report in *The Times*, 1 May 1891.

422. Pugh, *March*, 21-23.

423. Pugh, *March*, 76 and 111.

424. Rubinstein, *Different World*, 155.

425. Dora D'Espaigne Chapman, 'Lady Frances Balfour', *The World's Work 1906-07,* Vol. IX (December 1906-May 1907), London: Heinemann, 182-83. The article on Frances appeared in the January 1907 issue, No. 50, Vol IX.

426. Pugh, *March*, 32.

427. Ibid, 79, and AR, Central Committee, 1892.

428. Pugh, *March*, 79.

429. *The Times*, 28 April 1892.

430. Ibid.

431. Untitled and undated Notes in Philippa Strachey Papers, No 7PHS, Box 61.

432. AR, Central Committee, NSWS, 1892.

433. Pugh, *March*, 79.

434. *The Times*, 28 April 1892, and *Women's Herald*, May 1892.

435. Helen Blackburn, *Women's Suffrage: A Record of the Women's Suffrage Movement in the British Isles with Biographical sketches of Miss Becker,* New York: Source Book Press, 1902, 197.

436. Ibid.

437. AR, Central Committee, NSWS, 1895.

438. Blackburn, *Women's Suffrage*, 199.

439. Ibid.

440. FB to MGF, 16 December 1893, 9/01/0050.

441. FB to BB, 27 November 1893, 309.

442. BB to ABB, 15 June 1894, 310.

443. FB to MGF, 16 December 1893, 9/01/0050.

444. Blackburn, *Women's Suffrage*, 201.

445. FB to MGF, 22 February 1895, 9/01/0059.

446. Rosamund Billington, 'Women, Politics and Local Liberalism: From "Female Suffrage to Votes for Women,"' *Journal of Regional and Local Studies*, Vol 5, (1985), 8.

447. FB to MGF, 9 May 1895, 9/01/0062, and AR, Central Committee, 1895.

448. FB to MGF, 5 February 1895, 9/01/0056.

449. Mary Arnold Forster to MGF, 6 March 1894, GB/106/7/MGF, Box 90A/Cust.

450. MGF chronology at beginning of Box 90A/Cust.

451. FB to MGF, 15 March 1894, Box 90A/Cust.

452. Clipping from K Lyttleton to MGF, dated 24 September 1894, Box 90A/Cust.

453. FB to MGF, 19 March 1895, Box 90A/Cust.

454. Ibid, 25 March 1895, Box 90A/Cust. Fawcett noted that she had made no reply to Frances's letter.

455. FB to BB, 14 May 1894, 310.

456. "'I never forgive, but I always forget.'" Quoted in Dugdale, *Balfour*, II, 5.

457. See Ray Strachey's *Millicent Garrett Fawcett*, 118-120, and Rubinstein, *Different World*, 89.

CHAPTER SIX 'Can it get right with Alice?'

458. FB Diary, 17 December 1892, 406.

459. RBF to FB 9 July 1895, 313.

460. FB Diary, 3 April 1897, 411.

461. BB to FB, 14 November 1891, 305.

462. FB to BB 10 July 1892, 306.

463. FB to BB, 20 July 1895, 313. All the information about this election is taken from this letter.

464. RBF to FB 9 July 1895, 313.

465. RBF to FB, 11 July 1895, 313. For those familiar with her autobiography, (*Ne*, II, 205-206), Frances, who wrote mainly from memory, confused some of her efforts on behalf of Finlay's 1895 election with his loss in 1892.

466. FB Diary, 31 August 1895, 409.

467. Frances Balfour, 'The Election of 1895: II. Lessons from Scotland', *National Review*, XXVI, (September to February, 1895-96), 93-96.

468. Government records do not include information on Parliamentary Private Secretaries in the late 19th century. E-mail to author from Jean Fessey, hcinfo@parliament.uk. Received 25 February 2013 7:24.

469. BB, Note, 313. All the material later in this paragraph are taken from this Note.

470. BB to FB, 28 November 1891, 305. Letter by Lytton written 18 May 1891.

471. FB to BB, 15 November 1891, 305. That Frances was not the only child who experienced such wrenching emotions can be seen in Emily Lutyens (nee Lytton), *A Blessed Girl*.

472. Lutyens, *A Blessed Girl*, 182.

473. BB to FB 29 May 1892, 306.

474. FB to BB 18 October 1899, 321.

475. BB to FB 19 October 1899, 321.

476. 'A Friend', 'Lady Frances Balfour: An Appreciation', *The Times*, 3 March 1931.

477. Dugdale, *Family Homespun*, 75-76.

478. BB, Note, 309.

479. FB to BB, 21 July 1893, 308.

480. FB to BB, n d but internal evidence indicates 1893, 309.

481. FB to BB, 31 December 1893, 309.

482. *The Times*, 5 January 1894.

483. FB Diary, 6 January 1894, 408.

484. *The Times*, 6 January 1894.

485. FB Diary, 10 January 1894, 408.

486. Quoted in FB Diary, 9 January 1894, 408.

487. Quoted in FB to BB 22 August 1895, 313.

488. FB to BB, 31 October 1895, 314.

489. FB to Lady Salisbury 18 January 1895, H H Mss 3MCH/6d, no 14.

490. FB to BB 19 January 1895, 312.

491. FB to MGF, 17 January 1895, 9/08/144.

492. Quoted in FB to BB 19 January 1895, 312.

493. 'Eustace Balfour, Architect and Surveyor', prepared by William W Ellis for the author, February 1990, Estate Office of the Duke of Westminster.

494. FB to Miss Emily Faithfull, n d except 1890 but after 5 February 1890, when Eustace was offered the job. 7EFA/099, TWL.

495. Pevsner, *Buildings of England*, Vol I, (1973), 601.

496. *Survey of London: Grosvenor Estate, Mayfair,* Part I, Vol 29, 1977, 148.

497. Information supplied by Nigel Hughes.

498. This architectural rendering is held by the Greater London Record Office (Modern Records).

499. *Survey of London: Grosvenor Estate, Mayfair,* Part II, Vol 40, 1980, 333.

500. Ellis, 'Eustace Balfour', and Pevsner, *The Buildings of England*, I, 600.

501. 'Balfour & Turner', groveart.com (Oxford University Press, 2003).

502. 'The late Colonel Eustace Balfour', *RIBA Journal*, 18 February 1911.

503. *Survey of London: Grosvenor Estate, Mayfair*, Part II, Vol 40, 77.

504. Quoted in Ibid, Vol 39, 77.

505. EAJB to FB, October 1895, 314.

506. W B Richmond to 1st Duke of Westminster, 11 January 1896, 316.

507. *Survey of London: Grosvenor Estate, Mayfair,* Part I, Vol. 39, 1977, 79. '[M]any of the windows in their original tracery', including the West window designed by Eustace, as well as the columns and capitals were incorporated in the new church, which also received the choir stalls, font, organ, sanctuary paving, and rails.

508. FB Diary, 6 September 1895, 409.

509. Wake, *Princess Louise*, 312.

510. H H Asquith to Pamela McKenna, 7 December 1907, McKN 9/3, Churchill College Library, Cambridge University.

511. FB to BB, 29 May 1896, 316, and *The Times*, 22 May 1896, and 23 May 1896.

512. FB, *Ne*, II, 237.

513. FB to unnamed but AJB, undated but probably written 17 March (certainly after 14 March), in folder labeled '1897', 162. Approximate dates can be established from Frances's Diary and letters and from Alice's journal.

514. FB to AJB, 9 June 1897, 159.

515. FB to AJB, 17 March 1897, 162.

516. ABB Journal, 1897, 373.

517. FB to ABB, undated but 24 March 1897, 162.

518. Ibid.

519. ABB Journal, 1897, 373.

520. FB to AJB undated by after 12 March 1897, 162.

521. FB Diary, 3 April 1897, 411.

522. 'Draft' of letter from AJB to FB, 20 July 1897, 159.

523. FB to Ldy S, 30 December 1897, H H Mss. 3MCH/6d. No. 37.

524. See especially Mary Drew to AJB, 5 November 1899, 164.

525. Brander, *Eve Balfour*, 14.

526. Harris, *A J Balfour and Whittingehame House*, 61. All the information for this event was taken from this book.

527. Wake, *Princess Louise*, 316.

528. FB to AJB, undated but 9 June 1897, 159.

529. FB to BB, 6 and 7-9 November 1898, and BB to FB, undated but November 1898, 319.

530. FB to BB, 17 November 1898, 319.

531. She suffered her first stroke in late 1898. Roberts, *Salisbury*, 715 and 746.

532. Gwendolen Cecil to FB, 22 November 1899, H H CHE 58/92.

533. FB Diary, 20 November 1899, 413.

534. Gwendolen Cecil to FB, 22 November 1899, H H CHE 58/92.

535. Dugdale, *Family Homespun*, 160.

536. FB Diary, 17 September 1898, 412.

537. BB, Note, 320.

538. Dugdale, *Balfour*, I, 203.

539. Derek Hayward, <u>derekhayward@tantraweb.co.uk</u>, 2 February 2004.

540. FB, *Ne*, II, 262.

541. Roberts, *Salisbury,* 718.

542. FB, *Ne*, II, 299

543. On the value of war experience to the Volunteers, see Eustace's article 'The Employment

of Volunteers Abroad', *Contemporary Review*, 76 (November 1899), 759-760.

544. Beckett, *Riflemen Form,* 212.

545. FB, *Ne*, II, 434.

546. Ibid.

CHAPTER SEVEN 'No one dreamt of such Success'

547. FB to Baffy, undated but 5 February 1897, 318.

548. FB Diary, 19 May 1896, 410.

549. AR, Central Committee, NSWS, 1897, 11-12.

550. Minutes of the Combined Sub-Committee, 27 April 1896, GB/106/2/NWS/A2/1/2, 27 April 1896.

551. AR, Central Committee, of NSWS, 1896.

552. Blackburn, *Women's Suffrage*, 207.

553. Ibid, 208.

554. Quoted in AR, Central Committee of NSWS, 1896.

555. Hume, *NUWSS,* 4.

556. Quoted in AR, Central Committee of NSWS, 1896.

557. 'Women's Suffrage', *Englishwoman's Review*, 15 April 1896, 93.

558. Hume, *NUWSS*, 14.

559. MCSub-C, 17 June 1897.

560. Rubinstein, *Different World*, 136.

561. Ibid, 137.

562. Harold Smith, *The British Women's Suffrage Campaign, 1866-1928* (London: Longman, 1998), 18.

563. *Englishwomen's Review*, 15 January 1898, 25, and Pugh, *March of Women*, 80.

564. FB to Baffy, undated but 5 February 1897, 318.

565. Blackburn, *Women's Suffrage*, 212.

566. FB to S, 6 November 1896, H H Mss 3M/E.

567. *Pall Mall Gazette*, 23 July 1897.

568. AR, Central Committee of NSWS,1897, 11-12.

569. Pugh, *March of Women*, 80-81.

570. Hume, *NUWSS*, 15.

571. *Englishwomen's Review*, 15 April 1898, 107.

572. Hume, *NUWSS*, 16.

573. Minutes of Associate Scheme Sub-Committee, Central & East of England Society for Women's Suffrage, 8 April 1900, found in NWS/2A/2.

574. *The Times*, 7 June 1899.

575. FB to MGF, June 1899, 9/02/114.

576. FB to S, 16 June 1899, H H Mss 3M/E.

577. *The Times*, 27 June 1899.

578. Ibid, 7 July 1899.

579. *Parliamentary Debates* (Authorized Edition), 4th Series, Vol 73, 20 June 1899 to 5 July 1899, Column 562-563.

580. *The Times*, 1 July 1899.

581. Clipping, dated 22 October 1903, 325.

582. The Earl of Oxford and Asquith, *Memories and Reflections, 1852-1927* (Boston: Little, Brown and Company, 1928), I, 259.

583. FB to AJB, undated, but February 1901, 165.

584. 1901 article in *Fulham Observer*.

585. Hume, *NUWSS*, 194.

586. 1901 article in *Fulham Observer*.

587. Ibid.

588. *The Gazette*, 23 November 1901, 8.

589. *Englishwoman's Review*, 15 January 1902, 23.

590. Article in *Cooperative News*, March 15, 1902, contained in 2/CCN, OS7/3.

591. The women textile workers from Lancashire presented their petition to MPs in 1901. Jill Liddington and Norris, Jill, *One Hand Tied Behind Us: The Rise of the Women's Suffrage Movement* (London: Virago, 1978), 152.

592. *Cooperative News*, 15 March 1902, 311-312.

593. Jill Liddington, *The Life and Times of a Respectable Rebel, Selina Cooper, 1864-1946* (London: Virago Press, 1984), 106-107.

594. *Englishwoman's Review*, 15 October 1902, 248.

595. FB to AM, 18 March 1902. It is not known where she spoke.

596. AR, Central Society, 1902, Blackburn Papers, Girton College Archives.

597. Quoted in Crawford, *Women's Suffrage Reference*, 655.

598. *The Guardian*, 28 February 1914.

599. FB to AM, 22 February 1903, GD492/133.

600. Ibid, 12 November 1905, GD492/135.

601. *The Times*, 8 July 1899.

602. FB to *The Times*, 4 July 1904.

603. *Englishwoman's Review*, 15 July 1900, 151.

604. Crawford, *Women's Suffrage Reference*, 62.

605. *Englishwoman's Review*, 15 January 1900, 34.

606. Email from Anne Bridger to Kate Perry, Archivist, Girton College Library, dated 20 April 2007.

607. Letter from Miss Jessie Boucherett to Miss Antoinette Mackenzie dated 19 January

1903, in 'Notes' made on 6 March 2003 by Anne Bridger for Kate Perry.

608. AR, NUWSS, 1900, 3.

609. *The Times*, 2 August 1902.

610. AR, Central Society, 1902.

611. BB, Notes, 26 June 1902, 326.

612. Pitt Crawfurth Smith, 'Seventy Years of Service, 1901-1971', 5, known today as the League of Commonwealth Fellowship.

613. FB, *Ne*, II, 3, and Gordon and Doughan, *British Women's Organisations*, 147-148.

614. Smith, 'Seventy Years', 5.

615. FB, Ne, II, 383.

616. Ibid.

617. MEC, Central Society, 6 July 1904, OS7/5.

618. *Englishwoman's Review*, 15 January 1904, 87.

619. FB to MGF, 21 January 1903, 9/8/192.

620. *The Scotsman*, 4 April 1902.

621. Ibid, and *Englishwoman's Review*, 15 April 1902, 103.

622. Statement by Lady Knightley of Fawsley at meeting of Freedom of Labour Defence meeting, 25 June 1900, *Englishwoman's Review*, 16 July 1900, 146.

623. Olive Banks, 'Balfour, Lady Frances 1858-1930', *The Biographical Dictionary of British Feminists*, I: 1800-1930 (New York: NYU Press, 1985), 12.

624. FB to AM, 1 May 1904, GD492/134.

625. Quoted in FB to AM 16 May 1904, GD492/134.

626. *Englishwoman's Review*, 15 October 1903, 243.

627. FB to AM, 5 February 1905, GD492/135. Also see Gordon and Doughan, *British Women's Organisations*, 88-89.

628. Smedley, *Crusaders,* 54-55.

629. Ibid, 62.

630. FB Diary, 20 June 1904, 418.

631. Smedley, *Crusaders,* 68.

632. Quoted in Ibid, 73.

633. FB to AM, 5 February 1905, GD492/135.

634. *The Times*, 18 June 1904.

635. Smedley, *Crusaders*, 71-72.

636. Gordon and Doughan, *British Women's Organisations*, 89.

637. FB to BB, 7 February 2005, 331.

638. FB to AM, 5 February 1905, GD492/135.

639. FB Diary, 2 March 1905, 419.

640. FB to AM, 17 February 1907, GD492/137.

641. FB to AM, 21 March 1904, GD492/134.

642. Hume, *NUWSS*, 22.

643. *Women's Suffrage Record*, October 1902, 8.

644. MEC, NUWSS, 17 September 1903.

645. Ibid.

646. Ibid, 9 July 1903.

647. Hume, *NUWSS*, 23.

648. Ibid.

649. David Rubinstein, *Different World*, 137.

650. MEC, NUWSS, 17 September 1903.

651. *The Times*, 17 March 1904.

652. *Englishwoman's Review*, 15 January 1904, 87.

653. Article from *Ethics*, June 1905, in 2/CCN, OS7/3.

654. FB to AM, 31 January 1904, GD492/134.

655. FB Diary, 15 November 1905, 419.

656. *The Bailie*, 19 October 1904, 2.

657. *The Scotsman*, 2 October 1905.

CHAPTER EIGHT 'It is a changed Place'

658. FB to BB, 29 March 1909, 338.

659. FB to Alice Salisbury, 1 October 1903, H H 4 MCH 4/4.

660. FB, *Ne*, II, 158-159.

661. FB, *Ne*, II, 309.

662. Death Records, New Register House, General Register Office, Book 513.

663. Codicil dated 18 July 1899. See also Wake, *Princess Louise*, 326.

664. Wake, *Princess Louise*, 328.

665. FB to Dr James Robertson, 13 May 1900, 322.

666. HRH Queen Victoria to FB, 25 April 1900, 322.

667. MGF to FB, 25 April 1900, 322.

668. FB to Dr James Robertson, 3 May 1900, 322.

669. FB to MGF, 2 May 1900, 9/08/170.

670. Wake, *Princess Louise*, 336.

671. Ibid.

672. FB Diary, 1, 5, 8, 28 July; 25, 26 August; 5, 19, 27, 29 September, 1900, 414.

673. FB Diary, 10 March and 30 March 1901, 415.

674. Quoted in Thomas Pakenham, *Boer War* (New York: Random House, 1979), 492.

675. FB Diary, 5 October 1900, 414.

676. Roberts, *Salisbury*, 784.

677. Longford, *Queen Victoria*, 557-58.
678. FB, 'The Queen's Death', 31 January 1901, 324. All the comments about the events preceding the Queen's death are taken from this article.
679. FB to MGF, 13 February 1901, 9/02/124.
680. FB to BB, 27 March 1902, 326.
681. FB to AM, 8 November 1902, GD492/132,.
682. Ibid.
683. FB to AJB, n d but February 1903, 165.
684. Pugh, *March*, 77.
685. FB to BB?, 2 January 1903, 281.
686. Lady Kathleen Oldfield, RAL's youngest sister, asserted that she did not believe that 'Aunt Frances' actually spat on her brother. Interview September 1992.
687. FB to BB, 6 November 1898, 319.
688. FB Diary, 14 March 1903, 417.
689. FB Diary, 13 July 1903, 417.
690. FB to GWB?, undated but 1903, 281.
691. FB to Robert Cecil, 9 October 1903, H H CHE 58/14.
692. Ibid.
693. FB to Alice Salisbury, 1 October 1903, H H 4 MCH 4/4.
694. Both Frances, the Dowager Lady Fergusson, and Elizabeth Gibb, nee Milne, called their grandmother a 'Unionist' without any prompting or questioning from the author. Interviews with Frances, Lady Fergusson, 1987, 1988, and Elizabeth Gibb in the 1990s.
695. Dugdale, *Balfour*, I, 308.
696. FB Diary, 31 December 1895, 409.
697. FB to AM, 12 July 1904, 134.
698. Dugdale, *Balfour*, I, 277.
699. FB Diary, 12 February 1906, 420; FB to BB, 22 November 1905, 332.
700. *The Scotsman*, 21 November 1905.
701. Ibid.
702. 'The Reformer's Tree', *The Scotsman*, 23 November 1905.
703. *The Scotsman*, 21 February 1911.
704. Information supplied by Nigel Hughes.
705. BB Note, 330.
706. *The Scotsman,* 13 October 1909.
707. B to AM, 20 April 1902, 492, 132.
708. FB to Lord Robert Cecil, 16 January 1906, BM Mss 51158 f 49.
709. *The Times*, 28 February 1906.
710. FB, *Ne*, II, 158-159.

711. FB, *Ne*, I, 335

712. FB to BB, 29 March 1909, 338.

713. FB to *Westminster Gazette*, 21 July 1906. Also *Englishwoman's Review*, 15 October 1906, 258.

714. FB to Margot, 10 April 1908, Oxford, M S Eng C 6670.

715. FB, *Ne*, II, 158.

716. Ibid.

717. *The Times*, 2 March 1931, 8.

718. Quoted in Hattersley, *The Edwardians*, 166.

719. Quoted in R K Webb, *Modern England: From the 18th Century to the Present* (New York: Dodd, Mead, and Company, 1968), 459.

720. BB, Notes, 339, taken from FB to BB, dated 16 September 1909 (should be 10-11 November 1909).

721. Egremont, *Balfour*, 219.

722. Information provided by Dr Barbara Hazel Horn, retired librarian, NRS, e-mail December 8, 2006.

723. Ibid.

724. Dr Norman Maclean, 'Lady Frances Balfour', *The Scotsman*, 27 February 1931.

725. FB to Frank Balfour, 12 September 1906, 334.

726. Ibid.

727. The Census of 1911 identifies him as a mechanical engineer.

728. Frank to FB, 26 March 1907, 336.

729. Mark Bonham Carter and Pottle, Mark, ed., *Lantern Slides: The Diaries and Letters of Violet Bonham Carter, 1904-1914* (London: Weidenfeld and Nicolson, 1996), 116.

730. Arthur Conan Doyle to ABB, 24 September 1906, 273.

731. FB to Frank, 27 December 1906, 334.

732. Paraphrased by Rubinstein, *Before the Suffragettes*, 86.

733. BB, Note, 335.

734. *The Scotsman*, 16 May 1908, 11.

735. FB to Frank, 15 May 1908, 337.

736. Joan to FB, 14 February 1912, 344.

737. FB to AM, 4 June 1907, GD492/137.

738. Quoted in FB to AM, 4 June 1907, GD492/137.

739. Letter inserted in Ibid.

740. FB to AM, July 1907, GD492/137.

741. Jean Lindsay to author, 25 September 2007.

742. Quoted in Norman Maclean, *The Years of Fulfillment* (London: Hodder and Stoughton, 1953), 101.

743. FB to Frank, 5 June 1908, 337.

744. BB, Note, 338.

745. FB to BB, 26 January 1909, 338.

746. HRH King Edward VII to Mr Herbert Gladstone, 10 September 1909, Royal Archives, R.39/75.

747. Philip Magnus, *King Edward VII* (New York: Penguin Books, 1979), 542.

748. FB, *Ne*, II, 423.

CHAPTER NINE   '[N]ot playing the Game'

749. Quoted in Chapman, 'Lady Frances Balfour', 182-83.

750. FB, *Ne*, II, 141.

751. FB, 'Our Chances for the Future', *Common Cause*, 22 April 1909, 20.

752. Quoted in Mitchell, *Queen Christabel*, 63. Material in this paragraph is taken from this work.

753. FB, *Ne*, II, 143.

754. MEC, CS, 20 June 1906, 2/CCN, OS7/3.

755. Quoted in Hume, *NUWSS*, 30.

756. FB to MGF, undated except 1906, 9/01/0085.

757. Hume, *NUWSS*, 25.

758. AR, NUWSS, 1905-1906.

759. FB, *Ne*, II, 140. .

760. Ibid.

761. Quoted in Chapman, 'Lady Frances Balfour', 182-183.

762. Rosen, *Rise Up, Women*, 75-76.

763. Quoted from *The Daily Graphic*, 3 November 1906, 2/CCN, OS7/3.

764. Ibid.

765. FB to BB, 30 October 1906, 273.

766. *The Times*, 5 November 1906, and The *Women's Suffrage Journal*, November 1906, 2.

767. FB to BB, 30 October 1906, 273.

768. FB to BB, 6 November 1906, 334.

769. *Kensington News*, 7 December 1906, article found in 2/CCN, OS7/3.

770. Ibid.

771. Quoted in Chapman, 'Lady Frances Balfour ', 182-183.

772. 'Woman Suffrage', *Westminster Review*, Vol 166, December 1906, 623-625.

773. Chapman, 'Lady Frances Balfour', 182-183.

774. FB, *Ne*, II, 140.

775. Ibid, 169.

776. FB to Strachey, 21 June 1907, 9/01/0200.

777. There were 816 people in Inveraray and its surrounding area in 1891. Statistics taken from *Groome's Gazetteer*. E-mail from Alastair Campbell, 12/19/05. See also FB Diary, 13 December 1907, 421.

778. FB to AM, 15 December 1907, 137.

779. Quoted in MEC, CS, 17 October 1906, 2/CCN, OS7/5.

780. Mostly taken from Minutes of Sub-Commmittee on Re-organization, GB/106/2/NWS/A2/3.

781. Miss Sterling to Lady Frances Balfour, 6 March, 1906, 9/01/0112.

782. Edith Dimock to Miss Sterling. 3 January 1907, 9/01/0176.

783. Ibid.

784. MEC, CS, 26 September 1906, 2/CCN, OS7/5.

785. *The Tribune*, 11 February 1907, clipping contained in scrapbook 2/CCN, OS7/3. Though not officially represented at the event, the WSPU had a contingent in the procession led by Mrs Despard.

786. Ibid, 22 February 1907. They had anticipated only 2,000 women (FB to Frank, 6 February 1907, 335).

787. Hume, *NUWSS*, 34.

788. *The Times*, 15 February 1907.

789. Ibid, 9 March 1907.

790. Ibid, 13 June 1907.

791. *The Scotsman*, 7 October 1907.

792. The Edinburgh and Glasgow and West of Scotland National Societies agreed to participate in the procession only after an assurance that the march would be peaceful.

793. *The Scotsman*, 7 October 1907.

794. *Marylebone Mercury and West London Gazette*, 23 November 1907, 5.

795. *The Advertiser*, 28 November 1907, 3.

796. *Marylebone Mercury and West London Gazette*, 23 November 1907, 5.

797. Ibid.

798. FB to AM, 24 November 1907, GD492/137.

799. FB to BB, 20 November 1907, 336.

800. Ibid.

801. E-mail from Anna Kisby, TWL, 18 June 2008. Information taken from 2LSW/E/04/08.

802. *Women's Franchise*, 2 January 1908, 310.

803. FB to BB, 27 November 1907, 339.

804. Rubinstein, *Different World*, 242 and 253.

805. *Report of the Executive Committee of the London Society for Women's Suffrage, 1908. The Times*, 21 May 1908.

806. Hume, *NUWSS*, 48-49

807. Ibid.

808. Pugh, *March*, 163.

809. *Kensington News*, 29 March 1909, 2/CCN, OS7/4.

810. FB to MGF, 3 October 1908, 9/01/0442.

811. FB, *Ne*, II, 153. In her autobiography, Frances incorrectly dated this letter 1907. The debate took place in 1908 (FB Diary, 19 March 1908).

812. Quoted in David Mitchell, *Queen Christabel*, 120.

813. FB, *Ne*, II, 153.

814. *Women's Franchise*, 19 March 1908.

815. FB, *Ne*, II, 153.

816. Ibid, 152.

817. Crawford, *Women's Suffrage Reference*, 30.

818. Lisa Tichner, *Spectacle of Women*, (Chicago: University of Chicago Press, 2009), 69.

819. Janet Howarth, 'Fawcett, Dame Millicent (1847-1929)', *ODNB*, article 33096.

820. *The Standard*, 15 June 1908.

821. Tichner, *Spectacle*, 69.

822. *The Times*, 14 May [should be June] 1908, Scrapbook in 2/CCN, OS7/4, TWL. The Oaks horse race was, of course, won by a 'female' because it is a race for three-year-old fillies. Signorinetta, the filly which won the Derby in 1908, is one of only six to have won the Derby since its founding in 1780. E-mail from Sandie Bowden, July 18, 2006.

823. Talk by Elizabeth Crawford, entitled 'An Army of Banners', given on 14 June 2008 at The Women's Library, London. Email from Elizabeth Crawford, June 18 2008.

824. FB Diary, 17 October 1908, 422.

825. *Portsmouth Times*, 14 November 1908, 8.

826. FB to BB, 11 March 1909, 338.

827. *Common Cause*, 16 December 1909, 489.

828. Fawcett, *What I Remember*, 124.

829. FB to Emily Rathbone, 25 January 1909, Rathbone Papers, University Library, University of Liverpool.

830. Mrs Humphrey Ward was the Antis' best-known debater, and was challenged by Mrs Fawcett on one prominent occasion. However, Ward did not debate on a regular basis, as Pott did.

831. FB, *Ne*, II, 166-167.

832. *The Penrith Observer*, 12 October 1909, 7.

833. Ibid.

834. Marion Phillips to Miss [Catherine] Marshall, 4 October 1909, Cumbria Record Office (Carlisle), D Mar 3/9.

835. Maclean, *Years of Fulfillment*, 101.

836. Editor of *National Review* to Mrs Parker Smith, 18 January 1909, Strathclyde Regional Archive TD1, 541. It was Dr Elizabeth Garrett Anderson, sister of Mrs Fawcett, who 'poured ridicule' on Mrs. Parker Smith.

837. FB, *Ne*, II, 173.

838. Lindy Moore, *Bajanellas and Semilinas: Aberdeen University and the Education of Women, 1860-1920* (Aberdeen University Press, 1991), 94; R D Anderson, *The Student Community at Aberdeen, 1860-1939* (Aberdeen University Press, 1988), 79.

839. FB to BB, 15 October 1908, 337.

840. Ibid.

841. The Penrith Observer, 12 October 1909, 7.

842. *The Times*, 11 July 1908.

843. *Englishwoman's Review*, 15 July 1908, 176.

844. FB Diary, 2 November 1908, 422.

845. AR, NUWSS, 1909.

846. MGF to FB, 7 November 1908, 9/01/0444.

847. FB to BB, 4 April 1909, 338.

848. Copy of the agenda of the Annual Meeting of the LSWS held 10 November 1908 included in 3/CCN, OS7/4.

849. There are no minutes of the Executive Committee of the London Society for this period. *Common Cause*, 11 November 1909, 410, Hume, *NUWSS*, 53-55, and *The Englishwoman's Review*, 15 January 1910, 34-35.

850. Ray Strachey, *Women's Suffrage and Women's Service: The History of the London and National Society for Women's Service* (LNSWS, 1927), 23.

851. *The Englishwoman's Review*, 15 January 1910, 35.

852. MGF to FB, 18 December 1909, 9/01/0710.

853. FB to MGF, 4 October 1909, 9/01/0625.

854. FB, *Ne*, II, 141.

855. *The Glasgow Herald*, 9 October 1913.

856. FB to Frank, 2 April 1908, 337.

857. FB to Fawcett, 29 June 1909, 7MGF/A/1/040.

858. FB, 'Our Chances for the Future', *Common Cause*, 22 April 1909, 20.

859. Frances was one of six official delegates to the conference. *The Englishwoman's Review*, 15 July 1909.

860. *The Scotsman*, 29 April 1909.

861. FB to BB, 2 May 1909, 338.

862. *Common Cause*, 22 April 1909, 19.

863. Balfour Papers, 337, and Patricia Miles and Jill Williams, *An Uncommon Criminal: The Life of Lady Constance Lytton, Militant Suffragette, 1869-1923* (Privately printed by Knebworth

House Education and Preservation Trust, 1999).

864. Rosen, *Rise Up, Women!*, 130.

865. BB, Notes, 340.

866. For a time, Con was a salaried employee of the WSPU, as related by Betty to Victor Lytton, 21 June 1910, www.Knebworthhouse.com. See also Lyndsey Jenkins, *Lady Constance Lytton, Aristocrat, Suffragette, Martyr* (Biteback Publishing, 2015), 177.

867. Miles and Williams, *An Uncommon Criminal*, 24 and 26.

868. FB to BB, 8 April 1909, 338.

869. Betty explained in 'Note', 344, that 'the sisters' . . . were . . . not very much use except for their distinguished names – Balfour, Sidgwick, Rayleigh'.

870. Quoted in MGF to Miss Strachey, 8 August 1908.

871. A.J.R., *The Suffrage Annual and Women's Who's Who,* 177.

872. Leneman, *Guid Cause*, 88.

CHAPTER TEN 'The Kirk of the Crown of Scotland'

873. FB to AJB, 1 June 1894, 165.

874. Anon., '[An Account of the Connection of Scottish Churches in England with the General Assembly of the Church of Scotland . . .]', n.p. [unnumbered, loose, typed pages beginning with these words found in the church vault].

875. *The Scotsman*, 28 May 1885, and *The Times*, 28 May 1885.

876. FB to AJB n d but 27 May 1885, 165. Lord Aberdeen was Lord High Commissioner in 1885.

877. 'Disestablishment', *Dictionary of Scottish Church History*, (Edinburgh: T & T Clark, 1993), 246. Hereafter *DSCH.*

878. Burleigh, *Church History*, 380 and 399.

879. 'Story', *DSCH,* 799-779.

880. Ibid.

881. Statement by The Rev Mrs Jean Stewart, letter to author, 12 June 2007. Rev Stewart's father was Lady Frances' minister, the Rev Joseph Moffatt, of Crown Court Church, London, 1917-1962.

882. 'Story', *DSCH*, 798-799.

883. *The Times*, 21 May 1886.

884. 'Story', *DSCH*, 798-799.

885. Quoted in BB, Notes, 308.

886. Ibid.

887. FB to AJB, 1 June 1894, 165.

888. Ibid.

889. Ibid.

890. FB to BB, May 1895, 312.

891. FB to BB, 16 January 1909, 338.

892. 'Columba', *DSCH,* 196-197.

893. FB, *Lady Victoria Campbell,* 280-283.

894. See 'Iona and the National Trust for Scotland' by Donald Erskine; Anon, 'Iona', *Life and Work,* Vol 24 (1902), 246; 'Minutes of the General Assembly 1900 – Abridgment', Thursday, May 31, 1900, 58. Also *Lady Victoria Campbell,* 280-285.

895. T W Bayne, 'Story, Robert Herbert (1835-1907)', rev A T B McGowan, *ODNB,* article 36327.

896. *The Times,* 8 June 1900 and 28 May 1903. These words are not Story's but were consistent with his views expressed in this discussion.

897. *The Times,* 8 June 1900.

898. *The Times,* 4 June 1901.

899. 'Free Church of Scotland, Post-1900', DSCH, 338.

900. 'United Free Church', DSCH, 838.

901. 'Scottish Churches Act (1905)', DSCH, 756.

902. FB to AM, 31 July 1904, GD492/134.

903. Quoted in Ridley and Percy, *Letters of Arthur and Lady Elcho,* 19.

904. Dr Story co-wrote the letter which appeared in *The Times.* FB to AM 19 April 1903.

905. *The Times,* 21 April 1903.

906. FB to AJB, 12 April 1903, 328.

907. FB to Dr James Robertson, 29 May 1903, 328.

908. *The Times,* 12 May 1903.

909. I am indebted to the *London Journal* for permission to use much of the material that is in this chapter about the rebuilding. My article, entitled 'For Kirk and Crown: The Rebuilding of Crown Court Church, 1905-1909', appeared in the journal in Vol 17, No 1, 1992, 54-70.

910. [Frances Balfour], 'A Statement Concerning the Position of Crown Court Church, Covent Garden, London', (1906), 3.

911. FB, *Ne,* II, 443.

912. 'Statement', 1.

913. FB, *Ne,* II, 442-443.

914. Gavin Lang, Letter to the Editor of *The Scotsman,* May 14, 1909, Crown Court Church Archives (hereafter CCCA).

915. CCCA, Minutes of the Renovation Committee, 19 June 1905. Unless otherwise stated, information quoted is taken from these records with dates indicated in the text.

916. The published figures were taken from the *Daily News.*

917. 'Statement', 5. During Dr Cumming's ministry, Crown Court Church had 900 persons

on its Communion Roll. Frances Balfour, 'The Rev John Cumming, DD, Minister of the Scottish National Church, Crown Court, 1832-1879', *St. Columba's (Church of Scotland) [Magazine]*, xiv (April 1905), 38.

918. ' Anon., '[An Account of the Connection of Scottish Churches in England with the General Assembly of the Church of Scotland . . .] ', n.p. [unnumbered, loose, typed pages beginning with these words, found in the church vault]. 'Hereafter cited as 'Account '.

919. The Duke of Bedford's terms were quite generous, considering that the first decade of the 1900s was a time of rapidly rising real estate values in the Strand area of central London.

920. FB to AM, 11 August 1907, GD492/137.

921. Balfour, 'Memorandum to the Rev Dr Arcbibald Fleming', 18 August 1906, Crown Court Papers – Huffman Collection (CCP-HC).

922. Frances no doubt persuaded George to serve, although she later declared that their treasurer was 'a gloomy one; always forecasting that we should never raise the large sum needed'. FB, *Ne*, II, 445.

923. FB, *Ne*, II, 443.

924. FB to AM, 17 November 1907, GD492/137.

925. Though Renovation Committee members Balfour of Burleigh and James Campbell of Stracathro did not actively solicit funds from their friends and relatives, both men donated money to the cause. In fact, Campbell helped launch the campaign by making the first large donation of £1,000, which is acknowledged by a plaque in the church. After the death of her father, Campbell's daughter assisted Frances with the fund-raising.

926. FB Diary, 25 July 1907, 421.

927. BB, 'Note', 337. The Rev Jean Stewart explained that 'the word "begging" would have been totally unacceptable to Frances. [One] cannot beg for the King and Head of the Church and His Body on Earth'. Comments to author forwarded by Mrs Jean Lindsay, 9 November 2007. Betty was an Anglican.

928. FB, *Ne,* II, 443.

929. Arthur Balfour served as a trustee for the Carnegie Trust for the Universities of Scotland.

930. CCCA, Ren Com, 5 August 1908.

931. Andrew Carnegie to FB, 22 December 1909, CCP-HC.

932. CCCA Cuttings, 28 June 1908. The Duke of Bedford generously set the rent for the Church leasehold at a peppercorn for the rebuilding year.

933. 'Account'.

934. *Crown Court* (1969), 4. On 2 September 1990, Mrs Elizabeth Gibb (nee Milne), Frances

Balfour's favourite granddaughter, returned with the author to Crown Court Church for her first visit since her twin daughters were baptized there in 1943. On this occasion, she brought with her the key with which her grandmother had ceremonially re-opened Crown Court in 1909. Since the key was 'black', Mrs Gibb had polished it until the silver shone brightly. Later, when reading the programme of the Rededication ceremony, Mrs Gibb discovered that she had polished off the gold-plating. She subsequently had the key re-gold-plated.

935. Royal Institute of British Architects, Biographical Files (hereafter RIBA Files), *RIBA Journal*, 18 February 1911.

936. RIBA Files, *The Building*, 26 March 1909 and FB, 'the Rev John Cumming', 26. The design had the advantage of making a small congregation appear larger.

937. *Crown Court* (1969), 11.

938. FB to Frank, 3 July 1914, 347.

939. FB, *Ne*, II, 445.

940. Norman Maclean, *Years of Fulfilment* (London: Hodder and Stoughton, 1953), 100.

941. *Crown Court*, (1969), 18.

942. George Cameron explained in *Scots Church in London*, 176, that Frances used 'Lines' incorrectly. 'Lines' was a reference to a Disjointure Certificate which was issued to Church of Scotland members who were moving to a new church. Frances was apparently using 'Lines' to mean simply membership.

943. FB, *Ne*, II, 445.

CHAPTER ELEVEN   'The complete victory of Redmond'

944. FB Diary, 14 April 1910, 424

945. Quoted in FB, *Ne*, II, 429.

946. FB to 'My dear Constance', probably Lady Constance Battersea, 8 April 1911.

947. *The Times*, 6 May 1910.

948. FB to Frank, May 1910, 340. It is not clear why Frances believed this about the new monarch.

949. General Register Office Book 685, New Register House, NAS.

950. FB to Frank, 22 July 1910, 341.

951. 'Thackeray Turner', *The Architect and Building News*, 17 December 1937, 333; *The Builder*, 17 December 1937, 1109.

952. *Survey of London*, Mayfair, Vol 40, 228.

953. Ibid, Vol 39, 47.

954. F M L Thompson, 'Grosvenor, Hugh Lupus, first duke of Westminster (1825-1899)', *ODNB*, article 11667.

955. Quoted in *Survey of London, Mayfair*, 39, 38.

956. Thompson, 'Grosvenor, 1st Duke', *ODNB* article 11667.
957. *Survey of London, Mayfair*, 39, pt 1, 148.
958. *Survey of London*, 39, pt 1, 47-66.
959. FB, *Ne*, II, 447.
960. *Survey of London*, Mayfair, 39, pt 1, 148.
961. E-mail from Nigel Hughes, 18 October 2004.
962. Grosvenor Estate Book, 95.
963. George Arthur Codd, 'Statements on Policy and Factual Information on the Mayfair and Belgravia Estates as compiled in 1934', 24. Codd was an Assistant Surveyor under Eustace.
964. *Survey of London, Mayfair*, 39, 149.
965. Ibid, 40, 311.
966. 'Bourdon House', statement by Terry Garland, Architect with Aukett Ritzroy Robinson for Alfred Dunhill's renovation of Bourdon House undertaken in 2008-2009, prepared 9 August 2006.
967. *Survey of London, Mayfair*, 40, 187.
968. Thompson, Grosvenor, 1st Duke, ODNB article 11667.
969. Email from Nigel Hughes, 18 October 2004.
970. FB Diary, 26 November 1910, 424.
971. FB to Ettie Desborough, 13 January 1911, Desborough Papers, Hertfordshire Record Office, D/ERv C135/1.
972. FB Diary, 19 January 1910, 425.
973. BB, 'Note', 342.
974. 'Eustace James Anthony Balfour', Register of Deaths, Parish of Whittingehame, County of Haddington, 009743.
975. Copy of sermon included in Balfour Papers, 342, NAS.
976. *The Scotsman*, 15 February 1911. On his death, Alice entered Eustace's name without comment in the departure column of the Visitors' Book at Whittingehame. Item 3, *The Book of Bosh*, 1915.
977. Quoted in BB,'Note', 342.
978. Lord Haldane of Cloan to FB, 7 March 1911, 342.
979. 'Drug Use', Encyclopaedia Britannica, 2006. Encyclopaedia Britannica Online. 4 October 2006 http://www.britannica.com/article-40519.
980. Frances left a record of her menstrual cycles, the last of which was in 1910.
981. Frank to AJB, 28 February 1911, 477.
982. Ibid, 17 February 1911, 425.
983. FB to 'My dear Constance', probably Lady Constance Battersea, 8 April 1911.
984. Clipping in Balfour Papers, review of *Lord Esher's Journals and Letters,* 342.

985. Dugdale, *Balfour*, 46.

986. Ibid, 57.

987. Quoted in FB to BB, 11 November 1911, 343.

988. Lord Riddell Diaries, British Library, Add Mss 62969, fol 126-127.

989. FB to BB, n d but May 1911, 342.

990. FB to BB, 12 May 1911, 342.

991. 'Divorce Report, 1912, February 1912 and 7 March 1913, Vol 18, 235.

992. Gail Savage, 'Divorce and the Law in England and France prior to the First World War', *Journal of Social History*, 21 (Spring 1988): 449-514.

993. 'Divorce Report, 1912', 26 February 1910, 18, 400.

994. Ibid, 28 February 1910, 18, 402. *The Scotsman,* which carried a headline about the exchange, reported this verbatim on 1 March 1910.

995. Ibid, 26 February 1910, 18, 400. Also quoted in *The Scotsman*, 28 February 1910.

996. 'Divorce Report, 1912', 9 March 1910, 18, 598.

997. Ibid, 9 March 1910, 18, 598.

998. A James Hammerton, 'Victorian Marriage and the Law of Matrimonial Cruelty', *Victorian Studies*, Winter 1990, 272 [269-292].

999. H Gorell, Barnes, et al, *The Divorce Commission: The Majority and Minority Reports Summarized.*

1000. FB to BB, 12 May 1911, 342.

1001. The discussions that the Commissioners held among themselves in order to arrive at the final report were not published.

1002. FB to MGF, 14 June 1910, 9/01/0796.

1003. Stone, *Road to Divorce*, 16.

1004. Ibid, 393.

1005. 'Divorce Report, 1912', 18, 298.

1006. Brian Harrison, 'For Church, Queen and Family: The Girls' Friendly Society 1874-1920', *Past and Present*, No. 61 (November 1973), 124.

1007. FB Diary, 3 August 1911, 426.

1008. *The Scotsman*, 9 August 1911.

1009. *Oban Times*, 15 August 1911.

1010. FB to Frank, 1 August 1911, 342.

1011. Elizabeth Gibb, interview September 1993.

1012. BB, 'Facts of 1908', 337.

1013. *The Scotsman*, 12 June 1911.

1014. FB Diary, 12 June 1911, 426.

1015. Finlay's son and his wife moved into 31 Phillimore Gardens with him following Biba's death. Letter to author from Finlay's granddaughter, Lady Rosalind Hayes, 31 January

1991.

1016. FB to AJB, 20 August 1911, 343.

1017. Gentleman Cadet Register, Royal Military College, Sandhurst. E-mail from Dr A R Morton, Archivist and Deputy Curator, dated October 11, 2006.

1018. FB to BB, 29 November 1913, 346.

1019. *The Scotsman,* 19 January 1914, 12.

1020. FB to Frank, 20 January 1914, 347.

1021. Professor Emeritus Neil McIntyre of the Royal Free Hospital School of Medicine on the career of Ruth Balfour. E-mail August 28, 2008.

1022. FB to Frank, 10 June 1910, 340.

1023. Excerpts from letter by FB to Frank, n d but around 3 August 1911, 342.

1024. FB to Frank, 21 March 1912, 344.

1025. Ibid, October 1912, 344.

1026. FB to Hugh Cecil, 7 November 1912, H H Cecil Papers, QUI 15/170.

1027. FB to Ettie Desborough, D/ERvC135/2, Hertfordshire RO.

1028. 'Dr. Macgregor', Review by C Boyd, *The Bookman,* (London) 43: March 1913, 306.

1029. BB,' Note', 344.

1030. Records of the venerable publishing house were destroyed in World War II; thus, the financial terms for the biography of Lady Victoria are not available.

1031. *The Scotsman, 25 June 1912.*

1032. BB,' Note', in Eve Balfour to BB, early 1915, 354.

1033. Quoted in BB, 'Note', 344.

1034. Ridley and Percy, *Letters from Arthur to Mary Elcho,* 241.

1035. FB to Frank, 11 July 1912, 344.

1036. Savage to FB, November 1912, 344.

1037. Ibid.

1038. *The Scotsman,* 1 May 1913, 5.

1039. See letters from BB to AJB, one dated 14 April 1913, others just dated 1913, 164.

1040. See correspondence between FB and AJB, 14 April 1913 et al, 164.

1041. *The Scotsman,* 31 March 1913.

1042. FB to BB, 6 July 1913, 345.

1043. FB to Frank, 10 July 1913, 345.

1044. Ibid, 10 June 1913, 345.

1045. Frans Lasson, ed, Isak Dinesen, *Letters from Africa, 1914-1931* (University of Chicago Press, 1981), 451-52.

1046. Alison Milne to BB, 2 July 1913, 346.

1047. Anthony Clayton, 'Cholmondeley, Hugh, third Baron Delamere (1870-1931)', *ODNB* Article 32405.

1048. Lasson, Dinesen, *Letters from Africa,* 452.

1049. Ibid, xxxi.

1050. FB to BB, 20 May 1914, 347.

1051. Clayton, 'Cholmondeley', ODNB article 32405.

1052. FB to Eleanor Cole, 31 January 1922, 367.

1053. FB Diary, 12 January 1914, 429.

1054. FB to Frank, 8 January 1914, 347.

1055. FB Diary, 19 February 1914, 429.

1056. FB to Frank, 8 January 1914, 347.

1057. *The Scotsman,* 30 April 1914.

1058. Wake, *Princess Louise,* 385-386, and FB Diary, 28 April 1914, 429.

1059. Lady Frances Balfour, 'Ian, Duke of Argyll', *The Dunedin Magazine,* Vol II, No 3, July 1914, 130.

1060. Frances Balfour, 'The Late Duke of Argyll', *British Weekly,* 7 May 1914, 347.

1061. Quoted by BB, 'Note', 347.

CHAPTER TWELVE   '"No votes for Women"'

1062. Quoted in FB to BB, 30 March 1912, 344.

1063. Quoted in *Common Cause,* 8 June 1911.

1064. FB to Margot, 5 March 1912, Oxford, MS Eng C. 6670.

1065. AR, LS, 1910.

1066. Hume, *NUWSS,* 61; Fawcett, *Women's Suffrage,* 71.

1067. *Common Cause,* 13 January 1910.

1068. Ibid, 19 May 1910.

1069. *Englishwomen's Review,* 15 July 1910, 189.

1070. Quoted in Hume, *NUWSS,* 66.

1071. Ibid, 81.

1072. FB to MGF, 26 May 1910, 9/01/0778.

1073. AR, LS, 1910, 8.

1074. Hume, *NUWSS,* 78-79.

1075. Leneman, *Guid Cause,* 95.

1076. AR, LS, 1910.

1077. FB to MGF, 14 July 1910, 9/01/0828.

1078. *Common Cause,* 15 September 1910.

1079. Hume, *NUWSS,* 83.

1080. FB to MGF, 14 July 1910, 9/01/0828.

1081. AR, NUWSS, 1910.

1082. Quoted in AR, LS, 1911.

1083. FB to BB, 27 March 1911, 342.

1084. Fawcett, *Women's Suffrage*, 71.

1085. *Common Cause*, 5 January 1911.

1086. Ibid, 101.

1087. Ibid, 102.

1088. MGF to FB, 6 May 1911, 9/01/0945.

1089. AR, LS, 1911 and *The Times*, 18 June 1911.

1090. *The Scotsman*, 19 June 1911.

1091. FB, *Ne*, II, 171.

1092. Hume, *NUWSS*, 117; Fawcett, *Short History*, 81.

1093. Quoted in Ibid, 122.

1094. Ibid, 95 and AR, NUWSS, 1910.

1095. AR, NUWSS, 1912.

1096. MEC, NUWSS, 6 June 1912, GB/106/2/NWS/A1/4.

1097. Frances wrote about the organization in 'The Girls' Guildry', *Life and Work*, Vol. XLVI (1924), 126, but made no mention of what she did for the guild.

1098. *The Times*, 14 March 1914.

1099. *Coventry Standard*, 6-7 May 1910.

1100. Leah Leneman, *The Scottish Suffragettes* (Edinburgh, NMS Publishing, 2000), 34.

1101. *The Times*, 31 October 1910.

1102. Quoted in *Common Cause*, 8 June 1911.

1103. *East Grinstead Observer*, 8 July 1911, 2.

1104. *Common Cause*, 2 November 1911.

1105. *Common Cause*, 4 May 1911.

1106. Hume, *NUWSS*, 134.

1107. *Common Cause*, 1 February 1912.

1108. FB probably to BB, 4 March 1912, 344.

1109. Ibid.

1110. Quoted in Hume, *NUWSS*, 134.

1111. MEC, NUWSS, 21 March 1912.

1112. FB to MGF, 7 March 1912, 9/01/0993.

1113. The *Westminster Gazette*, 29 March 1912.

1114. Rosen, *Rise Up, Women,* 161.

1115. FB to MGF, 19 March 1912, 9/01/0995.

1116. FB to Margot, 5 March 1912, Oxford, MS Eng C 6670.

1117. *The Autobiography of Margot Asquith* (London: Methuen, 1985 [1962]), 153.

1118. Rosen, *Rise Up, Women*, 163.

1119. FB to BB, 30 March 1912, 344.

1120. D C Brooks, *The Emancipation of Women* (London: Macmillan, 1970), 15. Frances was not a 'suffragette', but few people made this distinction.

1121. *The Scotsman*, 25 May 1912.

1122. Hume, *NUWSS*, 139.

1123. Ibid, 145 and AR, NUWSS, 1912.

1124. Ibid.

1125. Pederson, Susan, *Eleanor Rathbone and the Politics of Conscience* (London: Yale UP, 2004), 130.

1126. MEC, LS, 5 March 1913 through 19 November 1913.

1127. Hume, *NUWSS*, 162.

1128. FB to BB, 22 January 1913, 345.

1129. Leneman, *Guid Cause*, 126.

1130. Hume, *NUWSS*, 181.

1131. MEC, NUWSS, 6 February 1913, and AR, NUWSS, 1912.

1132. FB to Frank, 14 February 1913, 345.

1133. Martin Pugh, *March*, 285.

1134. Ibid.

1135. *The Scotsman*, 5 June 1913.

1136. FB to Frank, 6 June 1913, 345.

1137. Email from Kate Perry, Archivist, Girton College, 20 April 2007 to author. With Bridger's permission, Perry shared 'Notes by Anne Bridger' dated 6 March 2003 with the author. See also Minutes of the Freedom of Labour Defence, 1912-1913, GCIP SPTW 4/4, Girton College.

1138. Ibid.

1139. AR, NUWSS, 1913, 13.

1140. Hume, *NUWSS*, 198.

1141. AR, NUWSS, 1913, 13-14.

1142. Fifth Annual Report, Richmond Branch, 1913.

1143. Annie E Wishart, WMP Secretary, to the LS, 15 August 1916 (Women's Municipal Party, 1915-1917, 2/LSW/364), and Amanda Mackenzie Stuart, *Consuelo and Alva: Love and Power in the Gilded Age* (London: Harpercollins, 2005), 333. Also *Norwood News*, 24 November 1916.

1144. Stuart, *Consuelo and Alva*, 33.

1145. Mrs H Fitzstephen O'Sullivan, 'The Women's Municipal Party: Formation and Work', 7. Mrs O'Sullivan was the founder and organizer of the WMP.

1146. Consuelo Vanderbilt Balsam, *The Glitter and the Gold* (Maidstone, George Mann, 1953), 156.

1147. Ibid.

1148. Stuart, *Consuelo and Alva*, 329.

1149. MEC, LS, 2 April 1913 through 19 November 1913.

1150. MEC, NUWSS, 2 April 1914.

1151. *The Scotsman*, 27 February 1914.

1152. Quoted in Ibid. Leah Leneman, *Guid Cause*, 199.

1151. *The Scotsman*, 6 March 1914.

1152. Copies of two newspaper articles from *The Scotsman* found in the Balfour Papers, 347.

1153. FB to Frank, 6 March 1914, 347.

1154. *Common Cause*, 28 August 1914.

1155. AR, NUWSS, 1913.

1156. Pugh, *March*, 211.

1157. FB to BB, March 1912, 426.

1158. FB to MGF, 10 February 1912, 9/01/0985.

1159. MGF to FB, 11 February 1912, 9/01/0986.

1160. Crawford, *Suffrage Reference*, 30.

1161. *Northern Times*, 11 September 1913.

1162. Leneman, *Guid Cause*, 157.

1163. *The Guardian*, 28 February 1914.

1164. Ibid.

1165. BB, 'Note', 21 February 1914, 347.

1166. MEC, NUWSS, 15 June 1916.

CHAPTER THIRTEEN 'We go from shock to Shock'

1167. FB to Frank, 7 June 1916, 357.

1168. BB, 'Note' from FB's letters, 20 September 1914, 348.

1169. *Daily Mail*, undated but 1914, in BP.

1170. "Notes," 4 August 1914, by BB, 347. Also Ian Beckett e-mail October 11, 2007.

1171. BB, Notes from FB's letters, 20 September 1914, 348.

1172. Oswald to ABB, 28 September 1914, 255.

1173. FB to Frank, 17 November 1914, 256.

1174. *The Scotsman*, 19 October 1914.

1175. FB to Frank, 3 December 1914, 349.

1176. Rose, *Later Cecils*, 223.

1177. FB to Frank, 5 November 1914, 349.

1178. 'Esher Journals and Letters, IV', *The Sunday Times*, undated article in Balfour Papers, 347.

1179. Beckett, *Riflemen Form*, 253.

1180. Rubinstein, *Different World*, 215.

1181. *Daily Mail,* undated but 1914, BP.

1182. Oswald to Nell, 15 May 1915, 352.

1183. Oswald to AJB and ABB, 16 May 1915, 255.

1184. FB Diary, 25 May 1915, 430.

1185. Oswald to ABB, 1 June 1915, 352.

1186. Oswald to FB, 26 May 1915, 352.

1187. Billy to Ruth, 15 May 1915, 352.

1188. Ibid, 22 May 1915, 352.

1189. Oswald to Baffy, 19 May 1915, 352.

1190. D George Boyce, 'Harmsworth, Alfred Charles William, Viscount Northcliffe (1865-1922)', *ODNB,* article 33717.

1191. FB to BB, 4 November 1915, 354.

1192. Richard Davenport-Hines, 'Vincent, Edgar, Viscount D/Abernon (1857-1941)', *ODNB,* article 36661.

1193. FB to BB, 8 August 1915, 353.

1194. FB to Ettie Desborough, 28 May n y but 1915, D/ERv C135/3, Hertfordshire RO.

1195. *The Scotsman,* 12 March 1915, 4.

1196. FB to BB, 11 December 1915, 355.

1197. FB to Frank, 20 August 1916, 357.

1198. A H M Kirk-Greene, 'The Sudan Political Service: A Profile in the Sociology of Imperialism', *The International Journal of African Historical Studies,* 15, 1 (1982), 23.

1199. Kirk-Greene, 'The Sudan PS', 25.

1200. Ibid, 28.

1201. Frank to FB, 27 January 1916, 356.

1202. Frank, 'Fiki Ali', SAD 303/8/26-39.

1203. Ibid.

1204. Sir Reginald Wingate to Frances Balfour, 8 January 1916, SAD 303/8/19-20.

1205. Alan Wakefield and Moody, Simon, *Under the Devil's Eye: Britain's Forgotten Army at Salonika, 1915-1918* (Gloucestershire: Sutton Publishing, Ltd, 2004), 99.

1206. Oswald to FB, 20 January 1917, 359.

1207. FB to Elizabeth Milne, 5 May 1921, GP.

1208. BB, 'Note', inserted in BB to Nell, 29 November 1916, 358. Also letter to author from her aunt, Jean Lindsay, 14 January 2008.

1209. FB to BB, 12-14 April 1916, 356.

1210. FB to Frank, 31 July 1916, 357.

1211. FB to Frank, 7 June 1916, 357.

1212. Billy to Ruth Balfour, 24 July 1916, 357.

1213. FB to Frank, n d except September, 1916, 357.

1214. Baffy to FB, 21 September 1916, 357.

1215. Wakefield, *Devil's Eye*, n p but IWM Q 32160 in the photographs; Tucker, *Great War*, 123.

1216. Egremont, *Balfour*, 280-281.

1217. Letter from FB to Herbert Henry Asquith, 13 December 1916, Oxford, Bodleian Library, MS Asquith 17, fols 25-26, 251-56.

1218. FB to Frank, 12 December 1916, 358.

1219. Quoted in Mackay and Matthew, 'Balfour, *ODNB* article 30553.

1220. FB to Frank, 15 April 1917, 359.

1221. Quoted in Mackay and Matthew, 'Balfour', *ODNB* article 30553.

1222. Interview with Frances, Lady Fergusson, 23 June 1987.

1223. FB Diary, 30 June 1917, 359.

1224. FB to Frank, 22 February 1917, 359.

1225. Janet Wallach, *Desert Queen* (New York: Doubleday, 1996), 191.

1226. Quoted in BB, Note, 11 July 1917, 359.

1227. Frank to FB, 29 July 1917, 359.

1228. Wallach, *Desert Queen*, 192.

1229. Ibid, 180.

1230. Ibid, 242.

1231. Frank, 'Mesopotamia 1917-1918' and Frank to FB, 8 April 1918, 256.

1232. Quoted in FB to BB, 24 April 1918, 361.

1233. Quoted in FB to BB, 8 September 1895, 314.

1234. Quoted in Virginia Cowles, *The Rothschilds, A Family of Fortune* (London: Futura Publications, 1975 [1973]), 190-191.

1235. FB Diary, 29 June 1918, 433.

1236. The Times, 4 March 1916.

1237. FB to Elizabeth Milne, 8 December 1919.

1238. Ibid.

1239. FB to Elizabeth Milne, n d but June 1918, GP.

1240. FB to BB, 13 November 1918, 362.

1241. FB to BB, 16 December 1918, 362.

CHAPTER FOURTEEN 'The triumphant Feminist'

1242. *The Scotsman*, 14 July 1921.

1243. FB to Frank, 4 June 1915, 353.

1244. *The [Wandsworth] Borough News*, 26 March 1915. Quoted in AR, LS, 1913-1914, 11.

1245. Rubinstein, *Different World,* 214.

1246. MEC, LS, 17 March 1915.

1247. FB to Frank, 4 June 1915, 353.

1248. AR, LS, 1913-1914, 11.

1249. Strachey, *Women's Suffrage and Women's Service*, 25-26.

1250. Leah Leneman, *In the Service of Life: The Story of Elsie Inglis and the Scottish Women's Hospitals* (Edinburgh: Mercat Press, 1994), 2.

1251. Fawcett wanted the hospitals to carry the name of the National Union of Women's Suffrage Societies, but Inglis, asserting that votes for women was a controversial issue and might alienate some supporters, vetoed the idea, though the SWH stationery did carry the name of the NUWSS.

1252. Scottish Women's Hospitals Records, GB/106/2/SWH/D5/2.

1253. AR, LS, 1915.

1254. *Cambuslang Advertiser* (Strathclyde), 11 November 1916.

1255. AR, LS, 1915, 12.

1256. *The [Wandsworth] Borough News*, 26 March 1915.

1257. Ibid.

1258. Daphne Glick, The *National Council of Women of Great Britain* (London: National Council of Women, 1995), 12.

1259. '[Preliminary] Report', Women's Advisory Committee: Reports and Correspondence, HO 185/258, Public Record Office (PRO).

1260. FB to BB, 24 October 1915, 354. Frances is listed as representing 'Scotland'. Mrs Creighton to members, 20 October 1915, HO 185/258, PRO.

1261. 'Report', WAC.

1262. Ibid.

1263. Ibid.

1264. Mrs Louise Creighton to Lord D'Abernon, 8 April 1916, HO 185/258, PRO. See also FB Diary, 31 March 1916, 432.

1265. "Third Report, Central Control Board, 1917-1918' [Cd.8558], 22.

1266. AR, LS, 1915-1916.

1267. AR, LS, 1916-1917.

1268. See AR, LS, 1915-1916.

1269. AR, LS, 1916-1917.

1270. Oswald to FB, 18 February 1918, 361.

1271. MEC, NUWSS, 2 March 1916.

1272. AR, LS, 1916-1917.

1273. Ibid.

1274. Ibid.

1275. Fawcett, *Remember*, 219.

1276. MGC, 27 November 1914, TAS.

1277. MGC, 20 April 1917, TAS.

1278. MGC, 17 January 1919.

1279. MEC, CCCWSS, 2 April 1917.

1280. FB to BB, 2 February 1917, 359.

1281. MEC, CCCWSS, 23 April 1917.

1282. On 19 June 1917, the Members voted 385 to 55 to reject Sir F Banbury's amendment which would have struck down Clause 4, in which women over the age of 30 got the vote.

1283. AR, NUWSS, 1916-1917, 12.

1284. *Common Cause*, 24 August 1917.

1285. Ray Strachey, *Women's Suffrage and Women's Service*, 29.

1286. FB to MGF, 3 January 1917, 9/01/227.

1287. Quoted in Fawcett, *Remember*, 247.

1288. The Lords rejected Lord Loreburn's amendment to omit women's suffrage from the Reform Bill. *The Times*, 11 January 1918. See also MEC, NUWSS, 17 January 1918.

1289. FB to BB, 19 [21?] January 1918, 361.

1290. FB, *Dr Elsie Inglis* (London: Hodder and Stoughton, 1918), 242.

1291. *The Scotsman*, 12 December 1918.

1292. FB, *Inglis*, 249.

1293. Ibid, 251, and Article in GB/106/2/SWH/D3.

1294. Fawcett, *Remember*, 250-251.

1295. BB to Nell, 8 March 1918, 361.

1296. MEC, NUWSS, 18 February 1915.

1297. MEC, NUWSS, 2 March 1916.

1298. Proceedings of Annual Council, NUWSS, 21-23 February 1917.

1299. *The Scotsman*, 3 December 1918.

1300. Ridley and Percy, *Letters of Arthur to Mary Elcho*, 318.

1301. Countess Markiewicz (Constance Gore-Booth) was elected in Ireland, but, as a Sinn Feiner, refused to take her seat in Westminster.

1302. *The Scotsman*, 3 December 1918.

1303. Rubinstein, *Different World*, 252.

1304. AR, LS, 1917-1918. See Minutes of Annual Meeting appended to the Annual Report.

1305. Fawcett repeated the phrase 'over 17 years' at a reception in Fawcett's honour on 6 March 1919. Quoted in *Common Cause*, 14 March 1919.

1306. E-mail from Archivist Lorna Cahill to author 14 January 2010.

1307. Ibid.

1308. FB, *Ne*, II, 167.

1309. Grace Brockington, 'History of the German Lyceum Clubs', http://www.lyceumclub. org/en/history.htm, accessed 21 January 2010.

1310. Gordon and Doughan, *British Women's Organizations*, 176.

1311. Glick, *NCW*, 7. The author was also aided by conversations with Glick.

1312. Ibid, 16.

1313. *The Scotsman*, 9 November 1918.

1314. I am indebted to Jane Hogan, Assistant Keeper, Archives and Special Collections at Durham University Library, Palace Green, for assistance with this matter.

1315. FB to Dr Robertson, 1 March 1919, 479, and *The Scotsman*, 27 May 1919.

1316. *The Scotsman*, 27 May 1919.

1317. FB, *Ne*, II, 132.

1318. Macdonald, *A Unique and Glorious Mission,* 15.

1319. FB to BB, 23 October 1923, 370.

1320. Ibid.

1321. *The Times*, 13 May 1920.

1322. *The Evening Dispatch*, 20 October 1923, and Balfour Papers, 370.

1323. *The Scotsman*, 6 July 1918.

1324. FB Diary, 3 June 1919, 434.

1325. *The Scotsman*, 14 July 1921.

1326. Ibid, 15 July 1921.

1327. Taken from 'Graduation Lists' in *Edinburgh University Calendar.*

1328. FB Diary, 27 September 1921, 436.

1329. *The Times*, 26 September 1922.

1330. Ibid and Glick, *NCW*, 29.

1331. Glick, *NCW*, 30-31.

1332. *The Times*, 26 September 1922.

1333. Programme and Agenda of the Annual Conference of the NCW, 1922, LMA, ACC/3613/5/1/69.

1334. Ibid.

1335. Annual Conference Records, NCW, 1923, LMA. All in para.

1336. Oswald to FB, 7 July 1923, 369.

1337. Annual Conference Records (ACR), NCW, 1923, LMA.

1338. Ibid.

1339. Ibid.

1340. *The Scotsman*, 20 October 1923.

1341. Quoted in Ibid.

1342. FB to Frank, 21 October 1923, 370.

1343. *The Times*, 20 July 1920.

1344. ACR, NCW, 1923, 8.

1345. Glick, *NCW*, 30-31.

1346. Glick, *NCW*, 251.

1347. BB, 'Note', n d except 1922, 367. Helen Louisa Kerry was on the Board of Management at the Royal Infirmary beginning in 1906.

1348. Crawford, *Suffrage Reference Guide*, 30.

CHAPTER FIFTEEN 'Everything Changes'

1349. FB to Frank, 4 May 1924, 371.

1350. *Paisley Daily Express*, 21 November 1918.

1351. Quoted by BB, 25 July, n y but 1930, 381.

1352. Margot Asquith to FB, 1 January 1919, 363.

1353. Gordon A Craig and Gilbert, Felix, Eds *The Diplomats, 1919-1939: The Twenties* (New York: Atheneum, 1968 [1935]), 20-27.

1354. Mackay and Matthew, "Balfour," ODNB article 30553.

1355. Baffy to FB, 20 July 1919, 363.

1356. Comment related by Joan.

1357. Arthur endorsed Nancy in a letter for publication. Sykes, *Nancy Astor*, 221.

1358. FB to Margot, 2 December 1919, MS Engl C6670, Western Manuscripts, Oxford.

1359. Quoted in Sykes, *Nancy Astor*, 136.

1360. Frank to FB, 2 November 1919 and 24 November 1919, 363.

1361. FB to BB, 7 April 1919, 363.

1362. FB Diary, 6 April 1919, 363.

1363. FB to BB, 21 October 1920, 365.

1364. FB Diary, 27 June 1919, 434.

1365. Quoted in Wallach, *Desert Queen*, 261.

1366. *Evening Dispatch*, 29 October 1923, 370.

1367. *The Scotsman*, 1 September 1920.

1368. Frank to FB, 5 August 1921, 363.

1369. FB to Elizabeth Milne, [n d except] March 1920, Gibb Papers.

1370. Ibid, 13 February 1920, Gibb Papers.

1371. Jean Balfour, 'Notes and Reflections', 57.

1372. FB to Elizabeth Milne, March 1920, Gibb Papers.

1373. FB to Mary Elcho, 6 September 1920, Neidpath Papers.

1374. Jean Lindsay, email to author, 27 December 2009.

1375. Note by BB, 25 July 1921, 366.

1376. Oswald to Joan, 17 March 1920, 365.

1377. *The Scotsman*, 6 July 1921.

1378. Ibid, 8 July 1921, and *Westminster Gazette*, 8 July 1921.

1379. Ibid.

1380. Oswald to FB, 25 December 1921, 366.

1381. FB to Frank, 29 May 1922, 367.

1382. *The Times*, 29 June 1917.

1383. FB, "The Problem of Divorce," *Edinburgh Review*, April 1923, 237:389-92.

1384. Email from Gail Savage to author, April 26, 2006.

1385. Oswald to FB, 3 August 1922, 368.

1386. Oswald to Arthur, 11 August 1922, 231.

1387. FB to Frank, 1 January 1923, 369.

1388. FB to Frank, 19 December 1921, 366.

1389. FB to Frank, 11 February 1922, 368.

1390. Ibid, 18 February 1922, 367.

1391. E-mail from Mary Sharp, Carleton Club, to author, 16 July 2010.

1392. FB to BB, 16 November 1922, 368.

1393. "Asquith", *ODNB* article 30483.

1394. Edith Picton-Turbervill, *Life Has Been Good* (London: Frederick Muller, 1939), 157.

1395. Quoted in Ibid, 158.

1396. Ibid.

1397. FB to Frank, 4 June 1923, 369.

1398. Ibid, 3 July 1922, 368.

1399. Quoted in FB, *Ne*, II, 189.

1400. FB to Frank, 23 May 1923, 369.

1401. FB to BB, 23 October 1923, 370.

1402. FB to Frank, 10 December 1923, 370.

1403. Margot Asquith to BB, 21 November 1923, 370.

1404. FB to Frank, 22 January 1924, 371.

1405. FB to BB, 22 January 1924, 371.

1406. Quoted in *Paisley Daily Express*, 21 November 1918.

1407. FB to Frank, 22 January 1924, 371.

1408. Ibid.

1409. FB to Frank, 1 February 1924, 371.

1410. FB to Frank, 14 April 1924, 371.

1411. Quoting Betty in FB to Frank, 18 February 1924, 371.

1412. FB to GWB, 6 May 1924, 267.

1413. *The Times*, 22 August 1924.

1414. Paul Addison, 'Churchill, Sir Winston Leonard Spencer (1874-1965)', *ODNB*, article 32413.

1415. FB to Frank, 2 February 1925, 373.

1416. Ibid, 29 March 1925, 373.

1417. Quoted in Egremont, *Balfour*, 330.

1418. Daly, M W, 'Stack, Sir Lee Oliver Fitzmaurice (1868–1924)', *ODNB*, article 36230.

1419. *The Scotsman*, 24 November 1924.

1420. Daly, 'Sir Lee Oliver Stack', *ODNB* article 36230.

1421. Frank to FB, 27 November 1924, 498.

1422. FB to Frank, 14 June 1924, 371.

1423. Ibid.

1424. Obituary of 'William James Stuart', *Lancet*, 7 March 1959, 527. E-mail to author from Laura Brouard, Lothian Health Service, 5 October 2010.

1425. Quoted in Alison to BB, 6 November 1924, 372.

1426. James O. Robinson, 'Treatment of Breast Cancer through the Ages', *The American Journal of Surgery*, Vol 151, March 1986, 330-331. Most of the material about the surgeon's treatment for Frances's breast cancer is taken from this article.

1427. BB to Frank, 8 November 1924, 372.

1428. Alison to BB, 6 November 1924, 372.

1429. BB to Frank, 8 November 1924, 372.

1430. FB to Frank, 7 December 1924, 372.

1431. Ibid.

1432. FB Diary, 29 March 1925, 441.

1433. FB to Frank, 10 November 1925, 373.

1434. BB, Note, 372.

1435. Joan to ABB, 29 March 1925, 373.

1436. Joan to ABB, 2 April 1925, 373.

1437. *The Scotsman*, 2 April 1925.

1438. Ibid.

1439. *Illustrated London News*, 11 April 1925.

1440. Joan to ABB, 6 April 1925, 373.

1441. *The Scotsman*, 9 April 1925.

1442. *The Scotsman*, 20 May 1925.

1443. FB Diary, 30 May 1925, 441.

1444. *The Scotsman*, 8 February 1926.

1445. FB to Frank, 1 December 1925, 373.

1446. *The Scotsman*, 26 February 1931.

1447. Quoted in the *New York Times*, 26 February 1931.

1448. FB to Frank, 4 May 1926, 374. All the rest of the narrative concerning the General Strike follows from this first letter.

1449. FB to AJB, 24 October 1927, 231.

1450. FB to BB, 17 December 1927, 376.

1451. FB to Whittingehame, 8 January 1927, 375.

1452. FB to George Saintsbury, 26 January 1929, 379.

1453. Frank to AJB, 2 March 1929, 231.

1454. Quoted by BB, 25 July, n y but 1930, 381.

1455. Ibid.

1456. FB to Frank, 29 April 1927, 375.

1457. FB to Frank, 6 May 1927, 375.

1458. FB to Margot, 11 February 1928, Western Manuscripts, Oxford.

1459. *The Book of Bo*sh, item 61, and FB to Frank, 31 July 1928, 377.

1460. FB to Frank, 21 August 1928, 378.

1461. Frances credited Baldwin with this suggestion.

1462. FB to BB, [n d] May 1929, 379.

1463. Ibid.

1464. *The Scotsman*, 2 October 1929.

1465. FB to BB, 1 October 1929, 379.

1466. Story related by telephone to author by John Balfour, son of Ruth and Bill Balfour, on 8 April 2008.

1467. FB to BB, 3 October 1929, 380.

1468. FB to BB, 5 October 1929, 380.

CHAPTER SIXTEEN   'Women are looking Up'

1469. FB to George Saintsbury, 23 March 1929, 379.

1470. Ibid.

1471. *The Scotsman*, 26 February 1931.

1472. *The Times*, 19 March 1924. All the quotes from this debate are from this article.

1473. FB to Frank, 4 April 1924, 371.

1474. Oswald to FB, 22 April 1924, 371.

1475. I am indebted to Frank Sharp for locating this photograph, No H-16437-S.

1476. *The Woman's Supplement*, October 1920.

1477. *The Times*, 24 July 1925.

1478. *The Times*, 1 March 1924.

1479. Quoted in Cheryl Law, *Suffrage and Power: The Women's Movement, 1918-1928* (London: I.B. Tauris Publishers, 2000 [1997]), 196.

1480. Quoted in Angela V Johns, *Turning the Tide: The Life of Lady Rhondda*, Cardigan, Wales: Parthian, 2013, 290.

1481. Ibid.

1482. Minutes of Conference Committee, 11 July 1927, Minutes of Bournemouth Branch, 1923-1930, NCW, LMA.

1483. FB to Miss Green, 1 October 1927, NCW Papers at LMA, Acc/3613/03/001/A.

1484. FB to ABB, 15 October, 1927, 376.

1485. This letter from Frances is entitled 'To the Editor of the Times', 11 March 1927, Acc/3613/03/001/A, LMA.

1486. FB to George Saintsbury, 23 March 1929, 379.

1487. Ibid.

1488. FB to BB, 7 August 1929, 380.

1489. FB, 'Mrs. Fawcett', *Contemporary*, 136 (September 1929), 313. (313-315)

1490. FB to George Saintsbury, 23 March 1929, 379.

1491. MGC, 23 January 1925, TAS.

1492. AR 1920, TAS.

1493. Glick, NCW, 1.

1494. MGC, 26 February 1886, TAS.

1495. MHS, 25 February 1920, TAS.

1496. MGC, 20 January 1928, TAS.

1497. MGC, October 1934, TAS.

1498. Minutes of Sub-Committee, Executive Committee of the TAS, 13 November 1893.

1499. MGC, 14 and 21 October 1938, TAS.

1500. 'The Travellers' Aid Society' and 'Merger of the N.V.A. and the TAS'.

1501. *The Times*, 11 March 1929.

1502. FB to Mary, Lady Wemyss, 13 March 1929.

1503. FB to Linky (Lord Hugh Cecil), 27 February 1929, H H QUI 37/120, Hatfield House.

1504. FB to Mary, Lady Elcho, 9 May 1929, Neidpath Papers.

1505. BB, Note, 379.

1506. BB to FB, 3 April 1929, 379.

1507. FB to BB, 28 September 1929, 380.

1508. Ibid.

1509. FB to Professor George Saintsbury, 15 June 1929, 379.

1510. Quoted by FB, *Ne Ob*, Preface, ii.

1511. *The Scotsman*, 3 February 1930.

1512. *The Illustrated London News*, 22 February 1930, 288.

1513. FB, *Ne*, I, 339.

1514. Ibid.

1515. Ibid, 340.

1516. Lady Alice Salisbury to BB, 3 February 1920, 380.

1517. Lord Robert Cecil to FB, 19 February 1930, 381.

1518. Joan Campbell to FB, 2 February 1930, 381.

1519. *The Scotsman*, 3 February 1930.

1520. Rough draft of material prepared by FB for the cover of her biography, 381.

1521. BB, Notes, 381. All the quotes in this paragraph are from these notes.

1522. FB to Etty Desborough, 29 March 1930, Hertfordshire Record Office.

1523. FB to Alice, Lady Salisbury, n d but shortly after 22 March 1930, H H 4 MCH 4/4.

1524. Jean Balfour to BB, 23 March 1930, 386.

1525. Quoted in Egremont, *Balfour*, 82.

1526. Ibid, 83, and Ridley and Percy, *Letters of Arthur to Mary Elcho*, 33-34.

1527. FB to BB?, 22 September 1930, 386.

1528. FB to BB, n d except January 1931, 387.

1529. *The Scotsman*, 16 January 1931.

1530. Interview with Mrs Elizabeth Gibb, September 1996.

1531. FB to BB, 24 January 1931, 387.

1532. Ibid, 12 February 1931, 387.

1533. BB, Notes, 1931. Her broadcast was later published under the title 'Scotland for Ever!' in *The Listener*, 1 April 1931.

1534. BB, Note, 383.

1535. Ibid.

1536. Death Certificate of Frances Balfour, No. Y123327, Registration District Kensington, Kensington South, County of London.

1537. *The Times*, 26 February 1931.

1538. *The Times*, 3 March 1931.

1539. Quoted in Wake, *Princess Louise*, 405.

1540. Notes entitled 'The Family Chronicle from 1931' by BB, 383.

1541. *The Scotsman*, 2 March 1931.

1542. *The Scotsman*, 26 February 1931.

1543. *The Scotsman*, 20 May 1931.

1544. Lesley Orr [Macdonald], 'Balfour, Lady Frances, n Campbell', *The Biographical Dictionary of Scottish Women from the Earliest Times to 2004,* (Edinburgh University Press, 2006), 25-26.

1545. Jean Balfour to BB, 3 March 1931, 383.

1546. Lady Gwendolen Cecil to BB, 2 March 1931, 381.

1547. Mrs Elizabeth Gibb explained her 'Will' to the author.

1548. 'In Memoriam The Lady Frances Balfour', AR, TAS, 1931.

1549. Janet Adam Smith, *John Buchan* (London: Rupert Hart-Davis, 1965), 173.

1550. H H Asquith to Pamela McKenna, 7 December 1907, MCKN 9/3, Churchill Archives Centre, Cambridge University.

1551. Constance Battersea, *Reminiscences* (London: Macmillan & Co., 1922), 218.

1552. Balfour, Jean, 'Notes and Reflections', 57.

1553. Knox, *Lives of Scottish Women*, 98, 101, 113.

1554. Stuart, *Consuelo and Alva*, 243.

1555. 'Party Political Women,' 181.

1556. Colin Matthew, ed, *The Nineteenth Century: The British Isles: 1815-1901* (Oxford: Oxford University Press, Short History of the British Isles, 2000), 189.

1557. 'Lady Frances Balfour,' *Every Woman's Encyclopaedia*, http://chestofbooks.com/food/household/Woman-Encyclopaedia-4/Lady-Frances-Balfour. Frances herself said – at least on one occasion – that she was 'usually a pessimist'. FB to Frank, 10 July 1913, 345.

1558. FB, 'Scotland for Ever!' BBC broadcast reprinted in *The Listener*, April 1, 1931, 546-547.

1559. Balfour, Jean, 'Notes and Observations'. 57.

For the Bibliography, see www.LadyFrancesBalfour.com

INDEX

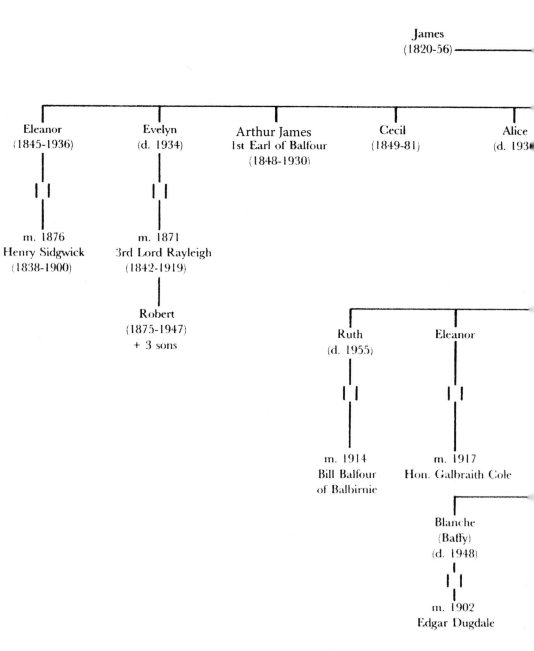

James
(1820-56)

Eleanor
(1845-1936)

Evelyn
(d. 1934)

Arthur James
1st Earl of Balfour
(1848-1930)

Cecil
(1849-81)

Alice
(d. 193●

m. 1876
Henry Sidgwick
(1838-1900)

m. 1871
3rd Lord Rayleigh
(1842-1919)

Robert
(1875-1947)
+ 3 sons

Ruth
(d. 1955)

Eleanor

m. 1914
Bill Balfour
of Balbirnie

m. 1917
Hon. Galbraith Cole

Blanche
(Baffy)
(d. 1948)

m. 1902
Edgar Dugdale

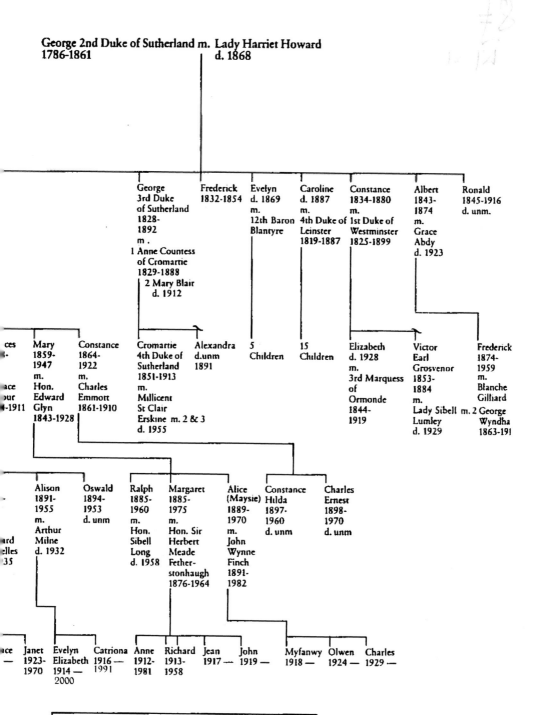

George 2nd Duke of Sutherland m. Lady Harriet Howard
1786-1861   d. 1868

George 3rd Duke of Sutherland 1828-1892 m. 1 Anne Countess of Cromartie 1829-1888 2 Mary Blair d. 1912	Frederick 1832-1854	Evelyn d. 1869 m. 12th Baron Blantyre	Caroline d. 1887 m. 4th Duke of Leinster 1819-1887	Constance 1834-1880 m. 1st Duke of Westminster 1825-1899	Albert 1843-1874 m. Grace Abdy d. 1923	Ronald 1845-1916 d. unm.

ces	Mary 1859-1947 m. Hon. Edward Glyn 1843-1928	Constance 1864-1922 m. Charles Emmott 1861-1910	Cromartie 4th Duke of Sutherland 1851-1913 m. Millicent St Clair Erskine m. 2 & 3 d. 1955	Alexandra d.unm 1891	5 Children	15 Children	Elizabeth d. 1928 m. 3rd Marquess of Ormonde 1844-1919	Victor Earl Grosvenor 1853-1884 m. Lady Sibell Lumley d. 1929	Frederick 1874-1959 m. Blanche Gilliard m. 2 George Wyndha 1863-191

	Alison 1891-1955 m. Arthur Milne d. 1932	Oswald 1894-1953 d. unm	Ralph 1885-1960 m. Hon. Sibell Long d. 1958	Margaret 1885-1975 m. Hon. Sir Herbert Meade Fether-stonhaugh 1876-1964	Alice (Maysie) 1889-1970 m. John Wynne Finch 1891-1982	Constance Hilda 1897-1960 d. unm	Charles Ernest 1898-1970 d. unm

ace	Janet 1923-1970	Evelyn Elizabeth 1914-2000	Catriona 1916-1991	Anne 1912-1981	Richard 1913-1958	Jean 1917—	John 1919—	Myfanwy 1918—	Olwen 1924—	Charles 1929—

ARGYLL FAMILY TREE